Risk Management

Edited by Muddassar Sarfraz
and Larisa Ivascu

Published in London, United Kingdom

IntechOpen

Supporting open minds since 2005

Risk Management
http://dx.doi.org/10.5772/intechopen.91067
Edited by Muddassar Sarfraz and Larisa Ivascu

Contributors
K. Srinivas, Pasqualina Porretta, Fabrizio Santoboni, Isabell Koinig, Yaser Rahimi, Arnaldo Marques de Oliveira Neto, Wael A. Zatar, Vladimir Gorbunov, Amparo Marin-De-La-Barcena, Dietmar Pfeifer, Vivien Langen, Lassaad Abdelmoula, Patrizia Riva, Ambra Garelli, Maurizio comoli, Fasilat Aramide Sanusi, Jordi Botet, Jeffrey M. Shepard, Katarina Holla, Eva Sventekova, Sami Boudabbous, Satirenjit Kaur Johl

First published in London, United Kingdom, 2021 by IntechOpen
IntechOpen is the global imprint of INTECHOPEN LIMITED, registered in England and Wales, registration number: 11086078, 5 Princes Gate Court, London, SW7 2QJ, United Kingdom
Printed in Croatia

British Library Cataloguing-in-Publication Data
A catalogue record for this book is available from the British Library

Additional hard and PDF copies can be obtained from orders@intechopen.com

Risk Management
Edited by Muddassar Sarfraz and Larisa Ivascu
p. cm.
Print ISBN 978-1-83968-905-5
Online ISBN 978-1-83968-906-2
eBook (PDF) ISBN 978-1-83968-907-9

For EU product safety concerns:
IN TECH d.o.o., Prolaz Marije Krucifikse Kozulić 3, 51000 Rijeka, Croatia, info@intechopen.com or visit our website at intechopen.com.

Meet the editors

Dr. Muddassar Sarfraz works as an assistant professor at Wuxi University, China. He completed a postdoctoral fellowship in Business Management at the Business School of Hohai University, China. He has published numerous papers in foreign authoritative journals and academic conferences at home and abroad. He is senior editor of Cogent Business & Management, associate editor of Frontiers in Psychology, Energies, and Future Business Journal, and guest editor of Frontiers in Environmental Sciences and INQUIRY. He is a member of the British Academy of Management, Chinese Economists Society (USA), World Economic Association (UK), and the American Economic Association, and an ambassador of the MBA program at Chongqing University, China. His research focuses on corporate social responsibility, risk management, strategic management, and business management.

Dr. Larisa Ivascu is an associate professor at the Politehnica University of Timisoara, Romania, with eighteen years of experience in programming, teaching, and research. She graduated with an MBA in Production and Transportation from the Faculty of Management, Politehnica University of Timisoara. She is a doctoral supervisor in the field of engineering and management. She is the head of the Entrepreneurship Office of Politehnica University of Timișoara, and director of the Research Center in Engineering and Management. She is the president of the scientific committee of the Academy of Political Leadership, and vice-president of the Society for Ergonomics and Work Environment Management. Ms. Ivascu has been involved in national and international projects and has published nine books and contributed scientifically to more than 190 scientific articles.

Contents

Preface

Modern globalization has accelerated business and increased competition among economies. Due to excessive industrialization, the world has disturbed its natural ecology, raising concerns about the environment. To mitigate environmental problems, corporate environmental responsibility measures have been suggested. In this regard, emerging economies have also compelled their organizations to adopt risk management measures emphatically. Sustainability is addressed globally due to the opposition between growing needs and limited natural resources. In this context of sustainable development and the dynamics of the business environment, risk management becomes an important process for organizations. An efficient risk management process contributes to achieving organizational goals and vision. These strategic elements, organizational objectives, missions, and visions are important for stakeholders. The sustainable development of an organization contributes to local, national, and global development. One cannot talk about development over a long period of time if organizational risks are not addressed. There are a few innovative methods for approaching risks and several attitudes towards risks. These nuances depend on the human personality and the organizational culture.

Significantly, firms adopt risk management strategies that not only sustain performance but also augment the firms' reputation. However, it is significant to analyze the role of corporate governance, which can accelerate risk management measures and orient upper management teams towards organizational environmental measures so that firms' reputation and growth may be sustained in the future.

This book identifies strategic challenges for risk management assessment and practices, examines potential factors that affect business growth, and offers new opportunities for enterprises. It covers several important topics in the context of global sustainability and environmental dynamics, as follows:

- role of technological innovation and corporate risk management
- challenges for corporate governance while launching corporate environmental management among emerging economies
- relationship between environmental risk management and sustainable management
- strategic corporate environmental responsibility under the influence of cultural barriers
- risk management in different countries (the international dimensions)
- global standardization vs local adaptation of corporate environmental risk management in multinational corporations
- approaches towards risk management strategies in the short and long term

Chapter 1, "Insurance Business and Sustainable Development," discusses how to control organizational risks as effectively as possible. It presents aspects of insurance in the context of sustainable development.

Chapter 2, "Environmentally Influenced Risk and Sustainable Management of State Controlled Transportation Assets", demonstrates the relationship between environmentally influenced risk management and sustainable management of state-controlled transportation assets in the United States. It addresses several key parameters including risk assessment, financial risk, and organizational behavior.

Chapter 3, "Risk Mitigation: Sustainable Management in Construction Industry" addresses important management issues in the construction industry. The construction industry is an important field in the context of current dynamics and customer requirements.

Chapter 4, "Basel IV: The Challenge of II Pillar for Risk Management Function", is based on the Supervisory Review and Evaluation Process (SREP) conducted annually by the supervisory authorities to verify that each bank (Significant/Less Significant) has implemented strategies, processes, capital, and liquidity assessment processes appropriate to the business model and overall planning activity and risk governance system.

Chapter 5, "Risk Management in the Area of Major Industrial Accident Prevention in the EU and Slovak Republic", is an important chapter for the development of European and national strategies. This chapter considers the latest approaches and presents an important study for risk management.

Chapter 6, "Risk Analysis in Engineering Projects", addresses the most important aspects of risk management in projects. The bibliographic study is an important foundation for experts in this field.

Chapter 7, "Social Impact Returns. Filling the Finance Gap with Data Value", presents a framework to measure social impact filling the finance gap. It demonstrates the range of opportunities that can be achieved by adopting data and Sustainable Development Goals (SDGs) as a core strategy.

Chapter 8, "Dealing with Unforeseen Circumstances. Implication of Risk Management in the COVID-19 Public Health Emergency", addresses important topics for the manufacturing industry. Public health is a major topic of interest in the business environment.

Chapter 9, "Risk Communication in the Age of COVID-19", is an important chapter in the current context. The pandemic period developed new forms of communication and profiles of individuals. This chapter presents the issue of communication risks.

Chapter 10, "Corporate Governance and ERM for SMEs Viability in Italy", addresses an important issue in the context of sustainable development. It addresses topics such as the role of the board of statutory auditors, the role of auditors, the Internal Auditor (IA) and the Internal Control and Risk Management System (IC and ERM), monitoring ESG risks in SMEs, and risk of overlapping and possible remedies.

Chapter 11, "The Management of Tax Risks in Mergers and Acquisitions - The Importance of Tax Due Diligence", provides an overview of the responsibility of company administrators in the management of tax risks and the importance of due diligence to mitigate them, especially in mergers and acquisitions.

Chapter 12, "Fuzzy Approach Model to Portfolio Risk Response Strategies", addresses an important topic. The first objective focuses on maximizing profits and efficiency of risk responses, and the second objective aims at minimizing project direct costs including machinery, human, and material costs to implement proper risk responses over a planning horizon under uncertainty.

Chapter 13, "Determinants of Job Satisfaction of Accounting Professionals in Tunisia", presents a study with global applicability. Determining the variables that contribute to job satisfaction is an area of interest for all entrepreneurs.

Chapter 14, "Discerning the Strategies for Exiting Your Business", addresses elements of strategic management. These elements are very important for achieving the vision and developing realistic strategic objectives.

Chapter 15, "Assessment of Top Management Commitment and Support on IS Risk Management Implementation in the Business Organization" presents directions and approaches to information management and technology. The information system for risk management implementation is an important direction in preparing the industry for the 5.0 revolution and for the dynamics of information technology.

This book is a useful resource t for specialists in the field as well as researchers. It also offers a series of introductory aspects for those who want to learn the concepts of risk.

The editors would like to acknowledge the help of all those involved in this project. Without their support, this book would not have been possible. First, we thank the contributing authors for their time and expertise. Second, we wish to acknowledge the valuable contributions of the reviewers whose comments improved the quality, coherence, and content of each of the chapters.

Dr. Muddassar Sarfraz
College of International Students,
Wuxi University,
Wuxi, PR China

Larisa Ivascu
Professor,
Faculty of Management in Production and Transportation,
Politehnica University of Timisoara,
Timisoara, Romania

Section 1

Risk Management and Sustainable Development

Chapter 1

Insurance Business and Sustainable Development

Dietmar Pfeifer and Vivien Langen

Abstract

In this study, we will discuss recent developments in risk management of the global financial and insurance business with respect to sustainable development. So far climate change aspects have been the dominant aspect in managing sustainability risks and opportunities, accompanied by the development of several legislative initiatives triggered by supervisory authorities. However, a sole concentration on these aspects misses out other important economic and social facets of sustainable development goals formulated by the UN. Such aspects have very recently come into the focus of the European Committee concerning the Solvency II project for the European insurance industry. Clearly the new legislative expectations can be better handled by larger insurance companies and holdings than by small- and medium-sized mutual insurance companies which are numerous in central Europe, due to their historic development starting in the late medieval ages and early modern times. We therefore also concentrate on strategies within the risk management of such small- and medium-sized enterprises that can be achieved without much effort, in particular those that are not directly related to climate change. We start this study with a general overview of the UN sustainable development goals and their implementation in the financial sector world-wide, with a major focus on climate change aspects of investments in a lower carbon economy and economic support of underdeveloped countries that were prevailing until very recently. Although the insurance sector can be considered as a particular branch of the finance industry there are several particularities which need a separate consideration. In the first place, insurance provides a protection of individuals and companies against severe material and non-material losses. Therefore the insurance premiums must be invested safely, in particular under actual insurance regulations like Solvency II. But the insurance industry is also faced with new emerging risks due to climate change, in both the life and non-life sector. Moreover, the European development of insurance regulation has very recently focused also on other sustainability aspects than those related to climate change. We discuss this aspect of risk management in a separate section of this study. Finally, we discuss in detail appropriate strategies how small- and medium sized insurance companies in Europe can handle the new challenges of insurance supervision without too much effort. Our suggestions are mainly driven by own experiences from practice.

Keywords: SDG, CSR, ESG, green finance, green insurance, sustainable development

1. Introduction

In 2015, the United Nations (UN) member states adopted a far-reaching resolution with the intention to transform the world [1, p. 7]. Under the impression that the targets that were originally formulated in the Millennium Development Goals (MDGs), which were the dominating political framework from 2000 to 2015, were seemingly not completely reached, the MDGs were replaced by the 2030 Agenda for Sustainable Development [2]. The eight MDGs were replaced by seventeen Sustainable Development Goals (SDGs) that should be achieved world-wide by 2030:

1. No Poverty
2. Zero Hunger
3. Good Health and Well-Being
4. Quality Education
5. Gender Equality
6. Clean Water and Sanitation
7. Affordable and Clean Energy
8. Decent Work and Economic Growth
9. Industry, Innovation and Infrastructure
10. Reduced Inequalities
11. Sustainable Cities and Communities
12. Responsible Consumption and Production
13. Climate Action
14. Life below Water
15. Life on Land
16. Peace, Justice and Strong Institutions
17. Partnership

A parallel initiative to these goals for long-range sustainable economic and business activities was the development of the concept of Corporate Social Responsibilities (CSR) [3]. "More specifically, CSR for example involves fair business practices, staff-oriented human resource management, economical use of natural resources, protection of the climate and environment, sincere commitment to the local community, and also responsibility along the global supply chain" [4], p. 3. PRI Association, an investor initiative in partnership with UNEP Finance Initiative and UN Global Compact, has introduced Environmental, Social, and Governance (ESG) issues in their principles for sustainable investments to varying degrees across companies, sectors, regions, asset classes and through time [5], p. 2. Some examples of ESG issues are [6], p. 3.

Environmental (E)	Biodiversity loss, greenhouse gas emissions, climate change, renewable energy, energy efficiency, environmental pollution, waste management, ozone depletion, changes in land use, ocean acidification, changes to the nitrogen and phosphorus cycles
Social (S)	Human rights, labour standards in the supply chain, child labour, workplace health and safety, freedom of association and freedom of expression, human capital management and employee relations, diversity, activities in conflict zones, controversial weapons
Governance (G)	Company board structure, size, diversity, skills and independence, executive pay, shareholder rights, stakeholder interaction, disclosure of information, business ethics, bribery and corruption, internal controls and risk management

In the course of time, CSR has moved from a type of international private business self-regulation, along the lines of the UN SDGs expressed through the ESGs, to a more generally accepted source of principles and mandatory schemes at regional, national and international levels, including bilateral investment treaties and free trade agreements [7].

2. The role of the financial sector in sustainable development

Climate change and ESG issues have strongly influenced the finance sector – both banking and insurance – world-wide in the last decades [8]. The manner in which institutional investors approach ESG issues is gaining increased attention in particular across OECD countries. Pension funds, insurers and asset managers have to understand and respond to potential risks and opportunities arising from ESG-related factors in order to safeguard the assets that they invest on behalf of their beneficiaries and clients. At the same time, regulators must be confident that institutional investors meet the required standards of prudence and care when they include ESG considerations in their portfolio decisions [9]. This is also stressed in the reports of the Global Sustainable Investment Alliance who define sustainable investing as an investment approach that considers ESG factors in portfolio selection and management [10].

Concerning climate change aspects, the Financial Stability Board Bank for International Settlements has established a Task Force on Climate-related Financial Disclosures (TCFD), which establishes recommendations for disclosing clear, comparable and consistent information about the risks and opportunities presented by climate change. Their widespread adoption will guarantee that possible effects of climate change become regularly considered in business and investment decisions. A routine use of these recommendations will also support companies in a better demonstration of their responsibility and foresight in climate issues [11]. Nearly 200 countries agreed in December 2015 to reduce greenhouse gas emissions and accelerate the transition to a lower-carbon economy. A particular issue here are investments in alternative clean, energy efficient energy sources, for example, windmills, solar energy or water power. The expected transition to a lower-carbon economy is estimated to require around $1 trillion of investments a year for the proximate future, thereby also generating new investment opportunities. The United Nations Environment Programme (UNEP) has been supporting the idea of creating a sustainable financial system since 2014 with a purpose of mobilizing capital for sustainable development and achieving a green and inclusive economy.

A particular strategy that has been singled here out is green finance. Globally speaking, developing economies face serious challenges concerning mobilizing capital related to green investments. For these countries, one source for external capital flow is represented by foreign direct investments (FDI), which generally target projects related to energy, waste, water, or agricultural development. In addition to FDI, other sources of external capital flow are concessional loans from international financial institutions, long-term commercial debts, aid and remittances. The major aim of issuing green bonds is raising financial resources for climate change initiatives. These fixed-income instruments are generally oriented to climate-friendly activities. The performance of green bonds issued in US dollars and Euros has been superior as compared to non-green bonds [12]. A recent study by the National Bank of Belgium has investigated this topic in more detail [13]. It is interesting to notice that the authors have applied sophisticated statistical methods to obtain their conclusions. In particular, their findings were:

- No statistically significant difference was seen between the overall distribution, the mean or median of bond's asset swap spread changes on individual bond pairs.
- There are indications that the volatility of some green-bonds is lower than their non-green counterparts.
- There are indications that sustainable investments like green bonds are potentially more immune to systemic crises.

Sophisticated econometric statistical methods were also the basis of the recent paper [12]. For their analysis, the authors used the variables domestic credit from banks and domestic credit from the financial sector in USA, Canada and Brazil. Gross domestic product (GDP) was used as a proxy for sustainability of economic growth, along with CO_2 and N_2O emissions, which are caused by manufacturing, agriculture, the use of forests and fisheries. According to their findings, bank credit is insufficient to achieve green financing. For the purpose of increasing economic growth and reducing global warming, the financial sector should assume a bigger role in increasing green investments. Their results show that the level of domestic credit within financial sectors contributes to green financing, while CO_2 emissions remain a challenge for reaching the 1.5 ° C target.

The use of science-based methods in the judgment of climate related risks is also stressed in the Technical Supplement by the TCFD [14]. In general, the most significant effects of climate change are probably emerging over a medium- to long-term time horizon, but their precise timing and magnitude are uncertain. This uncertainty induces challenges in understanding the potential effects of climate change on business, strategies, and financial performance. It is, therefore, important to investigate how climate-related risks and opportunities may potentially evolve and how they affect business under different conditions. One way to assess such implications is through the use of scenario analysis.

Scenario analysis is a well-established method for developing input to strategic plans in order to enhance plan flexibility or resiliency to a range of future states. The use of scenario analysis for assessing climate-related risks and opportunities and their potential business implications, however, is relatively recent. Given the importance of forward-looking assessments of climate-related risk, the Task Force believes that scenario analysis is an important and useful tool for an organization to use, both for understanding strategic implications of climate-related risks and opportunities and for informing stakeholders about how the organization is positioning itself in light of these risks and opportunities. It also can provide useful forward-looking information to investors, lenders, and insurance underwriters.

This topic has also been addressed in a Working Group of 16 banks piloting the TCFD Recommendations under a UNEP Finance Initiative, with a special emphasis on credit risk [15]. The physical aspects from a changing climate were accompanied by a follow-up study [16].

In the insurance and reinsurance industry, these aspects have already been the basis of judgments on the effects of natural catastrophes like windstorm, hailstorm or flooding on insured portfolios for a long time [17].

Another central aspect in this discussion is the public disclosure of sustainable business activities. In order to implement and internalize the sustainability by businesses, it should, first of all, be traceable and measurable. This is possible through sustainability reporting. Sustainability reports show that there are differences among countries and even among sectors. In developed countries such as the USA, the UK, and Australia, such reports contain – besides climatic and environmental aspects – qualitative information in social and governance areas such as number of employees, salary and bonuses, and employee training [18].

3. The role of the insurance sector in sustainable development

Insurance companies - life insurers as well as providers of property and casualty, health, and financial coverage - perform important economic functions and are big players in financial markets. They enable economic agents to diversify idiosyncratic risk, thereby supplying the necessary preconditions for certain business activities. They are a major source of long-term risk capital to the real economy, and are among the largest institutional investors [19]. The overall assets invested by the insurance sector in 2018 were more than 32 trillion US $ [20].

Although the insurance sector is generally seen as a part of the financial sector there are, however, some peculiarities. Essentially, insurance is the process of an exchange of unpredictable financial risks (whether for individuals or for institutions) against a fixed monetary premium. The statistical basis for insurance to work economically sufficient is the famous law of large numbers discovered by Jakob I Bernoulli in the late 17th century [21]. Therefore sophisticated actuarial risk models and elaborate statistical calculations are a fundamental basis of insurance [22]. While the actuarial processes for insurance have been in continuous development since early on, it really took until the second half of the twentieth century for a modern theory of insurance economics to emerge [23]. The central idea here is the concept of risk diversification, which also plays an essential role in insurance regulation. Since in particular life insurance requires an utmost degree of safety in financial asset investments, governmental regulation is of great importance here; and has been set to work in almost all developed countries over the world. In Europe, this was accomplished by the Solvency II project finalized in 2016 [24].

The investment strategy (asset management) of insurance companies is limited by regulations and driven by a number of internal and external factors [25].

Insurers must invest conservatively. They must ensure that they remain solvent throughout and are able to make their payouts to the policyholders with the highest probability at any time. Insurers have a fiduciary obligation to keep or augment the value of their 'policyholder' assets. This poses constraints on the industry's investment strategies.

Furthermore, insurance regulators impose risk-based capital charges on investments to ensure adequate capital levels to cover insurers' liabilities; the riskier the investment, the higher the capital charge. These vary by country and region. It is important to note that different lines of business are exposed to different risks. That is why financial risks associated with assets and liabilities are managed differently by life and non-life insurers. Specifically,

- Life insurers are typically 'buy and hold' investors. They aim to generate predictable and stable income to match cash flows of long-dated and generally predictable liabilities. Life insurance contract duration can range from ten years to several decades, involving payout patterns of 20 to 30 years [25]. Life insurers are deeply concerned about the asset-liability mismatch, with interest rate risk being a key issue.

- Non-life insurers are geared towards more liquid investments with shorter time horizons, typically one to three year in duration [26]. However, in some instances (e.g. asbestos-related), claims are paid out many years later, exposing them to interest rate risk.

The discussion of sustainable developments in the finance sector as outlined in the preceding section has, of course, also reached the insurance sector. Firstly, one can distinguish between sustainability risks and opportunities on the asset side and on the insurer's liability side [3].

Major issues that can potentially arise from sustainability risks on the asset side include credit risk, market risk, liquidity risk, insurance risk, strategic risk and reputational risk. The German supervisory authority BaFin [26], p. 18 provides the following ostensive examples:

i. Credit risk/counterparty default risk: A credit institution providing a loan to an entity with a business model that is significantly damaged by political decisions on ESG issues (such as a CO_2 charge).

ii. Market risk: A pension fund or investment fund could be invested in companies which do not demonstrate sustainable management or use the invested monies for transition towards sustainability. An abrupt change in market sentiment (e.g. to reflect the cost of regulatory measures) might lead to declines in value.

iii. Liquidity risk: After a catastrophic flood, tens of thousands of clients withdraw money from their accounts at a regional credit institution in order to finance damage repairs. The credit institution has to sell a high level of assets to cover these outflows.

iv. Insurance risk: Homeowners' insurance claims rise as a result of storms, floods or hail. Business interruption insurance claims may also rise. The increasing intensity and/or frequency of such events should be appropriately reflected in the assessment of technical provisions or premium risk. In this context it is also worth considering that insurance undertakings may be affected by the same sustainability risk on both the asset and the liability side.

v. Strategic risk: A credit institution specialized in financing coal mining loses the basis of its business.

vi. Reputational risk: An investment fund is invested in a clothing factory owned by a well-known brand in East Asia. The building burns down as a result of inadequate national safety standards, hundreds of workers die, reports circulating in the media name the investor. The sale of allegedly sustainable financial products (known as greenwashing) to those seeking ESG-compliant investments may also represent a reputational risk.

Important issues that can potentially arise from sustainability risks on the liability side include natural catastrophes due to windstorm, hailstorm and flooding. Beyond insured losses from physical climate damages, climate trends and shocks can cause far-reaching economic disruptions. The insurance "protection gap" for weather related losses remains significant, with roughly 70% of losses uninsured. This leaves significant burden on households, businesses, and governments. Uninsured losses arising from physical risks may have cascading impacts across the financial system, including impacts on investment companies and banks. Likewise, the availability of insurance – or risk of uninsurability due to high physical risk profiles – can have significant impacts on the performance of credit and investment across the economy (including, for instance, mortgage lending) [27]. Historically, insured risks from natural disasters were to a great extend covered by world-wide operating reinsurers with a high grade of global diversification. In the recent years, new financial products were created shifting insurance risks to the financial market, e.g. cat bonds or other climate related derivatives [28]. However, as the severity and frequency of significant natural disasters increases, the availability and cost of reinsurance cover for weather-related risks may become prohibitive for smaller insurers in certain markets – potentially leading to a reinsurance gap [27].

Another possible threat is a rise in mortality due to climate change. Extreme high air temperatures contribute directly to deaths from cardiovascular and respiratory disease, particularly among elderly people. In the heat wave of summer 2003 in Europe, for example, more than 70 000 excess deaths were recorded. High temperatures also raise the levels of ozone and other pollutants in the air that exacerbate cardiovascular and respiratory disease [29]. Life and health insurers are in many cases just beginning to explore the impacts of climate factors on their underwriting portfolios. The potential impacts of climate change on mortality – in particular due to extremes in weather events like excessive heat – are coming into the focus of actuarial associations, who are exploring the matter in relationship to insurance, annuity and pension programmes [27].

Besides the pure monetary aspects of climate change risks and their management, also other ESG criteria have recently come into the focus of the insurance industry and their supervisors. An important lesson learned is the need for financial supervisory authorities, as well as the supervised companies, to be deeply engaged in efforts that incorporate ESG risks into their business. This requires a profound change of mind-set within institutions. In order to attain this engagement, it is very important for supervisors to raise awareness of ESG issues through provision of information, guidance, and capacity building [27].

4. The European way for the insurance sector in sustainable development

In 2018, the European Insurance and Occupational Pensions Authority (EIOPA), received a request from the European Commission for an opinion on sustainability within Solvency II, with a particular focus on aspects relating to climate change mitigation [30]. According to EIOPA's understanding, the term "climate risks" aims to include all risks stemming from trends or events caused by climate change, i.e., *climate change-related risks*. This encompasses extreme weather events, including natural catastrophes, but also more general climate trends such as a general rise in temperature, sea level rise, or climate-related forced migration that could affect (re) insurance activity. Concerning the impact of climate change-related risks on non-life, health and life insurance, EIOPA tried to collect information from non-life (re) insurance business. This initial step was motivated by the consideration that non-life lines of business may be affected by climate change effects over a shorter time period than the life and health business. In addition, EIOPA started to collect additional evidence on the impact of climate change related risks on the morbidity and mortality risks through a public consultation. An integration of sustainability risks in Pillar 1 of Solvency II has to take account of capital requirements within the overall Solvency II framework which aims to ensure that undertakings can survive severe unexpected shocks (losses) and still meet their obligations to policyholders over a one-year period [31] (Article 101(3) of the Solvency II Directive [32]). The Solvency II Directive expresses this as the ability to withstand shocks with a 1 in 200 probability within this one-year time horizon.

Capital requirements in Solvency II are calibrated based on a one-year time horizon, while sustainability risks are generally considered to be long-term risks. In particular, climate change-related risks are expected to emerge over a longer time horizon which presents practical challenges for integrating them in the current Pillar 1 capital requirements.

Further, specifically for traditional non-life business, the insurance cover period (during which undertakings are liable for claims that occur) just spans the next 12 months, at the end of which, undertakings can theoretically adjust the pricing for the future, based on claims experience. This repricing is, in particular, enabled by the fact that the uncertainty on the final amount of natural catastrophe claims is limited, as they are usually settled within one year after their occurrence.

Unfortunately, market participants tend to believe that they have time to adapt their investment strategy within the next 10 to 20 years, and thus firms have limited incentives to consider climate change risks, in particular, transitions risks, in their asset portfolio today. This behavior refers to the so-called "tragedy of the horizon" coined by Mark Carney [8].

Accompanying the aforementioned aspects, the European Commission has initiated a Taxonomy Regulation (TR), agreed at the political level in December 2019, which was intended to create a legal basis for the EU Taxonomy, published as a directive in 2020 [33]. As explained in the final Report of the Technical Expert Group on Sustainable Finance (TEG) [34] the TR sets out the framework and environmental objectives for the Taxonomy, as well as new legal obligations for financial market participants, large companies, the EU and Member States. The EU Taxonomy is a tool to help investors, companies, issuers and project promoters navigate the transition to a low-carbon, resilient and resource-efficient economy. The TR will be supplemented by delegated acts which contain detailed technical screening criteria for determining when an economic activity can be considered sustainable, and hence can be considered Taxonomy-aligned.

Consistent with the EU Action Plan on Financing Sustainable Growth, finance is a critical enabler of transformative improvements in existing industries in Europe and globally. The OECD estimates that, globally, EUR 6.35 trillion a year will be required to meet Paris Agreement goals by 2030. Public sector resources will not be adequate to meet this challenge, and mobilization of institutional and private capital will be necessary [34].

A part of these reflections has, meanwhile, also found entry in the foremen-tioned Taxonomy Directive, in particular, in Articles 9 and 10 [33]. As environmen-tal objectives, the following topics are considered:

a. climate change mitigation;

b. climate change adaptation;

c. the sustainable use and protection of water and marine resources;

d. the transition to a circular economy;

e. pollution prevention and control;

f. the protection and restoration of biodiversity and ecosystems.

European insurance companies will be strongly affected by these political measures in the future, especially concerning their asset management. It will, however, be difficult to judge which investments are truly Taxonomy-aligned. E.g., in Solvency II, government and related bonds are considered to be the safest investment in Pillar I, but governments typically also engage in the armaments industry or fossil energy, like brown and stone coal mining in Germany, contradicting, in part, the above topics.

Recently, further ESG aspects other than mere climate change risks, have come into the focus of European insurance supervisors. For instance, the German supervisory authority BaFin compiles the following ESG topics as specific examples to be considered in the future by European insurance companies [26, p. 13]:

Environmental (E)	Climate mitigation; adjustment to climate change; protection of biodiversity; the sustainable use and protection of water and maritime resources; the transition to a circular economy, the avoidance of waste, and recycling; the avoidance and reduction of environmental pollution, the protection of healthy ecosystems; sustainable land use
Social (S)	Compliance with recognized labour standards (no child labour, forced labour or discrimination); compliance with employment safety and health protection; appropriate remuneration, fair working conditions, diversity, and training and development opportunities; trade union rights and freedom of assembly; guarantee of adequate product safety, including health protection; application of the same requirements to entities in the supply chain; inclusive projects and consideration of the interests of communities and social minorities
Governance (G)	Tax honesty; anti-corruption measures; sustainability management by the board; board remuneration based on sustainability criteria; the facilitation of whistle blowing; employee rights guarantees; data protection guarantees; information disclosure

These aspects were already partly addressed in the EU directive on non-financial disclosure in 2014, acknowledging the importance of publishing businesses information on sustainability such as social and environmental factors, with a view to identifying sustainability risks and increasing investor and consumer trust. Actually, disclosure of non-financial information is vital for managing change towards a sustainable global economy by combining long-term profitability with social justice and environmental protection. Thus, disclosure of non-financial information helps the measuring, monitoring and managing of undertakings' performance and their impact on society in order to take account of the multidimensional nature of corporate social responsibility (CSR) and the diversity of the CSR policies implemented by businesses matched by a sufficient level of comparability to meet the needs of investors and other stakeholders, as well as the need to provide consumers with easy access to information on the impact of businesses on society [35].

5. The role of small and medium sized insurance enterprises in Europe

Relatively little is, in general, known about CSR and ESG among small and medium sized enterprises (SMEs). Where SMEs are doing it, they may not use the language of CSR or ESG. Just as the best of SMEs are a source of innovation for business generally, so it can be assumed that the best of environmentally and socially responsible SMEs will offer CSR innovations. Efforts to engage more SMEs in CSR should be mindful of this fact. They should reflect the daily realities of SME life. They should work through channels as close to SMEs as possible, which SMEs already use and trust. This will involve a range of initiatives at local, regional, national, EU and sectoral levels. They will include initiatives from different stakeholder groups such as staff and consumers [36]. This is of special importance since the share of SMEs in total in the world is over 96%. This ratio is 99% in Germany, Japan, and France. Therefore, the place of SMEs in the economy is very important in general. It is known that SMEs play an important role in helping economic and social developments of countries as they rapidly adapt to the changing market conditions, have flexible production structures, achieve balanced growth among the regions, and help reduce unemployment [18]. In the insurance sector, typical SMEs are mutual insurance companies that reflect the original idea of insurance at best. Many of them were already founded in the late middle and early modern age as guilds or friendly societies in the Netherlands, Germany, France, England, and later, also in Northern America [37]. These institutions probably reflect the original insurance idea of a humanitarian protection against life or business existence threats at its best. In Germany, 241 out of a total of 535 insurance companies were organized in the form of a mutual company in 2019, which corresponds to 45% in number, although their share in the total premium income was only 14.7% [38].

With respect to ESG criteria, mutual SMEs can play an important role without much effort. We discuss several suggestions in more detail in the following section.

5.1 Environmental

A careful asset management can concentrate on investments that are veritably Taxonomy-aligned ("green assets"). However, there is a delicate balancing act between risky assets which require additional solvency capital according to Solvency II (like investments in alternative energy supply) and less risky assets, which are probably not, or only in part, Taxonomy-aligned (like government and related bonds).

A new initiative that has come up recently is a direct sponsorship of local environmental projects (e.g. planting trees in the company's environment) or the establishment of a "green" non-profit foundation that provides financial resources for various local and cross-regional programmes that are not only restricted to environmental aspects but also to SG. Such a foundation has been incorporated recently by the GVO Mutual Insurance Company. The idea here is to donate regularly a certain monetary amount (say 1 Euro) per contract and year to the foundation. Similar activities can also apply to the company's head office building (green roofing, CO2 neutral energy supply, an improved heat insulation and other architectural aspects), the use of local supply chains for stationery and other office supplies, or an environmentally friendly car fleet.

But also, innovative insurance products can contribute to environmental protection and sustainability ("green insurance"). For instance, concerning the household contents insurance, the policy could guarantee a replacement of damaged technical devices with corresponding devices of the highest available energy efficiency class, e.g. refrigerators, washing machines, stoves and other appliances. In Germany, it has turned out that such a kind of insurance products is appealing more and more to the younger generation who has a higher mental affinity to environmental and climate protection. Seemingly, this clientele is also willing to pay a slightly higher premium in the awareness of a constructive contribution to environmental and climate protection.

Similar reflections also apply to agricultural insurance products, which are for a large part, handled by mutual insurance companies. The idea here is a kind of premium gratification system for countrymen who, e.g., avoid excessive chemical fertilizers or who care responsibly about their livestock breeding.

A completely new generation of insurance products concerns the private traffic sector. Due to new technologies like blockchain [39], it becomes possible to create car liability insurance products where the premium depends on the individual driving behavior ("pay how you drive") [40]. This could give incentives to car owners to adapt their driving behavior to the environment (less fuel consumption, less deterioration). Even if insurance SMEs are, in most cases, not able to handle the technical challenges connected with blockchain products themselves, they can easily serve as insurance brokers. A new line of insurance products emerges actually with bicycle insurance comprehensive coverage in Germany, in particular for pedelecs and e-bikes. This might give incentives to people to abstain from using cars with combustion engines in cities in favor of environment-friendly mobility.

5.2 Social

SMEs are in general frequently characterized by flat management hierarchies. This facilitates to a great extent precaution measures for their employees, guarantees of equal opportunities and of workforce diversity, safety of workplaces, respecting a worker's council and the implementation of a staff unit for conflict management and whistle blowing.

On the personal side, SMEs can provide individual retirement arrangements, gratification programmes, support of continuing business education and honorary appointments, the establishment of an appropriate in-house television network for the employees, or in-house sportive activities within a general health programme. The GVO Mutual Insurance Company, for instance, sponsors general all sportive activities of their staff in-house and outdoor.

Social aspects are also immanent in many insurance products like life, accident, health, business interruption, and complementary insurance contracts.

5.3 Governance

Although several legislative regulations prescribed by the European Taxonomy and Transparency Directive concern only large companies say with more than 500 employees, insurance SMEs can of course decide for a voluntary disclosure of their ESG activities, in particular when they pursue outstanding environmental sponsoring programmes, as e.g. the GVO Mutual Insurance Company does. Personally, a typically small and responsible Board of Directors of an SME can serve as business ideal for the employees, thus preventing stimulation of misconduct and deception. Further, sustainability aspects can and must become an indispensable part of the whole business culture, which, in particular, insurance SMEs can easily implement due to their flat business hierarchy. This concerns, besides business processes and service regulations supervised by the CEOs, the complete in-house staff as well as the employed field staff or sales department and the IT department of the company.

It is important to state that an implementation of all of the aforementioned examples will in general not lead to an increase in the company's risk profile which would be crucial in the light of the Solvency II directive.

6. Conclusions

The world is rapidly changing due to an increase in climate variation and environment pollution, but also with respect to social problems like poverty, suppression and migration. In the awareness of these challenges, the UN has formulated several Sustainable Development Goals to be reached by 2030. As a reaction, the finance and insurance sector has initiated several activities to help overcoming these problems, accompanied by strong legal directives, particularly in Europe. A very important role here is played by insurance SMEs, which represent a significant number of companies in the insurance industry. Due to their flat management hierarchies and local business orientation, they are able to comply with almost all legal ESG demands without accumulating a higher risk profile, and can easily serve as forerunners in the propagation of ESG principles in the society. Thus, insurance SMEs can and will contribute to a promising way to reach the UN Sustainable Development Goals in the future.

Acknowledgements

We would like to thank the Board of Directors of the GVO Mutual Insurance Company for permanent support and many fruitful discussions.

Conflict of interest

The authors declare no conflict of interest.

Author details

Dietmar Pfeifer[1,2]* and Vivien Langen[2]

1 University of Oldenburg, Institute of Mathematics, Germany

2 GVO Mutual Insurance Company Oldenburg, Germany

*Address all correspondence to: dietmar.pfeifer@uni-oldenburg.de

References

[1] Deutsche Gesellschaft für Internationale Zusammenarbeit (GIZ). Inclusive insurance and the Sustainable Development Goals - how insurance contributes to the 2030 Agenda for Sustainable Development (2017). Available from: https://microinsurancenetwork.org/sites/default/files/Inclusive%20Insurance%20and%20the%20Sustainable%20Development%20Goals%20.pdf [Accessed: 2020-11-13]

[2] United Nations: Transforming Our World: The 2030 Agenda for Sustainable Development. A/RES/70/1 (2015). Available from: https://sustainabledevelopment.un.org/content/documents/21252030%20Agenda%20for%20Sustainable%20Development%20web.pdf

[3] Sheehy B. Understanding CSR: An empirical study of private regulation (2012). Monash University Law Review (Vol 38, No 2), 103-127

[4] Gatzert N, Reichel P, Zitzmann A. Sustainability risks & opportunities in the insurance industry. ZVersWiss 109 (2020). DOI:10.1007/s12297-020-00482-w

[5] PRI Association. Impact investing market map (2018a). Available from: https://www.unpri.org/download?ac=5426 [Accessed: 2020-11-13] PRI Association.

[6] PRI reporting framework - main definitions (2018b). Available from: https://d8g8t13e9vf2o.cloudfront.net/Uploads/d/t/z/ main definitions to pri reporting framework_127272.pdf [Accessed: 2020-11-13]

[7] Condon M. The Integration of Environmental Law into International Investment Treaties and Trade Agreements : Negotiation Process and the Legalization of Commitments (2015). Boston University School of Law. Available from: http://ssrn.com/abstract=2693207 [Accessed: 2020-11-13]

[8] Carney M. Breaking the tragedy of the horizon - climate change and financial stability (2015). Available from: https://www.bankofengland.co.uk/-/media/boe/files/speech/2015/breaking-the-tragedy-of-the-horizon-climate-change-and-financial-stability.pdf? la=en&hash=7C67E785651862457D99511147C7424FF5EA0C1A [Accessed: 2020-11-13]

[9] Organisation for Economic Co-Operation and Development (OECD). Investment governance and the integration of environmental, social and governance factors (2017). Available from: http://www.oecd.org/investment/Investment-Governance-Integration-ESG-Factors.pdf [Accessed: 2020-11-13]

[10] Global Sustainable Investment Alliance (GSIA). 2018 Global Sustainable Investment Review. Available from: http://www.gsialliance.org/wpcontent/uploads/2019/06/GSIR_Review2018F.pdf [Accessed: 2020-11-13]

[11] Task Force on Climate-related Financial Disclosures (TCFD): Final report: Recommendations of the Task Force on Climate-related Financial Disclosures (2017). Available from: https://www.fsbtcfd.org/wpcontent/uploads/2017/06/FINAL-2017-TCFD-Report-11052018.pdf [Accessed: 2020-11-13]

[12] Batrancea I, Batrancea L, Rathnaswamy M M, Tulai H, Fatacean G, Rus M-I. Greening the Financial System in USA, Canada and Brazil: A Panel Data Analysis. Submitted to MDPI mathematics, 2020, 8(12), 2217. DOI: 10.3390/math8122217

[13] Ma C, Schoutens W, Beirlant J, De Spiegeleer J, Stephan Höcht S, Van Kleeck R. Are green bonds different

from ordinary bonds? A statistical and quantitative point of view. Working Paper Research No 394, National Bank of Belgium, October 2020. Available from: https://www.nbb.be/doc/ts/publications/wp/wp394en.pdf [Accessed: 2020-11-13]

[14] Task Force on Climate-related Financial Disclosures (TCFD): Technical Supplement: The Use of Scenario Analysis in Disclosure of Climate-Related Risks and Opportunities (2017b). Available from: https://assets.bbhub.io/company/sites/60/2020/10/FINAL-TCFD-Technical-Supplement-062917.pdf [Accessed: 2020-11-13]

[15] UNEP Finance Initiative. Extending our horizons: Assessing credit risk and opportunity in a changing climate: Outputs of a working group of 16 banks piloting the TCFD Recommendations. Part 1: Transition-related risks & opportunities (2018). Available from: https://www.unepfi.org/news/themes/climate-change/extending-our-horizons/ [Accessed: 2020-11-13]

[16] UNEP Finance Initiative. Navigating a new climate: Assessing credit risk and opportunity in a changing climate: Outputs of a working group of 16 banks piloting the TCFD Recommendations. Part 2: Physical risks & opportunities (2018). Available from: http://www.unepfi.org/wordpress/wp-content/uploads/2018/07/NAVIGATING-A-NEW-CLIMATE.pdf [Accessed: 2020-11-13]

[17] Grossi P, Kunreuther H. Catastrophe Modeling: A new approach to managing risk (2005). Boston: Springer Science + Business Media, Inc.

[18] Şahin Z, Çankaya F. The Importance of Sustainability and Sustainability Reporting. In: Çalıyurt K T, editor. New Approaches to CSR, Sustainability and Accountability, Volume I. Singapore: Springer Nature; 2020. p. 45-59. DOI: 10.1007/978-981-32-9588-9_4

[19] *International Monetary Fund* (IMF). *Global Financial Stability Report* - Potent Policies for a Successful Normalization (2016). Washington, April *2016*. Available from: https://www.imf.org/-/media/Websites/IMF/imported-full-text-pdf/external/pubs/ft/gfsr/2016/01/pdf/_text.ashx [Accessed: 2020-11-13]

[20] Statista Inc. Total assests of insurance companies worldwide from 2002 to 2018 (2020). Available from: https://www.statista.com/statistics/421217/assets-of-global-insurance-companies/ [Accessed: 2020-11-13]

[21] Heyde C C, Seneta E, editors. Statisticians of the Centuries (2001). New York: Springer Science+Business Media

[22] Daykin C D, Pentikäinen T, Pesonen M. Practical Risk Theory for Actuaries (1994). London: Chapman & Hall

[23] Zweifel P, Eisen R. Insurance Economics (2012). Berlin: Springer. DOI: 10.1007/978-3-642-20548-4

[24] European Parliament and Council. Commission Delegated Regulation (EU) 2015/35 of 10 October 2014 supplementing Directive 2009/138/EC of the European Parliament and of the Council on the taking-up and pursuit of the business of Insurance and Reinsurance (Solvency II) (2015). Official Journal of the European Union L12/1-797

[25] The Geneva Association. Climate Change and the Insurance Industry: Taking Action as Risk Managers and Investors. Perspectives from C-level executives in the insurance industry (2018). Zürich.

[26] Bundesanstalt für Finanzdienstleistungsaufsicht (BaFin): Guidance notice on dealing with sustainability risks (2020). Available from: https://www.bafin.de/SharedDocs/Downloads/EN/Merkblatt/

dl_mb_Nachhaltigkeitsrisiken_en.pdf?__blob=publicationFile&v=5 [Accessed: 2020-11-13]

[27] International Association of Insurance Supervisors (IAIS). Issues Paper on Climate Change Risks (2018). Available from: http://www.unepfi.org/psi/wp-content/uploads/2018/08/IAIS_SIF_-Issues-Paper-on-Climate-Change-Risks-to-the-Insurance-Sector.pdf [Accessed: 2020-11-13]

[28] Gurenko E N, editor. Catastrophe Risk and Reinsurance. A Country Risk Management Perspective (2004). London, RISK Books, Incisive Financial Publishing

[29] World Health Organization (WHO). Climate Change and Health (2018). Available from: https://www.who.int/news-room/fact-sheets/detail/climate-change-and-health [Accessed: 2020-11-13]

[30] European Insurance and Occupational Pensions Authority (EIOPA). Opinion on Sustainability within Solvency II (2019). EIOPA-BoS-19/241. Available from: https://www.eiopa.europa.eu/sites/default/files/publications/opinions/2019-09-30_opinionsustainabilitywithinsolvencyii.pdf [Accessed: 2020-11-13]

[31] European Insurance and Occupational Pensions Authority (EIOPA). Technical Advice on the integration of sustainability risks and factors in the delegated acts under Solvency II and IDD (2019). Available from: https://register.eiopa.europa.eu/Publications/EIOPA-BoS-19-172_Final_Report_Technical_advice_for_the_integration_of_sustainability_risks_and_factors.pdf [Accessed: 2020-11-13]

[32] European Parliament and Council. Directive 2009/138/EC of the European Parliament and of the Council of 25 November 2009 on the taking-up and pursuit of the business of Insurance and Reinsurance (Solvency II) (2009) Official Journal of the European Union L335/1-155. Available from: https://eur-lex.europa.eu/legal-content/EN/TXT/PDF/?uri=CELEX:32009L0138&from=en [Accessed: 2020-11-13]

[33] European Parliament and Council. Regulation (EU) 2020/852 of 18 June 2020 on the establishment of a framework to facilitate sustainable investment, and amending Regulation (EU) 2019/2088 (2020). Official Journal of the European Union L198/13-43. Available from: https://eurlex.europa.eu/legalcontent/EN/TXT/PDF/?uri=CELEX:32020R0851&from=EN [Accessed: 2020-11-13]

[34] EU Technical Expert Group on Sustainable Finance (TEG). Taxonomy: Final report (2020). Available from: https://ec.europa.eu/info/sites/info/files/business_economy_euro/banking_and_finance/documents/200309-sustainable-finance-teg-final-report-taxonomy_en.pdf [Accessed: 2020-11-13]

[35] European Parliament and Council. Directive 2014/95/EC of the European Parliament and of the Council of 22 October 2014 amending Directive 2013/34/EU as regards disclosure of non-financial and diversity information by certain large undertakings and groups (2014). Official Journal of the European Union L330/1-9. Available from: https://eur-lex.europa.eu/legal-content/EN/TXT/PDF/?uri=CELEX:32014L0095&from=EN [Accessed: 2020-11-13]

[36] European Multistakeholder Forum on CSR (EMF CSR). Report of the Round Table on 'Fostering CSR among smes' (2004). Available from: https://docplayer.net/39820177-Report-of-the-round-table-on-fostering-csr-among-smes.html [Accessed: 2020-11-13]

[37] Van Leeuwen M H D. Mutual Insurance 1550-2015. From Guild

Welfare and Friendly Societies to Contemporary Micro-Insurers. London: Palgrave Macmillan, published by Springer Nature. DOI 10.1057/978-1-137-53110-0

[38] Gesamtverband der Deutschen Versicherungswirtschaft (GDV). Statistisches Taschenbuch der Versicherungswirtschaft 2020. Available from: https://www.gdv.de/resource/blob/62142/ac6287aeb67a3a336342e33f55992ffb/statistisches-tb-2020-download-data.pdf [Accessed: 2020-11-13]

[39] Raikwar M, Mazumdar S, Ruj S, Sen Gupta S, Chattopadhyay A, Lam K. A Blockchain Framework for Insurance Processes, 9th IFIP International Conference on New Technologies, Mobility and Security (NTMS), Paris (2018), 1-4. DOI: 10.1109/NTMS.2018.8328731.

[40] Lamberti F, Gatteschi V, Demartini C, Pelissier M, Gomez A, Santamaria V. Blockchains Can Work for Car Insurance: Using Smart Contracts and Sensors to Provide On-Demand Coverage. IEEE Consumer Electronics Magazine, vol. 7, no. 4 (2018), 72-81. DOI: 10.1109/MCE.2018.2816247

Chapter 2

Environmentally Influenced Risk and Sustainable Management of State Controlled Transportation Assets

Wael A. Zatar

Abstract

Federal and state transportation agencies across the world face a multitude of challenges to effectively maintain cost-effective core maintenance programs for managing a safe, yet sustainable transportation assets' program. The decision-making process involves several risk factors, and the prioritization of these factors could considerably affect both the level of utilization of these assets, as well as short- and long-term management protocols and plans for these agencies. The Moving Ahead for Progress in the 21st Century Act requires each state Department of Transportation in the United States to have a risk-based asset management plan in place to preserve the condition of their assets and improve the performance of the National Highway System. Many transportation agencies lack the financial and human resources to achieve their targets, and therefore they may opt to make trade-offs, lower targets, and perhaps drop some important objectives. Trade-off decisions can become clearer when objectives and targets are viewed through the lens of which options reduce the top-priority risks, such as reduced risk to safety, asset performance, or future costs. This chapter primarily focuses on emphasizing the importance of risk management in transportation networks and demonstrating the relationship between environmentally influenced risk management and sustainable management of state-controlled transportation assets in the United States. Several key parameters including risk assessment, financial risk and organizational behavior are addressed. Successful examples demonstrating how transportation agencies have identified how to best address a given risk, and in turn impact the resource allocation process are provided.

Keywords: state controlled transportation assets, environmentally influenced risk, risk assessment, financial risk, organizational behavior

1. Introduction

Federal and state transportation agencies in several countries face a multitude of challenges to routinely maintain effective and cost-effective core maintenance programs for their transportation assets. The focus on uncertainty and variability highlights the importance of managing both opportunities and threats to the agency's priorities. Risk management is a strategic approach that usually adapts to agencies' specific circumstances. It can primarily pave the road for better alignment between operations and the agencies' strategic objectives.

The Transportation Research Board's (TRB) National Cooperative Highway Research Program (NCHRP) Report 08–93 [1] lists levels of risk within transportation agencies including the enterprise, program, project and activity levels. Risk management heightens the identification of threats that could impede objectives, particularly threats to the public's safety and well-being. Seismic excitations, scour damage, frequent flooding, and increasing storm frequency and severity exhibit significant risks to agencies hoping to sustain high-risk assets and to meet their asset-condition targets. Benefits of risk management include the ability to think strategically, produce time savings, enhance the ability to manage uncertainties, shift from a reactive mode to a proactive mode, and make informed decisions.

2. Moving ahead for Progress in the 21st century act (MAP-21)

The Moving Ahead for Progress in the 21st Century Act (MAP-21), signed into law In the United States in July of 2012 [2]. It requires each state Department of Transportation (DOT) to have a risk-based asset management plan in place by 2015 to preserve the condition of their assets and improve the performance of the National Highway System. MAP-21 amended the 23 U.S. Code § 119 - National Highway Performance Program to require State Departments of Transportation (DOTs) to develop risk-based Transportation Asset Management Plans (TAMPs).

3. Transportation asset Management plans

The Federal Highway Administration (FHWA) produced several reports between 2012 and 2013 to detail the concepts and vision for risk-based transportation asset management plans [3–8]. FHWA adopted in 2017 a final TAMP rule that elaborates on the MAP-21 requirements. Both the statute and the FHWA rule identify the TAMP as a central part of the larger Federal performance management process [9]. The TAMP is one of a series of plans State DOTs are required to develop to achieve the Nation's transportation goals. State DOTs are tasked with the development of plans for highway safety, congestion and freight [9]. These plans will continue to influence and inform the larger transportation planning process and its products, Long-Range Statewide Transportation Plan (LRSTP), and Short-Term State Transportation Improvement Program (STIP). Looking at the current transportation funding environment, many transportation agencies lack the financial and human resources to achieve their targets. The agencies must make trade-offs, lower targets, and perhaps drop some important objectives. Trade-off decisions can become clearer when objectives and targets are viewed through the lens of which options reduce the top-priority risks, such as reduced risk to safety, asset performance, or future costs.

The objective of a risk based TAMP is not to avoid all risks. Rather, it is to acknowledge risks, assess and prioritize them, and allocate resources and actions based on the agency's risk tolerance and how the risks could affect the asset management objectives. Risk-based TAMPs acknowledge, identify, assess, and prioritize risks that affect performance. They should identify high-risk assets, such as structures prone to seismic waves, scour damage, frequent flooding and increasing storm frequency and severity [10]. Risk-based TAMPs help agencies make difficult trade-offs of scarce resources to address top-priority risks. By identifying risks, agencies can be more informed about managing their performance.

The FHWA finalized guidance documents for both Transportation Asset Management Plan Development Processes Certification and Recertification Guidance, and Transportation Asset Management Plan Consistency Determination Interim Guidance [11]. These documents were developed to provide implementation guidance on provisions of the MAP-21 and the Asset Management Final Rule, which requires a State department of transportation to develop and implement a risk-based asset management plan [11]. FHWA must certify that TAMP development processes established by a State DOT meet applicable requirements, and make an annual consistency determination, evaluating whether a State DOT has developed and implemented a State-approved TAMP that meets all applicable requirements [11].

4. TAMP goals and targets

TAMP managers and leads in transportation agencies are strong advocates who organize meetings, set schedules, and clearly articulate the group's objective. Their task focuses on identifying, analyzing, prioritizing, and describing how to manage risks to the agency's asset management objectives. It is always advantageous if the TAMP lead has no vested interest in the outcome of the exercise and can engage the entire group to think through the risk management process for all areas relating to the TAMP during the exercise. The type of data and information the group should compile include, but is not limited to: (a) asset management goals and targets; (b) the process for developing the goals and targets; (c) level of achievement of these goals and targets in the past; (d) level of matching with life-cycle planning; (e) checking if the goals and targets take into consideration the long-term effects and the desired State of Good Repair (SOGR); and (f) level of comfort of the staff about meeting these goals and targets [12].

5. Financial forecasting and planning

Transportation agencies perform financial forecasting to plan for future management of their infrastructure assets [13–15]. They examine: (a) types of revenues and bonds; (b) whether revenues are rising or falling; (c) duration and expiation of revenue sources; (d) new initiatives of expansion, safety or other agency high priorities that require funding and if they been considered in future projections; (e) fund availability for investing in assets; (f) level of confidence in the forecast; (g) past trend lines of asset conditions and the accompanying expenditures; and (h) whether the conditions trended positively or negatively, and how were those trends affected by programming decisions [16–19].

In addition, transportation agencies should gather information about major influences that will affect their TAMP and to examine if these agencies expect changes in population, traffic, contractor availability, climate, sea levels, or even revenues and appropriations, that could affect the TAMP. Moreover, the agencies consider the number of structurally deficient structures, aging assets, or deteriorated assets as these will significantly impact the financial planning. The financial planning's should incorporate sound key assumptions that are utilized in managing and forecasting bridges and pavements, as well as other asset investment needs [11–13]. Assumptions related to inflation rates, asset deterioration rates and material performance are included, and the level of accuracy or confidence in the forecasting models should be documented [11–13].

Studies or forecasts for environmental risks that could affect asset performance or agency costs and the likelihood and anticipated severity of seismic activity or extreme weather events should be examined. In accordance with the FHWA's Special Federal-Aid Funding—Implementation of 23 CFR Part 667: Periodic Evaluation of Facilities Repeatedly Requiring Repair and Reconstruction Due to Emergency Events [20], agencies should examine if their inventories include assets from past events that need to be addressed because of environmental conditions such as excessive floods that have created ponding and expedited asset deterioration or fires that have destabilized slopes.

Transportation agencies implement methodologies to describe the process that is used to incorporate the results of the FHWA's 23 CFR Part 667 evaluation into risk management. Each agency should develop and implement an emergency event risk register and prioritize the risks and create risk scores. The development of a risk register assists with the risk management process. The likelihood of the development of environmentally impacted events should be taken into account when developing a risk register. The register could include should cover varying levels of risks ranging from very low to very high ones. Risk scores are essential for making solid decisions for the programming needed to better manage and maintain the agencies' assets.

The TRB NCHRP Synthesis Report on 556 [21]. The objective of this synthesis report was to document practices by state DOTs to identify locations where highway assets have been repeatedly damaged and to identify considerations for mitigating the risk of recurring damage in those areas. The synthesis report focuses on identifying decisions and practices that support use of the results to improve achievement of asset management or performance management objectives [21].

6. Measuring success and continuous improvement

FHWA produced a report for incorporating risk management into transportation asset management in 2017 that depicts a risk management process [9]. It exhibits an iterative monitoring and review process where transportation agencies monitor the risks and update the risk management documentation once these risks are identified, analyzed, and a mitigation plan is developed. The process is generally consistent with ISO Standard 31000, as well as FHWA's requirements for state DOTs to assess risks to the National Highway System (NHS) assets in developing a TAMP.

Successful integration of risk into asset management plans and processes revolves around several key elements and relying on a high-level (top-down) support because risk management works best when it supports executive decision making and developing a robust analysis that demonstrates the long-term consequences of investment scenarios. In addition, successful risk-based, asset management processes should address resiliency through an accurate prediction and mitigating of external environmental risks including storm events, seismic events, flooding, and other natural events and environmental impacts [20]. Few agencies started their risk efforts with sufficient talent and experience while others started their efforts by acquiring the human resources and receiving needed training. Transportation agencies should develop a plan for measuring their level of compliance and the resulting level of success meeting their goals and targets. Continuous improvement of risk management skills and processes is gaining more attention day after day [11, 12].

7. Risk-informed resource allocation of transportation agencies

Resource Allocation is a key component of Transportation Asset Management (TAM) [22]. This chapter primarily focuses on emphasizing the importance of risk management in transportation networks and demonstrating the relationship between environmentally influenced risk management and sustainable management of state-controlled transportation assets in the United States.

The American Association of State Highway and Transportation Officials (AASHTO) developed a transportation asset management guide that describes essential components for resource allocation and prioritization process, cross-asset resource allocation methods, TAM financial plans, and work planning and delivery. Chapter 5 of the AASHTO Guide describes the resource allocation process and provides guidance on implementing a resource allocation process that makes the best use of asset data and systems to allocate scarce resources in a timely manner in support of TAM-related goals and objectives [23].

The AASHTO Guide includes several examples where it specifically stated that an organization may identify through its risk management approach areas where better data or improved processes are needed to best address a given risk, in turn impacting the resource allocation process. For instance, if uncertainty concerning future asset conditions is found to be a significant risk, this may result in efforts to improve the deterioration models in an agency's asset management systems and/or motivate data collection improvements to reduce uncertainty.

8. Successful examples for risk-based asset Management of Transportation Infrastructure

Many transportation agencies lack the financial and human resources to achieve their targets for the maintenance of their transportation assets and have started employing risk management in the management of transportation networks. The TRB recently produced NCHRP 08–103 in 2020. The report includes case studies in cross-asset, multi-objective resource allocation [24]. In addition, several studies were successfully conducted in the past few years to better assess the risk associated with elevated environmental challenges on various transportation assets. Collaborating with several transportation agencies, the following examples highlight the author's efforts and success for employing risk management in the asset management of federally and state transportation networks.

The United States Army Corps of Engineers (USACE) has a large inventory of navigation locks and dams that use gates to control water flow. Monitoring and inspecting components of locks and dams, such as Milter/Tainter gates, are generally performed by visual inspection. The visual inspection relies heavily on subjective assessments made by inspectors and significantly differ from one expert to another. Structural health monitoring (SHM) can assist making accurate condition assessment of infrastructure assets to perform their intended design function(s), based on sensor and inspection data, numerical engineering models, and statistical analyses.

SHM principles and technology provide continuous information to support maintenance, operation, and repair decisions. Though automated SHM systems are gaining acceptance, they have been applied in an ad-hoc manner to monitor navigation locks and dams. SHM uses dense sensor suites, which are designed to catch unforeseen events rather than being optimally designed to provide specific information.

Zatar et al. [25] carried out an extensive study that aimed at performing critical reviews of the effectiveness of SHM systems that have recently been employed for a few of the United States Army Corps of Engineers navigation locks and dams. **Figure 1** shows the vertically framed gates of the Miter dam and **Figure 2** shows a typical flow-chart for data analysis of dam structural health monitoring that is used for the Miter dam. The physical SHM system, sensing suite, data acquisition hardware, telemetry, and data anomalies are discussed and recommendations for improved SHM systems for the United States Army Corps of Engineers navigation locks and dams are provided.

Mid-Atlantic Transportation Sustainability University Transportation Center (MATS UTC) served as focal point in Region 3 of the United States Department of Transportation. The MATS UTC includes the District of Columbia (Washington D.C.) and five states including Delaware, Maryland, Pennsylvania, Virginia, and West Virginia. Transportation infrastructure in this region, particularly concrete highway bridges, are exposed to the deleterious effects of environmental attacks, leading to environmental degradation of the concrete materials [26]. This is due to, for example, carbonation and chloride contamination that eventually break the alkali barrier in the cement matrix, and the steel reinforcement in the concrete becomes susceptible to corrosion. As a consequence, the concrete deteriorates at the reinforcement level, leading to cracking and spalling of the concrete owing to volume increase of the steel reinforcement. Such degradation is exacerbated by the application of de-icing salts on highway bridges, and the freeze–thaw and dry-wet cyclic exposures causing accelerated aging of the structure over time.

Concrete deterioration in the United States and worldwide has motivated the development of new and innovative materials and methods for structural rehabilitation, since replacement of structures would be very costly and nearly prohibited [26]. FRP composite materials in the form of fabrics, laminates, and bars have been externally bonded to concrete structures to increase structural capacity and provide longer service-life. The goal of this project was to present the technical and economical effectiveness of externally bonded FRP composites for repair and retrofit of highway infrastructure, and particularly concrete bridges [26]. The application of this technology in practice has been highly successful in West Virginia (**Figure 3**).

Composite behavior of precast Ultra-High-Performance Fiber-Reinforced Concrete (UHPFRC) slabs connected to Fiber-Reinforced Polymer (FRP) I-shaped girders was examined as a potential sustainable and low-cost maintenance alternative for composite bridge construction. Two series of large-scale FRP-UHPFRC composite girders were tested monotonically under four-point

Figure 1.
Vertically framed Miter dam.

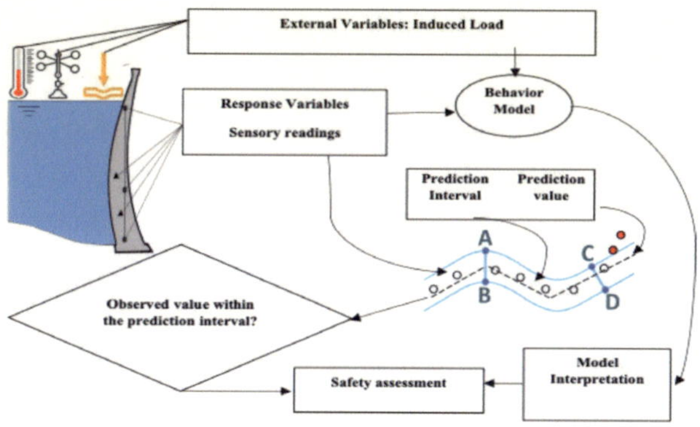

Figure 2.
Typical flow-chart for data analysis of dam structural health monitoring.

Figure 3.
Degradation and retrofitting of highway bridges in West Virginia. (a) Spalling of concrete and exposed rebars of bridge superstructures (curtesy of WVDOT–WVDOH); (b) retrofitting of highway bridge wing walls using GFRP wraps (curtesy of WVDOT–WVDOH).

flexural loading [27]. The test results showed promising indicators for short-span and pedestrian bridges. The developed girders were successfully employed in the construction of two demonstration pedestrian bridges in Japan. The established technology exhibited a sustainable and fast bridge construction solution in harsh environments [28].

The Region of Peel in Ontario, Canada, assesses needs and priorities across a diverse portfolio of Infrastructure that supports a variety of programs and services. These programs include solid waste management, water and wastewater treatment distribution, roadway network, and a variety of social, health and emergency services. The Region successfully integrated several efforts to enable an optimized investment methodology. The Region accounted for risk management, level of service, and life cycle management strategies to prioritize needs across its diverse infrastructure system [29].

The approach for allocating funding within the Caltrans State Highway Operation and Protection Program (SHOPP) in the State of California is a great example of a multi-objective, cross-asset resource allocation approach. SHOPP funds are used for repair, preservation, and safety improvements on the California State Highway System. The SHOPP programming cycle results in a multi-year program of capital projects that achieve the performance targets specified in the TAMP [24].

Other examples for successful transportation asset management efforts include: (a) Caltrans great example for TAMP-Practical Lessons from the Loma Prieta

Earthquake where the agency defined a separate program for seismic retrofits [30]; and (b) The Sustainable Solutions Lab at the University of Massachusetts Boston used a scenario-based approach to analyze the feasibility and potential risk reduction of Boston Harbor barrier systems to protect the Boston area from future flooding due to sea level rise [31].

9. Successful examples for risk-based TAMP in the state of West Virginia

9.1 Condition assessment of ground-mount cantilever highway weathering-steel overhead sign structures

Weathering steel (WS) is a high-strength, low-alloy steel and best known under the trademark COR-TEN or Corten steel. There are approximately 100 WS bridges and numerous WS overhead sign structures (WSOSSs) throughout the State of West Virginia, and inspection of these WS structures is essential to maintain public safety. Zatar and Nguyen conducted an expansive work that aimed at assessing 82 WSOSSs in the Charleston Interstate System in West Virginia [32]. A total of 26 comprehensive inspection forms were developed to objectively evaluate the current condition of 11 general types of sign structures. This part of the project focused on analyzing 25 single-armed and double-armed ground-mount cantilever WSOSSs (GMC-WSOSSs). **Figure 4** shows the locations of the overhead sign structures along I-64, I-79 and I-77 in Charleston, West Virginia.

A reliable ultrasonic testing technique was used to examine key components of the sign structures while the other components were inspected by visual inspection technique [33]. A rating methodology was developed to evaluate the sign structures at both the element level and their overall condition. The element condition was rated based on the developed rating criteria and score. The overall condition of each sign structure was then evaluated by the ratio between the total score of each structure and its maximum possible total score. It was concluded that all the GMC-WSOSSs performed relatively well after more than 40 years of service and exposure to moist weather condition of Kanawha County (climate zone 4A). The study found out that 52 percent of sign structures were found to be in fair condition and 48 percent were in good condition [33]. The rating system assisted the West Virginia Department of Transportation in making rational decisions about whether there is a need to repair or replace at-risk elements, connections, of these sign structures.

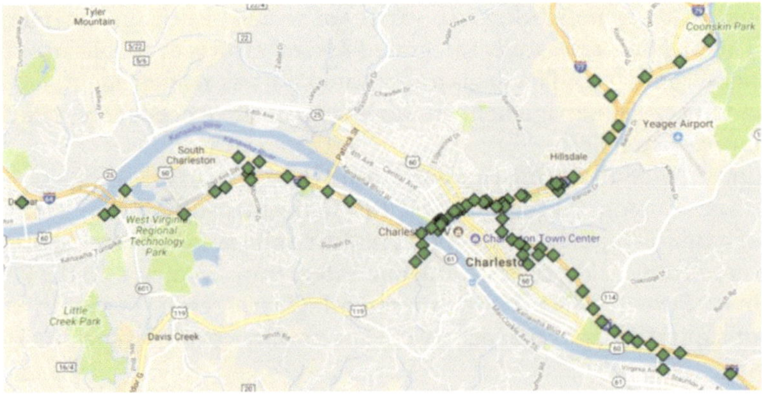

Figure 4.
Weathering-steel highway overhead sign structures along I-64, I-79 and I-77 in Charleston, West Virginia.

9.2 Performance of dual-shoulder-mount-truss highway weathering-steel overhead sign structures

Zatar and Nguyen conducted a study that focused on evaluating 15 dual-shoulder-mount-truss weathering steel overhead sign structures (DSMT-WSOSSs) in Charleston Interstate System in West Virginia [34]. A non-destructive testing technique was used to examine key components of the sign structures while the other components were inspected by visual inspection. **Figure 5** shows one of the dual-shoulder-mount-truss overhead sign structures. A rating methodology was developed to evaluate the sign structures at both the element level and overall condition. The element condition was rated based on developed rating criteria and score. The rating system assisted the West Virginia Department of Transportation in making rational decisions about whether there is a need to repair or replace at-risk elements, connections, or structures. All the DSMT-WSOSSs performed relatively well after four decades of service and exposure to moist weather condition of Kanawha County. Eighty seven percent of the sign structures are in fair condition and thirteen percent are in good condition [34].

9.3 Risk Management and rehabilitation of transportation infrastructure with FRP wraps

Concrete highway bridges in the State of West Virginia are exposed to the deleterious effects of environmental attacks, leading to degradation of these bridges as they age. The concrete deteriorates at the reinforcement level, leading to cracking and spalling of the concrete owing to volume increase of the steel reinforcement. According to 2017 National Bridge Inventory (NBI) database [9], West Virginia has 7,228 highway bridges and 19 percent of these bridges (1,372 bridges) were rated as structurally deficient. Of all the highway bridges in West Virginia, 1,394 bridges (19.3 percent) were rated as functional obsolete.

One solution to overcome steel corrosion in concrete for new construction is to use Fiber-Reinforced Polymer (FRP) materials for internal reinforcements instead of steel reinforcement. More significant is the beneficial application of FRP for structural rehabilitation of deteriorated concrete bridge structures. FRP composite materials in the form of fabrics, laminates, and bars have been externally bonded to concrete structures to increase structural capacity and provide longer service-life [26]. The application of this technology in practice has been highly successful [26].

Figure 5.
Dual-shoulder-mount-truss weathering-steel overhead sign structures.

Overall condition of all highway bridges in the State of West Virginia are reported where the data is extracted from the latest National Bridge Inventory by U.S. Department of Transportation and Federal Highway Administration. A few case studies for the use of FRP composites for rehabilitating bridge structures in West Virginia were examined. **Figure 6** shows two bridges in the inventory of West Virginia Department of Transportation. Cost of FRP-wrap projects by West Virginia Department of Transportation is addressed [35].

9.4 Non-destructive evaluation for risk and asset Management of Bridges

This project aimed at evaluating reinforced concrete bridge elements using two non-destructive evaluation (NDE) techniques, namely ultrasonic pitch and catch (UPC) and ground-penetrating radar (GPR). State-of-the-art literature reviews on multiple cutting-edge NDE techniques were carried out to identify potential knowledge gaps. **Figure 7** shows the basic principles of the UPC technique.

A validation test for a reinforced concrete slab specimen with embedded steel rebars and wire meshes was conducted to identify the advantages and limitations associated with the UPC and GPR techniques. **Figure 8** shows 3D visualization of the test specimen using NDT/NDE GPR and UPC (MIRA). **Figure 9** shows two-dimensional reconstructed image at an artificial delamination location. The high-resolution electromagnetic GPR technique accurately located almost all embedded reinforcements in the 3D slab volume tested.

The UPC technique detected rebars with large diameters while small diameter rebars and wire meshes could not be accurately detected. However, unlike the image obtained from the GPR data, 3D visualization reconstructed from the UPC's data showed very strong reflections of the slab bottom. The UPC technique usually requires multiple-point scanning for the targeted survey areas, resulting in a time-consuming data collection and processing. The research team recommended the combined use of the GPR and UPC techniques to comprehensively assess RC bridge elements, where the GPR is used to quickly evaluate questionable/defected regions while the UPC technique is used for an in-depth inspection/evaluation.

9.5 Evaluation of corrosion-induced risk and deterioration of concrete slabs using ground-penetrating radar and ultrasonic pitch-catch techniques

This project aims at evaluating corrosion-induced deterioration of RC bridge deck slabs using two non-destructive evaluation techniques, UPC and GPR. Experimental testing on RC slab specimens with pre-planned artificial defects was conducted to

Figure 6.
Two bridges in West Virginia Department of Transportation's inventory. (a) East Street Viaduct Bridge (curtesy of WVDOT - WVDOH bridge inspection reports 2012 and 2017); (b) Flag Run Bridge (curtesy of WVDOT - WVDOH bridge inspection reports 2016).

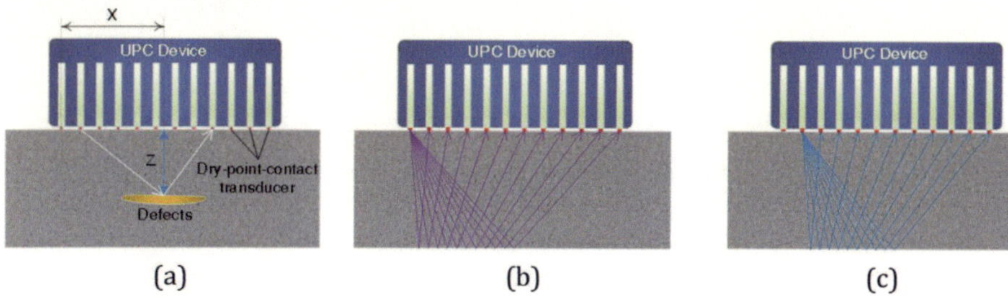

Figure 7.
Basic principles of the UPC technique: (a) transmitting and receiving transducers in UPC configuration; (b) the first channel transmit signals and the other channels receive the signals; and (c) the second channel transmit signals and the other channels receive the signals.

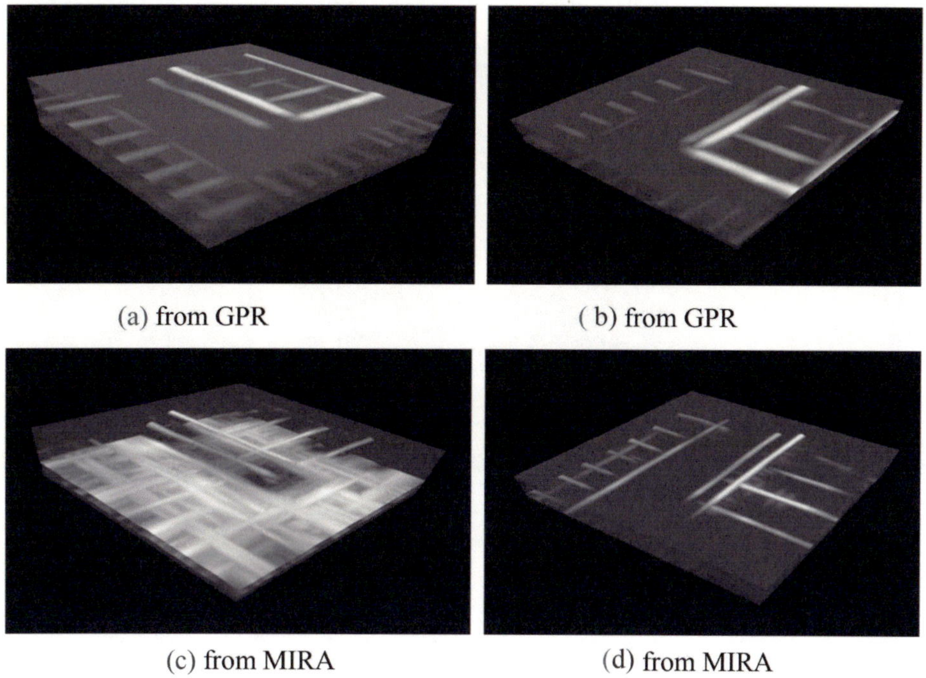

Figure 8.
3D visualization of the test specimen using NDT/NDE GPR and MIRA.

understand merits and disadvantages of each NDE technique. **Figure 10** illustrates the points at which data was collected for the RC slab using the UPC technique. **Figure 11** shows the signal amplitude versus depth of the delamination. The collected NDE data were used to generate both 2D and 3D images of layouts of reinforcements in the RC slabs [36]. The GPR effectively identified corrosion.

Potential areas of defects were generated using B-scan data. NDE data fusion approach was used to interpret the NDE data and to reconstruct the 2D/3D images. The GPR technique is not likely to be detect corrosion-induced concrete delamination. On the other hand, the UPC technique was found to be quite effective in determining and locating delamination, voids, reinforcing rebars, and pre-stressing tendons in the RC slabs. Major limitation of this technique is its sensitivity to the electrical properties of concrete such as the resistivity and dielectric constants. Therefore, the UPC is not suitable for detecting early signs of reinforcing bars corrosion. In addition, it requires a substantial amount of time to complete data

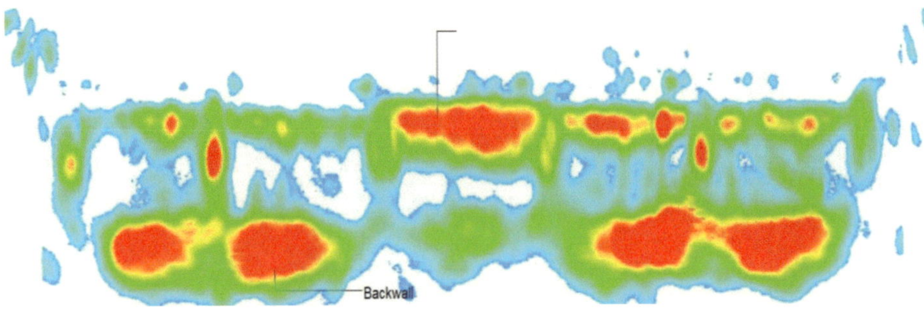

Figure 9.
Two-dimensional reconstructed image at an artificial delamination location.

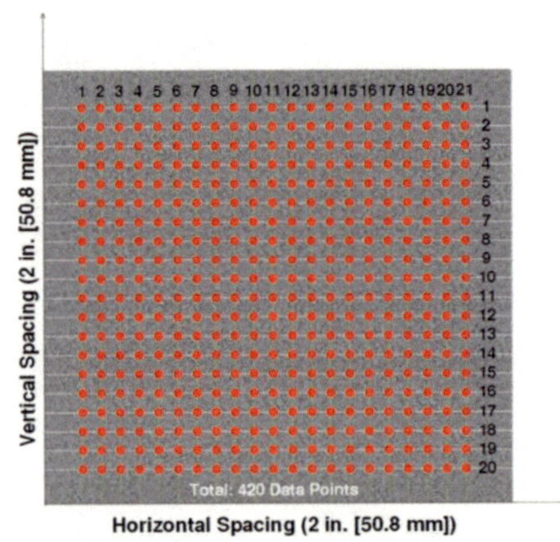

Figure 10.
Data collection on the RC slab using the UPC technique.

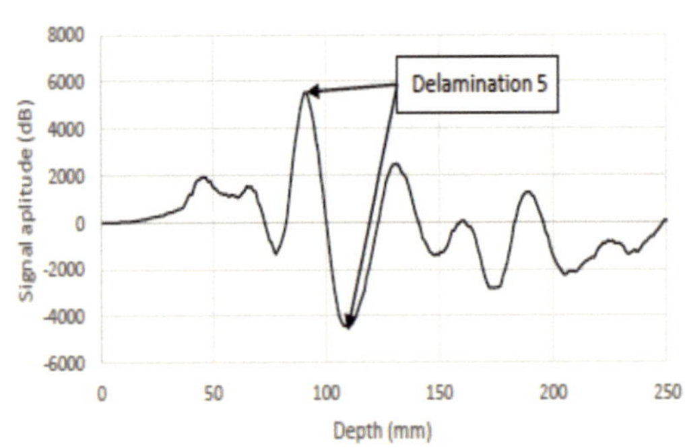

Figure 11.
Signal amplitude versus depth of the delamination.

collection. The GPR technique rapidly detected the highly corrosive regions in RC structures while the UPC technique can be used for in-depth evaluation and inspection of likely active corroding areas found by the GPR technique.

The project team recommended the combined use of GPR and UPC techniques for comprehensive assessment of corrosion-deteriorated bridge deck slabs [36].

9.6 Asset evaluation of concrete bridge deck slabs rehabilitated with composite Fiber-reinforced polymers

Fiber-reinforced polymer (FRP) materials have been widely accepted as an effective method in retrofitting deteriorated infrastructure (in shear, flexure and confinement applications). Despite the fast-growing and advanced technology in FRP materials and strengthening techniques, the monitoring and quality control of the FRP construction and installation remain challenging. For externally FRP-rehabilitated newly constructed and existing structures, it is critical to evaluate the potential for debonding failure and defects including cracks and voids surface on the concrete surface.

Accurate detection and evaluation of these defects is important to verify the structural capacity and to ensure appropriate durability of the FRP-strengthened structures. Experimental and theoretical non-destructive studies were conducted for concrete bridge deck slabs externally bonded with glass FRP, carbon FRP, and the combination thereof. **Figure 12** shows a sample reinforced concrete bridge deck slab specimen. Ground-penetrating radar (GPR) and infrared tomography (IRT) methods were utilized.

The results showed that the in-house developed software using an enhanced image reconstruction technique could provide high-resolution images of the FRP-strengthened reinforced concrete slabs in comparison to those obtained from the device's original software [37].

Figure 13 shows reconstructed images of the sample bridge deck slab specimen. The results obtained from the IRT camera indicated that this technology could accurately detect and locate near-surface defects such as debonding, cracks and voids. The study suggests that the combination of the GPR and IRT methods is effective in imaging internal defects of FRP-strengthened concrete structures.

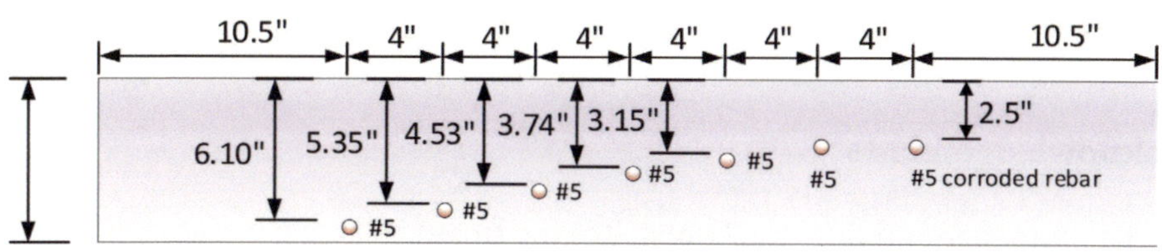

Figure 12.
Details of a sample reinforced concrete bridge deck slab specimen.

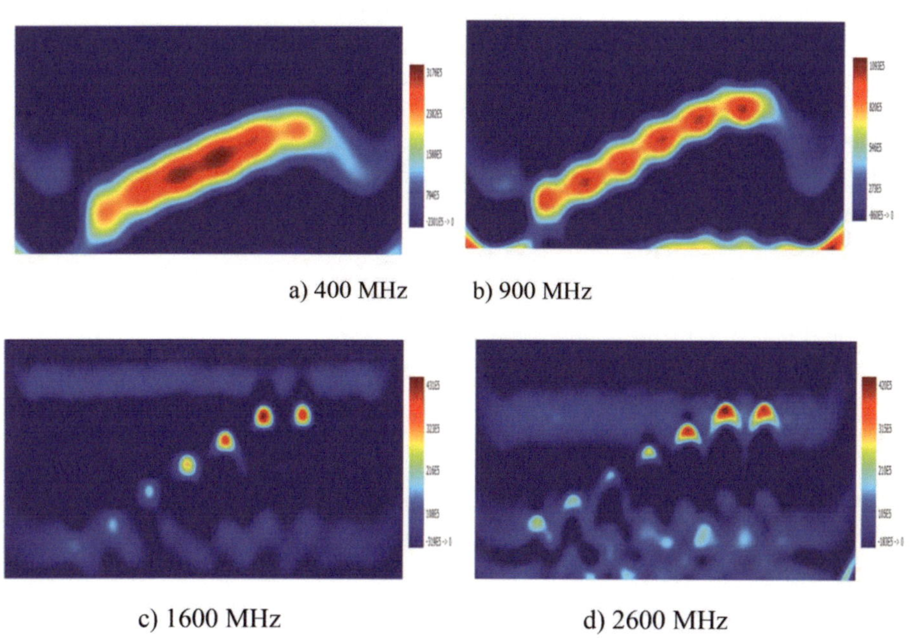

Figure 13.
Reconstructed images of the sample bridge deck slab specimen.

10. Conclusions and future works

Federal and state transportation agencies across the world are tasked with a multitude of challenges associated with routine, yet effective, maintenance and upgrade programs for the agencies' aging transportation assets. Challenging environmental conditions play a significant role in exacerbation the degradation, lowering the level of service, and increasing the risk of managing transportation agencies infrastructure assets. This is all happening at a time when limited funds are directed to sustain and enhance critical transportation assets. The chapter addresses the necessity to building and maintaining safe and sustainable transportation network for future generations, as well as highlights the implication of implementing life cycle cost measures to the process—as these measures add another level of complexity to the already difficult challenges facing transportation asset managers and decision makers.

The chapter stressed that the decision-making process involves several risk factors, and displayed the considerable effect of prioritizing these factors for both the level of utilization of these assets, as well as the short- and long-term management protocols and plans for transportation agencies. The relationship between environmentally influenced risk management and sustainable management of state-controlled transportation assets in the United States is demonstrated. Several key parameters including risk assessment, financial risks and organizational behavior are addressed, and multiple successful examples for risk-based transportation asset management in the State of West Virginia are highlighted.

Acknowledgements

The author would like to acknowledge the financial support and technical guidance provided by the West Virginia Department of Transportation–Division of Highways (WVDOH) while conducting several of the highlighted research studies.

The author would also like to acknowledge the diligent support provided by the research team members of the Encova Center for Engineering and Safety at Marshall University. The author would like to extend special thanks to Dr. Haroon Malik, Dr. Hai Nguyen, Dr. Hien Nghiem, Dr. Cumhur Cosgun, Dr. Tu Nguyen, and Dr. Kien Dinh for all their tireless efforts while conducting several of the studies highlighted herein.

The author would like to acknowledge the financial support provided through both the United States Army Engineer Research and Development Center and the Mid-Atlantic Transportation Sustainability Center University Transportation Center (MATS UTC). The successful collaboration and technical support provided by Dr. Osman Ozbulut from the University of Virginia, while conducting two of the highlighted research projects, are greatly appreciated.

Conflict of interest

The author hereby declares no potential conflict of interest with respect to the research of this article.

Author details

Wael A. Zatar
College of Information Technology and Engineering, Marshall University, Huntington, WV, USA

*Address all correspondence to: zatar@marshall.edu

References

[1] Proctor, G., Varma, S., and Roorda, J., "Managing Risk across the Enterprise: A Guide for State Departments of Transportation," National Cooperative Highway Research Program (NCHRP) Report 08-93, 2016. http://onlinepubs.trb.org/onlinepubs/nchrp/docs/NCHRP08-93_FullGuide.pdf

[2] MAP-21, the Moving Ahead for Progress in the 21st Century Act (P.L. 112-141), Federal Highway Administration (FHWA). https://www.fhwa.dot.gov/map21/#:~:text=MAP%2D21%2C%20the%20Moving%20Ahead,highway%20authorization%20enacted%20since%202005

[3] Risk-Based Transportation Asset Management: Evaluating Threats, Capitalizing on Opportunities, Report 1: Overview of Risk Management, Federal Highway Administration (FHWA) publications, 2012.

[4] Risk-Based Asset Management: Examining Risk-based Approaches to Transportation Asset Management, Report 2: Managing Asset Risks at Multiple Levels in a Transportation Agency, Federal Highway Administration (FHWA) publications, 2012.

[5] Risk-Based Transportation Asset Management: Achieving Policy Objectives by Managing Risks Report 3: Risks to Asset Management Policies, Federal Highway Administration (FHWA) publications, 2012.

[6] Risk-Based Transportation Asset Management: Managing Risks to Networks, Corridors, and Critical Structures Report 4: Managing Risks to Critical Assets, Federal Highway Administration (FHWA) publications, 2013.

[7] Risk-Based Transportation Asset Management: Building Resilience into Transportation Assets Report 5: Managing External Threats Through Risk Based Asset Management, Federal Highway Administration (FHWA) publications, 2013.

[8] Managing Risks and Using Metrics in Transportation Asset Management Financial Plans, FHWAHIF-15-020, Aug. 2015, accessible at https://www.fhwa.dot.gov/asset/plans/financial/hif15020.pdf.

[9] Incorporating Risk management Into Transportation Asset Management Plans, Federal Highway Administration (FHWA) publications, November 2017. https://www.fhwa.dot.gov/asset/pubs/incorporating_rm.pdf

[10] Integrating Extreme Weather into Transportation Asset Management Plans, an NCHRP 25-25 project, Sept. 21, 2015, accessible at https://apps.trb.org/cmsfeed/TRBNetProjectDisplay.asp?ProjectID=3723

[11] Transportation Asset Management Plan Development Processes Certification and Recertification Guidance; Transportation Asset Management Plan Consistency Determination Interim Guidance, A Notice by the Federal Highway Administration, Feb. 2018. https://www.federalregister.gov/documents/2018/02/22/2018-03618/transportation-asset-management-plan-development-processes-certification-and-recertification

[12] Using a Life Cycle Planning process to Support Asset Management, Federal Highway Administration Office of Asset Management, US Department of Transportation, November 2017. https://www.fhwa.dot.gov/asset/pubs/life_cycle_planning.pdf

[13] Proctor, G., and Varma, S., "Financial Planning for Transportation

Asset Management," Federal Highway Administration, 2015.

[14] National Highway Institute (NHI) Course on Financial Planning for Transportation Asset Management, Federal Highway Administration, Course Number FHWA-NHI-136002, 2019.

[15] Guidebook on Risk Analysis Tools and Management Practices to Control Transportation Project Costs, National Cooperative Highway Research Program (NCHRP) 08-60, Transportation Research Board, 2010.

[16] Work Planning and Delivery - A Guidebook for the Evaluation of Project Delivery Methods, Transit Cooperative Research Program (TCRP) Report 131, Transportation Research Board, 2016.

[17] Accelerating Transportation Project and Program Delivery: Conception to Completion, National Cooperative Highway Research Program (NCHRP) Report 662, Transportation Research Board B, 2016

[18] Alternative Technical Concepts for Contract Delivery Methods, National Cooperative Highway Research Program (NCHRP) Synthesis 455, Transportation Research Board, 2018.

[19] Construction Manager-at-Risk Project Delivery for Highway Programs, National Cooperative Highway Research Program (NCHRP) Synthesis 402, Transportation Research Board, 2010.

[20] FHWA's Special Federal-Aid Funding—Implementation of 23 CFR Part 667: Periodic Evaluation of Facilities Repeatedly Requiring Repair and Reconstruction Due to Emergency Events, 2017. https://www.govinfo.gov/content/pkg/CFR-2017-title23-vol1/xml/CFR-2017-title23-vol1-part667.xml

[21] National Cooperative Highway Research Program (NCHRP) Synthesis Report 556: Asset Management Approaches to Identifying and Evaluating Assets Damaged Due to Emergency Events, Transportation Research Board, 128 pages, 2020, DOI: https://doi.org/10.17226/25825.

[22] Transportation Asset Management (TAM) Guide, The American Association of State Highway and Transportation Officials, AASHTO 2020.

[23] The American Association of State Highway and Transportation Officials (AASHTO) Guide for Enterprise Risk Management—Chapter 5 Resource Allocation, First Edition, AASHTO 2016, available as an electronic document from the AASHTO Bookstore.

[24] National Cooperative Highway Research Program (NCHRP) 08-103: Case Studies in Cross-Asset, Multi-Objective Resource Allocation, Transportation Research Board, 2020, DOI: 10.17226/25684.

[25] Zatar, W., Haroon, M. and Nguyen, H., "Critical Review of Conventional Large Sensor Suites for Health Monitoring of Large Structures," Technical Report, U.S. Army Corps of Engineer, United States Army Engineer Research and Development Center, W912HZ-17-SOI-0031, 608 pages, 2020.

[26] Zatar, W., Nguyen, H. and Ozbulut, O., "Fiber-Reinforced Plastic (FRP) Wraps for Next Generation Sustainable and Cost-Effective Rehabilitation of Coastal Transportation Infrastructure in the Mid-Atlantic Region," Mid-Atlantic Transportation Sustainability Center University Transportation Center (MATS UTC), March 2018.

[27] Nguyen, H., Mutsuyoshi, H. and Zatar, W., "Hybrid FRP-UHPFRC Composite Girders: Part 1–Experimental and Numerical Approach," Journal of Composite

Structures, Elsevier, Vol. 125, pp.631-652, 2015.

[28] Nguyen, H., Zatar, W. and Mutsuyoshi, H., "Hybrid FRP-UHPFRC Composite Girders: Part 2–Analytical Approach," Journal of Composite Structures, Elsevier, Vol. 125, pp.653-671.

[29] Peel Enterprise Asset Management Plan, 2019, pp.141.

[30] Caltrans TAMP-Practical Lessons from the Loma Prieta Earthquake, p.174-180, 2018. https://www.nap.edu/catalog/2269/practical-lessons-from-the-loma-prieta-earthquake

[31] Feasibility of Harbor-wide Barrier Systems Preliminary Analysis for Boston Harbor, Sustainable Solutions Lab, University of Massachusetts Boston, May 2018, PP.250, https://www.greenribboncommission.org/wp-content/uploads/2018/05/Feasibility-of-Harbor-wide-Barriers-Report.pdf

[32] Zatar, W. and Nguyen, H. Evaluation of Weathering steel Overhead Sign Structures in West Virginia. Marshall University, 2014.

[33] Zatar, W. and Nguyen, H. Condition Assessment of Ground-Mount Cantilever Weathering-Steel Overhead Sign Structures. Journal of Infrastructure Systems, 2017, 23(4), p. 05017005.

[34] Zatar, W. and Nguyen, H., "Performance of Dual-Shoulder-Mount-Truss Weathering-Steel Overhead Sign Structures in West Virginia," BIT 5th Annual World Congress of Smart Materials, Rome, Italy, 2019.

[35] Zatar, W. and Nguyen, H., "Rehabilitation of Transportation Infrastructure in West Virginia with FRP Wraps," 5th International Conference on Sustainable Construction Materials and Technologies (SCMT5), Kingston University, London, UK, July 2019.

[36] Zatar, W., Nguyen, H. and Nghiem, H., "Ground-Penetrating Radar Reconstructed Image for Identifying Steel Rebars and Artificial Defects in Concrete Structures," Journal of Nondestructive Testing and Evaluation, Submitted, October 2020.

[37] Zatar, W., Nguyen, H. and Nghiem, H., "Non-Destructive Evaluation of Reinforced-Concrete Slabs Rehabilitated with CFRP/GFRP," American Concrete Institute Fall Convention, Atlanta, accepted, 2021.

Chapter 3

Risk Mitigation: Sustainable Management in Construction Industry

K. Srinivas

Abstract

Various parameters which are interactive in nature are exerting a negative influence on the existence of planet earth. Excessive urbanization, runaway global warming, unbridled generation of waste and pollution of air, water and soil has resulted in depletion of natural resources. As a result of threat to ecosystems and irreversible degradation, the growing evidence that the earth's ability to sustain life is getting eroded needs to be taken seriously. Major parameter which is responsible for substantial contribution to global warming and degradation of environment is the construction industry. The construction industry consumes about 40% of extracted materials and is responsible for about 35% of total carbon dioxide emissions. Rapid economic development coupled with unplanned construction has resulted in choking of cities/towns, with little or no lung space and over-exploitation of natural resources. This paper seeks to address the methods to mitigate the adverse effects on environment by way of implementation of sustainable management in the form of green and intelligent building which will facilitate the planet earth to be a liveable place for future generation while simultaneously pursuing the agenda of sustainable development.

Keywords: sustainable development, sustainable construction, sustainable design, green building, intelligent buildings

1. Introduction

The concept of sustainability is embedded in the fact that it enhances the quality of human life while carrying on our activities within the carrying capacity of supporting ecosystems. A responsible and proactive decision-making and innovation that minimizes negative impact and maintains a balance between ecological resilience, and economic prosperity to ensure a desirable planet for all species for the present as well as for the future is the core of sustainability. Sustainable development consists of balancing local and global efforts to meet basic human needs without destroying or degrading the natural environment.

Sustainable construction is the practice of creating a healthy environment that's based on ecological principles Sustainable Construction focuses on principles namely: 1) Conserve, 2) Reuse, 3) Recycle/renew, 4) Protecting nature and 5) Miinimising the use of toxic substances. The process of sustainable construction commences well before the start of actual on-site building activity and extends to post construction activities such as commissioning and asset management thus covering the entire project development cycle.

2. Literature survey

Albert Borgstein [1] conducted a research on Sustainability and concluded that sustainability is defined as a strategy for conducting operations in a manner associated with governance standards, which meet existing needs without compromising the needs of future generations.

Endersbee [2] conducted a study on Global Challenges and New Challenges for Civil Engineers and concluded that life cycle costing and life cycle management of resource splay an important role in development of a sustainable construction and that emergence of zero energy buildings and sustainable structures will reduce dependence on fossil fuels which is the primary source of global warming.

Hermawan et al. [3] conducted a study on Identification of Source Factors of Carbondioxide emissions in concreting of Reinforced concrete and the research findings show that there are seven factors namely scope, time, cost, quality, resources, procurement and material transfer which contributed to carbondioxide emissions in a construction project which will enhance the energy performance of buildings and thermal comfort as compared with light weight materials.

Nielsen [4] on Carbon foot print of Concrete Buildings seen in Life Cycle Perspective has researched that even though concrete has high carbondioxide emission during production, it is of paramount importance to include the service life of buildings in this type of calculations as at the end of service period, concrete will carbonate and will absorb carbondioxide from atmosphere.

Kim [5] researched on principles of sustainable design and findings indicate that per capita consumption of resource is linked with per capita income and has proposed three principles of sustainability namely: 1) Reduction, reuse, and recycling of the natural resources that are input to a building, 2) Life Cycle Design for analyzing the building process and its impact on the environment and 3) focus on humane Design for interactions between humans and the natural world.

Kilbert [6] has examined the future of sustainable construction and concluded that ecological design, the key concept in creating high performance buildings is in its infancy and needs to be articulated to be truly called as green building, the concept of green building needs to be further defined and methods for their evaluation needs to be developed and better conservation of resources and adjustments of social expectations will be an important factor in development of more sustainable built environment.

Planning Commission, Govt of India [7] in their study on Sustainable development has stated that in our society, every material is either derived from a mineral product or made using intermediate goods and may not be possible for the society without drawing mineral resource from our environment. Hence, the negative impact on the environment is to be limited and to reverse the damage done to the maximum extent possible through appropriate technological/management practices and procedures. The study concluded highlighting Sustainable development as an important concern for mankind.

Mehta [8] in his key findings on study on reducing the Environmental Impact of Concrete is that in a finite world the model of unlimited growth, unrestricted use of natural resources, and uncontrolled pollution of the environment is ultimately a recipe for planetary self-destruction and that greatest challenge that the concrete industry faces during the 21st century is to achieve a sustainable pattern of growth.

The task is formidable but it can be accomplished provided we make a paradigm shift from the culture of accelerating construction speeds to a culture of conservation of energy and material.

Penttala [9] in study on concrete and sustainable development has stated that the global warming caused by the green house effect are visible and hence new evaluation of building materials according to their ability to fulfill the requirements of sustainable development may have to be done. Taking into consideration the production and operational phases, the energy consumption and green house gas emissions of concrete in residential buildings needs to be examined. The concrete buildings brings ab significant energy and emission savings compared to buildings in which light materials have been used. Which enhances improves the ecological balance of concrete and lifts it to the group of building materials which burden environment least.

Ambuja Technical Literature Series [10] in its study has stated that building industry consumes 40% of the extracted materials and is responsible for 33% of carbondioxide emissions. Use of green and smart buildings can reduce the impact of energy consumption and that a thorough life cycle analysis of and management of building materials is necessary for selection of materials for high performance green buildings. Use of fly ash, silica fume and slag can contribute of sustainable construction.

3. Methodology

The methodology adopted for this paper is depicted in **Figure 1**.

4. Contribution of construction industry to global emissions

The contribution of various materials of construction to carbon dioxide emissions is furnished in **Figure 2**.

One of the largest industries in developing and developed countries in terms of investment, employment and contribution to GDP is the construction industry. Consequently, the impact of the construction industry on the environment in terms of loss of soil/agricultural land, the loss of forests/wetlands, air/water pollution, etc. is considerable. Contribution of eight major categories to environmental burden varies from 12 to 40%. The details are furnished in **Table 1**.

The embodied carbon in various aspects of construction is furnished below in **Figure 3**.

The construction sector is having negative impacts on the environment in the following manner:

- Almost two fifths of the Demolition Waste and Green House Gas is produced by construction industry.

- The environmental impact on buildings is spread throughout their entire life cycle.

- Construction of buildings is having impact by way of depletion of resources such as ground cover, forests, water, and energy.

- In providing comfort to occupants, energy is consumed for lighting, space conditioning and water heating.

- Continuous extraction of raw materials like limestone and ground water has caused irreparable and irreversible damage to the environment in the form of:

- Water stress.

- Reduction in the availability of fresh water due to potential decline in Rainwater.

- Threat to agriculture.

- Food scarcity in regions of excess extraction.

- Threat to biodiversity with adverse implications for forest dependent activities.

- Unscientific and uncontrolled method of limestone mining in various parts of the country have caused various adverse environmental impacts on the surrounding area leaving the region scarred with irregular patches, loss of vegetation cover, emergence and growth of xerophytes, instability of the mountains and esthetic degradation of the area, depletion of forest cover, depletion in plant diversity due to the stripping off, random digging and quarrying.

- Mining has also affected water resources severely both in terms of its quantity and quality. Changes in water levels and flow, availability of potable and

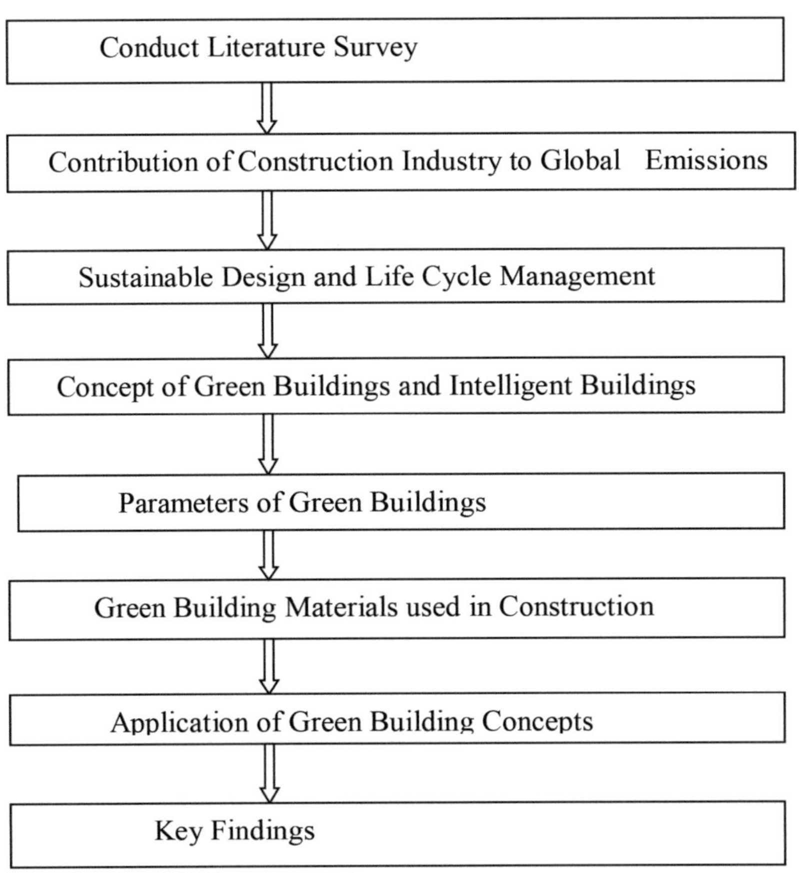

Figure 1.
Methodology Adopted.

irrigation water, degradation of water quality, reduction and degradation of habitat of aquatic flora and fauna and decrease in abundance and diversity of aquatic species are some of the adverse impacts of mining. In regions where mining is carried out, water resource are polluted, diverted/disturbed from their natural conditions as a result of mining activity making water unfit for consumption.

- There is high content of calcium, bicarbonates, sodium and chloride salts in the water of streams and rivers receiving a significant volume of mine water generated from open cast limestone mining areas.

- Cement on an average produces 0.9tonnes of carbon dioxide per ton of clinker and on an average, globally 3.5 billion tonnes of cement is utilized and hence the contribution to green house gas emissions is obviously quite large.

- Sand, Gravel and crushed rock is used at the rate of 10–11 billion tones every year which leads to excessive mining of soil components resulting in loss of water table.

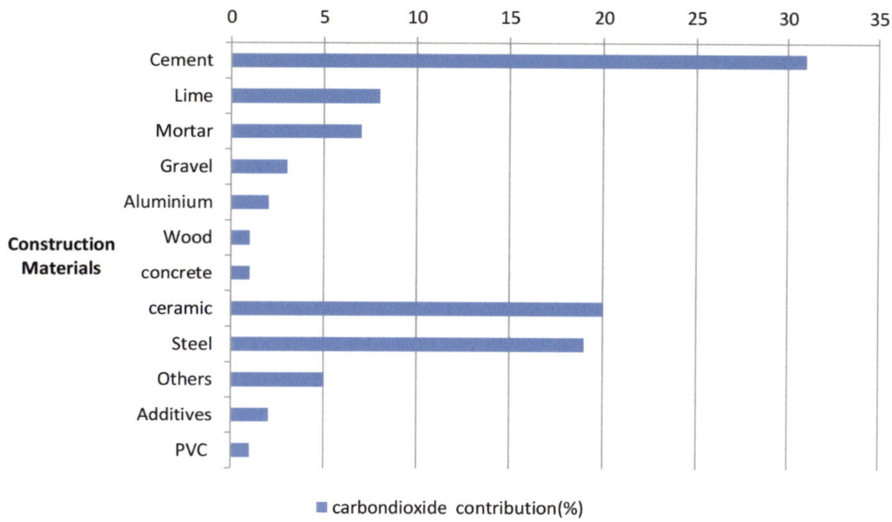

Figure 2.
Source: www.construct.com/carbon-emisisons-in-construction-materials.

Parameter	% Contribution
Use of raw materials	30
Energy	42
Water	25
land	12
Atmospheric emissions	40
Water effluents	20
Solid waste	25
Other releases	13

Table 1.
Contribution of major categories of construction to environmental burden.

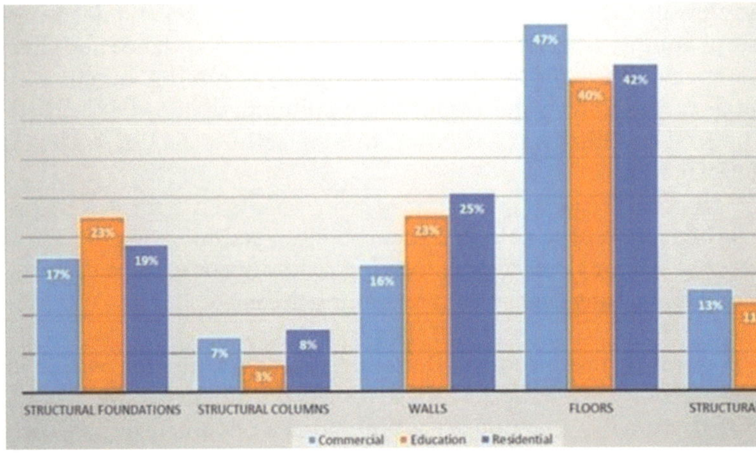

Figure 3.
Source: www.construct.com/carbon-emisisons-in-construction-materials.

Considering the above cited factors, it is imperative that in line overall objective of bringing down the green house gas emissions by 40% from the level of 1990 by 2030, the construction industry has no choice but to adopt innovative measures to bring down its carbon foot print substantially.

5. Sustainable design

In comparison to any human endeavor, the built environment had adverse and long lasting impacts on the environment. Approximately 10% of the global economy is earmarked for construction activities as it consumes 50% of global resources. On an average, buildings account for:

- 39% of total energy use
- 68% of total electricity consumption
- 30% of landfill waste
- 38% of carbon dioxide emissions
- 12% of total water consumption

Effective approaches for life cycle design and management of construction that will ensure their sustainability as regards improved physical performance, cost effectiveness and environmental compatibility is to be developed to address the challenges. This should achieve an optimal balance between the following criteria namely:

- Engineering Performance which encompasses Safety, Serviceability and Durability
- Economic Performance in terms of minimum life cycle costs and minimum user cost
- Environmental Performance by way of minimum green house gas emissions, reduced materials consumption, improved energy efficiency)

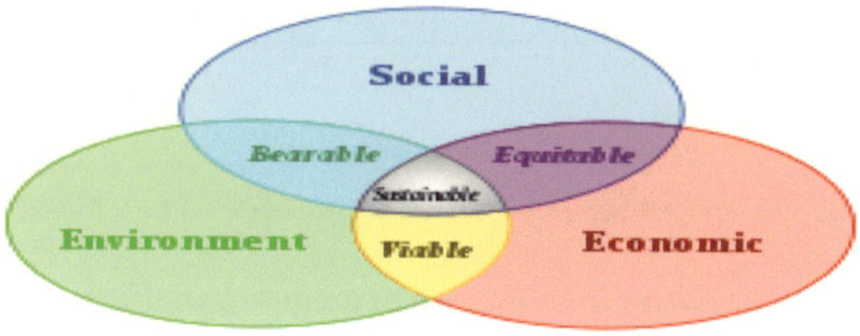

Figure 4.
Major aspects of sustainability.

Design professionals may be aware of the first two criteria but the last criteria has impact on the way the design is thought of. Sustainable design means developing products with improved performance in all phases of the product life cycle. Sustainable design has to consider three major aspects of sustainability, i.e., Social, Economic and Environmental. The relationship is depicted in **Figure 4**.

Consideration for design of sustainable building:

- Resources should be discarded at the speed at which local eco-systems can absorb them and should be utilized ed. at the pace at which they naturally regenerate.
- Resources naturally available on the site such as solar and wind energy, natural shading and drainage, etc. should be incorporated in site planning to lessen the local and global impact.
- Minimisation of energy and material waste throughout the life cycle of a building.
- Considering factors such as day lighting, passive ventilation, efficient material and design strategies, internal load, local climate, etc. buildings should be designed.
- Occupant's health and productivity should be maximized by design.
- Waste reduction and recycling should be supported by operation and maintenance systems.
- Judicious use of water considering it as a finite resource.
- Location and systems should optimize employee commuting and minimize the use of single occupancy vehicles. These include alternative work modes such as telecommuting and teleconferencing, etc.

6. Green building

A green building is one which:

- Consumes less water
- Optimizes energy efficiency

- conserves natural resources
- generates less waste and
- Provides healthier spaces for occupants, as compared to a conventional building.

Research has shown that a green building can give benefits by way of:

- Reduced energy use by 20–40%
- Reduced Carbon dioxide emissions by 37%
- Reduced Water use by 40%
- Reduced Solid Waste by 70%
- Enhances and protects ecosystems
- Conserves and restores natural streams
- Enhances esthetic qualities
- Minimum strain on local infrastructure and reduced operating costs
- Optimizes life cycle economic performance
- Improves air and water quality
- Enhances the productivity of occupant

7. Intelligent buildings

An intelligent or smart building is one that uses technology and processes to create space that is safer and more productive for its occupants. In such a building, network of electronic devices monitor and control the mechanical and lighting systems to reduce energy and maintenance costs. Lighting is controlled by sensors, which can detect the presence of occupants and relative darkness and can modulate lights accordingly. To monitor the temperatures, sensors are placed in rooms and air ducts. Such buildings are provided with hot water systems for supplying heat to the air handling unit and chilled water systems for cooling its air and equipment with optimum level of temperature being maintained by sensors. Intelligent buildings also have alarm capabilities and alarms for reporting critical faults in mechanical and electrical systems.

8. Factors of green building

8.1 Location

- Selection of a green building site should be based on how easily it can integrate into the existing electric, gas, water and sewage utilities.
- It should have minimal impact on the existing energy, water, sewage and road systems.

DOI: http://dx.doi.org/10.5772/intechopen.100215

Figure 5.
Wool brick.

8.2 Orientation

- A green building should organically fit into the surrounding area, making best use of existing roads, sidewalks, alleys, site specific resources.

8.3 Daylight

- Day lighting is the controlled admission of natural light—direct sunlight and diffuse skylight into a building to reduce electric lighting and saving of energy. Day lighting is an important element of sustainable design (**Figure 5**).

8.4 Renewable energy

- A green building uses maximum of renewable energy like solar, wind, geothermal, biofuels, etc. thereby bringing down the quantum of usage of non-renewable energy.

8.5 Rainwater harvesting

- The main purpose of rainwater harvesting system is to collect and store rainwater falling on the ground which can be further be used during times of drought and scanty rainfall.

8.6 Waste water management

Waste water management has a direct impact on the biological diversity of aquatic ecosystems, disrupting the fundamental integrity of our life support systems, on which a wide range of sectors from urban development to food production and industry depends.

9. Various green building materials

9.1 Wool brick

- Obtained by adding wool and a natural polymer found in seaweed to the clay of the brick.

- 37% More strength than burnt bricks.

- Resistant for cold and wet climate.
- Researchers have added wool fibers to clay material used to make bricks and combined these with an alginate, a natural polymer extracted from seaweed. This resulted in bricks that are stronger and more environmentally friendly.
- Wool Bricks are comprised of clay, wool, and alginate.
- Clay can be found in estuaries, coastal plains, continental shelves and offshore islands.
- It can easily be found anywhere in the world.
- Unlike regular brick, wool bricks they do not crumble suddenly, they develop small cracks and deform slowly before giving way.
- In addition, since these bricks contain sodium aliginate it can easily become biodegradable.
- Wool Brick can be manufactured without firing which contributes to energy saving.
- Zero-carbon product.
- These fibers improve the strength of compressed bricks, reduce the formation of fissures and deformities as a result of contraction, reduce drying time and increase the bricks' resistance to flexion (bending) (**Figure 6**).

9.2 Sustainable concrete

- Fine and coarse aggregates can be replaced with 10% of with recycled glass (Soda-lime glass used for bottles washed and crushed to fine and coarse aggregate sizes for use in the concrete mixes).
- Resulted in better properties in fresh and hardened states at ambient and high temperatures than those with larger replacement.
- Concretes made with Fine Waste Glass aggregates had satisfactory compressive strengths as well as initial and final setting time of concrete.
- 25% reduction in weight of concrete.
- 30% reduction in carbon dioxide emissions and 40% reduction in repair costs.

Figure 6.
Concrete made of FWG aggregates.

DOI: http://dx.doi.org/10.5772/intechopen.100215

9.3 Cellulose insulation

- Recycled paper products and a very high recycled material content of 82–85% and forms the basis of cellulose insulation.
- The paper is reduced to small pieces and then fiberized, which creates a product that packs tightly into building cavities and inhibits airflow.
- Sometimes mineral borate is blended with the less costly ammonium sulfate, to ensure fire and insect resistance.
- Cellulose insulation typically requires no moisture barrier and, cannot settle in a building cavity (**Figure 7**).

9.4 Triple glazed windows

- A triple glazed window is a window that comprises of 3 layers of windows.
- Exhibits strong insulation performance.
- Triple glazing has grown in preference over the years, and has gradually gained a lot of acceptance.
- Triple-glazed windows are great at taking in the warmth of sunlight and then getting it into the rooms.
- Best suited for bigger windows, these windows also contain a glass pane that has solar control and self-cleansing characteristics.
- They are durable and rigid.
- Reduces sound transmission, saves energy and gives more comfort (**Figure 8**).

9.5 Pre-cast concrete slabs

- Saves energy, water and building materials
- Rapid construction on site

Figure 7.
Cellulose insulation.

Figure 8.
Triple glazed window.

Figure 9.
Pre-cast concrete slabs.

- Good quality control
- Safety and Protection
- Low impact construction
- Esthetically appealing structure (**Figure 9**)

9.6 Bamboo

- Bamboo is being used in columns, walls, beams, doors, roofs, fencing, staircases and boundary walls
- Bamboo fiber reinforced concrete is used for construction of sla bs which proves to be lighter than conventional concrete
- They are 3 times cheaper than steel and has great tensile strength
- Upto 70% of steel can be replaced by bamboo for a structure
- Disadvantages are that it can swell and rot if untreated and it can shrink which can lead to segregation of concrete (**Figure 10**)

Figure 10.
Bamboo reinforcement.

9.7 Concrete alternatives

- Papercrete and Hempcrete are two examples of concrete alternative.
- These two building materials also use cement or clay.
- This concrete uses more environmental friendly aggregates as against of the nonrenewable aggregates used in traditional concrete
- Concrete-like materials for building is produced by repulped paper fiber, hemp and even bits of wood or sawdust.
- Environmental impact would be amazing if f interior walls of new buildings were replaced with this material.
- For papercrete in particular, raw materials aren't expensive.
- The heat and sound insulation found in papercrete is much better than traditional concrete.
- Papercrete has a high compressive strength and is light weight enough to be used as a roofing alternative.
- Disadvantage is that there are waterproofing methods that can be applied to the materials, but it's still made of paper (**Figure 11**).

9.8 Acetylated wood products

- This is an eco-friendly material which is alternate to the use of toxic pressure-treated wood.
- Wood is modified through a acetylation to create a product which is resistant to rot and improved thermal insulation, stability and longer lifespan.
- This is gorgeous and certified non-toxic (**Figure 12**).

Figure 11.
Papercrete concrete.

Figure 12.
Acetylated wood product.

9.9 Polyurathenes

- The most important application of polyurethanes in buildings is insulation.
- Polyurethanes are regarded as an affordable, durable and safe way of reducing carbon emissions.
- Polyurethanes can dramatically reduce heat loss in homes and offices in cold weather.
- During the summer, they play an important role in keeping buildings cool, which means air conditioning is needed less.
- They can be used in cavity walls, roofs, around pipes and floors (**Figure 13**).

9.10 Green roofs

They are vegetated roofs consisting of a waterproofing membrane, growing medium (soil) and vegetation (plants) overlying a traditional roof (**Figure 14**).

9.10.1 Benefits of green roofs

- Average life expectancy of a green roof is 40 years, as compared to an average expectancy of 17 for a conventional roof.
- Green roofs can act as an insulating layer and reduce heat flux by up to 72%.

Figure 13.
Polyurathenes in construction.

Figure 14.
Green roofs.

- The energy efficiency factor of green roofs reduces demand for power, thereby decreasing the amount of Carbondioxide being released into the atmosphere.
- Green roofs can reduce outside sound penetration by 40–60 decibels.
- Increased efficiency means an increase in property value. Also green roofs contribute to green building movement.
- Green roofs can retain 70–90% of precipitation in the summer and 24–40% in the winter.
- Green roof means added biodiversity, esthetic appeal, and more green space for relaxing, stress relief, and even gardening.

9.11 Environment friendly industrial by-products

- Iindustrial by-products such as flyash, blast furnace slag and silica fume as cementitious materials in concrete structures leads to significant reductions in consumption of energy, quantity of cement needed to make concrete and reduced emissions.

- Flyash which is difficult to dispose is substituted for over 30% of cement volume and blast furnace for more than 35%.
- High volume flyash concretes with 50–70% of cementitious content is found to be feasible in certain situations.
- Use of these products has resulted in substantial improvements in properties of both fresh and hardened concrete'.
- The proportion of blended cement has increased by more than 80% in a decade from 2005 onwards and is likely to increase further in the coming years.

10. Application of green concepts-landmark structures

- Biodiversity Conservation India Ltd. (BCIL), Bangalore (India).
- This is the first residential apartment in the world to be certified under 'Platinum Category' by LEED (Leadership in Energy and Environmental Design).
- No home at BCIL TZed (Towards Zero Energy Development) use incandescent lamps, halogens and fluorescent tube lights.
- Lighting reduced by nearly 70%.
- Green project spread over 5.5 acres (**Figure 15**).

Figure 15.
BCIL building.

11. ITC Green Centre-Gurgaon (India)

- This was the first 'Platinum' rated building in India with a built-in area of 1.8 lakhs sq.ft.
- The building features, storm water management system, solar thermal technology, reflective high-albedo roof paint, minimal exterior lighting, separate smoking rooms with exhaust system and zero-water discharge.
- About 10% of the building materials were refurbished from other construction sites and two fifths of the materials were procured with least transportation cost (**Figure 16**).

Figure 16.
ITC Green Centre.

12. Druk White Lotus School, Ladakh (India)

- It is a school is situated in desert landscape of severe climatic conditions, 3,500 meters above sea level.
- This structure is recipient of the Best Asian Building, Best Education Building and best green building awards.
- It combines the best of traditional Ladakhi architecture with 21st century engineering excellence.
- Traditional mud brick masonry is used internally to provide increased thermal performance and durability (**Figure 17**).

13. Confederation of Indian industry, Hyderabad (India)

- Below mentioned are some Green features of this structure.
- Potable water use is reduced 35%.
- Energy savings to the extent of 50% and reduced lighting consumption by 88%.

Figure 17.
Druk White Lotus School.

Figure 18.
CII building.

- Four fifths of the materials used are recycled/recyclable.
- Photovoltaics provide one fifth the building's energy requirement.
- Use of aerated concrete blocks in facades resulted in 15–20% less load on AC.
- It's a Zero water discharge building.
- 90% of building uses daylight and 75% of the occupants have outside view (**Figure 18**).

14. Key findings

Our planet earth is at peril due to plethora of factors like population explosion, unplanned urbanization, excessive energy use, water scarcity and inefficient waste management. It is pertinent to note that construction industry substantially consumes energy and other resources produced by the world as well as a major contributor to Green House Gas emissions. Green and Intelligent buildings with LEED certification, life cycle costing and life cycle management of resources play an important role in sustainability of the construction industry. Unless strong and efficient measures are adopted to bring the concept of green buildings within the affordability of a common man, the concept of sustainable construction will be confined to mere pipe dream. It is the responsibility of the current generation to bequeath a liveable planet to the next generation by cutting down of carbon dioxide emissions and adoption of pro-green measures. The window of opportunity to cut down the emissions is closing on us and unless we act fast, it may be too late to reverse the damage that has been inflicted on the environment by the construction industry.

Author details

K. Srinivas
National Academy of Construction, Hyderabad, India

*Address all correspondence to: ksrinivasap@gmail.com

References

[1] Albert Borgstein, A. (2017). South Africa JSE Listed Company Perspective of Sustainability and Sustainability Reporting. DOI:10.13140/RG.2.2.36269.33761

[2] Endersbee, L. (1989). Global challenges and new challenges for civil engineers. Journal of Professional Issues in Engineering 115(1):29-44.

[3] Hermawan, Puti Marzuki, Muhamad Abduh, and R. Driejana (2015). Identification of source factors of carbondioxide emissions in concreting of reinforced concrete. In: 5th International Conference of Euro Asia Civil Engineering Forum EACEF-5. Indonesia: Proceedia Engineering No. 125. pp. 692-698.

[4] Nielsen, C. V. (2008). Carbon foot print of concrete buildings seen in life cycle perspective. In: Proceedings of NRMCA 2008 Concrete Technology Forum, Denver.

[5] Kim, J. J. (1998). Introduction to sustainable design. The Master Builder 3(6):34-44.

[6] Kilbert, C. J. (2005). Sustainable Construction, Green Building Design and Delivery. NJ: John Wiley and Sons, Inc.

[7] Planning Commission, Govt of India (2012). https://niti.gov.in/planning commission.gov.in/docs/reports/sereport/ser/isid_mining%20_report1206.pdf

[8] Mehta, P.K. (2001). Reducing the environmental impact of concrete. Concrete International 23(10):61-66.

[9] Penttala, V. (1997). Concrete and sustainable development. ACI Materials Journal 94(5):409-416.

[10] Ambuja Technical Literature Series (2008). Sustainable Challenges and Solutions, No: 130.

Chapter 4

Basel IV: The Challenge of II Pillar for Risk Management Function

Pasqualina Porretta and Fabrizio Santoboni

Abstract

The book is based on Supervisory Review and Evaluation Process (SREP) is conducted annually by the Supervisory Authorities to verify that each bank (Significant/Less Significant) has implemented strategies, processes, capital, and liquidity assessment process appropriate to the business model and overall planning activity and risk governance system. Analysis of the aims, the features, and the different phases of SREP and the proportionality principles on which the Single Rulebook is based. Some reflections about proportionality principle of Single Rule Book and new skills required to Risk Management function. The research emphasised the need for a holistic approach also in Risk Management and the bank's business activity.

Keywords: SREP, PILLAR 2, Business Model Analysis, Risk Management

1. Introduction

The *Single Supervisory Mechanism*[1] (SSM), the *Single Resolution Mechanism*[2] (SRM) and the *European Deposit Insurance Scheme*[3] (EDIS) are the three pillars of the European Banking Union, which together form a single set of rules that must be applied to all EU Member States. The European Banking Union is the response to the international financial crisis (first subprime crisis, then liquidity crisis of financial markets and sovereigns) aimed at establishing a single market for banking services and safeguarding financial stability, helping to overcome tensions (mainly fuelled by the intertwining of banking and sovereign risks), restore confidence in the European banking sector, strengthen integration and support economic growth. This objective has yet to be achieved and has been pursued with a massive amount of regulations, guidelines and technical principles (Single Rulebook), which have undoubtedly burdened the cost structure of financial intermediaries in their quest for stability. The three pillars of the Banking Union are closely interrelated and

---

[1] Council Regulation (EU) no. 1024/2013 of 15 October 2013 conferring specific tasks upon the European Central Bank concerning policies relating to the prudential supervision of credit institutions.

[2] Regulation (EU) no. 806/2014 establishing uniform rules and procedures for the resolution of credit institutions and certain investment firms under the Single Resolution Mechanism and the Single Resolution Fund.

[3] Directive 2014/49/EU of the European Parliament and of the Council of 16 April 2014 on Deposit Guarantee Schemes.

interdependent. However, a single supervisory system could not have been imagined without building a system capable of intervening in crises when they occur. Similarly, where a crisis cannot be resolved without bank failure and liquidation, a common deposit protection system is needed for all EU Member States. The keystone of the Banking Union, the pillar of change in terms of profound changes in policy and law, is the latter. The pursuit of financial stability has become even more urgent during the COVID pandemic because of the global health emergency's impact on the economic and financial system.

As defined in the Guide to Banking Supervision, the European Central Bank (ECB) has identified three objectives to be achieved by the *Single Supervisory Mechanism* (SSM):

- The safety and soundness of the European banking system.
- Integration and stability of the financial sector.
- The increased consistency of banking supervision across the Euro area.

The Single Supervisory Mechanism (SSM) has no legal personality and its purpose is the prudential supervision of banking activities. It consists of the ECB, which also plays the lead role, and the national competent authorities (NCAs) of the participating countries. Although the ECB has the ultimate responsibility for decision-making, it carries out its supervisory tasks under the MVU in close cooperation with the NCAs. Working with the NCAs, the ECB performs direct supervision of institutions defined as Significant (SIs). On the other hand, the supervision of Less Significant institutions (LSIs) is carried out directly by the NCAs in a unified supervisory approach guided by the general guidelines and instructions given by the ECB. In addition, all supervisory tasks that are not conferred within the MVU, such as consumer protection or anti-money laundering, remain with the NCAs. The criteria for determining whether banks can be considered significant – and therefore subject to direct ECB supervision – are defined in the MVU Regulation.

To qualify as significant, banks must meet at least one of these criteria[4]:

- The total value of assets exceeds €30 billion or, unless the total value of assets is less than €5 billion, exceeds 20% of national GDP.
- Be one of the three most significant credit institutions in a Member State.
- Receive direct assistance from the European Stability Mechanism.
- The total value of assets exceeds €5 billion and the ratio of cross-border assets in more than one other participating Member State to total assets exceeds 20%, or the ratio of cross-border liabilities in more than one other participating Member State to total liabilities exceeds 20%.

The ECB may decide at any time to classify a bank as significant to ensure that high supervisory standards are applied consistently, and conducts periodic reviews of all licenced banks within the SSM. The classification of banks may be changed due to the normal operations of credit institutions or as a result of extraordinary

[4] Regulation (EU) no. 468/2014 of the European Central Bank of 16 April 2014.

events such as mergers or acquisitions. In such cases, the ECB and the national supervisory authorities involved coordinate the transfer of supervisory responsibilities. The purpose of balancing the regulatory requirements for institutions of different sizes is to promote the stability of the financial system and to ensure a level playing field within the financial system and an appropriate comparison of risk, capital and liquidity profiles between intermediaries of different sizes and operational complexity.

For significant institutions, the ECB carries out its supervision through a specific methodology, the periodic assessment of their economic and financial situations, the verification of compliance with prudential rules, the adoption of any necessary supervisory measures, and the performance of stress tests. All of this is done by the Joint Supervisory Teams (JST) composed of staff from the ECB and the NCAs of the significant institutions' countries of establishment. The JST is responsible for drafting and organising the supervisory review programme, as well as for performing day-to-day supervision at consolidated, sub-consolidated and individual levels (assessments of the institutions' risk profiles, business models and strategies, risk management and control systems and internal governance). JST members may also participate in on-site inspections and investigations of internal models.

In our country, the supervision of less significant banks and banking groups is instead exercised directly by the Bank of Italy with a view to unitary supervision under the guidelines and general instructions given by the ECB. Among the less significant banks are the so-called "High Priority" banks for which the exchange of information between the BoI and the ECB is more intense. (These are the first banks "below the threshold" of €30bn in assets.) However, the BoI retains full and autonomous competence in the areas of consumer protection, combating money laundering and terrorist financing, supervision of payment services and markets for financial instruments, and supervision of non-banks and branches of non-EU banks.

As regards SIMs and OICR managers, the Consolidated Law on Finance (TUF) assigns to the Bank of Italy supervisory tasks for risk containment, stability and sound and prudent management, and to Consob those for the transparency and propriety of the conduct of these intermediaries in offering investment products.

The First Pillar of the MUV (SSM) is based on the so-called Basel framework, or rather on the following regulatory sources:

- CRR (*Capital Requirements Regulation*), which is directly applicable in all participating countries.

- CRD IV (*Capital Requirements Directive*) as transposed into national law.[5]

Starting from 2021, the two regulatory packages will be gradually replaced by the new CRR II and CRD V, whose regulatory changes define the final structure of the new "*Basel IV*". This expression, replacing the previous "*Basel III*", indicates the important process of change that has taken place over the last three years to the current regulatory framework. The changes, which affect several areas of prudential supervision of the banking sector (credit risk, market risk, operational risk, liquidity, leverage ratio, etc.) will become fully effective in 2027. The regulatory texts that make up Basel IV are as follows:

[5] In Italy, CRD IV has been implemented by Circular No. 285 of the Bank of Italy.

1. CRR II and CRD V.[6]

2. Basel III: Finalising post-crisis reforms.

3. EU Regulation 2017/2401–2402 (*Securitisation*).[7]

The prudential supervisory framework for risk and capital (Basel IV) has always been ideally divided into three pillars:

1. **Pillar 1** regulates the calculation of the capital requirement,[8] i.e. the mandatory capital provisions that each intermediary must have for the following regulated risks: credit risk, market risk and operational risk.

2. **Pillar 2** is a set of rules governing the Supervisory Review Process, i.e. an integrated process of supervision and management of risk-capital-liquidity. In technical terms, it is the combined ICAAP/ILAAP, SREP and RAF process.

3. **Pillar 3** is devoted to the transparency obligations incumbent on all banking intermediaries.

In general terms, the MUV is based on the European single rulebook, which therefore consists – in addition to the Regulation and the Directives (Directive 2013/36/EU-CRD IV, EU Regulation no. 575/2013 - CRR, Directive 2014/49/EU - *Deposit Guarantee Schemes Directive*, Directive 2014/59/EU -*Bank Recovery and Resolution Directive*) – also of the binding technical standards and guidelines of the EBA. The chapter want to analyse the aim, the features and the different phases of Supervisory Review Process.

2. Is proportionality enough?

The entire structure of the Single Supervisory Mechanism is based on a principle of proportionality aimed at achieving a uniform application of the rules while respecting the diversity of banks' business models, identities, size and operational complexity. However, the operational implementation of this principle does not always seem to have been able to fully achieve these objectives, which is why the application of this principle continues to be a priority on the agenda of European authorities.

However, the approach of European supervision has historically been oriented towards the definition of a set of rules equal for all, in order to ensure homogeneity of treatment for different banks: the principle of "one size fits all". However, this approach, while further tightened in the immediate post-crisis years, has been revisited from a proportional perspective (at least in theory) with the introduction of the current CRR and CRD IV and the future entry into the scene of the new CRR II and CRD V.

The application of the principle of proportionality within the Single European Supervisory Mechanism is therefore substantiated by the application of the same

[6] Update of the CRD 4 Directive and the CRR Regulation by the EU Commission, made through a first proposal on 23 November 2016, and which will address market risk, interest rate risk, leverage ratio, Net Stable Funding Ratio, TLAC/MREL requirements, large exposures, counterparty risk, SME support factor, exposure to CCPs.

[7] The Regulation will amend certain aspects of securitisation procedures carried out by banks.

[8] It must be calculated and reported quarterly to the Supervisory Authorities.

Priority classes	Intermediary
Very High	Any LSIs identified as O-SIIs
High	High priority LSI
Medium	Medium priority LSI
Low	Low priority LSI

Source: Bank of Italy.

Table 1.
Classification of LSIs into priority classes.

rules to all banking intermediaries, but with a "depth" and an articulation proportionate to the significance and/or operational complexity. The significance of an intermediary is relevant to the identification of the competent Supervision Authority, even though, in this regard, an intense collaboration between the European Central Bank and the NCAs is foreseen to guarantee the harmonised application of the Community rules. Specifically, the SSM provides that, with regard to the supervision of the *Significant Institutions*, the ECB presides over working groups technically defined as *"Joint Supervisory Teams"* (which are composed of both representatives of the ECB and representatives of the NCAs), while for the supervision of the Less Significant Institutions it is the NCAs that calibrate the regulatory requests on the banks they are responsible for. The method used by the ECB, in its capacity as a harmoniser of EU supervisory practices, to ensure the proper application of the proportionality principle by national authorities is based on the classification (reviewed annually in cooperation with the NCAs) of LSIs into[9] priority classes that, based on their impact on the financial system and their inherent riskiness, consist of (**Table 1**).

Based on this classification, the NCAs establish the intensity of Pillar II assessments, supervisory expectations and information requirements at the data collection stage, calibrated according to the classes.[10] Supervisory activities for less significant institutions consist of regular assessments conducted jointly by the ECB and the NCAs of the Member States, with the aim of making the best use of the information available to the national authorities. Moreover, for high priority LSIs, the ECB examines the supervisory procedures and relevant draft decisions established by the NCAs themselves[11].

The subject of the proportionality of the rules of supervision and surveillance in the European banking system is of strategic importance, also due to the fact that the LSIs represent a pillar of the European real and financial economy, even though 80% of these institutions are concentrated in nine countries (primarily Austria, Germany and Italy, but also Croatia, Denmark, Luxembourg, Poland, Slovakia and Slovenia).[12] It is interesting, in this context, to observe how the principle of proportionality is implemented overseas.

[9] The objective is to determine an order of priority of individual LSIs to be applied in the allocation of supervisory resources within the MVU, both for NCAs and the ECB.

[10] MVU's SREP methodology for LSIs. ECB, 2018.

[11] MVU Supervision Manual. ECB, March 2018.

[12] As of 2016, the average size of European LSIs stood at around €1.5 billion, with German institutions accounting for a large part of this with €5.5 billion in assets (ECB, 2017). Moreover, the business models of less significant European intermediaries, although predominantly oriented towards a retail banking approach, are characterised by variety and by the market segments concerned. In fact, they are also present in sectors such as real estate or private banking, depending on the national context of reference.

In fact, US banking regulations basically implement the Basel standards for large banks, while the provisions of the reform known as the "Wall Street Reform" or also the "Dodd-Frank Act"[13] establish a series of rules tailored to the size of small and medium-sized banks, which make up about 95% of US credit institutions. From the outset, the main objective of the definition of new common rules was to guarantee greater stability to the US financial apparatus and above all to avoid the spread of systemic risk. Although this objective was perfectly consistent with that of European legislators, the approach used on the other side of the Atlantic was more oriented towards defining more stringent rules for large banks (identified as those with total assets of over $50 billion), and therefore by definition carrying systemic risk, while a set of new, less onerous rules proportionate to their operations was envisaged for community banks. In addition, in 2018, the Dodd-Frank Act was revised and amended with a view to further calibrating it towards a more pervasive application of the proportionality principle. For example, while initially the more stringent rules on stress testing, MREL requirements and the weakening of the role of advanced internal models were only applicable to institutions with assets in excess of $50 billion, from 2019 they would be limited to institutions with assets in excess of $250 billion. In the case of smaller banks, the legislature instead focused its attention on the need to hold high capital requirements, which – especially initially – resulted in the closure of smaller, underperforming banks [1].

With regard to Community banks, however, the principle of proportionality does not take the form of applying the same regulatory requirements with a different degree of depth, but rather provides for total exemption from certain supervisory standards (this is the case for banks with assets of less than $10 billion, which are not subject to the macroprudential stress tests that are mandatory for all larger institutions, including those with assets of between $10 and $50 billion). The application in the United States of the regulatory standards envisaged by Basel III applies, with due differentiation, to two categories of credit intermediaries: *internationally active* banks, identified as banking institutions with at least $250 billion in assets or an amount of foreign exposure of at least $10 billion; and *global systemically important banks* (G-SIBs), whose identification is based on a comparison of key indicators of systemic risk.

Table 2 summarises the regulatory capital and liquidity requirements for different types of banks operating in the US system.

A comparison of the regulatory indicators in the US and European systems reveals some differences in the proportionate application of supervisory rules with respect to bank size. First, while US regulation provides for a full exemption from stress testing for community banks, in Europe this exemption does not apply to LSIs. With respect to capital requirements, however, the main difference is that while the EU framework allows NCAs to require even smaller institutions to hold an additional countercyclical capital buffer in good times, this only applies to banks with assets greater than $250 billion in the US. Ultimately, evidence of different application of the proportionality principle can also be found with respect to liquidity requirements. Specifically, while in the US full compliance with the LCR

[13] The Wall Street reform known as the Dodd-Frank Act is a complex intervention sought by the Obama administration to promote a stricter and more complete regulation of US finance while encouraging a protection of consumers and the US economic system. Source: Borsa Italiana.

Applicable Regulations	**Current Tailoring of Rules**				
	G-SIB	**Int'l Active ($250b+)**	**Regional ($50-250b)**	**Mid-size ($10-50b)**	**Small (<$10b)**
Comprehensive Capital Analysis & Review (CCAR)					
Global market shock for trading	Yes (6/8)	No	No	No	No
Counterparty default scenario	Yes (8/8)	No	No	No	No
Qualitative Fed-run process review	Yes	Yes	No	No	No
Quantitative Fed-run stress tests	Yes	Yes	Yes	No	No
Fed ability to object to capital plans through CCAR	Yes	Yes	Yes	No	No
DODD-Frank Act Stress Tests (DFast)					
Quantitative Fed-run stress tests	Yes	Yes	Yes	No	No
Company-run stress tests	Yes	Yes	Yes	Yes	No
Annual stress test	Yes	Yes	Yes	Yes	No
Mid-year stress test	Yes	Yes	Yes	No	No
Capital Standards					
Risk-based					
G-SIB capital buffers	Yes	No	No	No	No
Countercyclical capital buffer	Yes	Yes	No	No	No
Including AOCI changes in capital	Yes	Yes	No	No	No
Risk-based (i.e., Base III)	Yes	Yes	Yes	Yes	Yes
Leverage ratio					
Enhanced Supplementary leverage ratio (eSLR)	Yes	No	No	No	No
Supplementary leverage ratio (SLR) of 3%	Yes	Yes	No	No	No
U.S. leverage ratio	Yes	Yes	Yes	Yes	Yes
TLAC and long-term debt requirement	Yes	No	No	No	No
Liquidity Requirements					
Liquidity coverage ratio (LCR)	Yes	Yes	No	No	No
Modified LCR	No	No	Yes	No	No
Net stable funding ratio (NSFR), proposed rule	Yes	Yes	No	No	No
Modified NSFR, proposed rule	No	No	Yes	No	No

Source: U.S. Treasury (A Financial System That Creates Economic Opportunities - Banks and Credit Unions. Pag.41. www.treasury.gov).

Table 2.
Breakdown of the main regulatory obligations in the US system.

Supervisory obligations	USA: application to CBs	Europe: application to LSIs
• Stress test	NO	YES
• Countercyclical buffer	NO	YES
• LCR	NO	YES
• NSFR	NO	YES
Source: Author elaboration.		

Table 3.
Differences between the US and the EU in the application of the principle of proportionality.

(Liquidity Coverage Ratio[14] [2]) and NSFR (Net Stable funding Ratio)[15] [2] is only required for banks with assets greater than $250 billion, and less stringent application is demanded of institutions with assets between $50 billion and $250 billion, in Europe compliance with an LCR of at least 100% is mandatory for all intermediaries. In addition, as of 2021, compliance with an NSFR of at least 100% will also be mandatory for all intermediaries, although a simplified version will be available for small and less complex institutions. **Table 3** below summarises the differences just discussed.

Finally, the application of the principle of proportionality in the US banking system manifests its effects also in the phase of resolution of banks in crisis, contrary to what actually happens in the European Banking Union. In Europe, in fact, as highlighted by Masera [3], while the SSM provides for the assignment of the tasks of supervision on the LSIs to the NCAs, the performance of this activity is effectively limited only to the banks in ordinary administration, and as highlighted in paragraph 3.2, in the cases in which a Less Significant bank shows signs of vulnerability, the ECB has the right to take over the supervision of the institution, making the principle of subsidiarity prevail over that of proportionality. In the US, on the other hand, resolution interventions are led by the Orderly Liquidity Authority for banks subject to *enhanced supervision* (i.e. less than 5% of credit intermediaries), while small and medium-sized banks are subject to a special procedure coordinated by the Federal Deposit Insurance Corporation, which is entrusted with the necessary powers for proportionate interventions according to the characteristics of the institutions in crisis. The greater operational flexibility of the aforementioned US authorities compared to the European authorities is also accompanied by the lack of a single deposit insurance scheme for the resolution of small banks and by the provision of a limit of $250,000, well above the €100,000 envisaged by the future CDGS (which the ECB is also considering modulating over time for interventions

[14] The LCR rules for European banks are defined in the CRR (Articles 411 to 416). The concept and requirements of LCR were devised by the Basel Committee of Banking Supervision in 2009 as a response to the 2008 financial crisis, which was caused by banks issuing risky loans and other egregious banking activities. Liquidity coverage ratio or LCR refers to the percentage amount of cash, cash equivalents, or short-term securities that large banks are required to hold as reserves to meet their short-term financial obligations during a crisis event. The LCR is calculated by dividing a financial institution's most liquid assets by its cash outflows over a 30-day period. Banks must maintain a ratio of 100% to satisfy the requirement.

[15] NSFR is a liquidity ratio requiring banks to hold enough stable funding to cover the duration of their long-term assets. For both funding and assets, long-term is mainly defined as more than one year, with lower requirements applying to anything between six months and a year to avoid a cliff-edge effect. Banks must maintain a ratio of 100% to satisfy the requirement.

limited to institutions in countries in financial difficulty), for the guarantee of depositors in the banking system.

In this context, it should be noted that the definition of the identification threshold for banks to which size-related measures are to be applied is not straightforward and can hardly be standardised. The difficulty lies primarily in defining criteria that are adaptable to the financial systems of different jurisdictions, which are different from each other. Policymakers and the literature have provided much food for thought [3–5] on the effective application of a two-tiered approach to less complex institutions identified through parameters such as:

3. The SREP process and the holistic approach to supervision and management of the banking business

Article 97 of the CRDIV (Directive 2013/36) requires supervisors to review the organisation, strategies, processes and methodologies that banks put in place to address the range of risks they face.

The Supervisory Review and Evaluation Process (SREP) is conducted annually by the supervisory Authorities to verify that each bank has implemented strategies, processes, capital and liquidity appropriate to the risks to which it is or might be exposed and that they have appropriate capital and organisational safeguards in place to address the risks they face, ensuring overall balance of operations and market resilience.

The SREP process is not new, as it has always been carried out before the SSM by national supervisors with different and non-homogeneous methodologies and practices. For this reason, the European regulation intended to standardise the SREP methodologies and practices used by the different Authorities at the level of the Banking Union.

SREP entered into force in 2016 for IS and only from 2018 became mandatory first for high priority LSIs and then for other LSIs. Following the harmonisation of the SREP process for LSIs, national authorities have been given full flexibility regarding the definition of Pillar 2 guidelines (P2G) [6]. Finally, one of the focal points of the MUV is the possibility for the ECB to take over the supervision of LSIs that are more vulnerable, for example due to a change in materiality profile or due to a choice by the Central Bank as a result of new assessments of the impact the institution might have on the financial system. Supervision of less significant institutions takes the form of periodic assessments conducted jointly by the ECB and the national supervisory authorities of the Member States, with the aim of making best use of the information available to the national authorities. Moreover, for high priority LSIs, the ECB examines the supervisory procedures and relevant draft decisions established by the NCAs themselves [6].

The SREP is a process by which the European Central Bank and the NCA specifically:

- Review and assess the ICAAP (Internal Capital Adequacy Process).
- Review and evaluate the ILAAP (Internal Liquidity Adequacy Process).
- Carry out Business Model Analysis (BMA).
- Analyse the bank's risk individually and in the aggregate, including under stressed conditions, and its contribution to systemic risk.
- Evaluate the corporate governance system, the organisational structure and the system of internal controls.

- Monitor compliance with all prudential rules.
- Make an overall assessment of the bank and initiate corrective action where appropriate.

At the end of the process, the supervisory Authorities send the banks a letter (called a "SREP decision") specifying the objectives and areas to be addressed and corrected within a defined time frame[16].

The SREP is an articulated process that develops through a continuous dialogue and confrontation between supervisor and supervised in order to make an overall assessment, from an integrated perspective, of the stability and resilience of the latter. The inspectors' findings and the on- and off-site supervision feed the subsequent SREP cycle. In this perspective, the SREP is not a control and assessment activity carried out by the Supervisor once a year, but rather a process of second-pillar prudential control, which unfolds continuously and starts from the identification of the category[17] to which the bank belongs (with respect to which to calibrate the intensity of the supervisory activity) against which the intensity of the SREP assessment is established, the supervisory expectations and the information required during the data collection phase, calibrated according to the classes [7] to finally arrive at the so-called SREP decision. The classification is calibrated according to the systemic impact of the intermediary, based on: size, structure, internal organisation, type, purpose and complexity.

The classification of institutions is followed by monitoring of indicators for changes in financial conditions and risk with the objective of updating the assessment of SREP elements. If monitoring reveals a deterioration in the institution's risk, the Supervisor investigates the causes and may revise the assessments of the SREP elements. Vigilance develops different sets of ratios based on the different specificities of banks, including: ratios for all risks subject to SREP. All ratios used for regulatory requirements (see EU Regulation 575/2013 and Directive 2013/36/EU), minimum requirements on own funds and eligible liabilities under Directive 2014/59/EU (bank recovery), market indicators (equity price, CDS spread, etc.), recovery indicators. The frequency of assessment of all items of the SREP process is calibrated according to the category that the financial intermediary belongs to.

The four central blocks covered by the SREP assessment are: business model analysis, the governance and risk management framework, the capital adequacy framework (ICAAP) and the liquidity management framework (ILAAP).

For each of the four main blocks covered by the SREP, banks are assessed by the Supervisory Authorities on a scale of 1 to 4.[18] The outcome of the assessment constitutes the basis for the overall assessment of the SREP: the SREP decision, which

[16] The normative sources of reference for the SREP process are: - *Guidelines on common procedures and methodologies for the supervisory review and evaluation process (SREP) (EBA/GL/2014/13)* issued on 19 December 2014 – Applicable from 1 January 2016 - *Guidelines on the revised common procedures and methodologies for the supervisory review and evaluation process (SREP) and supervisory stress testing* issued 19 June 2018.

[17] Banks are divided into four categories:

- Category 1: Global systemically important institutions (Global SIFIs) and other systemically important institutions (article 131 of Directive 2013/36/EU.
- Category 2: large-medium entities.
- Category 3: small and medium-sized entities.
- Category 4: small entities.

[18] For each block, the Authority is asked to assign a score on a scale from 1 to 4, with 1 being the best and 4 the worst.

Business Model Analysis	Degree of feasibility (within the year) and sustainability (over a three-year horizon) of the business model declared by the bank. Identification of the key elements of the Business Model and assessment of the main areas of vulnerability.
Governance and Risk Management Assessment	Adequacy of the governance model including the main control functions (risk management, internal audit and compliance). Adequacy of the Risk Management system/infrastructure and degree of establishment of a "risk culture".
Assessment of risks to Capital	Adequacy of capital to cover specific risk categories (e.g. credit, market, operational and interest rate risk in the banking book). Overall assessment of ICAAP (documentation, data quality, risk measurement processes, capital planning, ...).
Assessment of risks to Liquidity and Funding	Adequacy of overall liquidity management processes/governance; Funding capacity.

Table 4.
SREP process::Building blocks.

is the basis for supervisory measures. The SREP decision is the final summary of the entire Pillar 2 supervisory review process, which reports the bank's overall score (compared to the assessment of the four main blocks) and, if anomalies are found, any corrective measures of an organisational, capital or liquidity risk containment nature or **other early intervention measures**. Interventions depend on the severity of the deficiencies, the need for timeliness, the degree of awareness, capacity and reliability of the corporate governance, and the availability of human, technical and capital resources at the intermediary. In the case of organisational deficiencies, additional capital requirements will be imposed if the bank does not appear to be able to ensure the removal of the deficiencies within an adequate period of time. The SREP decision is also a strategic moment of reconciliation between the MUV Pillar II process and the BRRD because it provides for the possibility of activating early intervention measures in case of trigger events foreseen by the BRRD.

Early intervention measures may be triggered by events that could have a significant prudential impact[19] on the institution's financial condition. They should be considered if the institution's overall or individual SREP score is 4 and even if the SREP score inclusive was 3, but individual elements for governance and internal control, business model strategy, capital adequacy or liquidity score were instead 4. However, the early intervention measures are the result of ongoing monitoring of compliance with the requirements of the CRR and CRDIV with respect to the anomalous situations foreseen by the BRRD in the supervisory activity.

In the SREP decision the Authorities also define the so-called Pillar 2 Requirement (P2R), which **is applied in addition to the minimum** Pillar 1 **requirement in** order to cover all risks that are underestimated and not considered in internal risk governance. The P2R is one of the outcomes of the SREP and is legally binding. As part of the SREP process, an additional capital **requirement is** also identified, known as Pillar 2 Guidance or P2G, which is not legally binding, but which indicates to banks the level of capital deemed adequate to cope with stress situations and is defined by the Authorities downstream of the supervisory macro stress testing process (EU-wide stress test).

By its very nature, the entire process of Pillar 2 prudential supervision gives shape and content to the fundamental moments of intermediaries' strategic planning, business choices, capital and liquidity allocation, funding plan, governance

[19] For example, a severe operational risk due to improper business operations, fraud, natural catastrophes, severe cyber incidents, a significant deterioration of the minimum requirement for MREL eligible capital and liabilities, or rating downgrades.

and organisational structure. The SREP is certainly a holistic approach to supervision that calls for an equally integrated approach by individual intermediaries to business choices, risk, capital and liquidity management both in normal and stressed conditions (Crisis and Recovery Risk Management), governance and the overall Risk Management framework. In this perspective, the SREP certainly represents a regulatory "stimulus" to a significant qualitative leap in the functions that deal with risks, capital and liquidity in the bank, recognising them as having a primary role in the strategic planning of the bank, as well as a flexible and proactive integration of the corporate control functions (**Table 4**).

3.1 Business model analysis (BMA) and viability assessment

Within the SREP process, one of the main moments of assessment is represented by the analysis of the business model of financial intermediaries and the related operational and strategic risks (Business Model Analysis) aimed at establishing the economic (viability) and strategic sustainability of the business model[20] of the institution based on its ability to generate acceptable profits over the next 12 months and over a three-year horizon. With the BMA, legislators attempt to investigate in detail the profitability of the current and prospective business model, but also to assess its resilience and weaknesses, which could jeopardise the future survival of the bank and which may not be highlighted by other elements of the SREP. The business model is not to be confused with the concept of "intermediation model". On closer inspection, the former refers to a broader concept that encompasses both the issue of the intermediation model and other aspects such as the use of technology, the creation of value for the set of stakeholders and the management and operation of the most relevant processes (Maurizio [8]). The business model describes the logic with which an organisation creates, distributes and captures value [9]. However, there is no unambiguous definition of the business model in the literature, nor have European legislators ventured to define it in relation to the financial intermediation sector (Di [10]).

From this perspective, it is clear that the introduction of the BMA within the SREP process is a clear sign of the importance that European lawmakers assign to strategic planning and therefore to the choice of the intermediary's business model, which, as is well known, has a large impact on the levels of profit produced. The latter is an issue of strategic importance given the negative trend in profitability in the context of the low profitability of Italian and European banks caused by the international financial crisis and the strong tightening of prudential supervisory obligations on risk, capital and liquidity, which require a thorough review of the intermediary's strategic choices along possible lines of development of intermediation margins (Artificial Intelligence, attention to sustainable or rather ESG-oriented finance, etc.). The possibility for a bank to exploit resources with a high technological content, albeit following significant initial investments, allows it to achieve cost-reduction objectives, especially with regard to traditional credit activities, but in general for all activities whose costs (e.g. personnel costs) are not adequately remunerated by the revenues generated [11].

While it is true that business model choices have an impact on the profitability of individual banks, they also have important implications for the stability of the

[20] The EBA defines the concepts of economic and strategic sustainability as follows:

- The viability of the entity's business model is its ability to generate acceptable profits over the next 12 months.
- The sustainability of the institution's strategy is its ability to generate acceptable profits over a time horizon of at least three years, depending on its strategic plans and financial forecasts.

entire financial system (through funding structure,[21] revenue composition, cost composition, ownership structure), which is why the BMA has been given an important role in the overall Pillar 2 prudential control process.

The BMA starts with a preliminary assessment of the environment the bank operates in, with particular reference to its core activities. In this initial step, the supervisor is required to assess a number of parameters (total revenues/costs, market position, etc.) and monitor their evolution over time in order to have a clear picture of the condition of the institution and to establish the relevance of its business areas in the context of reference. Competent authorities should use this preliminary assessment to establish the materiality of business lines/areas (i.e. determine which geographic areas, subsidiaries/branches, business lines and product lines are the most relevant based on profit contribution, risk and/or organisational/regulatory priorities -specific requirements for public sector banks to offer certain products- identify the peer group based on competing product/business lines that target the same source of profits/customers, support the application of the proportionality principle.

After the preliminary macroeconomic assessment, the competent authority should focus on the current business model, on the business lines that are most important in terms of viability or future sustainability of the current business model and/or that are most likely to increase the institution's exposure to existing or new vulnerabilities, whereby they should assess the relevance of the business lines, previous SREP findings, findings and observations of internal and external audit reports, the importance of strategic plans identifying any business lines to be substantially increased or decreased, results of topical supervisory reviews, observed changes in the business model and peer comparisons (i.e. whether a business line has performed atypically compared to peers). As outlined in the EBA guidelines on the SREP process, the areas for which authorities are tasked with conducting analysis should include, at a minimum, an assessment of the trend in profits and losses in recent years, looking at the most significant indicators of banking activity such as net interest income, net banking income, cost-to-income ratio and loan impairment rate; the composition of the balance sheet in recent years, with particular attention to the composition of liabilities; the concentration of assets by customer, sector or geographic area; an assessment of the intermediary's risk appetite, taking into account the formal definition of the current limits and the real tendency to respect them in practice; and finally an assessment that takes into account both internal and external factors capable of impacting on the functioning of the business model.

It should be made clear that the BMA has as its ultimate goal:

- The feasibility/viability of the current business model over a 12-month horizon.

- The sustainability of strategic plans over a three-year horizon.

In other words, the supervisors' "ultimate" objective is to assess whether the financial intermediary, with its business model and strategy, is credibly capable

[21] As an example, as can easily be guessed the risks associated with the structure of the funding assume greater weight if the funding is wholesale, while they have less impact with reference to funding mainly based on deposits, which is more stable by definition. A market-oriented model certainly hides more pitfalls than a traditional credit intermediation model due to the greater volatility of its results. Finally, with regard to the last two points, situations of instability can certainly derive from cost inefficiency and from ownership policies oriented more towards satisfying shareholders rather than practices consistent with the objective of stability and profitability in the short and medium term. See Financial Stability Review. ECB, May 2016.

of generating acceptable returns over a short (12-month) and long-term (three-year) time horizon.

The BMA does not aim to give a rating to the possible business models since the choice of these remains the responsibility of the management body, but to assess viability and sustainability, therefore verifying the bank's ability to generate "acceptable returns" in the time horizons considered (12 months and 36 months). With regard to viability, having carried out the preliminary analysis, the Supervisor considers:

- **RoE vs CoE** (i.e. whether the business model considered allows for a higher RoE than CoE on a structural basis).

- **Adequacy of the funding mix** with respect to the bank's business model and strategy.

- **Risk appetite**: supervisors must assess whether the institution's business model or strategy is consistent with acceptable levels of risk, including in relation to its peer group.

After the preliminary assessment, that of the entrepreneurial context, the detailed analysis of the current business model for the purposes of assessing the viability thereof, the Authority must **analyse the forward-looking strategy and financial plans**: the competent authorities should carry out a quantitative and qualitative analysis – over a period of at least three years – of the financial projections and the strategic plan of the entity to understand the assumptions, plausibility and riskiness of the business strategies. With regard to sustainability, the following are considered:

- The **credibility** (plausibility) of the assumptions underlying the strategic plans and the economic-financial projections with respect to the view of the super-investors in relation to the current and expected business environment.

- The impact of supervisors' estimates on the business environment (if different from that assumed by the bank).

- The level of **risk of the strategy**, both in relation to ambition with respect to the business context and in terms of execution risk.

The most obvious problem that arises in the assessment phase of the financial intermediary's business model concerns the existence of documents capable of providing comprehensive information to the supervisory authority on the subject in question. Indeed, in many cases it is difficult to find the documentation relating to the detailed description of the business model adopted or, again, a definition of the responsibilities of the corporate functions involved in the implementation of the activities aimed at complying with the regulatory obligations on the subject. After the process described above and at the end of the BMA process, the authority will have the task of formulating an overall opinion on the business model adopted by the intermediary, highlighting any critical points identified.

3.2 Governance assessment and the strategic role of risk management: the risk culture

The second assessment of the SREP process is devoted to the following areas: Internal governance framework; Risk management framework and risk culture; Risk infrastructure and data and reporting.

At this stage of the assessment, the main objective of the supervisory authority is to evaluate whether the bank's governance system and risk management process are adequate and consistent with the adopted business model and with what is planned in the risk appetite framework. More specifically, the suitability of the governance is assessed and whether the governance is adequately informed about the risks assumed by the bank, the risk management policies, the impact of the risk management policies on the banking activity as well as the level of capitalisation and whether this level is in balance with the risks assumed. It also assesses whether the bank has remuneration policies that comply with applicable regulations and whether the bank has an adequate system of internal controls (focusing on the risk management and compliance function), and in particular whether: (a) risk management policies have been properly defined and documented; (b) whether operational limits to the risk that can be taken are properly defined for the various business units and the bank's risk appetite; (c) whether these limits are complied with; (d) whether the risk management function is able to measure, control and manage the risks the bank is exposed to; and (e) whether the bank in its operations complies with the rules affecting its business and internal regulations. Finally, in order for the analysis to be complete, the authority examines the technological infrastructure supporting the risk management process, as well as the quality of the data and the data collection mechanism. In fact, it is easy to see how scarce or irrelevant information can compromise the proper operation of the banking business, especially in terms of risk management and control. In summary, the areas impacted by this analysis are:

1. Overall internal governance framework.

2. Corporate and risk culture.

3. Organisation and operation of the management body.

4. Remuneration policies and practices.

5. Risk management framework, including ICAAP and ILAAP.

6. Internal control framework, including the internal audit function.

7. Information systems and business continuity.

8. Recovery planning arrangements.

Particular attention is paid to the assessment of the Risk management framework and the diffusion of an adequate risk culture at all organisational levels of the bank. The attention paid by supervisors to the three corporate control functions and in particular to the Risk Management function highlights the strategic role assumed by this function in recent years: there is no possibility of planning the opening of new branches, offering new products, changing the funding plan without taking into account the impact of these choices on the governance of risks, capital and liquidity. Given the strategic role that this function plays in the overall governance of the bank, it is clear that it must be staffed with adequate professionalism to oversee the various tasks and responsibilities that regulation has greatly articulated in recent years. In carrying out its activities, the Risk Management then has the moral obligation to spread the culture of risk at every organisational level; it is the culture of risk that is the real engine of change to guide the bank in the current hyper-regulated, volatile and complex market context. As pointed out by FSB [12][22] "*weaknesses in risk culture are often considered a root cause of the global financial crisis, headline risk and compliance*". A sound risk culture should be able to ensure:

- An appropriate risk–return combination, consistent with the financial institution's risk appetite.

- An effective system of controls, commensurate with the size and complexity of the financial institution.

- The quality of risk models, the accuracy of data, the ability to measure risks accurately, using appropriate tools.

- Limit possible violations of the policies followed.

A sound and widespread risk culture is the *sine qua non* for an effectively integrated risk governance that is capable of bringing together, in a reasoned manner, the supervisory and management views, the current and forward looking perspectives, and the *business-as-usual* and stressed perspectives. The board should continually promote, monitor and evaluate the institution's risk culture, assess the impact of the institution's risk culture on financial stability, risk profile and sound governance and make adjustments where necessary; and provide risk-taking rewards and penalties for those individuals within a bank who are in a position to make decisions regarding the risk they are managing.

For this reason, the culture of risk, being the humus of the sound and prudent management of a bank, cannot remain the exclusive property of the relative Risk Management function, but must become part of the common language and cultural baggage of the other actors involved in the governance of the company at any organisational level. In this perspective, it seems useful to clarify the skills and professionalism required by the corporate control functions, and therefore also by the Risk Management.

3.3 First conclusions: towards new skills and expertise. EBA and ESMA view

On 26 September 2017, EBA and ESMA [13] issued guidelines pursuant to article 9(1) of Directive 2014/65/EU (MiFID II) and article 91(12) of Directive 2013/36/EU (CRD IV). The Guidelines explicitly identify *Key Function Holders* (KFH), i.e. those responsible for certain key functions in the governance of the bank, as individuals to be assessed with the same criteria as corporate officers. They provide the criteria to be considered in the assessment of corporate officers and key function holders, outline the direction along which the supervisory authority develops the assessment of governance and key control functions in the context of the SREP process and aim to harmonise at a European level and improve the effectiveness of the assessment process for members of corporate governance and key function holders of banks, and therefore to strengthen the suitability of the governance structures of the European banking system. The guidelines came into force in June 2018 and are in any case inspired by the principle of proportionality, so its prescriptions must be calibrated in relation to the nature, size and operational complexity of the financial intermediary.

[22] FSB in *A Framework for Assessing Risk Culture* (2014).

The guidelines are addressed to board members, heads of corporate control functions, Chief Financial Officers (CFOs), and heads of business lines that otherwise exert influence on the bank's direction and governance.

In compliance with the guidelines, banking and financial institutions must ensure and assess that KFH have an appropriate level of reputation, honesty, integrity, knowledge, skills and experience:

- When applying for the authorisation;
- When appointing a new KFH (within one month of appointment);
- When necessary to ensure "ongoing" monitoring, in particular when "events" occur that make it appropriate to reassess the fitness of KFH (changes in the organisational structure, occurrence of episodes with reputational impact, changes in the business model).

In this regard, banks and financial institutions should establish their own fitness policy, including an appropriate induction plan (for new appointments) and ongoing training to ensure that they are familiar with the required areas and have the necessary skills. The Guidelines outline a perimeter of competencies for the fitness assessment of KFHs that includes not only their previous experience but also technical competencies[23] (banking and financial markets, legal requirements, regulatory framework, strategic planning, etc.) and a very articulated set of soft skills including: independence of mind, decision-making ability, authenticity (consistency with stated values), communication and judgement skills (examines, recognises and understands the essential elements of issues with respect to which he/she is able to weigh different courses of action and project himself/herself beyond his/her area of responsibility), customer and quality orientation (of products, services, relationships), leadership, loyalty (identifies with the company, its value system defends the interests of the company and operates objectively and critically with a sense of involvement), stress resistance, negotiation skills, awareness of the external context (he/she is well informed about financial, economic, social and other relevant developments at a national and international level that may affect the company), ability to work in a team, persuasiveness, strategic acumen (he/she is able to develop a realistic vision of future developments by translating it into long-term objectives, e.g. by applying scenario analysis), ability to chair meetings efficiently and effectively creating an open atmosphere that encourages everyone to participate.

Independence of mind should not be confused with the independence required of members of the management body. In the latter case, reference is made to the fact that a member of the body in question must not have had any present or recent relationship or connection of any kind with the intermediary that could influence the latter's ability to take balanced and independent decisions in the performance of his/her functions. For example, the fact that a member of the board of directors is

[23] In this regard, it should be noted that the amended article 26 of the Consolidated Law on Banking specifies that "persons performing administrative, managerial and control functions in banks must be fit for the performance of their duties.... The officers must meet the requirements of professionalism, good repute and independence, satisfy criteria of competence and propriety, and devote the necessary time to the effective performance of their duties, so as to ensure the bank's sound and prudent management.... The management and supervisory bodies of banks assess the fitness of their members and the overall adequacy of the body, documenting the analysis process and providing reasons for the assessment".

considered to be "independent" does not mean that the member simultaneously has independence of mind [14]. The latter is in fact a set of necessary behavioural skills, including courage, conviction and strength to effectively evaluate and challenge the proposed decisions of other board members, the ability to ask questions of board members and to resist group-think.

Author details

Pasqualina Porretta* and Fabrizio Santoboni
Faculty of Economics, Sapienza University, Rome, Italy

*Address all correspondence to: pasqualina.porretta@uniroma1.it

References

[1] Masera (2019): *Community banks and land banks: can the hiatus on both sides of the Atlantic be bridged?* Ecra editions. Page 35.

[2] Porretta P., Santoboni F. (2016), *Liquidity ratio e liquidity pillar 2. Prescrizioni regolamentari e impatti gestionali nelle banche,* CEDAM, ISBN 9788813363987.

[3] Masera (2019): *Community banks and land banks: can the hiatus on both sides of the Atlantic be bridged?* Ecra Editions. Page 48.

[4] Dombret Andreas (2017), *Sometimes small is beautiful, and less is more - a Small Banking Box in EU banking regulation*.

[5] Sabine Lautenschläger (2017), *Is small beautiful? Supervision, regulation and the size of banks.* IMF seminar, 14 October.

[6] ECB (2018a), *MVU's SREP methodology for LSIs*, https://www.bankingsupervision.europa.eu/banking/lsi/srep_for_lsis/html/index.en.html.

[7] ECB (2018b), *SSM LSI SREP Methodology 2018 edition,* https://www.bankingsupervision.europa.eu/ecb/pub/pdf/ssm.srep_methodology_booklet_lsi_2018.en.pdf.

[8] Maurizio Pierigè (2018): "Banks, the business model to come". *Risk Management*magazine, September-December.

[9] Alexander Osterwalder, Yves Pigneur (2012): *Creating business models*. FAG Editions. Page 14.

[10] Antonio M., Nieri L., Costa E., Guggiola G. (2019), "Banks' strategy and business model analysis: a proposal between rules and management principles". *Bancaria*, June. Bancaria editrice, Basel Committee on Bankjoint eing Supervision (2019): Proportionality in bank regulation and supervision – a survey on current practices, www.bis.org.

[11] Vacca C., Sibilio N.I, Cusmano L, P. Soprani (2016), Banking business models: analysis and evolutionary perspectives. Bancaria, April. Bancaria editrice.

[12] FSB in *A Framework for Assessing Risk Culture* (2014).

[13] EBA and ESMA (2017a), *Joint ESMA and EBA Guidelines on the assessment of the suitability of members of the management body*, https://eba.europa.eu/eba-and-esma-provide-guidance-to-assess-the-suitability-of-management-body-members-and-key-function-holders.

[14] EBA and ESMA (2017b), cit, para. 9.

Chapter 5

Risk Management in the Area of Major Industrial Accident Prevention in the EU and Slovak Republic

Katarina Holla and Eva Sventekova

Abstract

The SEVESO II and III Directives relate to approximately 12,000 EU establishments working with the hazardous substances. The majority of EU member states implement new requirements of the SEVESO III Directive to their legal environment. The third revision goes hand in hand with the enforcement of the CLP legislation, concerning the Classification, Labelling and Packaging of chemical substances and mixtures. Risk Management is appearing as one of the most important challenges nowadays to raise the prevention level in these establishments. The book chapter analyses the industrial accidents and identified consequences and impacts whose results can be implemented to the effective prevention. The benefit of this chapter is the summarisation of the legal regulations, information systems and especially the statistics of the industrial accidents in Slovakia and the EU. The risk assessment is one of the problem areas of prevention therefore, it was necessary to present the methods and techniques utilised here and to clarify the approach used in the Slovak Republic. The programme ALOHA is most frequently used for modelling the consequences and therefore we presented its possible utilisation on a particular example at the end of this article. The main goal of this chapter is to show how is important to proceed risk management in establishments with hazardous substances is, what kind of methods should be use here to decrease risks and possibilities for modelling its impacts.

Keywords: risk management, industrial accidents, prevention, Seveso, Slovakia, modelling

1. Introduction

The major industrial accidents are phenomena whose effects threaten the human lives, property and environment. The EU decided to solve this problem in 1982 through the legal tool known as SEVESO I that has been amended three times so far. Currently the SEVESO III Directive is valid and in 2015 Slovakia issued a law about the major industrial accident prevention as amended. These legal regulations determine the rules for handling with hazardous substances and fulfilling procedures connected with their handling procedures in the companies exceeding the amounts defined by the law. The transposition of the new SEVESO III Directive has created the necessary space for modifying the problem areas – also the risk management of the industrial processes.

The major industrial accident (MIA) prevention is a specific topic for preventing, planning and solving the crisis phenomena not only in Slovakia but also on the international level. In spite of the fact that in most EU countries, in the years 2008–2018 there was a decrease in the number of people injured in accidents at work and in fatal accidents in industrial processes, it is necessary to pay attention to this area [1, 2].

The risk management that consists of the risk assessment and risk treatment is one of the most important pillars of preventing the accident development [3]. The great amount of approaches, methods and techniques in this area make it often chaotic, however, the most substantial assumption is to understand the philosophy of assessing and managing the risks the how to implement it. The calculation mechanisms and formulae serve only as an aid for defining the risk and determining its acceptability or unacceptability. The objective of this chapter was the clarification of the procedures that will be understandable and usable [4–6].

This chapter deals with MIA prevention concerning only the SEVESO III companies. The under-threshold establishments are not taken into account.

The following information was taken into consideration for analysing the accidents:

- The number of injured/dead people and damages of the property,
- The accident during the validity of the SEVESO I, II and III.

The data collection process also utilised the semi-structured interviews with the employees of the Ministry of Environment of the Slovak Republic and the Slovak Environment Agency. The databases collecting the data about the MIAs according to the classification life/health, property and environment were analysed for identifying the causes and effects.

In the framework of the case study, we utilised the on-site observations and subsequently the software for simulating the consequences and impacts.

2. Industrial accident prevention

The constant increasing of the technological progress brings also development of the industrial accidents more and more frequently. The industrial accidents belong to the anthropogenic phenomena whose occurrence can be determined with a certain probability. The need of its legal adaptation became inevitable in the 1980s.

Bahr says that the accident is an unplanned development of events that lead to undesirable injuries, losses of lives, to damaging the property and environment. He also declares that it is necessary to differentiate the so called near-miss – the nuclear accident Three Mile Island can serve here as an example. During this crisis phenomenon not that big amount of radioactivity penetrated to the environment that would have threatened the lives of the citizens, however, the investigation showed a lot of shortages that drew lessons from this near-miss [7].

Marvin Rausand says that during the recent decades a lot of large accidents have drawn attention of the general public to the need of increasing the awareness about the risks that are connected with the technological systems and activities. The industrial accidents also affected the stance of the competent authorities concerning the safety in this area. The companies themselves are also aware of the need of implementing the principles of an effective prevention in the enterprises especially in connection with the high financial costs and losses of lives in the case an accident develops. The **Table 1** brings examples of major accidents with hazardous substances (HS) [8].

In spite of the negative effects and impacts, these accidents give us precious information for improving the prevention effectiveness in this area.

The overview in the **Table 1** was created from a file including the accidents and it should serve as a reminder that safety must never be on the second place and also the risks with a low probability bring frequently serious impacts. Macza analyses some of these accidents and the responses and perception of the society to each of them in connection with the changes of the legal regulations and other interactions [11].

In the further text we will deal only with accidents in the chemical enterprises that utilise hazardous substances in their processes.

Ostrom says in his book that several types of the primary and secondary crisis phenomena can develop in the industrial operations working with hazardous substances. They can cause an accident with the following consequence:

- the leakage of a hazardous substance outside the plant (small or large),
- the leakage of a hazardous substance in the plant (small or large),
- the fire or explosion (small or large),
- the injuries of the employees (acute, chronic),
- the traffic accident in the company,
- the terrorist activity,
- the secondary ones (e.g. damaging the company's reputation) [12].

The industrial accidents are connected especially with the uncontrolled leakage and spreading the hazardous substances that threat the life and health of people, damage the property and pollute the environment [13]. The hazardous substances causing the industrial accidents are of the chemical or radioactive origin and can come either from disrupting the stability of the stationary source of the hazardous substance (production of the equipment, warehouses, equipment using the hazardous substance in the process) or the mobile sources (cars or railway carriages determined for transporting the hazardous substances) [14].

In the EU framework there are different legal regulations for the nuclear and chemical premises that are subsequently transposed to the legal system of the member states. Just the development of the industrial accidents and investigating their causes aroused the efforts to adapt the given area through the legal regulations and thorough inspection in this field (see the **Table 2**).

The aforementioned accidents were the principal milestones for creating the safety standards of the industrial processes and application of the changes in the SEVESO Directive framework.

2.1 Industrial accident prevention

2.1.1 Prevention of major industrial accidents in the EU

2.1.1.1 The legal environment in the area of prevention of major industrial accidents in the EU

The afore-mentioned industrial accidents as well as a whole range of others showed the failure of the technology and operators that caused the death of a lot of

Place of the accident	Year	Effects	Impacts
Seveso, Italy	1976	Leakage of dioxin to atmosphere	2,000 poisoned people, environment pollution, mass evacuation
The North Sea, Norway	1977	Leakage of crude oil from oil platform	Significant sea pollution
Three Mile Island, USA	1979	Near-miss, a potential for leaking a larger amount of radioactivity	Without any serious impacts
Bhopal, India	1984	Leakage of toxic methyl isocyanate	3,800 dead people, 20,000 injured people, 200,000 evacuated people
Mexico City, Mexico	1984	Explosion and fire of LPG container with subsequent pressure wave,	500 dead people, material damages
Basel, Switzerland	1986	Leakage of chemicals from the Sandoz plant to the Rhein river	River contamination, serious environmental damage, cross-border impacts
Zeebrugge, Belgium	1987	Accident of the British tanker Herald of Free Enterprise	209 dead people, material damages
The North Sea, UK	1988	Explosion and fire on the oil platform "Piper Alpha"	167 dead people, extensive damage
Pasadena, USA	1989	Explosion and fire with subsequent pressure wave and heat radiation	23 dead and 100 injured people
The Baltic Sea	1994	Overturning the ferry Estonia	853 dead people, serious environmental damage
Longford, Australia	1998	Explosion and fire with subsequent pressure wave and heat radiation	2 dead people, Melbourne without gas for 19days
Brittany, France	1999	Sinking the tanker Erika with extensive leakage of HS to the sea	Extensive leakage of oil substances to the sea and its pollution
Enschede, the Netherlands	2000	Explosion and pressure wave in the company for pyrotechnic production	22 dead people, 1,000 injured people, more than 300 destroyed houses
Toulouse, France	2001	Explosion and fire with subsequent pressure wave and heat radiation	30 people dead, 2,000 injured people, 600 destroyed houses
Galicia, Spain	2002	Sinking the tanker Prestige with extensive leakage of HS to the sea	Extensive leakage of oil substances to the sea and its pollution
Texas, USA	2005	Explosion and fire with subsequent pressure wave and heat radiation	15 dead people, 180 injured people
Hertfordshire, Great Britain	2005	Explosion and fire with subsequent pressure wave and heat radiation	43 injured people, extensive damage
Gulf of Mexico	2010	Explosion of the oil rig Deepwater Horizon	11 dead people, 17 injured people, destroyed equipment, leakage of oil slick to the sea
Great Britain	2013	Explosions and a fire on a slab casting machine in a steel works	Damage to property more than 2 mil.Euros, 12 injuries

Place of the accident	Year	Effects	Impacts
Germany, Eltmann plant	2017	Explosion resulting in fire in a rolling element manufacturing plant	1 dead, 3 critically injured, 21 at risk, 150 000 Euros damage.
Spain	2020	Ammonia release in chemical establishment (upper tier)	the death of a worker, another one was critically injured, 15 workers were mildly injured

Table 1.
The most famous industrial accidents worldwide – An overview [9, 10].

people or the accident effects caused them durable consequences for their health and losses of the material values and the environment that can be of a long-term character but also irreversible. Therefore the number one issue is the prevention of such events and the implementation of the preventive measures in the industrial environment. The EU tries to regulate this environment and to determine the rules for the companies that are the most dangerous ones from the point of view of the hazardous substances concentration. The SEVESO Directive is such a tool – it has been amended several times and currently the SEVESO III Directive is valid.

The SEVESO III Directive creates the basic framework dealing with the prevention of and preparedness for overcoming the major industrial accidents of hazardous substances. Due to the rapid technological development and globalisation the updating process of this directive is under way in certain time intervals – from the SEVESO I to SEVESO III Directives. The overview of the most important updating of this directive is as follows:

- Council Directive 82/501/EEC of 24 June 1982 on the major-accident hazards of certain industrial activities (known as SEVESO I Directive),
- Council Directive 96/82/EC of 9 December 1996 on the control of major-accident hazards involving dangerous substances (known as SEVESO II Directive). This directive that became effective on 3rd February 1997 cancelled the SEVESO I Directive,
- Directive 2012/18/EU of the European Parliament and of the Council of 4 July 2012 on the control of major-accident hazards involving dangerous substances, amending and subsequently repealing Council Directive 96/82/EC.

2.1.1.2 The competent bodies responsible for the legislative processes and control of the industrial enterprises in the EU

The unified implementation and thorough fulfilment of the SEVESO III Directive provisions in the whole EU requires a close collaboration between the corresponding bodies of all member states and the European Commission. The competent bodies responsible for the major industrial accident prevention in the EU are:

- The competent institutions in the area of the major industrial accident prevention (CCA)
- The UN agency – the environmental section (UNEP)
- The UN economic commission (UNECE)
- The office for major industrial accidents (MAHB)

2.1.1.3 The information systems of industrial accidents in the EU

The information systems of the industrial accidents are a useful tool for supporting the decision-making process of prevention and also the solution of the major industrial accident prevention. Currently these information systems contain databases that concentrate data about the emergencies and participate in preventing

Accident	Accident cause	Accident consequences	Measures
Bhopal (1984) Union Carbide for production of the insecticide SEVIN	• Water penetrated the container of methyl isocyanate with subsequent exothermal reaction, • storing hazardous substances in large containers instead of in small barrels.	• Leakage of 20–30 tons of methyl isocyanate, • 3,787 victims, • deaths of the farm animals, • damages approximately 20 billion USD, • the surroundings contaminated even today.	• Increasing requirements on safety of the operation in the developing countries (by the multinationals), • improving the citizen protection against the effects of the hazardous substances.
Seveso (1976) Chemical plant ICMESA	• Increased temperature in the boiler and subsequent chemical reaction with leakage of poisonous gas (cloud) to the atmosphere.	• 37,000 people exposed to the toxic cloud, • Death of 3,300 animals and later deaths of 78,000 animals, • The decontamination price - 32 billion USD.	• Adopting the SEVESO Directive that is valid (with certain limitations) also today.
Baia Mare (2000) Golden Mine Aurul	• Building a barrier from insufficiently tough material, • long-lasting strong rains – destabilisation of the barrier, • leakage of mercury to the air during gold separation, • combination of highly dangerous manufacturing procedures with insufficient safety provisions for technological procedures.	• Contamination of the rivers Sasal, Tisa and Danube, • mass fish kill, deaths of other organisms in these rivers, • a cross-border accident, Hungary required a financial compensation.	• Amendment of the SEVESO II Directive (including the ecological accidents to major industrial accidents), • exempting selected activities from the Mining Act and moving them under the SEVESO II Directive, • increasing the safety measures in this area.
Buncefield (2005) oils warehouse terminal	• Failure of level gauge that indicated an incorrect petrol level, • failures of other technical barriers and warning devices.	• Injuries of more than 40 people, • enormous damages of the company property and in the surroundings.	• Thorough and quality assessment and risk management with an emphasis on analysing the influence of the human factor, • integrating other protection elements for limiting the accident (detectors and cameras), • good safety culture and employees´ motivation.

Table 2.
Causes and consequences of selected industrial accidents [15, 16].

similar crisis phenomena. The Major Accident Hazards Bureau (MAHB) ensures the summarisation of the data form analysing the major industrial accidents in the EU. The MAHB provides the basic research and scientific support to the EU in the area of formulating, realising and monitoring the EU policies with the goal to check the risks of developing major industrial accidents.

The industrial accidents are gathered in the national and multinational databases. The most useful databases concentrating the data about the accidents are:

- MARS (Major Accidents Reporting System) [15].
- SPIRS (Seveso Plants Information Retrieval System) [17].
- ARIA (Analyse, Recherche et Information sur les Accidents) [16].
- FACTS (Failure and Accidents Technical Information System) [18].
- ZEMA (Enterprise Data Management) [19].

The MARS database collects data about the major industrial accidents and near misses in the SEVESO III companies in the EU. The purpose of the database is to provide data for the statistic assessment with the goal to avoid development of such events and it also serves as a source of lessons from the accidents. Based on the in advance defined rules of the responsible institutions in the EU the EU member states provide information about the major industrial accidents and near-misses to the Joint Research Centre of EC in Ispra through the electronic database MARS. The report of the event to the MARS database is obligatory for the EU member states in the case of an event that fulfils the criteria of a major industrial accident presented in the Appendix IV of the SEVESO III Directive.

The MARS database can be utilised by the bodies of the state administration of the EU member states, the industrial and trade associations, Trade Unions, etc. Currently there is at disposal also the interactive version of the database, the so-called eMARS version that is available at the internet.

	Type of Accident			
Year	**Major Accident**	**Near Miss**	**Other Event**	**Total**
2010	30	7	1	38
2011	22	0	3	25
2012	28	9	5	42
2013	21	7	5	33
2014	23	2	0	25
2015	22	4	2	28
2016	13	3	1	17
2017	12	1	1	14
2018	11	2	3	16
2019	1	0	1	2
Total	183	35	22	240

Table 3.
Contingency table of accidents according to type and year [15].

The **Table 3** brings the classification according to the types of the accident and the year when the given type of accident developed during 2010–2019. As we can see the largest amount of the most serious accidents developed in 2010–2030 accidents. The lowest number of the major accidents was registered in 2019 – only one accident. However, during the last three years, not all accidents have been recorded and therefore the amount of the accidents can increase. The near-miss is another type of the accident. The highest number of the near misses was in 2012–9 accidents. The lowest amount of the near misses is registered in 2011 and 2019–0. However, the number can be changed in 2019 – similarly as in the case of the major accident. The last accident type is the so called another event. The highest number is recorded in the years 2012 and 2013–5, on the other hand there was none in 2014. In 2012 we registered the highest amount of all the aforementioned types – 42 accidents, on the contrary the lowest amount was in 2019 – only two of them. Also in the case of the year 2019, the number of the accidents can be changed due to registering other accidents.

Another directive directly connected with the SEVESO III Directive is the SPIRS database (SEVESO Plants Information Retrieval System). This database gathers especially the data identifying the SEVESO establishments (their name, address, location in the framework of the country's territory, hazardous substances in the company and their volume, number of employees, number of citizens in the circle of 5 and 10 kilometres, the distance from the nearest water course, the company activity, etc.).

There are several other databases worldwide gathering the data about the industrial accidents. One of them is also the ARIA database formed by the Bureau for Analysis of Industrial Risks and Pollutions (BARPI) in 1992 by the French Ministry of Ecology, Sustainable Development and Energy [16].

The database FACTS is a functional one in the Netherlands and includes data about more than 23,000 industrial accidents with hazardous substances globally during the recent 90 years. It contains not only the accidents that happened but also the near-misses from the point of view of their seriousness and consequences. The most serious ones are processed in the form of reports that are available and provide a data flow for assessing the risk and preventing the failures [18].

Germany has a database for the industrial accidents called ZEMA. It comprises data about small accidents but also about serious ones affecting seriously the population, environment and property [20].

2.1.1.4 Major industrial accident prevention in the Slovak Republic

The Slovak Republic is a small country; however, the industrial accidents occurred also in its territory. The legal framework for the major industrial accidents in the SEVESO III context began to be solved after the Slovak Republic had entered the EU in 2004. In Slovakia, there are about 80 SEVESO establishment and they are divided to the categories A and B [21]. Their number can be changed due to recategorising of the companies.

The legal regulations controlling the area of protection against the consequences of industrial accidents have an important place in the Slovak legal system. Their goal is to protect people, the environment and material values against the negative impacts of the industrial accidents but also other crisis phenomena connected with leaking hazardous substances to the air, soil or water.

The Ministry of Environment of the Slovak Republic is responsible for the preparation of the legal regulations in the area of preventing and removing the consequences of the industrial accidents, however, partial tasks in this area are also fulfilled by the Ministry of Interior of the Slovak Republic or the Ministry of Economy of the Slovak Republic. Besides the legal regulations that are generally obligatory, there are also technical standards that are only recommended.

The following legal regulations solve the area of the major industrial accident prevention:

- the law No. 128/2015 Coll. about major industrial accident prevention as amended and the implementing regulations that complete this law (further the law about the Major industrial accidents (MIA) prevention),

- the decree of the Ministry of Environment of the Slovak Republic No. 198/2015 Coll. that realises some provisions of the law No. 128/2015 about major industrial accident prevention as amended.

There are several subjects in the area of the MIA prevention that are mutually interactive:

- State administration in the MIA prevention area,

- SEVESO establishments,

- Evaluators [21].

In the further text, we will characterise the individual competencies of all represented subjects that participate in the major industrial prevention in practice.

The most intensive collaboration takes place between the Ministry of Environment of the Slovak Republic, Slovak Agency of Environment and district offices in the seat of the regions.

According to the law about MIA prevention the companies are divided into two categories – the A category (the upper tier) And B category (the lower tier). The number is equal, it can change regarding to the re-categorisation of the companies from the A to the B group or including a new enterprise under the law about MIA prevention. The companies differ from each other especially in the area of the defined obligations that have to be fulfilled and the categorisation itself is realised according to the total number of the hazardous substances in the enterprise (according to the Appendix 1 in the law of MIA prevention) [21].

The threshold quantities defined in the tables in the first and second part of the law about MIA prevention relate to each enterprise. The quantities that are to be taken into account are the maximal amounts that are present or can probably be present at any moment. The hazardous substances present in the company amounting 2% or less than 2% of the corresponding threshold quantity are not taken into consideration for calculating the total present volume if their location in the company cannot cause any major industrial accident in another part of the enterprise [21].

If the company has no hazardous substance in an amount that is greater or equals the corresponding threshold quantity the following rule for defining the fact whether the company is under the law about MIA prevention is used.

The law relates to the companies of the B category, if the sum:

$$N = \frac{q_1}{Q_{B1}} + \frac{q_2}{Q_{B2}} + \frac{q_3}{Q_{B3}} + \frac{q_4}{Q_{B3}} + \frac{q_5}{Q_{B5}} + \ldots + \frac{q_x}{Q_{BX}} \geq 1 \quad (1)$$

N = is the sum of the relative quantities of two or several hazardous substances present in the company, qx = is the amount of the hazardous substance x (or the present hazardous substances of the same class/category) according to the part 1 or 2,

QBX = is the corresponding threshold quantity for the hazardous substances or the class/category "x" from the column 3 – part 1 or from the column 3 – part 2.

The law relates to the companies of the B category, if the sum:

$$N = \frac{q_1}{Q_{A1}} + \frac{q_2}{Q_{A2}} + \frac{q_3}{Q_{A3}} + \frac{q_4}{Q_{A4}} + \frac{q_5}{Q_{A5}} + \ldots + \frac{q_x}{Q_{AX}} \geq 1 \quad (2)$$

N = is the sum of the relative quantities of two or several hazardous substances present in the company,

qx = is the amount of the hazardous substance x (or the present hazardous substances of the same class/category) according to the part 1 or 2,

QAX = is the corresponding threshold quantity for the hazardous substance or the class/category "x" from the column 2 – part 1 or from the column 2 – part 2 [21].

2.1.1.5 Information systems of the industrial accidents in Slovakia

Currently there are two information systems serving for registering the industrial accidents in Slovakia – the Information System of MIA Prevention and the Information System of the Industrial Accidents. Both information systems serve for gathering, recording, listing, searching, utilising, saving and transferring information about the industrial accidents in Slovakia [14].

3. Risk management of the industrial processes

The risk assessment and risk management are problematic areas in the area of the MIA prevention. The existence of a whole range of the systematic procedures, methods, techniques and software means increases the uncertainty rate for comparing the results of various companies in the framework of processing the safety documentation. Therefore the scientific and research activities in this area should bring new knowledge and approaches that will bring optimal solutions.

3.1 Position and importance of the risk management in the area of MIA prevention

The risk assessment and management is an interdisciplinary filed that is used in a lot of areas of the social life. Every company has to fulfil both the strategic and operational objectives in the individual sectors of its activity. The manufacturing process management, HR, management of the financial processes, quality and safety and a whole range of others belong here. The safety management as one of the non-profit company activities seems to be superfluous if there are no crisis phenomena until anything happens. The safety management is realised with an emphasis on the area of Safety and Protection of Health at Work, on the environment but also the accident prevention if we work with the hazardous substances in our processes. The risk assessment and management is the basis for implementing the preventive measures and reducing the risk of developing the crisis phenomena.

The risk assessment and management is of the key importance from the point of view of minimising the damages and losses of our interests. The protection of life, property and environment cannot be ensured without identifying the risk sources, their analysis and assessment from the point of view of undesirable effects of the hazardous substance.

3.2 Approaches and systematic procedures of the risk assessment utilised in the companies

In general we can say that the risk management process consisting of assessing and managing the risks can be implemented in every area of the social life. The unbinding standards in the form of the ISO standards are transposed to the legal standards of several countries worldwide. ISO 31 000 Risk Management was issued in 2019 and was implemented to the individual EU member states. This process can be implemented for the whole organisation and all processes that are realised in its framework. Sometimes the organisations evaluate and manage the risks only up to a certain level. This standard defines several principles that are to be fulfilled for the process to be effective. Its main aim is the development, implementation and continual improvement of the framework whose purpose is to integrate the risk management process to the company management, to its strategy and planning processes, management and also to the process of reporting, policies and other activities.

According to STN ISO 31 000, the risk management process represents a systematic implementation of the policies, procedures and implementation of practice for these specific activities (see the **Figure 1**) [23].

The **Figure 1** depicts the overall risk management process. In practice the organisations manage the risks through identifying, analysing and assessing them and subsequently they evaluate which means to use to reduce the unacceptable risks to an acceptable level. During the whole process they communicate and consult with the interested parties and monitor the risks and then the measures that were implemented. The standard used the term risk treatment; however, the MIA prevention area uses the term risk management.

The risk management of the industrial processes is realised especially in connection with fulfilling the legal requirements. The most frequent reason for its realisation is the employees' protection in the framework of the safety and protection of health at work. It is more complicated to assess and manage the risks in the case of

Figure 1.
Risk management process [23].

the accident development prevention, especially in those conditions that have to fulfil the requirements of the law about MIA prevention.

The risk assessment process in the industrial enterprises (according to the law about MIA prevention) consists of:

- identifying the dangers (risk sources) and events that can arouse a major industrial accident,
- quantifying the probability or frequency of the MIA development,
- estimating the extent and seriousness of the consequences on the MIA for people's health, environment and property, assessing the risk and evaluating the risk acceptability [21].

The risk assessment as an independent phase is part of the operator's documentation in compliance with the law and therefore it is important for the company representatives to understand this process and to be able to realise it appropriately. The risk assessment and management can be realised by a whole range of approaches, however, the idea algorithm has certain parallels. The logic of the overall procedure is the same almost in any environment; it is different only in the points that are specific for the given area. If the person (expert) that carries it out will understand its essence and usability, he/she is able to implement this process and to choose the optimal methods and techniques of the individual steps of this approach.

The following items can be utilised for the risk assessment:

- the systematic procedure,
- the method or a set of techniques,
- the mathematical calculation.

3.2.1 Systematic procedures for the risk assessment

The systematic procedures are complex algorithms that utilise the methods, techniques and mathematical formulae in the individual steps. The most frequently used are:

- PRA,
- CPQRA,
- ARAMIS [22–27].

3.3 Assessing the MIA prevention in the conditions of Slovakia and shortages detected

There are several problems that create a space for the scientific and research activity in the area of the MIA prevention. The improvement of the safety level of the SEVESO establishments in Slovakia by creating a complex model of the risk assessment of the industrial processes using the quantitative methods, with its harmonisation with the EU standards and subsequent implementation in the Slovak conditions has been the basic aim of the scientific and research activity at the FSE UNIZA during the recent years.

Based on the currently valid documents and approaches that are utilised in practice the risk management can be divided into two basic phases as follows:

- the risk assessment,
- the risk treatment.

These both phases of the risk management are in the mutual interaction. From the point of view of the sequence the risk assessment has to be realised first, then it is necessary to reduce the unacceptable risks and subsequently to monitor the reduced risks and all of that represents their treatment/management.

The risk assessment can be characterised as a systematic activity of an individual or a group of people (experts) whose main goal is to state the acceptability or unacceptability of the risks on the basis of criteria defined in advance. From the functional viewpoint we divide the risk assessment process to two phases:

- the preparatory phase,
- the realisation phase.

The preparatory phase of the risk assessment has a character of realising the decisions and preparatory activities connected with this phase whose selected outputs are connected with the individual steps of the realisation phase of the risk assessment. The realisation phase of the risk assessment is an implementation activity into which the data from the preparatory phase enter and then we implement the selected procedures, methods and techniques in the individual steps by the working group (evaluators) for assessing the risks of a particular process. A list of the acceptable and unacceptable risks that are subsequently reduced and as the residual risks they enter the process of monitoring the risk is created. Every phase has its steps that are logically interconnected. The **Figure 2** depicts the whole risk assessment process.

The quality of the preparatory phase is closely connected with the quality of the outputs that are obtained at the end of the realisation phase. It depends especially on the professionalism and assumptions of the human factor (working group) that participates both in making decisions in individual phases or steps and realising the analysis itself (expert evaluation) of the given system. The human factor is also connected with the rate of uncertainty that enters the process and can affect the analysis results and cause deviations. The highest rate of uncertainty influences the results in the risk assessment phase due to the calculations that are part of the implemented methods. These deviations are connected with the rate of knowledge of the evaluators and the information that is available at the time of the analysis.

The complex model was one of the main outputs of the FSE UNIZA's research activity. It was created on the basis of several sequential steps using methods, approaches and tools from other projects solved at our faculty. During its creation it was necessary to define the main risk management phases of the complex model (the risk assessment and management) and then to determine the individual steps. The solution process was aimed at the risk assessment phase that was then analysed and developed. The existing systematic procedures, methods and techniques for the risk assessment in the industrial environment of the Slovak Republic and worldwide were evaluated for the necessary identification, analysis and assessment of the risk.

Based on several assessment criteria we chose some parts and calculations of the systematic approach ARAMIS, QRA method, Boolean algebra, failure tree, event tree, etc. We utilised also the results of the tasks solved in the project framework for defining the input and output parameters of the model:

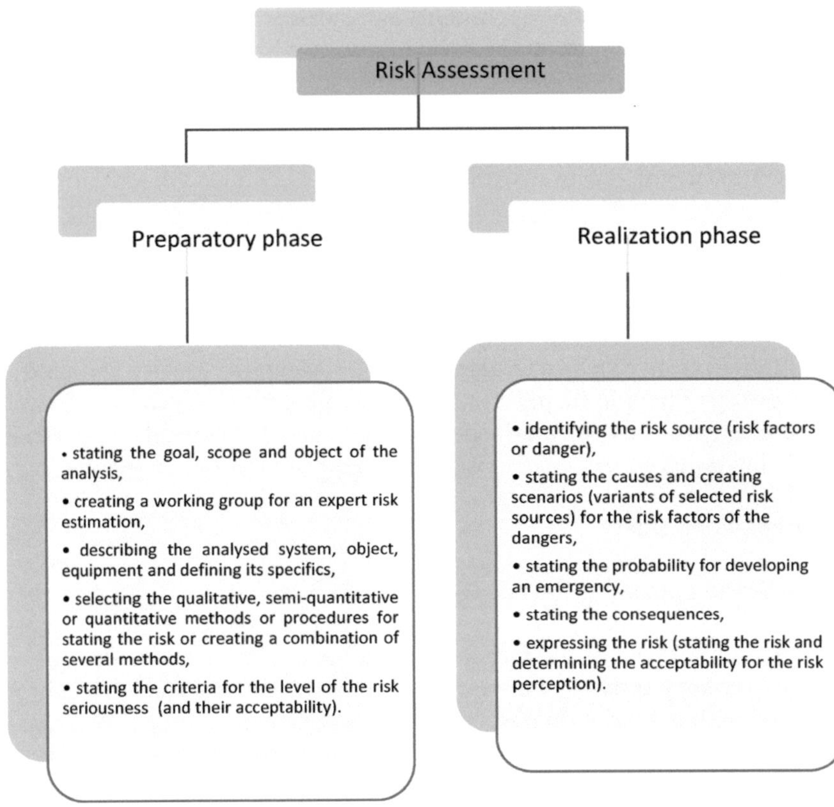

Figure 2.
Basic phases and steps of the risk assessment.

- analysing and synthesising the conclusions of the research of the SEVESO establishments in the form of the research report – Statistical Research of SEVESO Establishments.

- the working meetings.

We selected the methods and calculation mechanisms that were then implemented in the model. The project team's key procedure was the ARAMIS method that consists of two key methods – the Methodology for the Identification of Major Accident Hazards (MIMA) that identifies the risk sources of the major accidents and defines the highest risk potential of the equipment. The second method is called the Methodology for the Identification of Reference Accident Scenarios (MIRAS) that is a methodology for identifying the safety measures and procedures for scenarios identified by MIMAH.

The output of the whole analysis is the determination of the risk, designing suitable measures followed by an investment or organisational aim in the area of improving the operation safety.

4. Modelling the effects and impacts of the accidents

The current software tools used for modelling the effects and impacts are on a very good level. Their main task is to simulate (based on the models) the formation and development of the accident. These simulated accidents are subsequently included to the map material which can show us the impact of the accident in dependence on time and quantity. Thanks to these software means it is possible to identify the negative effects of the accidents and take the necessary preventive measures. These simulation programmes work with various databases thanks to which we can simulate the accidents as realistically as possible.

However, it is necessary to say this software cannot create a fully accurate model of the real world and define all parameters, e.g. the structure of the terrain, location of the buildings and equipment, etc.

Today there are a lot of simulation programmes determined for simulating the accidents, e.g. ALOHA, EFFECTS, BREEZE, TEREX, ROZEX, SAVE II, etc. They can be used for various types of accidents – the simulation of explosions, fires, leakages of hazardous substances to the air, evaporation of the hazardous substances, etc. [28, 29].

In the Czech Republic they most frequently utilise the simulation programme EFFECTS but the programmes ALOHA and SAVE II are also used. Only exceptionally they make use of the programmes TEREX and ROZEX. On the contrary, in Slovakia we often utilise ALOHA.

For simulating the type scenario in the emergency plan framework we chose the software ALOHA, particularly the version 5.4.7. The faculty student Lukáš Dančo participated in realising this simulation. The software simulated a leakage of a hazardous substance from a storage container. The software MARPLOT that is directly connected with ALOHA was subsequently used as a map basis for transferring the graphical outputs from ALOHA and thus for depicting the expansion of the hazardous substance fumes.

The particular company deals with manufacturing the basic chemicals and chemical products and its basic products are the essential amino-acids. Based on exceeding the threshold value of the hazardous substance present in the company, it belongs to the B SEVESO category.

Particularly, it is the hazardous substance ammonium hydroxide – the ammonia.

The ammonia stored in this company has a concentration higher than 25%. It presents a risk for the life and health of people only in the case of leaking from the storage containers or pipelines due to releasing the gaseous ammonia bound in water. The gaseous ammonia or the anhydrous ammonia (according to the law about MIA prevention) is the hazardous substance mentioned in the law in the Appendix 1, part 2. The substance is dangerous based on its classification as the toxic and ecotoxic material.

It is a caustic liquid with bad smell. Its colour range is from colourless to yellow or slightly turbid. This substance causes failures of the central nervous system and irritates mainly the respiratory system. The gaseous ammonia released from this liquid can be easily recognised already in a low concentration thanks to its strong odour. The exposure to a high concentration of the gaseous ammonia can cause the respiratory arrests.

The leakage of this hazardous substance can develop either in the storage containers or during pumping the hazardous substance from the tank truck. We aim at the storage containers, particularly at one of the containers, during the simulation of the hazardous substance.

We chose this device due to the fact it is the only storaging object in the company with a larger amount of the hazardous substance and it is the most dangerous equipment in the enterprise.

4.1 Input data

For us to be able to simulate the type scenarios we needed to define the input data in the software. The data about the territory were defined on the basis of the approximate position of the hazardous equipment. It is a locality in the Banská Bystrica region with an altitude of 370 metres above the sea level. The time and date of the emergency was fictitious only for the needs of the simulation – 14th May 2020 at 11:00 am (**Table 4**).

4.2 Simulating the hazardous substance leakage by software ALOHA

Our simulation of the emergency scenario took into account the formation of a crack on the surface of one of the containers causing a leakage of the whole volume of the ammonium hydroxide (63 m3) to the emergency tank (280 m3) during two minutes. Therefore we simulated the emergency scenario as the spill evaporation from the emergency tank (280 m3) on the basis of the defined atmospheric data.

However, it is necessary to say it was not possible to define the atmospheric data accurately as the emergency tank is located under the terrain level and this fact can affect the spreading of the gaseous ammonia. The surrounding buildings and terrain are not accurately defined in the simulation and it can also affect the spreading of the gaseous ammonia [30].

Input Data	
Data about Territory	
Locality	Banská Bystrica region
Altitude	370 m above sea level
North latitude	48°44′ N
East latitude	19°14′ E
Date of accident	14th May 2020
Time of accident	11:00
Chemical Data	
Hazardous substance	Ammonium hydroxide
Concentration	30%
Atmospheric Data	
Wind speed	4.5 m/s
Wind direction	North-west
Height of measuring the wind speed	10 m
Cloudiness	5 – semi-cloudy
Air temperature	19°C
Stability class	C
Inversion	None
Air humidity	70%
Data about Source	
Source	Spill
Size of the spill	280 m2
Volume of the spill	63 m3

Table 4.
Input data.

Based on the defined input data from the **Table 3** the software ALOHA graphically assessed the safe zones with a different concentration of the hazardous substance – see the **Figure 3**.

For us to understand the designations better, the following text describes the individual effects in the case of exposures to the hazardous substance to one of the zones.

ERPG 1 – Under this concentration the exposed persons can expect a low, insignificant and temporarily fugitive effect to their health within one hour or to perceive a clearly defined odour.

ERPG2 - Under this concentration the exposed persons can expect an irreversible effect to their health within one hour or less or any symptom that would reduce their ability to realise their personal protection.

ERPG 3 - Under this concentration the exposed persons can expect life-threatening effects to their health within one hour [3].

The abbreviation ppm means the amount of the volume parts of the given hazardous substance per million volume parts of the air.

Subsequently these graphical ALOHA outputs were transferred to the map material through the programme MARPLOT for the direction and reach of spreading the hazardous substance from the leakage source to be depicted. This depiction can be seen in the **Figure 4**.

The **Figure 4** shows the zone of the direct threat in the framework of which the persons can be exposed to the life-threatening effects can be found only in the operator's premises or it can partially hit the areas of the surrounding area. The next threat-zone covers several buildings with the services for the citizens. They are especially the bus stop, public road and staff quarters - here we can assume the occurrence of people. The last yellow zone covers only the uninhabited area where no people's occurrence is assumed. The **Table 5** shows the assumed distance of the reach of the threat-zones.

Our model example processed in the software ALOHA presents our attempt to show the risk of the leakage of ammonium hydroxide from the storaging premises in the company. Based on the assigned parameters we worked out a type scenario of leaking the toxic fumes of this hazardous substance. However, as it has been already mentioned, the software is not able to model certain parameters that would affect the spreading of the toxic fume – e.g. the terrain or the building layout.

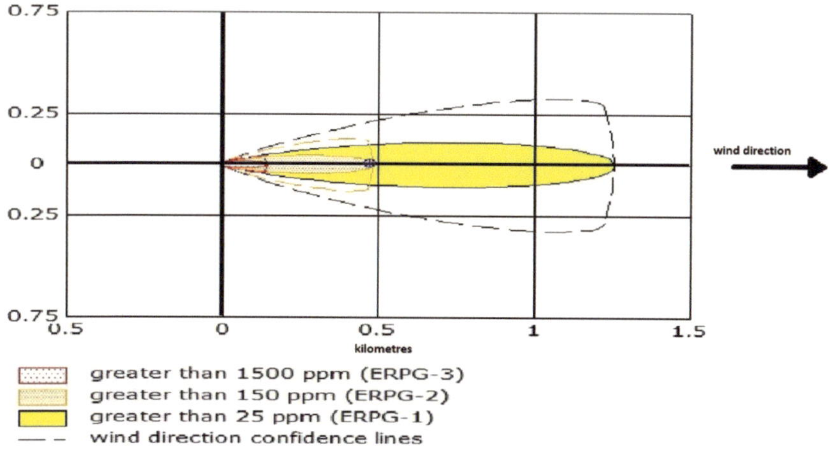

Figure 3.
A graphical depiction of the dangerous zones with the given concentration of the hazardous substance [30].

Figure 4.
The reach of the toxic fumes in the map [30].

Threat-zones			
Red	ERPG – 3	1500 ppm	144 metres
Orange	ERPG – 2	150 ppm	487 metres
Yellow	ERPG – 1	25 ppm	1,300 metres

Table 5.
The distances of the threat zones.

Certain safety systems in the company are to be taken into account, e.g. detecting the hazardous substance leakage, warning the employees in the case of the leakage and their subsequent immediate evacuation from the threatened surroundings, etc. Besides these facts there are also the emergency units that are able to affect the spreading process by their immediate response.

Based on the emergency scenario and the aforementioned facts which are not involved in the type scenario we can assume that the leaked toxic fume of the ammonium hydroxide should not exceed the company premises and to threaten the persons in the plant surroundings. We do not assume any impacts on the health of the persons and employees in the company due to their preparedness for such a scenario.

This type scenario was worked out for the needs of depicting the simulation possibilities in the software ALOHA.

5. Discussion and conclusion

Based on the analysis of the risk assessment approaches and type scenarios in the selected EU countries it is possible to say:

- The idea that on the basis of the identified risks in the industrial processes it is necessary to determine the protection zone for the population, its property and the environment for the case of the MIA is essentially the same in the whole EU. However, the approach of determining these zones is different.

- The analysis identified the selected member countries utilised various approaches to this area. Particularly they are the approaches based on the consequences/impacts, the approaches based more on the probability or on a combination of these two approaches.

- Each country has different criteria for the risk assessment and for determining the threat zones. It would be suitable to compare these approaches and to assess them on the EU level and subsequently to choose one approach which would be compulsory and the countries would implement it to their legal environment.

We would like to recommend utilising one type of software for modelling and simulating the type scenarios in all EU member states. Although the majority of the software process is based on the basic physical dispersion models, their outputs and thus the distances of the threat zones are frequently not identical. The ALOHA software is a complex tool.

The MIA prevention is one of the assumptions of ensuring the civil safety in the framework of the expanding technological development. The number and effects of the hazardous substances change permanently and therefore the risk assessment and the subsequent risk treatment/management in the industrial processes is the basic prevention principle. The MIA prevention is a complex and interdisciplinary area that is involved both in the European directives and in the regulations of the EU member states that transpose these requirements to their legal environment. In fact it is a tool that is an important attribute during processing the safety documentation of the SEVESO establishment.

Our complex model is based on the routine procedures and provides a broader interface for its implementation. Its verification confirmed the possibility to utilise the methodology especially in the SEVESO establishment by the specialist for the MIA prevention [32, 33]. In spite of the fact, the new law does not define a unified methodology of the risk assessment; the effort of the EU is oriented on creating a unified approach. The advantage of such a procedure would be the possibility of comparing the results of the SEVESO establishments if the same methodology was used.

The main benefit of this article is a complex analysis of the MIA prevention that is created by the legal environment (regulations and technical standards), by the participating parties (the state administration bodies, SEVESO establishments, etc.). The processes that are under way (the managerial and technical ones) and the methods and tools that are utilised (the information systems, methods and techniques of the risk assessment, etc.) both from the EU and the Slovak Republic's point of view. The area of the MIA prevention system is analysed and summarised in this work for the first time since the adoption of the new SEVESO III Directive and the subsequent adoption of the new law about the MIA prevention (2015) in the Slovak Republic.

5.1 Study limitations, implication and future research directions

Our main aim in this study was to show the importance of the MIA prevention. In spite of the fact the preventive measures are increased, its amount does not decrease and it can be caused mainly by the increasing number of the enterprises and the hazardous substances (the new ones) used. The prevention improvement has a direct impact on making the occupational safety of the company but also the public in its close surroundings more effective [31–33]. The company is able to process the risk assessment and subsequently to model it into the visual form better by using the structured procedures and utilising the available software (e.g. ALOHA).

The insufficient information occurring in individual database systems is the possible limitation. The identified causes of the accident and its consequences are often processed insufficiently and it is impossible to identify them. The limitation of the ALOHA system is the extent of its utilisation in the area of spreading the hazardous substances and it is a problem to model the fires and explosions.

Regarding to the created procedures for the risk assessment it would be suitable to integrate the calculation mechanisms to individual steps of the risk assessment. It would be also suitable to aim at utilising the tree methods for determining the causes and effects, especially by using the bow-tie diagrams. Another opportunity is also to create the corresponding methods of the risk assessment for the domino effects or zoning and permission activities.

Acknowledgements

This article was created as a one of research project outcomes VEGA 1/0581/19 Stating the Social and Individual Risk of Employees and Public Resulting from Impacts of the Domino Effects Caused by Industrial Accidents and Methods of Reducing their Possible Escalation.

Author details

Katarina Holla* and Eva Sventekova
University of Zilina, Faculty of Security Engineering, Zilina, Slovakia

*Address all correspondence to: katarina.holla@fbi.uniza.sk

References

[1] BahooToroody, F.; Khalaj, S.; Leoni, L.; De Carlo, F.; Di Bona, G.; Forcina, A. Reliability Estimation of Reinforced Slopes to Prioritize Maintenance Actions. Int. J. Environ. Res. Public Health 2021, 18, 373. https://doi.org/10.3390/ijerph18020373

[2] Dźwiarek, M., Latala A., International Journal of Occupational Safety and Ergonomics, 2021 Pages 186-192. https://doi.org/10.1080/10803548.2015.1129154

[3] Srinivas, K., Process of Risk Management, In book: Perspectives on Risk, Assessment and Management Paradigms, 2019, DOI: 10.5772/intechopen.80804

[4] Terje, A. Risk assessment and risk management: Review of recent advances on their foundation. European Journal of Operational Research, Volume 253, Issue 1, 2016, Pages 1-13, ISSN 0377-2217, https://doi.org/10.1016/j.ejor.2015.12.023.

[5] Jacxsens, L., Uyttendaele, M., Meulenaer, B.: Challenges in Risk Assessment: Quantitative Risk Assessment, Procedia Food Science, Volume 6, 2016, Pages 23-30, ISSN 2211-601X, https://doi.org/10.1016/j.profoo.2016.02.004.

[6] Buganova, K., Hudakova, M., Dvorsky, J.: The Assessment of the Impact of the Security Risk on the Small and Medium-sized Enterprises in the Slovak Republic 2nd International Conference on Management Innovation and Business Innovation (ICMIBI 2014), Volume 44. 2014.

[7] Bahr, N.J., 1997. System safety Engineering and Risk Assessment. CRC Press. ISBN 9781560324164.

[8] Rausand, M., 2011. Risk Assessment: Theory, Methods, and Applications . Wiley publisher. ISBN: 978-0-470-63764-7.

[9] Ostrom, L. T, 2012. Risk Assessment: Tools, Techniques, and Their Applications. John Wiley and Sons, Inc., Publication. ISBN 978 – 0 – 470 – 89203 – 9.

[10] eMARS - Major Accident Reporting System, 2020 [online]. [cit. 2020-02-20]. Available: https://emars.jrc.ec.europa.eu/en/emars/accident/search

[11] Macza, M., 2008. A Canadian perspective of the history of process safety management legislation. 8th Internationale Symposium Programmable Electronic System in Safety-Related Applications September 2 – 3. Cologne, Germany.

[12] Polorecka, M. ; Kubas, J. ; Danihelka, P.; Petrlova, K. ; Stofkova, Repkova, K.; Buganova, K. Use of Software on Modeling Hazardous Substance Release as a Support Tool for Crisis Management. SUSTAINABILITY. Volume: 13 Issue: 1 DOI: 10.3390/su13010438. MDPI, ST ALBAN-ANLAGE 66, CH-4052 BASEL, SWITZERLAND

[13] Occupational Safety and Health During Rescue Activities By: Osvaldova, Linda Makovicka; Petho, Martin. Conference: 6th International Conference on Applied Human Factors and Ergonomics (AHFE) Location: Las Vegas, NV Date: JUL 26-30, 2015 6TH INTERNATIONAL CONFERENCE ON APPLIED HUMAN FACTORS AND ERGONOMICS (AHFE 2015) AND THE AFFILIATED CONFERENCES, AHFE 2015 Book Series: Procedia Manufacturing Volume: 3 Pages: 4287-4293 Published: 2015

[14] Kuracina, R. a M. Ferjenčík, 2006. Tools for Risk assessment evaluation and accidents investigation. Conference

paper, Actual questions of HSE issues. ISBN 80-8073-649-9. [online]. [cit. 4.3.2012]. Available from: http://www.sjf.tuke.sk/kbakp/cinnocti/konferencie/obrazky/zbornikBOZP.pdf

[15] About eMARS, 2017 [online]. European commission [cit. 2020-03-04]. Available from: https://emars.jrc.ec.europa.eu/en/emars/content

[16] ARIA. [online]. [cit. 2.2.2020]. Available from: https://www.aria.developpement-durable.gouv.fr/the-barpi/the-aria-database/?lang=en

[17] SPIRS (Seveso Plants Information Retrieval System), online]. [cit. 2.7.2012]. Available from: https://op.europa.eu/sk/publication-detail/-/publication/919764ca-a426-11e7-9ca9-01aa75ed71a1

[18] About FACTS, [online]. FACTS Hazardous materials accidents knowledge base [cit. 2020-03-04]. Available from: http://www.factsonline.nl/Home/AboutFacts

[19] ZEMA Search, 2020 [online]. [cit. 2020-02-21]. Available: https://www.infosis.uba.de/index.php/en/site/13947/zema/index.html

[20] Uth HJ, Wiese N. Central collecting and evaluating of major accidents and near-miss-events in the Federal Republic of Germany--results, experiences, perspectives. J Hazard Mater. 2004 Jul 26;111(1-3):139-145. doi: 10.1016/j.jhazmat.2004.02.022. PMID: 15231359.

[21] Information system for the prevention of major industrial. Available online: accidents. https://app.sazp.sk/SevesoPublic/Podnik13.aspx (accessed on 18th Jun 2018). (in Slovak)

[22] Law 128/2015 Col. on the Prevention of Mayor Industrial Accidents. Available from: https://www.zakonypreludi.sk/zz/2015-128.

[23] ISO 31000: 2019. Risk management. Slovak institute of technical normalization.

[24] Duijm, N. J. 2004. Aramis project: Effects of Safety Management´s structural and cultural factors on barrier performance. Loss prevention 2004. Czech society of Chemical Engineering.

[25] Nomen R., Sempere J., Mariotti V. QRA including domino effect as a tool for engineering design. Procedia Engineering 2014, 84, 23-32.

[26] HAAG, U. et al., 2005. Guidelines for quantitative risk assesment [online]. Ministerie van verkeer en waterstaat [cit. 2020-21-04]. Available from: https://content.publicatiereeksgevaarlijkestoffen.nl/documents/PGS3/PGS3-1999-v0.1-quantitative-risk-assessment.pdf

[27] Basta, C., M. Struckl a M. CHristou, 2008. Overview of Roadmaps For Land-Use Planning In Selected Member States [online]. Italy: European commision [cit. 2020-21-04]. Available from: https://minerva.jrc.ec.europa.eu/EN/content/minerva/e4a15f3d-3069-4fb2-bae9-68296a0072a4/luproadmapsoverviewpdf

[28] Sluka, V., 2019. Accidents disaster land use planning in Czech republic. Occupational Safety Research Institute, Praha. Personal communication [2019-07-30].

[29] Zajacová, E., 2020. Information for the public. [online]. [cit. 2020-16-05]. Available from: https://www.fermas.sk/files/INFO_PRE_DOTKNUTU_VEREJNOST.pdf

[30] Dančo, L.: Land use planning for industrial accident in EU. Master Thesis. Supervisor: Katarina Hollá. 2019.

[31] Representative scenarios, 2020 [online]. Enviroportal [cit. 2020-16-05].

Available from: https://www.enviroportal.sk/uploads/2011/05/page/environmentalne-temy/star_19/9_metod_02_12_part_2.pdf

[32] Hudakova, Patrik Lahuta. Human errors as a source of personnel risk in the enterprise environment. In: Economic and social development : 62nd international scientific conference on economic and social development. - ISSN 1849-7535. - 1. vyd. - Varazdin: Varazdin Development and Entrepreneurship Agency, 2020. - s.142-149. - Spôsob prístupu: https://www.esd-conference.com/upload/book_of_proceedings/Book_of_Proceedings_esdLisbon2020_Online.pdf

[33] Osvaldova, L., Petho, M.: Occupational Safety and Health During Rescue Activities. Conference: 6th International Conference on Applied Human Factors and Ergonomics (AHFE) Location: Las Vegas, NV Date: JUL 26-30, 2015 6TH INTERNATIONAL CONFERENCE ON APPLIED HUMAN FACTORS AND ERGONOMICS (AHFE 2015) AND THE AFFILIATED CONFERENCES, AHFE 2015 Book Series: Procedia Manufacturing Volume: 3 Pages: 4287-4293 Published: 2015

Chapter 6

Risk Analysis in Engineering Projects

Vladimir Gorbunov

Abstract

Modern business processes are characterized by a large number of random factors that can affect the characteristics of internal and external processes. The created models use the method of calculating output parameters as an operation with random characteristics of factors that affect the final results. The processes and factors of the project are divided into permanent and random. Random processes are characterized by individual distributions and characteristics. The mathematical model of a business project is formed by a program that performs operations with the characteristics of random factors and risk factors that form the business project. The generated model allows you to calculate financial flows and balances at all stages of the project implementation, and determines various indicators of its effectiveness. To optimize these indicators, it is planned to introduce anti-risk measures. The model allows you to optimize the number of such activities, taking into account their cost and the degree of impact on the project performance indicators. Using the proposed method of analyzing business projects allows you to take into account possible random factors and risk factors and make the most optimal management decisions.

Keywords: risk assessment, discount rate, Probabilistic, simulation, distribution

1. Introduction

Innovative business projects require a thorough analysis of their implementation. For this analysis, a business plan is drawn up, the most important element of which is the financial model of the project. Typically, a business plan uses deterministic characteristics of the project's processes and objects. However, it is impossible to accurately predict the values of these processes, since they relate to the future time and are subject to market influences. By their nature, they refer to random processes with their individual characteristics and distributions. Just as random are the potential risks that may occur during the implementation of the project. The peculiarity of the considered method of constructing a financial model of the project is that all the initial data of the project components are recorded as random variables, if they are such. To quantify the characteristics of random variables, the program uses the ModelRisk add-in. The implemented program allows you to learn the output characteristics of a business project as random variables with their distribution law. This form of results allows you to more accurately determine the risks of project implementation.

IntechOpen

2. A functional model of a business process

The financial plan of the project involves the construction of business models, which shows all the actions performed with reflection used material values, labor cost, duration of execution of all intermediate operations.

IDEF0 refers to functional project presentation techniques that treat an organization as a set of functions that transform an incoming flow of information into an output one. The process of converting information consumes certain resources. The main difference from the object methodology is the clear separation of functions (data processing methods) from the data itself.

To build such models using special modeling languages, e.g. UML (Unified Modeling Language) [1]. Remedies such language describes the simple components of the procedure of a business process and reveals the relationship between the internal sub-processes and external data streams. Example view model of the company's activities (IDEF0 methodology), planning the development of a training course and sell it through the online shop shown in **Figure 1**.

The main part of the methodology is given in the diagram. The main conceptual principle of the IDEF0 methodology is the representation of any system under study as a set of interacting and interrelated blocks that reflect the processes, operations, and actions occurring in the system under study. In IDEF0, everything that happens in the system and its elements is usually called functions. Each function is assigned a block.

Function blocks in diagrams are represented by rectangles representing named processes, functions, actions, or operations that occur over time and have recognizable results. Each block contains its own name and number. The block name must be an active verb, a verbal phrase, or a verbal noun denoting an action.

The blocks in IDEF0 are arranged in order of importance, as the author of the diagram understands. This relative order is called dominance. Dominance is

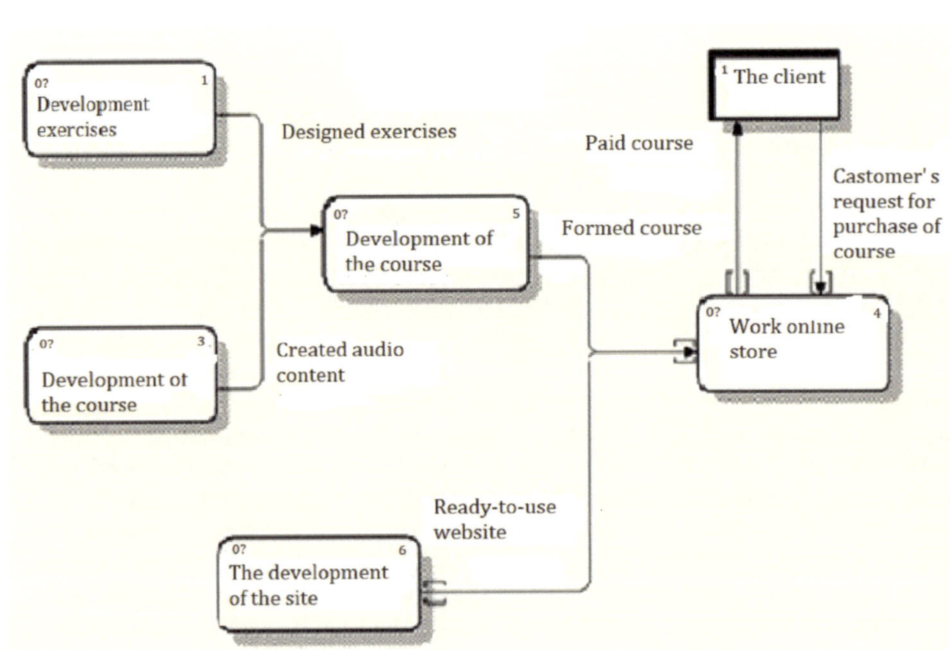

Figure 1.
IDEFo business model.

understood as the effect that one block has on the other blocks in the chart. The most dominant block is usually located in the upper-left corner of the chart, and the least dominant block is located in the right corner.

The interfaces through which the block interacts with other blocks or with the external environment of the simulated system are represented by arrows entering or exiting the block. Each side of the functional unit has a default value from the point of view of when the block arrows [2, 3].

IDEF0 distinguishes five types of arrows:

1. input data - the material or information that is used or transformed by the function block to obtain the result (output). It is assumed that the job may not have any entry arrows.

2. Governance - the rules, strategies, procedures, or standards that govern a business unit. The control acts on the block, but is not transformed by it.

3. Output-the material or information that is produced by the block. A block without a result does not make sense and should not be modeled.

4. the mechanism of the resources that perform the block, for example, the staff of the plant, machinery, equipment, etc. At the analyst's discretion, the mechanism arrows may not be displayed in the model.

5. Call - a special arrow pointing to a different work model. The call arrow is used to indicate that some work is being done outside of the simulated system.

The model includes three types of documents (graphical charts, Glossary, text), which refer to each other. In the graphical diagrams with blocks and arrows, and their connections displays information about the system. The blocks represent the basic functions of the model elements. These functions can be broken down (decomposed) into its component parts and presented in the form of more detailed charts. The decomposition process continues until the subject is described at the level of detail necessary to achieve the objectives of a specific project. The Glossary is created and maintained by a set of definitions, key words, explanations for each element of the chart and describes the essence of each element. The text gives additional description of the operation of the system.

The model of the business process allows the financial models to determine cost characteristics of the processes, their interaction in time.

The financial plan of the project should reflect all costs associated with its preparation, take into account the cost of manufactured goods or services and determine income from the sale of the goods or services. The projects differ by the time interval during which there is a formation of business, its development and completion. During the project the prices of goods, raw materials, debt capital can change and in financial terms, these changes must be taken into account.

Many characteristics and parameters of the processes included in the project cannot be defined by constant values. This is due to the dependence of these parameters on the set of internal processes that form these parameters. Many of these processes are random in nature. The business plan and financial model of the project are drawn up for the coming period. In the period of market relations, it is possible to predict the indicators of economic and technological processes only as indicators of random processes. At the same time, in many cases it is possible to determine the characteristics of random processes that are included as components in the analyzed business process. For example, when drawing up projects related to the production of agricultural products, accumulated statistical characteristics can be used that link the effectiveness of production with climatic conditions.

For an analytical model of business processes, it is necessary to describe the procedures used and set the input parameters of the process in an analytical form. The complexity of this approach lies in the analytical transformation of input parameters in accordance with the ongoing business processes.

When using the Monte Carlo method in a model, as a rule, the most influential parameters of the model found during the sensitivity analysis are involved. Within the framework of modeling, a large number of model implementations are carried out with a joint random change of the selected parameters. The determination of the distribution law is based, if possible, on historical data of the selected value. The user sets the number of implementations of the method, and for each selected parameter, the limits of its change and the distribution law of the corresponding random variable. If the selected parameters depend on each other, then you must set the correlation coefficient between them.

The Monte Carlo algorithm is associated with a sequence of operations:

- Select a set of variable parameters (risk factors).
- Set the boundaries of change and the distribution laws of each of the factors.
- Refine the correlation matrix for the factors that depend on each other.
- Run the output parameter calculation for the desired number of experiments (usually at least 1000). Form statistical characteristics of the output distribution.

Monte Carlo analysis allows you to understand the degree of uncertainty of the analyzed final value (characterized, for example, by setting a 90% confidence interval). Also, the user can focus only on the values that interest him, setting them when determining the interval instead of the % probability. In the results table, information is usually displayed in percentiles. The percentile is the percentage or

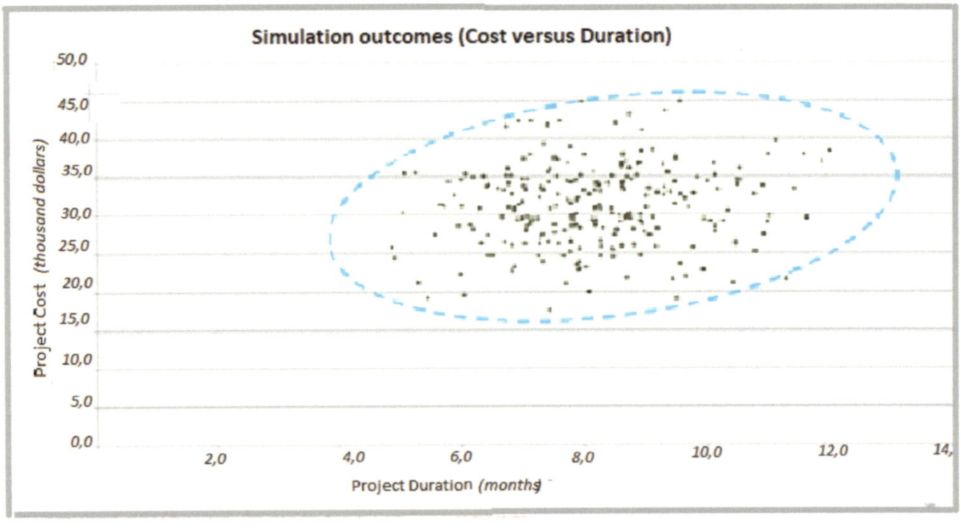

Figure 2.
Distribution of simulation results.

probability that the forecast value will be less than or equal to the value for a given parameter.

The Monte Carlo algorithm can become a necessary tool for all analysts, and their reports will contain not just General arguments about "potential risks", but also a separate section with a discussion of the results of the Monte Carlo analysis.

In many projects, the risks are determined not only by financial losses, but also by the failure of project deadlines. In such cases, risks can be assessed on a two-dimensional plane: cost, time of implementation.

When using Monte Carlo simulation on this plane, a set of results is formed, determined by the distribution laws of random input variables (**Figure 2**). the distribution Density of these calculations determines the probability of obtaining results corresponding to the coordinates on the plane under consideration.

All results can be divided into areas related to successful and unsuccessful project implementation.

3. Market and specific risks, feature of their account

A financial plan is an important document containing detailed information about cash flow on current operations as well as investment and financing activities of the enterprise. Properly plan the Manager may obtain information:

- about the source of funds and directions of their use;
- about the excess cash in the accounts of the enterprise, about the extent to which the enterprise extension is provided at the expense of own and borrowed funds;
- does enterprise in additional borrowing.

When making a report on cash flows for previous periods the entrepreneur uses the actual data available in the accounting records. The preparation of the forecast for the coming period requires more detailed analysis of the current situation and trends of its change. Often entrepreneurs are planning the distribution of funds to the best and worst case and also for the most real situation.

When planning the activities of small enterprises can be taken into account the probabilistic nature of the factors influencing its activity. In this case, the calculation of the indicators for the future period is not reduced to the calculation of the three moments of development, and to the calculation of a single process, which mathematically defines the probability of achieving the possible result of activity of the enterprise depending on the identified characteristics of the involved processes. Such forecasting will enable the entrepreneur to choose the right development strategy of the enterprise, ensuring the timely payment accepted debt.

Such figures as the price of the traded goods or services, the cost of materials or components, labor cost, etc., are connected with mathematical dependencies with the performance of the company. The variation of the initial indicators requires to re-produce the calculations. In this regard, there is a need for automated means of calculation that established procedures to instantly output when the source data changes.

To help developers to speed up the preparation of the business plan, to provide the necessary for the investor the level of quality of design documents, the entrepreneur offers specialized programs for financial planning. Traditionally, such systems are developed versions of the document templates. Most popular systems provide capabilities very far removed from the program Excel, and all of their value for the user lies in a well-chosen list of topics, filling it out, he will get more or less acceptable financial plan. As an example, the most popular system of this group is the program for Business Plan Pro with hundreds of thousands of users.

In connection with acceleration of rates of economic development, of particular importance is the ability of some of the programs on financial planning to take into account the risk factors. Such programmers can be placed on the program "E Project" [4, 5]. The program has the following features:

- the program incorporates a probabilistic calculation of the business processes;
- the program uses a widespread and reliable software packages;
- openness of the program provides the ability to navigate freely in calculation methodology, adapted to specific user requests by creating their own forms of source data and calculation algorithms;
- ability to enter data in the form of arbitrary shapes, and the results of calculations in the form of required reports. There are good editors for the formation of forms and reports;
- performed advanced analysis of the creditworthiness of the project, i.e. the dependence of results of calculation and changes in loan terms;
- a probabilistic calculation of the financial risk of the project depending on the probability characteristics of the source data;
- the results of the calculations are formed in the form of tables and diagrams.
- has the ability to convert data in HTML format.

The software package "E-Project" consists of two related programs: program of the calculation of economic indicators, realized in the program Excel, and textual blanks business plan that is implemented in Word.

In the analysis module using an input form, enter all of the source digital data for the project, it calculates the results, determine the course of economic processes associated with the implementation of the project.

Working with a design file starts with the opening title page of the project, where the author writes the project name, author name, choose project start date, the interval calculation of the project (month, quarter) and the duration of the calculated period. In this form, you select the currency format, in which to engage in financial calculations (RUB, thousand RUB, USD, thousand USD, etc.).

After filling in and confirming the passport data, the program displays a main form, consisting of ten control buttons (**Figure 3**).

The first eight control buttons provide a data input on the project.

The data input forms will be used to determine the financial flows required to support the production of products or provision of services to chart and plan-schedule of works for project implementation, for the computation of the aggregate depreciation at any point in your project.

A form of "Investment costs" it is designed to estimate all costs associated with the organization of projects. It is a list of all activities that must be performed to implement the project. For each of these events the data is entered at its cost (discusses options for average, minimum and maximum value), data at the

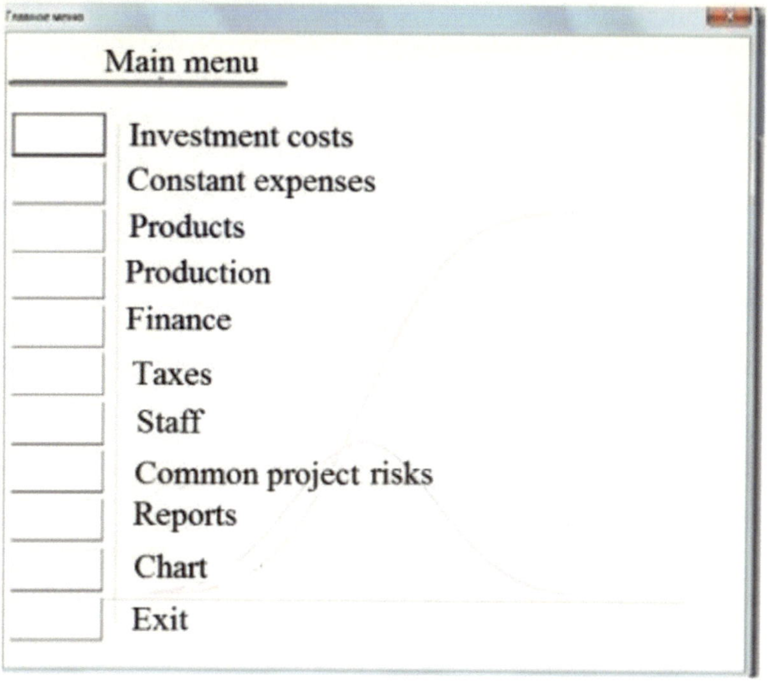

Figure 3.
The main menu of the project.

beginning of the activity and its duration, availability of plant and equipment associated with the event and the rate of depreciation for each fixed asset group.

To estimate fixed costs that are not related to the costs of producing the main products, use the form "Constant expenses". Such expenses include costs associated with building maintenance, payment for utilities, communications, transportation, security, etc.

Form "Products" associated with the data describing income and expenses for each planned type of product or service. It includes all the costs associated with the release of each type of product. The form provides for entering values for material and labor resources. The values of the tax and time delays for the preparation of production, for the production and for the sale of the product are determined.

Form "Production" is the total spent for marketing researches and answers the question, how much and when will be implemented the manufactured products listed in the form of "Products ". Since sales in the future period are random data, they are entered with the characteristics of this random process. To more accurately determine the process characteristics, use the ModelRisk add-in. The sales in this form shall be submitted in the number of products, the characteristics of which are presented in the form of "Products".

For enter initial data on the financial activities and considers such indicators as equity, loans, repayment of loans, interest on loans, grants and government funding, the payment of dividends used Form "Finance".

The procedure of payment and the amount of taxes depends on the legal form of the enterprise, accepted the forms of accounting and tax reporting. Input form "Taxes" specifies the source data for the calculation of the tax planning. In this form, the authors of the draft introduce the adopted tax rate for the primary taxable base indicators: payroll, income, imputed income, profit, property.

To determine the financial flows associated with staff wages, receiving a set salary, is a "Staff". In this form indicates the period during which the employee will work in the project, his position and set salary. You can plan rates without names when you do not know the names of the professionals who will be involved in the project.

The financial model allows us to assess the impact of the considered risk factors, taking into account the possible impact on the business process, taking into account the activation time of the risk factor. To calculate the impact of risks the software uses the input form of the "Common project risks". All risks of the project can be divided into two categories: market and special. Market risks due to fluctuations in price parameters, the instability of the market. These indicators can change from its average value both upwards and downwards. Such risks must be characterized by the standard parameters for random distributions (expectation, variance), which are determined by the entered data, reviewed the input forms. The second type (special risks) associated with the specific situation in the project, which can with some probability to occur and this will cause the appropriate financial changes.

№	Risk (Finance)	PQ	P_1Q_1	Event	Q_2	K
1	Revenue from employee training will not increase	10	4	Prepare present information and analytical materials for training staff	20	0
2	Support high production costs per unit of output	10	15	To Introduce the automation system to reduce cost of production	60	0
3	Will Not decrease the average collection time of accounts receivable	20	6	To Automate SIS theme collection of receivables	30	1
4	Will Not increase the net income of the main contract	60	12	Change mane contract	30	1
5	Reduced advertising agency sales growth	50	15	To Perform a range of promotion to increase sales	10	1
6	Administrative costs will increase	30	20	To Introduce the machine to the area	60	0

Table 1.
Risks and measures for compensation of financial risks.

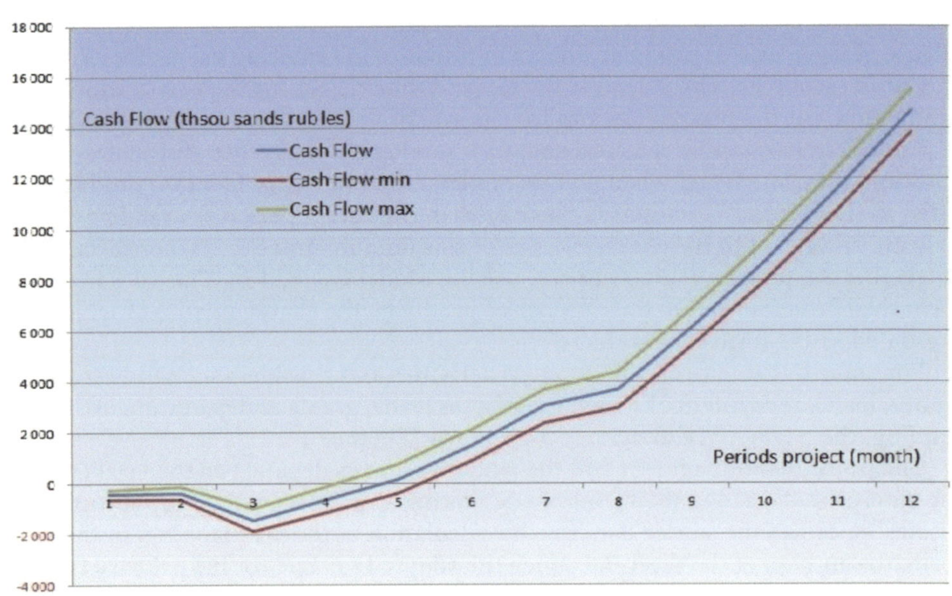

Figure 4.
Example of chart "The Cash flow project".

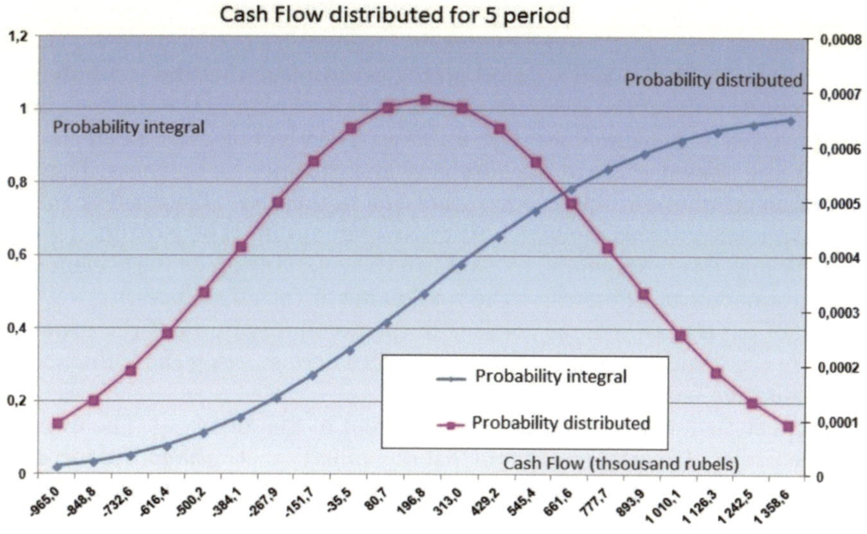

Figure 5.
Example of chart "Cash Flow Distribution".

To assess the impact of the special risks are considered characteristics such as the period of manifestation of this risk factor, the probability of a risk situation R, the financial cost upon the occurrence of a risk situation Q. For the construction of rose risks should be allocated considering the risk factor to one of the accepted categories: technical, organizational, financial, environmental, technological, etc. The Program includes measures to reduce the impact of risks. The effect of these events will change the parameters P and Q on P1 and Q1. Those events are recorded in the form of Investment measures the cost of these activities Q2 and their execution time. **Table 1** reflects the approach to risk assessment and events. A Boolean variable K can take the value 0 or 1. When K = 1 is performed event risks are characterized by the product of P1Q1, K = 0 event fails, and the risk perceived with the parameters R Q.

Introduction data in the form ends with the formation of the financial model of the project. The results for the generated models can be observed on the output reports that are in accordance with the selected algorithm and the results are given in tables (button on the main menu "Reports") or graphics (click main menu "Chart"). An example of the output graph shown in **Figures 4** and 5.

4. Measurement of risk using the discount rate, expert assessments, indicators of sensitivity

Discount rate is widespread to account for the risk through the introduction of special allowances to the risk-free discount rate.

Calculation formula for discount rate is:

$$NPV = \sum_{t=1}^{T} \frac{CF_t}{(1+i)^t} + \frac{CF_{(T+1)}}{i-g} * \frac{1}{(1+i)^T}, \tag{1}$$

NPV — net present value of future cash flows; T is the number of settlement periods within the planning horizon; CT_t — cash flow over the t- period; $CF_{(T+1)}$ cash flow terminal of the first period; i — the value of the discount rate, g is the growth rate of cash flow in the post-planning period (percent per annum) [6].

To build value models of the company and its elements may be used in the simplified model developed by the magazine Business Valuation Review [7] for emerging markets. This model is based on the assumption that the yield on government Eurobonds reflects the risks associated with investing in the share capital of "ideal companies", i.e. companies with no flaws. Disadvantages of a real company are equal to the risks specific to the company and the specific business. These flaws are marked as premium to the discount rate due to these risk factors. For the practical application of this model for risk management must be expanded given the types of risk into its components, to establish the relationship of these elements with the parameters and determine the total value of the allowances.

Method of expert estimations consists in the possibility of using the experience of experts in the analysis process of the project and considering the influence of diverse qualitative factors.

Formal peer-review process often comes down to the following. The management of the project (firm) develops the list of evaluation criteria in the form of the expert (polling) sheets containing the questions. For each criterion are assigned (at least - are calculated) and the corresponding weighting coefficients, which were not disclosed to the experts. Then for each criterion, the compiled answers, the weight of which is not known to the experts. The experts should have full information about the evaluation project and, through the examination to analyze the questions and mark the chosen answer. Next, the completed expert sheets are processed accordingly (on the basis of well-known computer packages for the processing of statistical information) and the output or results of the examination.

Not all risk factors can be digitally assessed. The reason for this may be the lack of experience with such factors. In these cases, the risk assessment can be carried out by experts using relatively rough estimates. Important to comparative analysis, which experts use to assess the occurrence of risk events simplified scale of gradations. For example, place each of the events on the graph in the axes of "impact" is "probability". The diagram consists of 9 cells, each of which corresponds to a single set of estimates (**Figure 6**). For example, the event characterized by the estimated "low impact, low probability" should be displayed in the lower left cell of the chart, and event assessments "low impact, high likelihood" should be displayed in the lower right cell, etc.

The whole chart is divided into 3 approximately equal parts. Three cells of the diagram located at the bottom left, is an area of insignificant risk. Three cells of the diagram in its upper right part, is an area of significant risk. The remaining part of the diagram (3 cells), it is an area of medium risk. Thus, the risk associated with event A is insignificant, the risk events B - average, risk events C is substantial. The resulting diagram, which, in accordance with expert assessments applied to all risk events, called risk maps. This map shows what risk events can take place, what is the correlation between different types of risks and how risks should be given maximum attention (in this example, risk events C). This approach is widespread in the practice of risk management companies in the real business. Risk managers typically use 3 or 5 (rarely 7) grades for probability of exposure and materiality.

		The probability		
		Low	*Medium*	*High*
The Impact	*Strong*			Event C
	Average	Event A	Event B	
	Weak			

Figure 6.
The risk maps.

Described card r is a convenient way to visualize risk. In practice, there are other ways of visualization, such as using a circular or a color chart.

Sensitivity analysis and scenario analysis is the sequential steps in quantitative risk analysis, the latter allows to get rid of some of the shortcomings of sensitivity analysis. However, the scenario method is most effective can be applied when the number of possible values for NPV of course. However, as a rule, when carrying out a risk analysis of the investment project, the expert is faced with an unlimited number of different scenarios. The actual method of assessing individual risk of the project help to solve this problem (simulation), the basis of this method is the probabilistic assessment of the occurrence of various circumstances.

By using specialized software packages for the calculation of economic efficiency of projects evaluation of impact of risks is obtained in the form of output tables and graphs reflecting the impact of risk factors on project output.

5. Digital risk assessment in entrepreneurship

Risk- category probability, so in the process of assessing uncertainty and quantifying risk it is possible to use probabilistic calculations. The most important indicator of the measure of financial risk of enterprise is its level.

In entrepreneurship, financial success is often associated with innovative solutions in projects. But any innovative solution is based on new approaches, on the use of new technologies or organizational structures. The success of the use of the original solutions in projects is not guaranteed. A huge number of new projects do not achieve financial success due to the fact that the solutions used in them did not take into account the peculiarities of market mechanisms, the demand for new solutions is not always confirmed by the market, and unplanned factors that prevent its implementation are encountered on the way to project implementation. In projects that are funded by venture capital, which are characterized by increased risk, there is one successful project for ten projects, the profit from which covers the costs of the nine remaining projects. And four out of ten projects are unprofitable. This ratio is a consequence of the impact of risks that were not taken into account during the initial organization of projects.

Financial risks of projects consist of a combination of internal and external risk factors that affect the planned business process. Many of these factors are random and cannot be predicted in the initial planning. Some random factors have formed statistics of their manifestation and can be taken into account in the project through known statistical indicators. Accounting for risks through digital indicators allows you to build a more accurate business process model. To form such a digital estimate, a certain number of indicators are used:

The level of financial risk Ur. is defined as the product of the probability of occurrence of this financial risk Pl by the amount of possible financial losses in the implementation of the considered risk Fl:

$$Ur = Pl * Fl$$

The complexity of determining losses from this relationship is often reduced to the complexity of determining the probabilistic characteristics of risk factors. Often, the probability of occurrence of a risk factor depends on a set of external factors and is characterized by a certain law of distribution of its occurrence. The law of distribution of risk factors can be characterized by a number of indicators.

In practice this algorithm makes the size of possible financial losses usually expressed by an absolute amount and the probability of occurrence of financial risk

– one of the coefficients the measurement of this probability (the coefficient of variation, beta coefficient, etc.). Accordingly, the level of financial risk when it is calculated according to the following algorithm will be expressed absolute indicator, which significantly reduces its basis of comparison when considering alternative options.

The variance σ^2 characterizes the degree of variability of the studied indicator (in this case the expected income from realization of financial operations) with respect to its average value. Then the fluctuations grow, the greater the risk. The variance is calculated according to the following formula:

$$\sigma^2 = \sum_{i=1}^{n} \left(R_i - \overline{R}\right)^2 * P_i,$$

Ri – specific value of the possible variants of the expected income for the financial transactions; R̂ - the average expected value of income under financial transactions; P_i – potential frequency (probability) of obtaining separate variants of the expected income on financial transactions; n is the number of observations.

Dispersion does not give a complete picture of the deviations $\Delta X = X - \hat{R}$, more pronounced for the risk evaluation. However, the job dispersion allows establishing a link between linear and quadratic deviations using the well-known Chebyshev inequality.

The probability that a random variable X deviates from its expectation by more than a given tolerance $\varepsilon > 0$, does not exceed its variance, divided by ε^2, i.e.

$$P\left(\left|X - \overline{R}\right| > \varepsilon\right) \leq \frac{D}{\varepsilon^2}.$$

This shows that a small risk of dispersion deviation corresponds to a small risk according to a linear deviation of point X are likely to be within ε – neighborhood of the expected values.

A more common estimate of probabilistic processes is the standard deviation. This characteristic of a random process has the same dimension as the random variable. For example, if the profit is measured in dollars, then the standard deviation is measured in the same values. Just like the variance, the standard deviation characterizes the spread of random parameters and is determined by the following dependence:

The root mean square (standard) deviation is one of the most common in assessing the level of individual financial risk as the variance determines the degree of absolute variability and is calculated by the following formula.

$$\sigma = \sqrt{\sum_{i=1}^{n} \left(R_i - \overline{R}\right)^2 * P_i}$$

The advantage of standard deviation is that when you reach the observed distribution (e.g., distribution of investment income) to normal this parameter can be used to determine the boundaries in which with a given probability, one should expect the value of a random variable.

The coefficient of variation CV lets you define the level of risk if the average expected income from financial operations differ [6]. The calculation of the coefficient of variation is carried out according to the following formula:

$$CV = \pm \frac{\sigma}{\overline{R}} * 100\%,$$

For the characteristics of random processes, the coefficient of variation CV is used. The peculiarity of this indicator is that it is a dimensionless quantity. With it, you can even compare the fluctuation of features expressed in different units of measurement. The coefficient of variation varies from 0 to 100%. The larger the coefficient, the greater the fluctuation (the spread of values of a random variable). The following qualitative assessment of various values of the coefficient of variation is established: up to 10% - weak fluctuation, 10–25% - moderate fluctuation, over 25% - high fluctuation.

The coefficient of variation CV – a dimensionless quantity. With it, you can even compare the variability of traits, expressed in different units of measurement. The coefficient of variation varies from 0 to 100%. The greater the ratio, the greater the variability. Established the following qualitative assessment of the different values of the coefficient of variation: 10% - weak variability, 10–25% moderate variability, over 25% - high variability.

The beta coefficient (β) is a parameter that allows you to assess the systematic financial risk of an individual project in relation to the level of risk of the financial market as a whole. This indicator is usually used to assess the risks of investing in individual securities and is calculated using the formula.

The beta coefficient (β) allows you to evaluate individual or portfolio systematic financial risk in relation to the risk level of the financial market as a whole. This indicator usually used to assess the risk of investing in individual securities and is computed by the formula

$$\beta = \frac{K \times \sigma i}{\sigma_p},$$

where β is the beta coefficient; K – the degree of correlation between the level of profitability on individual type of securities (or their portfolio) and the average level of profitability of the group equity instruments at the market as a whole; σi– standard deviation of return on the individual securities (or on their portfolio as a whole); σ_p – standard deviation of return on the stock market as a whole.

The level of financial risk for individual securities is based on the following values of beta coefficients: β = 1 – average; β > 1 – high level; β < 1 is low level.

Of particular interest for the assessment of entrepreneurship are methods that allow using the probabilistic method to assess the risk not only of a particular transaction, but also of the project as a whole, analyzing the dynamics of its income over a certain period of time. The choice of specific methods for evaluating long-term projects is determined by the availability of the necessary information base and the level of qualification of management personnel.

Using the probabilistic evaluation method can be assess the risk not only of a particular transaction, but also the business of the company as a whole (analyzing the dynamics of its income) for a certain period of time. The choice of specific assessment methods is determined by the availability of necessary information base and skill level of management personnel.

In the last decade has been the development of a new methodology for evaluating measures of financial risk through the use of the indicator "cost of risk" or "var" (Value-at-risk, VAR).

Value at risk is a measure of the statistical estimation expressed in the monetary form the largest possible size of financial losses in the prescribed form of the probability distribution of the factors influencing the value of the assets (tools) and a given level of the probability of occurrence of these losses over the estimated period of time.

From the above definition it is clear that the methodology of the calculation of VAR consists of three main elements. One of these elements is set by the risk Manager species a probability distribution of risk factors affecting the value of the assets (tools) or their total portfolio. Such can be the normal distribution, Laplace distribution, t-test etc. One of the definitions of VAR is set the risk-Manager level of probability that maximum possible size of financial losses will not exceed the estimated value of this indicator. In the terminology of financial risk management this specified probability is characterized by the term the confidence level. The specific value of the confidence level for the model of calculation of VAR is chosen by the risk Manager based on his risk preferences. In the modern practice of financial risk management this level is usually in the range of 90–99%.

A visual representation of the formation of a VAR gives the plot shown in **Figure 7**.

As can be seen from the graph in **Figure 7**, revenue curve illustrates the normal probability profit distribution on the financial instrument in a predetermined billing period of time. The field inside this graph between the -2σ and + 3σ corresponds to the chosen confidence level (90% of the area under the curve), and the between -3σ and-2σ — characterizes the value of possible losses beyond the confidence level (10%). On the chart, the VAR determined in the amount of –732,6 thousand rubles. This corresponds to a maximum size of possible financial losses on the financial instrument under the given confidence level and estimated valuation period, the value of VAR in the diagram separates the value of income beyond the limits of the confidence interval (10%).

To use the VAR measure to assess project risks, you need to specify the probability (small enough to consider an event "almost" impossible) for which the value of a random variable is determined. This value of the variable corresponds to the boundary value of the variable that is characteristic of the given probability of the process. Most often, in practice, they set a probability of 5%, respectively, they talk about a confidence level of 95% (100–5%) and denote the result in the form of VAR95% (pronounced "VAR at the level of 95%"). The 95% level is quite conditional, each individual sets this level based on their own attitude to possible unlikely

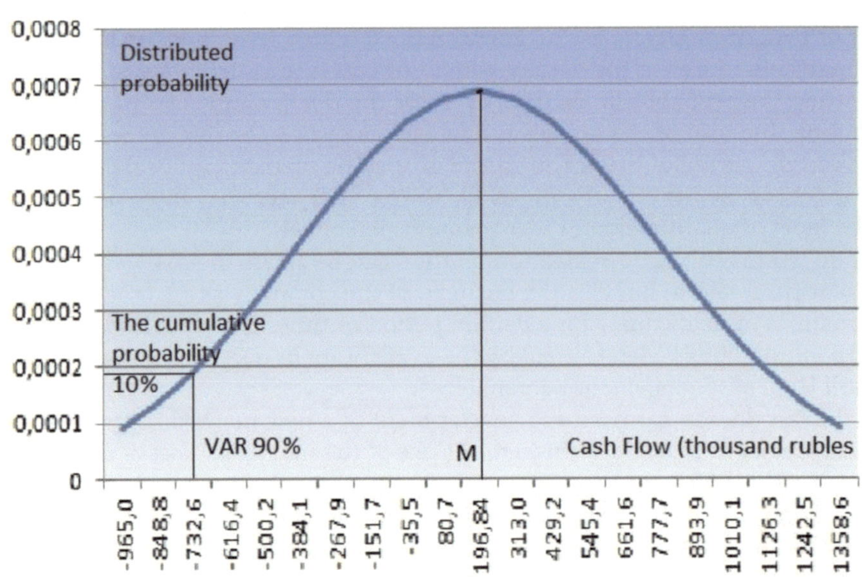

Figure 7.
Graphic method of determining the value indicator "value at risk" [VAR].

events and their understanding of what is considered an "almost" impossible event. Other confidence levels can also be used, such as 90% or 99% (then we talk about VAR90% or VAR99%).

When evaluating or calculating VAR, in practice, the time horizon of the project (financial transaction) is set. Therefore, the risk is referred to as the minimum result that will be obtained with a certain confidence probability within a specified period of time.

Here is an example. The phrase "evaluation of the VAR of the risk of lower returns during the next weeks is minus 3% at a confidence level of 95%" or briefly "a week VAR95% = - 3%" means that:

- weekly loss of over 3% is possible with a probability of 5%;
- with a probability of 95% loss for the week will not exceed 3%;
- with a probability of 95%, the yield of the planned operation will be at least −3% for the week.

Different distributions of random processes have certain relations with the VAR parameters. The normal distribution is defined by two parameters M and σ, and any characteristic of this distribution (in particular, any quantile) is also defined by these two parameters. This means that for a normal probability distribution, the relationship between variance and VAR at any confidence level is unambiguous and has the form:

$$VARi = M[X] - Z(1 - i),$$

where Z(1 - i) - quantile of order (1 - i) standard normal distribution.

The values of the tabulated quantiles, we present several important special cases:

$$\begin{aligned} VAR\ 90\% &= M[X] - 1,283 * \sigma \\ VAR95\% &= M[X] - 1,645 * \sigma \\ \mathrm{VAR}\ 99\% &= \mathrm{M[X]} - 2,326 * \sigma. \end{aligned} \tag{2}$$

These ratios can be effectively used to evaluate complex business processes. Complex processes are a set of procedures that are different in nature, and the distribution of such complex processes is likely to approach the normal distribution.

This assumption is close to the truth for games in the financial markets, since the prices of many important assets are determined by a variety of random factors, often acting in an inconsistent and multidirectional way. Even if the probability distribution of the results of each of these random factors is not normal, their combined distribution will tend to be normal.

The input data of business processes are characterized by individual distribution laws. The complexity of using this characteristic in the information model lies in the analytical representation of the input parameters in accordance with the ongoing business processes. By accepting some restrictions on input effects, you can simplify the analytical analysis procedure.

By adopting some limitations on input actions, it is possible to simplify the analytical analysis. For example, in the E-Project [2] as the parameters of the random input signals are used only two characteristics of M – mathematical expectation and D - standard deviation. Operations such variables are performed according to the rules of operations with random variables [3]:

- for any two random variables and the expectation of their sum M(X + Y).

$$M\ (X+Y) = M(X) + M(Y) \tag{3}$$

- the variance of sum of two random variables is equal to the sum of their variances plus twice the correlation time of the *K*xy:

$$D(X+Y) = D(X) + D(Y) + 2Kxy \tag{4}$$

- the mathematical expectation of the product of two random variables is equal to the product of their mathematical expectations plus the correlation time of the *Kxy*:

$$M(XY) = M(X) * M(Y) + Kxy \tag{5}$$

- the variance of independent random variables.

$$D(XY) = D(X) * D(Y) + M(X)2 * D(Y) + M(Y)2 * D(X) \tag{6}$$

Most of the results of typical business processes are built on the combination of operations of addition, subtraction, and multiplication can be defined by Eqs. (3)–(6).

Typically, a business process involves a large number of random variables, and the final result is a complex combination of these inputs. For such processes, the output results tend to be distributed according to the normal law. In the "E-Project" program, an assumption is made about the distribution of total values in accordance with the normal law. Rate the difference between the results of modeling the business process using the analytical model and method of simulation. For example, for changing the law Trian input data (**Figure 8**), the distribution of the output can be represented by a distribution by a normal distribution (**Figure 9**) [8, 9].

From this figure it is seen that model business processes at various distributions of the input parameters allow the output process to describe the distribution of the normal law. The standard deviation of all the distributions differs by a negligible amount. An approximation to these distributions will be more accurate the more processes will affect the output parameters.

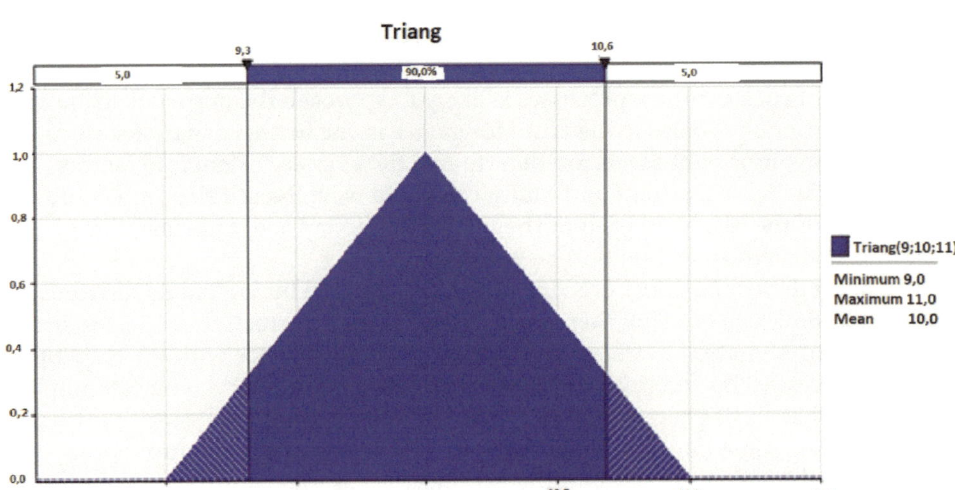

Figure 8.
The distribution of the input parameter "sales".

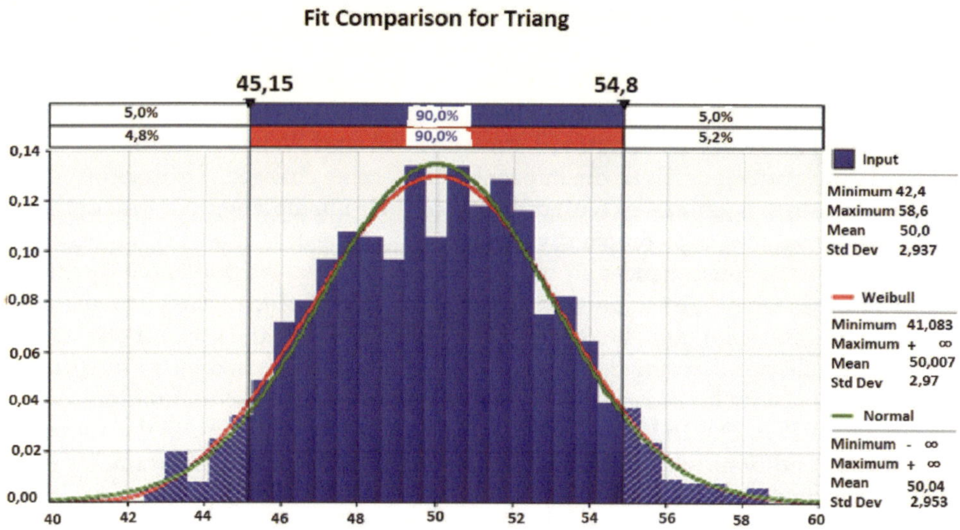

Figure 9.
The distribution of the output parameter of the business process in the distribution of the input data based on Triang.

For non-symmetric distributions of input data, final results, built according to the dependencies of the Eqs. (2)–(5) output a distribution with less asymmetry than the input.

It is interesting to evaluate the distribution of the output parameter of a business process with the participation of a set of input processes that are different in distribution. In **Figure 10** presents the simulation result of the mixture of the input data, distributed over 6 different laws. In this case, normal distribution has a matching mathematical expectation and standard deviation with the result from the simulation values of the distribution of the output parameter. The simulation results show that the model of the business projects can be based on analytical relations

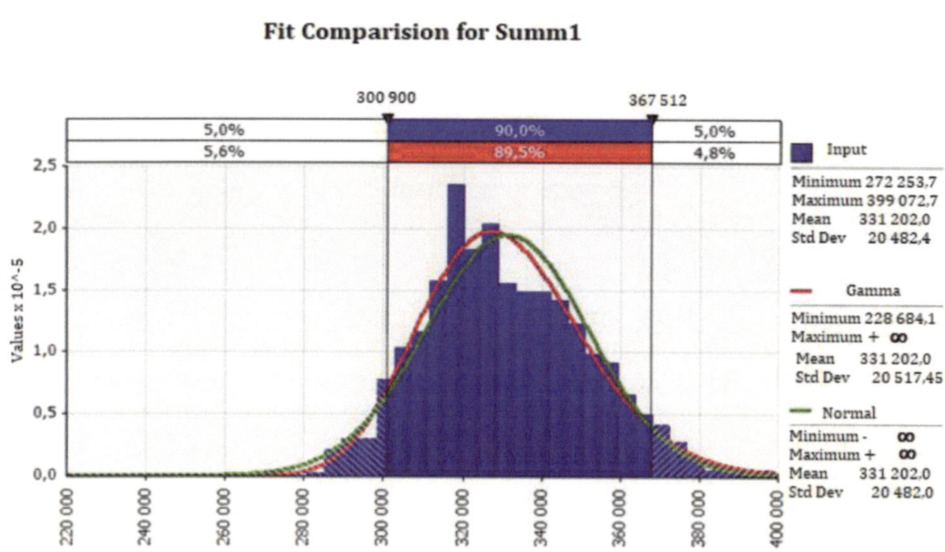

Figure 10.
The distribution of the outputs of the business process while increasing aggregate sales from various distributions of input data.

(3)–(6), with simplified analytical calculations and process simulations. Output parameters business processes in analytic calculations heavily depend on the accuracy of determining the statistical characteristics of the input parameters.

An important step of risk management is to optimize costs to reduce the impact. To reduce the impact of risks, anti-risk measures are used. When performing these measures, the characteristics of the impact of risk factors change. The organization of anti-risk measures is associated with the costs of their implementation. Risk optimization can be reduced to a comparative assessment of the cost of anti-risk measures and changes in the consequences after the occurrence of risk factors caused by the use of anti-risk measures. With a limited budget, it is not advisable to carry out all anti-risk measures, it is enough to limit yourself to those that give the greatest effect.

The feasibility of carrying out certain anti-risk activities based on an integrated assessment of the financial results of the project with different combinations of parameter K (**Table 1**). In E-Project uses a special add-in that enables the adopted criteria and conditions of restrictions to choose the optimal value of parameter K for all the risks involved.

When reducing the impact of risks, first of all, anti-risk measures are planned with the greatest efficiency [10]. **Figure 11** shows the dependence of financial loss from the implementation of the 24 anti-risk measures and the costs of implementation of these activities.

Anti-risk measures can be selected for implementation according to different rules. The limiting factor may be the allocated budget for these activities or the selection of activities whose effectiveness exceeds the established threshold. **Figure 12** shows the result of such optimization, where the financial losses from the initial risks and the same indicator is presented for a project with risk measures.

The proposed method allows to assess the impact of risk factors on the efficiency of the project, to assess the impact on financial performance anti-risk activities and to choose those which provide the greatest effect according to the chosen criterion of project evaluation.

A variant of estimating the influence of random parameters of input variables on the final results of modeling is obtained by using the "E-Project" program implemented in Excel with the ModelRisk add-in and using the simulation method.

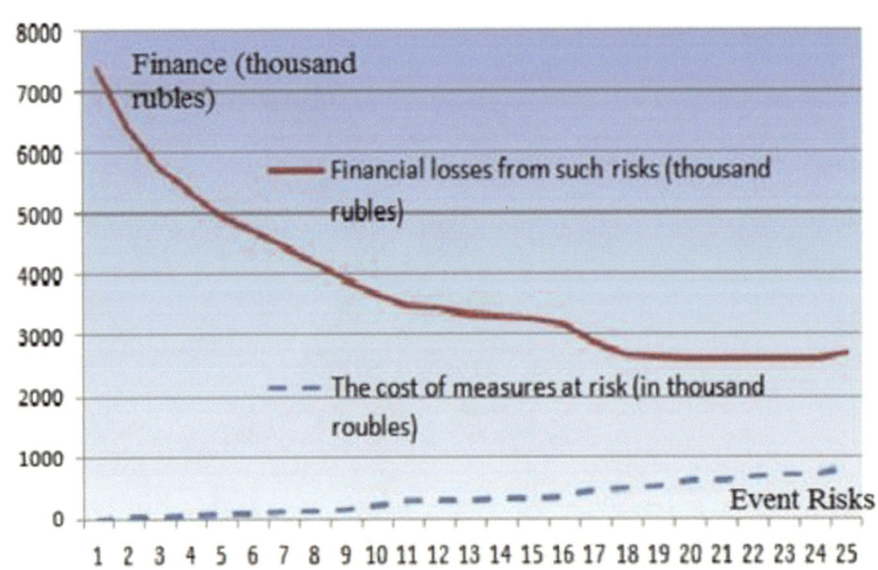

Figure 11.
Losses from risks and the cost of measures from them.

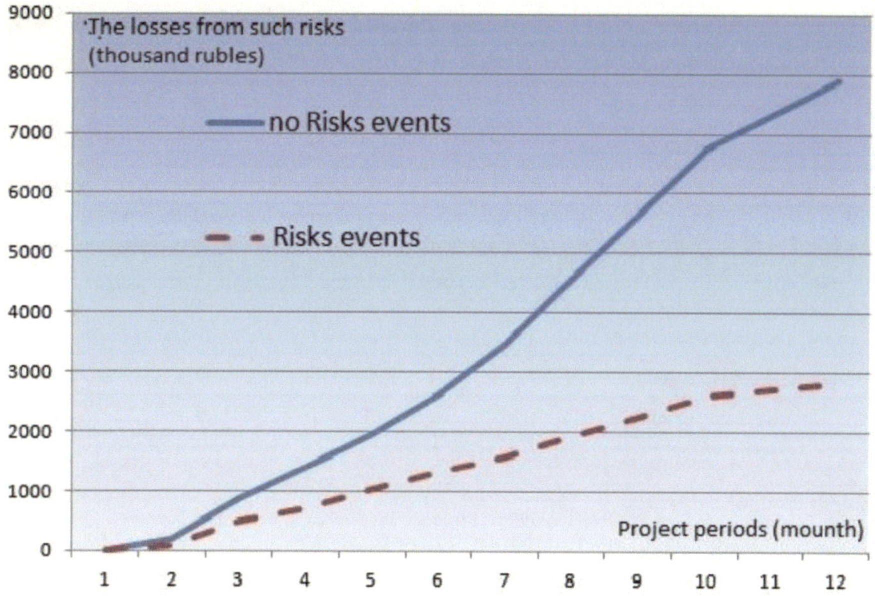

Figure 12.
Losses from risk source and risk after special events.

The "E-Project" program assumes a normal distribution of output data. This assumption is possible in cases where a large number of random variables are involved in the business process and the final result is a complex combination of these input actions.

For the presented graph, the duration of the process can be defined as a random variable that depends on the random parameters of individual operations. The use of the Monte Carlo simulation method when using statistical data for individual operations will allow you to obtain probabilistic estimates of the project duration. The probabilistic model of a business process involves the use of input variables with known distribution laws. For many models, these distribution laws are constructed in an expert way, in some cases they can be constructed on the basis of accumulated statistical material. The most common laws of distribution of random input variables for business processes can be considered as the following:

Normal distribution law, when a variable is formed under the influence of many random factors;

Discrete distribution law, when an input variable can take a certain number of values and the probabilities of these values are determined;

Asymmetric distributions, for which one extreme value is determined by some limiting factors, and the other may differ significantly from the first one by the distance from the value of the mathematical expectation.

For all input variables, an individual distribution can be given that corresponds to the nature of the input variable in question. For each given input variable, the distribution parameters are determined in the form of values of the minimum, maximum, average, mathematical expectation, variance, standard deviation, skewness indicators and quantile probability distribution. For the selected input variables, the skewness index in this example was at least 0.3.

For a particular sequence of operations, a critical path can be defined, which is the sequence of the longest sequence of network graph activities. Activities related to the critical path have the value K = 1. the Mathematical expectation of the time of the project being executed (**Table 2**).

№	The event	Beginning	Duration (T)	The critical path(K)	σ_i	D_i
1	Purchase Of Equipment	5	2	1	0.55	0,30
2	Preparation of the room	3	3	0	0.5	0,25
3	Connection of communications	3	3	1	0.62	0,38
4	Debugging of equipment	7	2	1	0.93	0,86
5	Product testing	9	4	1	1.07	1,14
6	Recruitment	7	5	1	0.93	0,86
7	Development of the technical process	9	4	0	1	1
8	Market analysis	4	5	0	1	1
9	Advertising campaign	2	7	0	2	4

Table 2.
Time characteristics of the project.

$M = \sum Ki * Di = 16$ weeks.

The variance of the project execution time is determined by the equation.

$D_P = \sum Ki * (\sigma_i)^2 = 3.54$ respectively $\sigma_p = 1.88$.

The ModelRisk add-in allows you to obtain the probability distribution of the output value using the Monte Carlo method. In this case, all input variables with a given distribution are assigned random values and the value of the output parameter is determined for these values according to the generated business process model. The procedure is usually repeated significantly more than a thousand times and the distribution of the output function is constructed for the obtained output values. In the example under consideration, the output function will be determined by the sum of time indicators of critical path events (for which K = 1). The program generates the distribution of the output function and displays the main indicators of the resulting distribution. In the example under consideration, for five random numbers with significant asymmetry (each of the input functions had an asymmetry index of at least 0.3), the resulting distribution of the profit received was calculated and it had an asymmetry coefficient of −0.04. This fact confirms that the output distribution formed as a result of the interaction of many random variables with an asymmetric distribution tends to a normal distribution with a low asymmetry index. As the number of operations and random variables increases, the deviation from the normal distribution law will decrease.

For calculating economic indicators, "E-Project" allows you to visualize information about the time of implementation and financial indicators of the project using built-in charts. For this purpose, the parametric system of ellipse equations is used:

$x = a * \cos \alpha;$

$y = b * \sin \alpha;$

where $\alpha \in (0; 2\pi)$,

a. first semi-axis of the ellipse corresponding to the deflection range of the financial parameter from its mathematical expectation,

b. the second axis of the ellipse corresponding to the deflection range of the temporary project setting its mathematical expectation.

As semi-axes in this equation, it is necessary to substitute the root-mean-square deviations of the cash flow and the project implementation time. Financial flows are

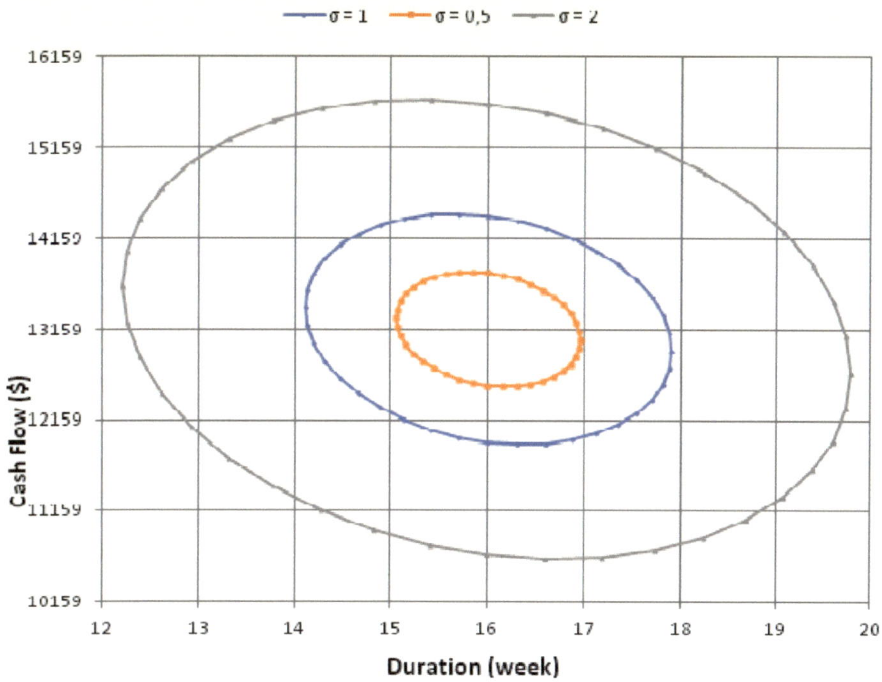

Figure 13.
Distribution of financial and time indicators of the project.

calculated in the "E-Project" based on the initial data. Taking into account that the center of the ellipse is located in the coordinates corresponding to the mathematical expectation of the planned profit (P_1) and the mathematical expectation of the project execution time (t_1), the system of equations will take the form:

$$x = t_1 + \sigma_t * \cos t; \quad y = (P_1 + \sigma_{p1} * \sin t) + C * (t_1 - x);$$

where σ_t - the standard deviation of the project implementation time; σ_{p1}– standard deviation of the cash flow taking into account risks; t_1– the average time of the critical path; P_1– the average value of the cash-flow, taking into account the risks; C– fixed costs per unit of time.

The diagram for the values of variables equal to 0.5, 1 and 2 standard deviations for both parameters (cash flow and time) is shown in **Figure 13**.

This diagram shows the ranges of cash flow and project implementation time within a certain value of the standard deviation of each of the parameters.

The area inside the smaller ellipse corresponds to the probability of achieving such a result at 65%, the average – 76% and the external-94%. The values obtained can serve as a guide for project adjustments if the financial or time characteristics do not meet the requirements of the project being implemented. Such financial and time estimates can be made not only for the end date of the project, but also for any of its internal intervals.

6. Conclusion

Most well-known financial models of projects use deterministic data to describe the internal processes of the planned business. Risks are inherently random processes. The model under consideration works with random numbers and allows you to take into account these random risk factors. The model allows us to assess the impact of anti-risk measures on the project performance indicators and limit ourselves to the most effective set of these measures.

Model the business process based on risk allows you to more accurately plan the development of the business. Before the start of the project has the opportunity to develop activities that improve the final result of the project with minimal cost.

Author details

Vladimir Gorbunov
National Research University of Electronic Technology, Moscow, Russia

*Address all correspondence to: nbia@mail.ru

References

[1] Sommerville I. Software Engineering. 6th Edition Addison-Wesley, 2001, 693 p

[2] Standart-idef0-primery-idef0-... pravila-postroeniya/[Internet]. Available from: *https://technolakpiter.ru/en//* [Accessed: 2020.12.10]

[3] Polgraphics/opisanie-funkcionalnoi-mod...snovnye-metodologii/ [Internet]. Available from: https://polarize.ru/en/ [Accessed: 2020.9.12]

[4] Gorbunov V. L. Business planning with risk and efficiency assessment of projects : Scientific-practical manual / V. L. Gorbunov. - M. : RIOR : Infra-M, 2013. - 248 with

[5] Gorbunov V. L. a Database "AE-Project" Certificate of registration No. 2004629261 from 09.09.2004 Y.

[6] V. B. the discount Rate in the evaluation. The magazine "Russian business newspaper", n 90, 2002, pp. 147-150.

[7] Gracheva M.V. Risk Analysis of the Investment Project. M/ UNINI-DANA, 2001

[8] Nersesian. Energy Risk Modeling. Palisade Corporation. In: NY USA. 2013

[9] James R. Morris, John P. Daley. Introduction to Financial Models for Management and Planning Textbook - 756 Pages - 316 B/W ISBN 9781420090543 - CAT# C0542 Illustrations 2009 by Chapman and Hall/CRC

[10] Gorbunov V. L. Accounting balanced scorecard of the enterprise in the system of business planning. SB. proceedings of the international conference "Innovative approaches to solving technical and economic problems," M. MIET. 2014

Chapter 7

Social Impact Returns. Filling the Finance Gap with Data Value

Amparo Marin de la Barcena Grau

Abstract

Sustainability, regulation and environmental issues such as climate change and resource scarcity are emerging as key trends with decisive impact on company's Risk management, value creation and growth strategy. This combination represents one of the biggest opportunities to Society as a whole, including organizations, Governments and citizens. Typically, companies possess vast amounts of data, most of it unutilized. Many are now making investments in digital transformation, which generates even more data. The issue is how to generate social impact returns. The use of data and data analytics is centuries old, but with Artificial Intelligence (AI), Machine Learning (ML), jointly with other distributed ledger technologies (Blockchain, Cloud) that are advancing rapidly, there are major opportunities to capture value better, cheaper and faster. Speed is of the essence, and success depends on how fast organizations understand the need for non-financial risks management and respond to data-driven intelligence by reallocating resources to accomplish what needs to be done more efficiently. The reason for impact returns is understanding the benefit as a common value, not exclusive to companies, but it also has to distribute value among individuals, communities, and why not, to contribute to regenerate our planet based on a new economy.

Keywords: Social Impact Return, Sustainability, Risk Management, Data Science, Quantitative Modeling, Competitive Intelligence, ESG, Advanced Analytics, Profit Enhancement

1. Introduction

The future is already here. Several new players have already begun to understand the state-of-the-art Sustainability, while others are still in its infancy. There are new tools and techniques to respond to data-driven needs constantly appearing, and at the same time the demand for environmental, social and governance compliance is racing ahead.

The idea of sustainability dates back to the Industrial Revolution, early 20th century, when two opposing factions emerged within the environmental movement: the conservationists and the preservationists. The conservationists focused on the proper use of nature, whereas the preservationists sought the protection of nature from use. In the 1970s sustainable development was a key theme of the United Nations Conference, where the concept was coined to suggest that it was possible to achieve economic growth and industrialization without environmental damage. In the last decades the concept was further refined as 'development that meets the needs of the present without compromising the ability of future generations to meet their own needs' [1].

In essence, the problem today to be addressed has three main elements: 1) unsustainability of current social lifestyles; 2) new regulation on non-financial reporting; 3) introduction of alternative means of payment to exchange transactions.

According to recent studies unsustainability of consumption and production poses a major social problem. If the population reaches 9.6 bn by 2050, we'll need 3 planets to sustain current lifestyles [2]. The proliferation of brands and parties that compete towards a market that is limited in resources induces fierce competition. This is no longer sustainable for customers, who must face increasing costs and prices, but also for small and medium businesses which end up running out of business. Beyond customers and companies there is even one more overarching and vulnerable affected target by environmental accelerated destruction: the community.

Envisioning a gap to evaluate performance and develop a responsible approach to business, the European Commission amended the law to require large companies to disclose certain information on the way they operate and manage social and environmental challenges [3, 4].

Increasing importance of non-financial performance requires large companies to measure and report such type of indicators, namely social and environmental impacts of their activities.

Tracking impact performance and alternative frameworks to shape a better future offer the potential of standardizing metrics and catalyzing value creation towards common goals.

The focus of rewards is no longer just economic and thus customers are increasingly demanding new ways to interact with companies in exchange of a promise for future service [5]. At this point operationalizing value capture from high impact data comes in. This is also known as Operationalized Data Monetization (ODM).

Data and data analytics are accelerating exponentially. According to one survey, 55% of IT leaders named data analytics as one of their main priorities in 2019. (Only security was ranked higher, at 57%). Additionally, 3 of the Top 13 Priorities for Executives and Board Members were related to Data [6] (**Figure 1**).

The rise of digital technologies is reshaping customers' habits and company strategies. And to stay competitive, enterprises – usually responding to suggested digital transformation strategies and "best-in-class" digital benchmarks – are racing to respond to these trends.

Jolted by the resounding success and sheer scale of the 21st century AI and ML-driven digital behemoths (such as Google, Amazon, Alibaba, Tencent, Alipay, Baidu, and dozens of fintech and insurtech startups), companies have plunged headlong into digital transformation [7–10] in the hope of stemming the long-term disruption to their businesses. However, the success rate of digital transformation has proved to be very low. According to recent studies [11, 12], more than 80 percent of analyzed companies have faced limitations in making successful digital changes to their business.

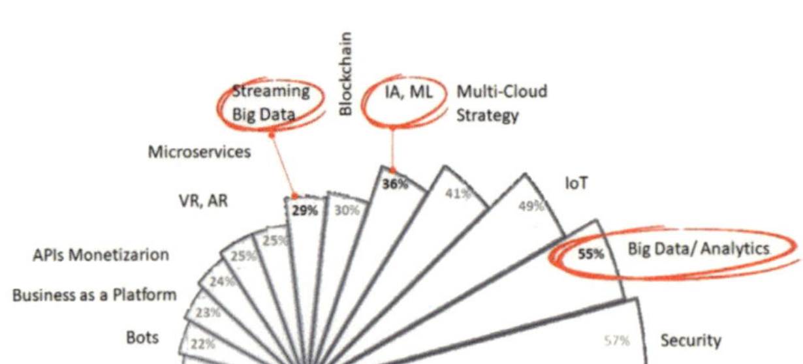

Figure 1.
Top technology investments for 2019. Source: MuleSoft.

Most of these companies have missed out on the high-impact value-creation opportunities because of a failure to differentiate between digital transformation and data value capture to generate social returns. Digital transformation, in addition to improving the customer journey, also produces quantities of internal and external data. Data value capture, on the other hand, is the use of data to create economic value and social returns. Survival and let alone sustainable growth require companies to reach the minimum high impact data levels; as of today, there is still a long way to go.

A framework to measure social impact filling the finance gap has been woven into this article. It demonstrates the range of opportunities that can be achieved by adopting data and Sustainable Development Goals (SDGs) as core strategy.

The increasing importance of sustainability for organizations is backed, not only by the fact that most corporate leaders are incorporating environmental, social, and governance (ESG) issues in their agenda but also sustainable funds more than doubled 2019 records, reaching over $51 billion in new investments, accounting for 25% of global new investments [13].

Executives and Leaders understand that taking responsibility for each of the sustainability pillars (economic, environment and social) implies accountability and impact on people, planet and profits; thus business performance and results.

Performance and results are mainstream measured and evaluated from the financial dimension; which is not comprehensive. This study aims to bridge that gap and raise awareness of the need to introduce the non-financial dimension. Such dimension can be easily understood in the current context of the COVID-19 pandemic situation; which has demonstrated that non-financial risks can pose further damage and in a more significant way than any of the precedent economic crisis.

Duality of models and frameworks is not yet a common practice but combination of quantitative and qualitative metrics is the path to superior and sustainable performance through continuous improvement. Filling the finance gap is challenging but undertaking a proper approach is also doable. And in this context is where technology as a facilitator is key to make it happen.

2. Social impact returns

2.1 Call to action. Solution is duality

The use of data and data analytics is centuries old. Developing technologies and tools together with decreasing data costs have eased that firms increasingly use data as support for decision making.

The cost of computation is roughly one hundred-millionth what it was in the 1970s. And the cost per megabyte of data storage has fallen from US$85,000 in 1956 to just $0.00002 today in constant dollars. Furthermore, connection speeds of hundreds of megabits per second now cost only tens of dollars per month [12, 14]. As a result, organizations have installed a myriad of systems – computers and software – to enhance their services, resulting in the capture and storage of enormous amounts of data, most of which remains underutilized [15].

It can be empirically and statistically observed that reliance on just quantitative (data based) models and attempting to exploit and understand all the data investing heavily in Data Lakes and Advanced Analytic tools does not work. The qualitative component, which includes counting on the right people and skills, is essential to enhance decision making.

Towards the end of the 16th century, insurance companies were formed on the basis of the monetization of shipping data [16–18]. Actuarial science applied to longevity and health are the backbone of the life and health insurance industries and have been around for decades [16, 19]. The same is true for the linkage between weather forecasting and commodity trading [20, 21]. There are many other familiar examples where the true value is captured through the combination between quantitative and qualitative aspects. This is what we refer to as need for duality.

Duality is present in every aspect of our lives: humans are rational and emotional; animals have a physical and psychological component; customers are no longer just interested in products but also in user experience; major risks caused by extrinsic and non-business related causes may result even more harmful by those that can be measured by traditional economic KPIs. All in all, we are shifting from the "what" to the "how" and this can have a clear impact on profitability and performance.

Defining and quantifying Key Performance Indicators (KPI) and undertaking these as the basis for operating decisions must be done. But to succeed, beyond just quantitative data, there is a need to introduce a qualitative component to understand which is the minimum data required for high impact decisions (**Figure 2**).

2.2 Quanti- vs. quali?

The answer is both. There is no single vision for Sustainability nor one definition for social impact return. Many will link these concepts with Corporate Social Responsibility (CSR), others with environmental problems, and very few will get it right by understanding that it is simply "the act of generating measurable economic benefits from available data sources".

To illustrate the call for quanti- + quali- based models, let us take the financial sector. The need for such combined framework emerged and materialized with the reform of the Basel Accord (1988), relying on three pillars: capital adequacy requirements, centralized supervisory and market discipline [22, 23].

For the purpose of understanding the framework proposed, we can draw the following analogy:

- Quantitative level = > companies must provide data (KPIs) that comply with required thresholds.

- Qualitative level = > Data needs to be qualified, certified and understood under common and homogeneous supervisory criteria.

- Relationship and correlation of both = > results at one level (e.g. quantitative) impact and are interdependent with the other (e.g. qualitative) and vice versa. If no relationship is drawn between both and results at one level are not used to

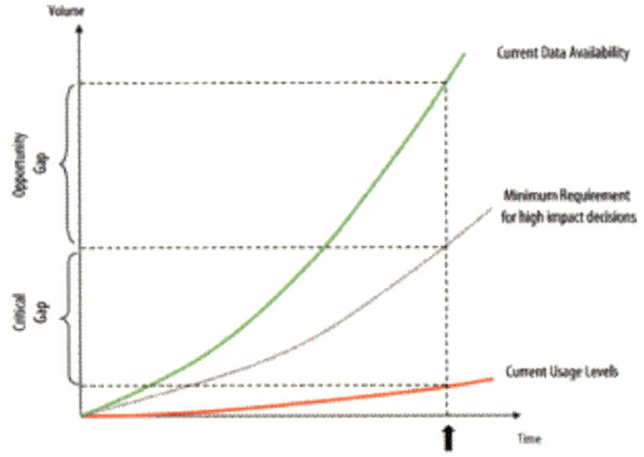

Figure 2.
The data intelligence gap. Source: The Gartner group, Essex.

feed back the complementary level, the ability to systematize a dynamic of continuous improvement and sustained profitable growth will be limited. This was precisely one of the core reasons for the amendment of Basel Accord [24, 25].

2.3 Non-financial risk management

The Non-Financial Reporting Directive (2014/95/EU) requires large public interest entities with over 500 employees (listed companies, banks, and insurance companies) to disclose certain non-financial information. As required by the Directive, the Commission has published Non-Binding Guidelines to help companies disclose relevant non-financial information in a more consistent and more comparable manner. However, to date it is unclear for companies how to comply with the Regulation and at the same time it is also unclear who/how to certify that companies are compliant with the Regulation.

How to respond to these challenges? In this regard we have developed a solution for non-financial reporting based on a dual model (quantitative + qualitative KPIs) that makes converge people, technology and social impact.

Social return can be measured by the value enterprises create by utilizing their data to develop and implement their products and services profitably while they contribute to attain the Sustainable Development Goals (2030 Agenda) [26]. To achieve this, companies will need to embark on a shift in organizational behavior, designed to opt for more sustainable ways of working that reduce enterprise complexity, excess of consumption and facilitate impact on society. This transformation entails converting insights into actions. It tackles the following key dimensions (**Figure 3**).

(1) Regulation.

Companies must report non- financial indicators. Such Regulation approved by the European Parliament implies that companies need to adapt and adequate their current reporting.

(2) Social.

Applicability and measurement of company data to contribute towards the Goals of the 2030 Agenda (17 SDGs) demands convergence between People, IT and Social Impact.

Sustainability entitles that companies' investment must generate returns which can be re-invested in producing further improvements. Returns materialize either increasing revenues, reducing costs or aiding in risk control.

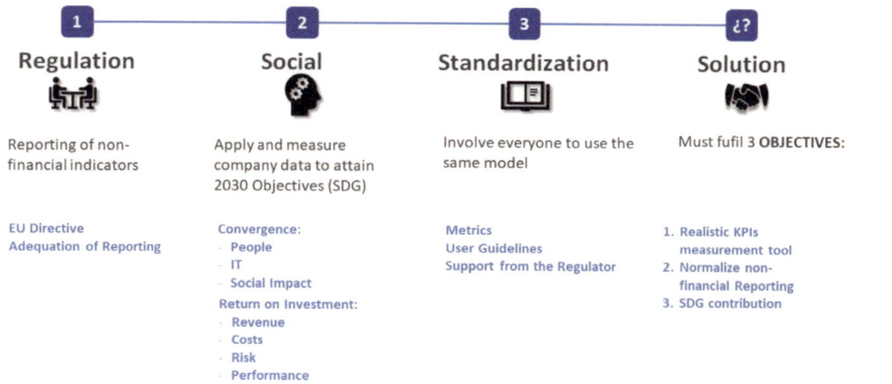

Figure 3.
Key components to generate transformation within an organization (specific orientation towards social impact return). Source: Own elaboration.

(3) Standardization.

This dimension is key to avoid complexity and inefficiencies. It promotes co-opetition (collaborate + compete to develop the best) and increase of productivity.

Homogeneous metrics and user guidelines allow to join forces between companies with the potential to generate synergies and multiply social impact returns.

(4) Solution.

To deliver impact, the solution should cover three main objectives:

1. Realistic tool of KPIs measurement

2. Normalization of non-financial reporting

3. Contribution to SDGs

2.4 Diagnose. Bridging the gap

A successful build-up of the financial gap that is tied to social impact generation implies 2 key elements.

1. A thorough diagnose of the macro-context understanding the trends that are shaping the environment

2. Proper identification of key stakeholders

Analysis of the macro-environment unveils that five trends are emerging as those requiring attention from companies due to their impact on costs and profitability; and therefore sustainability (**Figure 4**).

1. The new Era of Return. Transitioning from the "What" to the "How". There is increasing demand for user experience, values, hyper-personalization ...

2. New Technologies. IT has become a facilitator of business transformation and new ways of working.

3. Operationalization of Data value capture. Identify high-impact data that can generate a return on companies' investments is imperative.

Figure 4.
Key trends with impact on sustainability.

4. New Regulation. Need to adopt and comply with the laws and emerging norms that are becoming stricter.

5. Non-financial risks. Their relevance for business and markets is gaining momentum.

Additionally, who are the parties that need to be part of the solution and what is the role in the overall ecosystem? (**Figure 5**).

We have identified three main categories:

1. Companies: that have the obligation to report

2. Administrations and Regulators: who must certify companies' compliance

3. People/Society: demand information and benefits

All these are part of a model ecosystem whose sustainability needs to be evaluated from different standpoints. First, responsible production; second it needs to rely on a sound supervision and governance model that brings trust, ownership and non-repudiation; third it must look for efficiency optimization; and fourth, continuous improvement needs to be at the core.

2.5 Use case

Many organizations now have analytics departments that can generate data-driven insights. But conversion of these insights into implementable actions is often painfully slow. To make it happen organizations need to interiorize a truly data-driven culture [27–30]. And to accomplish the transformation required, companies will have to take a far more radical approach – less of the old jargon and hierarchical behavior; more data-driven intelligence and a relentless focus on Agile-grounded speed of execution.

Companies subject to the European Regulation for non-financial reporting will undergo the following scenario:

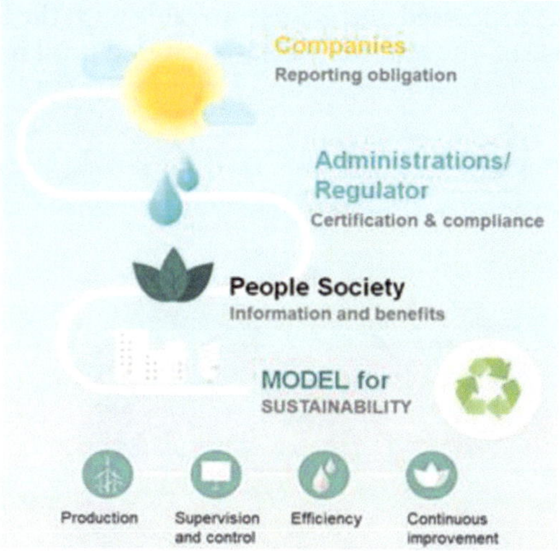

Figure 5.
Identified key stakeholders.

1. Company X needs to report social impact indicators.

2. Employees/people should feel committed to contribute towards the company's sustainable development goals and continuous improvement of associated indicators.

3. The generation of indicators should be automated.

4. Evolution and visualization of performance should be available for society and rewards for accomplishing the goals and producing returns should be rewarded.

The building blocks that can be put together to approach this situation are presented in **Figure 6**.

1. Organizational context. Macro-level. Represents the quantitative dimension.

2. People. Micro-level. Touches upon the qualitative level that will feed back and complement the quantitative results.

3. Dashboard. Critical tool to monitor performance

4. Technology. Is the facilitator.

5. Data.

6. Gamification. To secure user engagement and the overall sustainability of the model.

HOW DOES IT WORK?

Figure 7 provides an overview of the overall process flow and how the relationships between the different components.

At organizational level, the company would need to select quantitative social impact metrics to be included on its report. Those KPIs should be preferably related to the accomplishment of SDGs and aligned with EU reporting standards in a format that can be processed and is interoperable with the Supervisory Board. Specifically, in the case of our solution we have selected html format enriched with

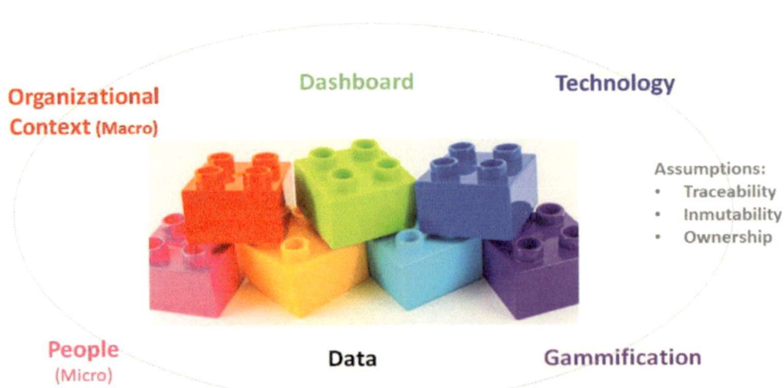

Figure 6.
Building blocks of the proposed approach.

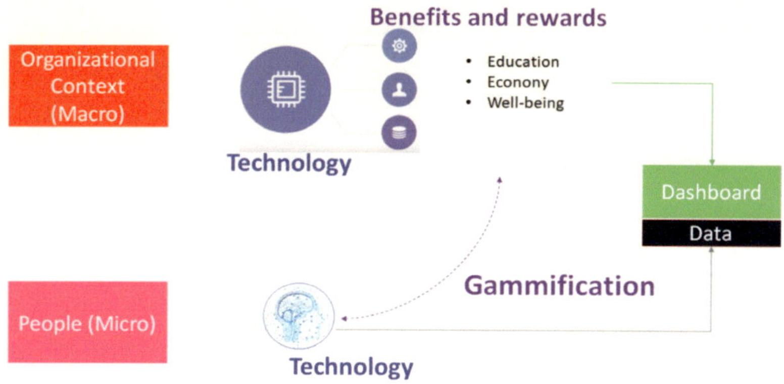

Figure 7.
Process flow. Relationship between components.

XBRL tagged metrics, as an extension of the standard that is already used in financial reporting. The reason for this selection is to ease company's adoption of something they are already familiar with, while lowering barriers from the Supervisory Board to introduce new standards.

As we are in a Regulatory context the need for ownership, traceability and non-repudiation is imperative. Additionally, the technology must be able to address the three pillars of Basel II Accord (Data, Certification and Transparency). Considering its intrinsic characteristics, we opted for Blockchain to provision the Social Impact Reports. Blockchain, beyond its ability to prove trust and immutability of data, it provided another added value: current absence of a Regulatory Body that feels responsible for certifying social impact reports. In a traditional approach, this need would have reflected in additional resources and staff, which we have been able to optimize by means of technology.

As companies are complying with regulatory requirements, they need to receive something in exchange. In our model, we will reward companies with tokens for complying with the regulation. But beyond regulatory compliance we want to incentive companies' alliances to contribute towards the 2030 Agenda SDGs. For this purpose, in our model, companies will also receive rewards for meeting the United Nations' thresholds to attain the expected results.

Results will be accessible on a Dashboard to monitor performance and ensure transparency and fairness of the reporting. But there is something still missing to guarantee the sustainability of the model: people involvement; the qualitative dimensions that provides feedback to the overall model. Based on gamification and AI we generate user engagement to contribute to improve the indicators and benefit from the social impact returns. **Figure 7** shows the overall process flow and the relationships between the different components while **Table 1** shows the value proposition that the model brings for each of the stakeholders.

2.6 PoC: balancing policy measures vs. economic activity

The Challenge.

Find the balance between mitigating policy measures and maintaining economic activity.

The Climate Act calls for a 49% reduction in greenhouse gas emissions by 2030, compared to 1990 levels, and a 95% reduction by 2050. The National Climate Agreement contains agreements with the sectors on what they will do to help achieve these climate goals.

Stakeholder	Added Value
Companies	Solution for non-financial reporting Regulatory compliance Social reputation
Administration and Regulators	Standardization Ease certification Transparency
People	Rewards for contributing towards sustainability Social benefits

Table 1.
Value proposition.

Participating sectors.

Build environment, Electricity, Traffic and transport, and agriculture and land use.

Proposed indicators (**Tables 2** and **3**).

Methodology and approach.

Our proposed solution is inspired by duality and the concept of system of systems [31]. Duality is twofold and implies:

- Use of AI and ML techniques that can emulate the learning capability and at the same time work with complex and large datasets; without forgetting gamification to foster commitment and people involvement.

- From a data perspective, using a combination of privately held and public data to monitor the economic impact of climate change policies in a timely manner allowing agile and balanced policy adjustments.

KPI	Unit of measure
Direct GHG emissions from sources owned or controlled by the company (Scope 1)	Metric tons CO2e
Indirect GHG emissions from the generation of acquired and consumed electricity, steam, heat, or cooling (collectively referred to as "electricity") (Scope 2)	Metric tons CO2e
GHG absolute emissions target	Metric tons CO2e achieved or % reduction

Table 2.
Proposed Indicators for GHG (green house gas emissions).

KPI	Unit of measure
Total energy consumption and/or production from renewable and non-renewable sources	MWh
Energy efficiency target	Percentage
Renewable energy consumption and/or production target	% increase of the proportion of renewable energy consumed/ produced from base year

Table 3.
Proposed indicators for energy.

Due to its capability of learning complex structures in large datasets, deep learning has been applied to many problems in financial markets and sustainability, such as analysis and data modeling to design strategies for investment and trading, prediction of prices, identification of market trends and customer behavior and even maximizing profits and returns. There are even examples of applications of AI algorithms to analyze robotic behavior in Smart cities and to understand the impact of news and information on human decisions and arbitrage [32–45].

The quantitative & qualitative factors both reflect on the solution framework. Beyond the quantitative level based on pure mathematical methods, it incorporates human attributes and capabilities of neurons and human learning. Narrowed to practice, our methodology combines a semi-supervised learning method with Generative Adversarial Imitation (GAIL) and Recurrent Neural Networks (RNN). The figure below illustrates the operationalized framework (**Figure 8**).

The framework is structured into three parts: (1) environment, (2) RNN and (3) GAIL. The environment is a virtual place in which we emulate how the

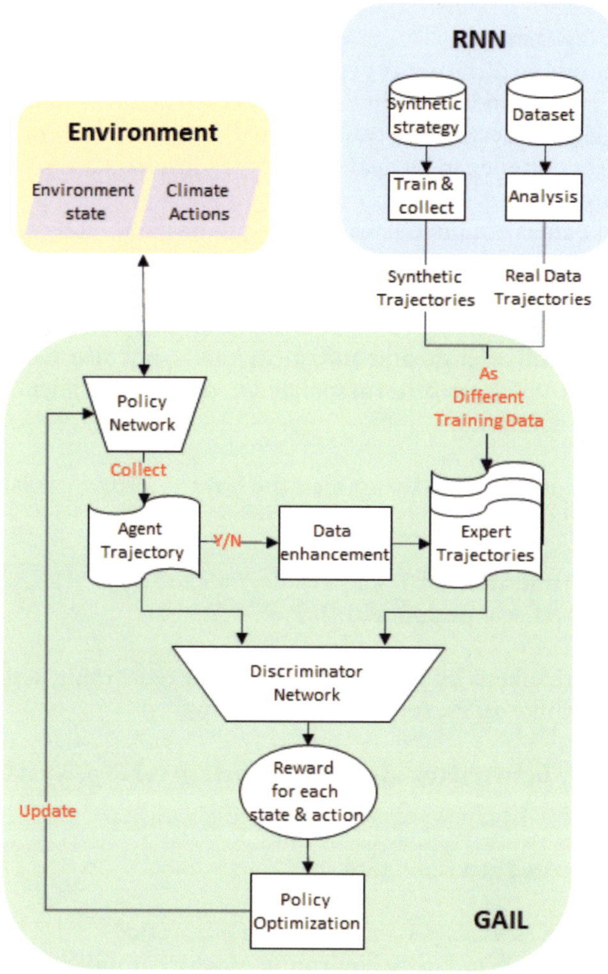

Figure 8.
Operationalized effective management framework to balance policy measures of climate change vs. economic activity.

environment is changing, the impact of climate change and the status of actions and initiatives, etc. Such emulation of the reality helps us practice and identify how Policies can influence and improve the economy. To simulate a realistic market, the environment provides its status (environment state) and the portfolio of climate actions (actions state). The RNN acts as an expert trajectory generator. It produces expert trajectories from raw data (in our problem, training data). Two types of data sources are used in our method: synthetic strategy and real monitored data. During the process of GAIL, we also provide data enhancement to overcome the defects in real data and at this stage we incorporate the gamification factor providing rewards for each state and action.

The actors where this PoC is framed play a crucial role due to their high sensitivity on such a matter as Sustainability and Climate Change, that can have a huge impact on people, the environment and the overarching economic system.

Due to the volatility of datasets, the information from the latest 6-months is generally outdated. Since we are combining privately held and public data to monitor the economic impact of climate change policies in a timely manner, these need to be aligned. Therefore, for the purpose of obtaining relevant results, our approach suggests taking week or few months timeframes, rather than many months or years.

Leveraging on Big Data.

The need to combine different types of data and imitate human learning to excel at decision making, demands putting Big Data at the core. It enables to analyze, extract information in a systematic way and deal with large and complex data sets that are too large or complex to be dealt with by traditional data-processing applications and software.

Privately held data is obtained from mobile phone data, internal company engagement surveys, NPS, satellite imaging, while Public data is sourced from National Statistics office, National banks, fiscal studies.

Based on Big Data platforms we are not only able to cope with data with many fields (columns), which offer greater statistical power, but also avoid leading to false discovery rates which are often associated to data with higher complexity (more attributes or columns).

Algorithm.

For the gamification module we applied the Loyalty Program Liabilities and Point Values algorithm

- We consider a timeframe of T + 1 periods, indexed by $t \in \{1, ..., T + 1\}$; a period corresponds to a fiscal period with $T \rightarrow \infty$

- Citizens acquire tokens by purchasing in cash or redeeming actions towards sustainability (bike miles, recycling plastic caps, ...)

- An equivalency between tokens q_t and monetary value p_t is established: $\theta t = p_t / q_t$ (θt =0,196€)

- Tokens are awarded at a fixed rate (λ)

Distributed Ledger Technologies – why are they important?

This PoC tackles the Regulatory environment which implies traceability, non-repudiation and ownership of the results. As of today, in the same way that there are clear responsible Institutions for Financial Reporting Supervision, there is no Organism in charge for non-financial reporting.

In absence of this figure, a solution is to rely on Technology: Blockchain. This technology not only provides the necessary principles of traceability, non-repudiation and ownership stated above, but also have proven to be the only alternative to deal with cases that need to combine Regulation and Economic factors.

In such sensitive context where information needs to be immutable, but at the same time there is no one institution responsible for ensuring this, our proposed solution is that each of the agents are responsible for their own information. All in all Blockchain, due to its intrinsic nature, will play the global role that is yet officially unassigned.

3. Results and discussion

The table below shows a simulation to estimate the social impact of the proposed model (**Table 4**).

With a correlation of 0.87 the model has proven potential to drive social impact returns at SME level, large corporations or country level. The key for the success of such framework is citizen adoption and engagement. All in all, since the model has been developed looking to universal global reporting standards (GRI) and traceability guaranteed by Distributed Ledger Technologies (DLT) it could be extended and tested Worldwide.

In this study, we examined the contribution of non-financial risks to society. When asking companies what is their social impact and the return of their sustainable investments, we often meet a silence. For the first time, with this model, a business that needs to answer this question the next time will be able to provide a quantitative metric. For instance, based on our calculations, a citizen living in a country of an advanced economy, assuming an adoption rate of 65% within a country, could contribute to reduce CHG emissions by 0,97 t during the next 10 years, which would mean that if all countries followed the same example, the objective set by the Climate Act (49% reduction of CHG emissions by 2030) would be feasible to achieve.

It's worth outlining that the backbone of this model is not only the maths and rationality behind, but also adoption and commitment towards a common specific goal. It is considered that for this model to work, a key prerequisite must be satisfied, namely having a joint/compatible goal or problem to solve materialized in a specific metric or KPI everyone understands (it is not enough that parties have their own individual goals and track them in a non-standard way).

It is hoped that this introduction to a new way to measure returns, complementary to traditional finance, will create reflection and commitment to a greater sustainable sensitivity when businesses and event citizens consider how their change of behavior may affect other people, the planet and profits.

Scope	Adoption rate	Rewards per citizen	Social impact return (↓GHG)
SME (100 employees)	80%	203,889	4,5 Tons
Large Corp (35.000 empl)	90%	407,778	3.325 Tons
Country (65 m citizens)	65%	543,704	6,3 mill Tons

Table 4.
Simulation. Social impact returns.

4. Conclusions

As our case study shows, there is an opportunity to use data to fill in a gap in the regulatory and social contexts. Capturing the value of data combined with an appropriate architectural framework and use of technology can rapidly help companies overcome a current compliance challenge while at the same time it can produce social returns that pay for previous years of heavy IT investment that has not yet been monetized.

The value proposition of the proposed approach is understanding benefit as a common value not exclusive to the organization, but it also has to distribute value among customers, workers, the community and, why not, to contribute to regenerate our planet based on a new economy.

Companies need to realize that the future is already here. Data-driven companies that have understood the importance of combining quantitative and qualitative models, Alipay, Tencent, Baidu, Huawei, Samsung, Apple, Amazon, Facebook, Google, and Walmart, to name a few, are rapidly grasping profit enhancement and social impact generation opportunities and filling the wide-open gap left by traditional players. Google (and Baidu in China) is used by every person on the planet who is connected to the internet. Facebook has over two billion customers. Baidu, Apple, Tencent, and Samsung's customer bases are close to one billion customers each. These companies have scale and very satisfied customers whom they really understand. They are essentially ready to deal with upcoming challenges which demand rapid adaptation (e.g. need for Regulatory Compliance with little guidelines for companies on how to report, VUCA (Vulnerable Uncertain Complex Ambiguous) environments which lack Supervisory Competence Boards).

We are living through a paradigm change, driven by new rules of competition in terms of both the speed of product development and the speed of obsolescence of products and services. Adopting new technologies and operationalizing the capture of value from data as the core strategic is imperative to maintain competitiveness. Digital transformation investments without focus on social impact returns has a very low success rate.

In this article, we have emphasized the need for an integrated, systematic approach, incorporating continuous improvement and constant feedback. The framework we propose is firmly based on empirical evidence, including both quantitative data and qualitative experience. As the PoC demonstrates. Implementing the framework can result from individual to country-wide contributions and improve sustainable development goals.

The framework described is in line with global reporting standards and at the same time, flexible enough to be tailored to each business's specific context, and if necessary, it can be implemented progressively, modulating the adoption rate. The higher the adoption rate, the more rapid profit enhancement and social impact returns. Crucially, though, customized solutions generally start delivering transformation in as little as three months.

As per the contribution of this research to sustainability, we have covered the applicability of modeling to non-financial risks management, and particularly in the field of sustainable finance. Conclusions point out that duality is the solution to capture the essential value of data and have an impact on planet, people and profits, which are associated to the three main pillars of Sustainability: Environment, Social and Governance (ESG).

Developing a framework is the first step towards systematization that can help businesses to generate value and impact in a recurrent way. Our framework is built under a pragmatic, universal and adaptable philosophy, which demands completion and commitment from the adopters' side. One of the main contributions of this model is that when companies are often asked what is the impact of their social investments, a silence is met. Next time, it is hoped that our solution represents a starting point that can be enhanced in a collaborative way, fostering open innovation and preempting any efforts to reinvent the wheel.

Capture of the essential data value, beyond data analytics, to generate returns and profit enhancement is the basis of all our work, which enables convergence between people, technology and value creation. One of the main limitations we faced is the volatility of data and its reliability and relevance. Most Large Corps., in order to comply with the EU Directive on non-Financial Reporting, have developed their own solutions. The problem is that lack of alignment and comparability of KPIs result in inefficiency of results when attempting to measure progress and achievement of targets. At this stage there is an urgent call to action to adopt standards that allow companies to co-pete (Collaborate and Compete), helping each other to improve and learn. Unless a shared strategy, goals and metrics are in place, actions will lead to sub-optimal results.

Finally, technology as a facilitator, plays a key role when it comes to the capture and exploitation of data value. In the las three years, investment in Digital Transformation accounts for $1 Trillón but only 12% of companies obtained a return. Decoupling Data Value capture from Digital Transformation is imperative. Companies need to understand which metrics are relevant and can generate an impact and then, adopt a data driven strategy. This framework is aimed to enable companies differentiate such aspects and start putting the right pieces together to capitalize the data value opportunity.

Acknowledgements

Universidad Politécnica de Madrid (UPM).
Instituto de Empresa (IE Business School).
Essex Lake Group (ESSEX).
Alastria.
WStartup Community.
Kunfud.
ClimateTrade.
MujeresTech.
SWN

Notes/thanks/other declarations

Thanks in an unprecedented year! Specially to my family and people that have provided support and advice at all times.

Nomenclature

AI	Artificial Intelligence
DLT	Distributed Ledger Technologies
ESG	Environmental Social and Governance
EU	European Union
GHG	Green House Gas emissions
GRI	Global Reporting Initiative
KPI	Key Performance Indicators

ML	Machine Learning
ODM	Operationalized Data Monetization
PoC	Proof of Concept
SDG	Sustainable Development Goals
SME	Small and Medium Enterprise
SWN	Santander Woman Network
UN	United Nations
UPM	Universidad Politécnica de Madrid
VUCA	Vulnerable Uncertain Complex Ambiguous

Author details

Amparo Marin de la Barcena Grau
Universidad Politécnica de Madrid (UPM), Madrid, Spain

*Address all correspondence to: amarin.alumno.ie@gmail.com

References

[1] Socialwatch (2011) What is sustainable development? The evolution of the idea [Online]. Available: https://www.socialwatch.org/node/12477

[2] United Nations (2020, Mar. 08) 17 Goals to Transform our World. [Online]. Available: https://www.un.org/sustainabledevelopment/

[3] European Commission (2020, Mar. 07). Non-financial reporting, EU rules require large companies to publish regular reports on the social and environmental impacts of their activities. [Online]. Available: https://ec.europa.eu/info/business-economy-euro/company-reporting-and-auditing/company-reporting/non-financial-reporting_en

[4] European Parliament and of the Council. Directive 2013/34/EU", OJ L 182, 29.6.2013, p. 19-76 (BG, ES, CS, DA, DE, ET, EL, EN, FR, IT, LV, LT, HU, MT, NL, PL, PT, RO, SK, SL, FI, SV). Special edition in Croatian: Chapter 17 Volume 3 p. 253-310. June 2013. Available: http://data.europa.eu/eli/dir/2013/34/oj

[5] Chun SY, Iancu DA, and Trichakis N. Loyalty Program Liabilities and Point Values. Informs PubsOnLine, October 2019. Published Online: https://doi.org/10.1287/msom.2018.0748

[6] Raconteur, Digital Transformation Survey of IT Leaders from Global Enterprises," MuleSoft 2019.

[7] Gottlieb J, Rifai K. Fueling growth through data monetization. McKinsey Insights, December 2017.

[8] Gandhi S. et al. Demystifying Data monetization. MIT Sloan Management Review. November 2018. [Online]. Available: https://sloanreview.mit.edu

[9] Rembert E. Banks Spend $1 Trillion on Digital, But Few Reap the Rewards. Bloomberg. June 2019. https://www.bloomberg.com/news/articles/2019-06-20/banks-spend-1-trillion-on-digital-but-few-benefit-study-says

[10] De la Boutetière H, Montagner A and Reich A. Unlocking success in digital transformations. McKinsey Insights. October 2018. https://www.mckinsey.com/business-functions/organization/our-insights/unlocking-success-in-digital-transformations

[11] Rembert E. Banks Spend $1 Trillion on Digital, But Few Reap the Rewards. Bloomberg. June 2019. https://www.bloomberg.com/news/articles/2019-06-20/banks-spend-1-trillion-on-digital-but-few-benefit-study-says

[12] Ramirez A. Digitalízate o desaparece. Gestión 2000 Grupo Planeta 2017. Isbn: 974-84-9875-459-9

[13] Morningstar (2020). Annual Landscape Report. [Online]. Available: https://www.morningstar.com/lp/sustainable-funds-landscape-report

[14] Parkings D. The world's most valuable resource. The Economist. May 2017.

[15] <Author unknown>, Drastic falls in cost are powering another computer revolution. The Economist. September 2019. [Online] Available: https://www.economist.com/technology-quarterly/2019/09/12/drastic-falls-in-cost-are-powering-another-computer-revolution

[16] Toesland F. How five brands learned from digital transformation failure. September 2018. [Online] Available: https://www.raconteur.net/digital-transformation/digital-transformation-failure

[17] Vaughan EJ, Vaughan T. Fundamentals of risk and insurance, 10th edition. John Wiley & Sons, Inc., 2008, ISBN: 978-0470087534

[18] Klein B. The World's first Insurance Company," IRMI. Expert Commentary. July 2001. [Online] Available: http://irmi.com

[19] Kingston C. Marine Insurance in Britain and America, 1720-1844: A Comparative Institutional Analysis. The Journal of Economic History. 67 p. 379-409. 2005.

[20] Piperdy Y, Rushing S. Past, Present and Future of Risk Factors: The History of Life Insurance Risk Assessment. RGA, November 2018. [Online] Available: https://rgare.com/knowledge-center/media/research/past-present-and-future-of-risk-factors

[21] Abawi GY, Smith RJ, and Brady DK. Assessment of the value of long-range weather forecasts in wheat harvest management. Journal of Agricultural Engineering Resources, 62 p 39-48, 1995

[22] E. Craft E. Economic History of Weather Forecasting. EH.Net Encyclopedia, edited by Whaples R, October 2001 [Online] Available: https://www.economist.com/technology-quarterly/2019/09/12/drastic-falls-in-cost-are-powering-another-computer-revolution

[23] Al-E. Basel M. The Three Pillars of Basel II: A Diffusion Model with Jumps of Banking Regulation. Journal of Money, Investment and Banking, ISSN 1450-288x Issue 19. 2011. [Online] Available: http://www.eurojournals.com/JMIB.htm

[24] Decamps JP, Rochet JC, Roger B. The three pillars of Basel II: optimizing the mix. Journal of Financial Intermediation. Volume 13, Issue 2 p. 132-155. April 2004. [Online] Available: https://doi.org/10.1016/j.jfi.2003.06.003

[25] Ferreira C., Jenkinson N. and Wilson C. IMF Working Paper. From Basel I to Basel III: Sequencing Implementation in Developing Economies. WP/19/127. JEL Classification Numbers: G21; G28. [Online] Available: www.imf.org › Publications › WPIEA2019127

[26] United Nations. Transforming Our World. The 2030 Agenda for Sustainable Development. 2015 [Online] Available: https://sustainabledevelopment.un.org/content/documents/21252030%20Agenda%20for%20Sustainable%20Development%20web.pdf

[27] De la Boutetière H., Montagner A. and Reich A., Unlocking success in digital transformations. McKinsey Insights. October 2018. https://www.mckinsey.com/business-functions/organization/our-insights/unlocking-success-in-digital-transformations

[28] Gottlieb J., Rifai K., Fueling growth through data monetization. McKinsey Insights. December 2017.

[29] Gandhi S. et al, "Demystifying Data monetization. MIT Sloan Management Review. November 2018. [Online]. Available: https://sloanreview.mit.edu

[30] Marin de la Barcena A. Quantitative models applied to the financial and strategic environments [thesis]. Universidad Politécnica de Madrid; 2020-2021.

[31] Wiley (2009). System of Systems engineering. Innovations from the 21st century. Wiley Series in Systems Engineering and Management. ISBN 978-0-470-19590-1

[32] Chong (2017). E. Chong, C. Han, and F.C. Park. "Deep learning networks for stock market analysis and prediction: Methodology, data representations, and case studies," in Expert Systems with Applications, vol. 83. Pp. 187-205. 2017

[33] Zhang (2018). R. Zhang, Z. Yuan and X. Shao. "A new combined cnn-rnn model for sector stock price analysis," in 2018 (IEEE 42nd Annual Computer Software and Applications Conference

(COMPSAC). vol 2. IEEE. 2018. Pp. 546-551

[34] Kraus (2017). M. Kraus and S. Feuerriegel. "Decision support from financial disclosures with deep neural networks and transfer learning," in Decision Support Systems, vol. 104, pp.38-48, 2017

[35] Jiang (2017). Z. Jiang, D. Xu, and J. Liang, "A deep reinforcement learning framework for the financial portfolio management problem," in arXiv preprint arXiv: 1706.10059, 2017

[36] Musciotto (2018) F. Musciotto, L. Marotta, J. Piilo, and R. N. Mantegna, "Long-term ecology of investors in a financial market," Palgrave Communications, vol. 4, no. 1, pp. 1-12, 2018.

[37] Liu (2018) Y. Liu, W. Zhang, S. Pan, Y. Li, and Y. Chen, "Analyzing the robotic behavior in a smart city with deep enforcement and imitation learning using iort," Computer Communications, vol. 150, pp. 346-356, 2020.

[38] Robin (2012). T. Robin and M. Bierlaire, "Modeling investor behavior," Journal of Choice Modelling, vol. 5, no. 2, pp. 98-130, 2012

[39] Ho (2017). J. Ho and S. Ermon, "Generative adversarial imitation learning," in Advances in Neural Information Processing Systems, 2016, pp. 4565-4573.

[40] Barber (2013). B. M. Barber and T. Odean, "The behavior of individual investors," in Handbook of the Economics of Finance. Elsevier, 2013, vol. 2, pp. 1533-1570.

[41] Beschwitz (2020). B. von Beschwitz and *M. Massa*, "Biased short: Short sellers' disposition effect and limits to arbitrage," Journal of Financial Markets, vol. 49, p. 100512, 2020.

[42] Financial studies (2007). ——, "All that glitters: The effect of attention and news on the buying behavior of individual and institutional investors," The review of financial studies, vol. 21, no. 2, pp. 785-818, 2007.

[43] Grinblatt (2009). M. Grinblatt and M. Keloharju, "Sensation seeking, overconfidence, and trading activity," The Journal of Finance, vol. 64, no. 2, pp. 549-578, 2009.

[44] Starmer (2000). C. Starmer, "Developments in non-expected utility theory: The hunt for a descriptive theory of choice under risk," Journal of economic literature, vol. 38, no. 2, pp. 332-382, 2000.

[45] Hussein (2017). A. Hussein, M. M. Gaber, E. Elyan, and C. Jayne, "Imitation learning: A survey of learning methods," ACM Computing Surveys (CSUR), vol. 50, no. 2, p. 21, 2017.

Chapter 8

Dealing with Unforeseen Circumstances. Implication of Risk Management in the COVID-19 Public Health Emergency

Jordi Botet

Abstract

Any production plant can be affected by a disaster. Emergency management plans are the best ally to overcome disasters in an adequate way. The present COVID-19 public health emergency can be assimilated to a disaster because of its effects on production and, thus, it requires a contingency plan too. The purpose of this study is to develop a model of contingency plan based on Risk Management (RM) concepts. The methods and analysis used in this development are based on those proposed in international pharmaceutical guidelines. The author, a consultant of the pharmaceutical industry, uses RM tools to provide a practical roadmap to detect problems and implement consistent palliative solutions in any type of manufacturing plant.

Keywords: Absenteeism, confinement, emergency management plan, FMEA, monitoring, PHA, supply

1. Introduction

1.1 Handling a disaster: "the remedy can be worse than the disease"

Any manufacturing site can be affected by a disaster, caused either by natural phenomena (flood, earthquake, fire, landslide, typhoon, tsunami, etc.) or by people (theft, arson, terrorism, vandalism, etc.).

Experience demonstrates that in the situation of stress, which follows a disaster, people are prone to take wrong decisions that could even aggravate the consequences of the incident.

Mismanagement can be avoided if a site has previously developed an "emergency management plan", intended as a roadmap for the satisfactory treatment of a given incident and for preventing the implementation of arbitrary measures.

This study develops a model of rationale to prepare a hands-on plan based on risk management.

1.2 COVID-19, another kind of disaster

A new single-strain positive (+) RNE virus, belonging to the Coronaviridae family, was detected in 2019. It was called SARS-CoV-2 and the respiratory disease that it causes became known as COVID-19 (Coronavirus Disease 2019) [1].

The dissemination of this virus on a planetary scale has created a global situation of "Public Health Emergency by COVID-19", which we will shorten in PHEC-19 [2].

Although we cannot anticipate the evolution and the final consequences of this pandemic, we already know that it has dramatically upset human activities in a completely unexpected way and we can consider it another type of disaster for many manufacturing plants that were forced to manage a problem for which they were not prepared.

We are going to analyze how PHEC-19 can affect the functionality of manufacturing plants and propose a management model derived from the general model proposed for disaster handling.

2. Methodology, the risk management model

When taking decisions, our aim is to take the right ones. However, because of human limitations in terms of information, knowledge, skills, etc., this is easier said than done and, thus, we are obliged to be pragmatic and "take as little risk of being wrong as possible". To meet this end we use risk management (RM), which is defined as the process of assessing, controlling, communicating and reviewing risks affecting the object of study [3].

We speak of quality risk management (QRM) when risk management focuses on protecting the quality of the products.

As shown in **Figure 1**, any RM process starts by defining the object of study or "action field" (item, procedure, unit) and then, getting as much as possible

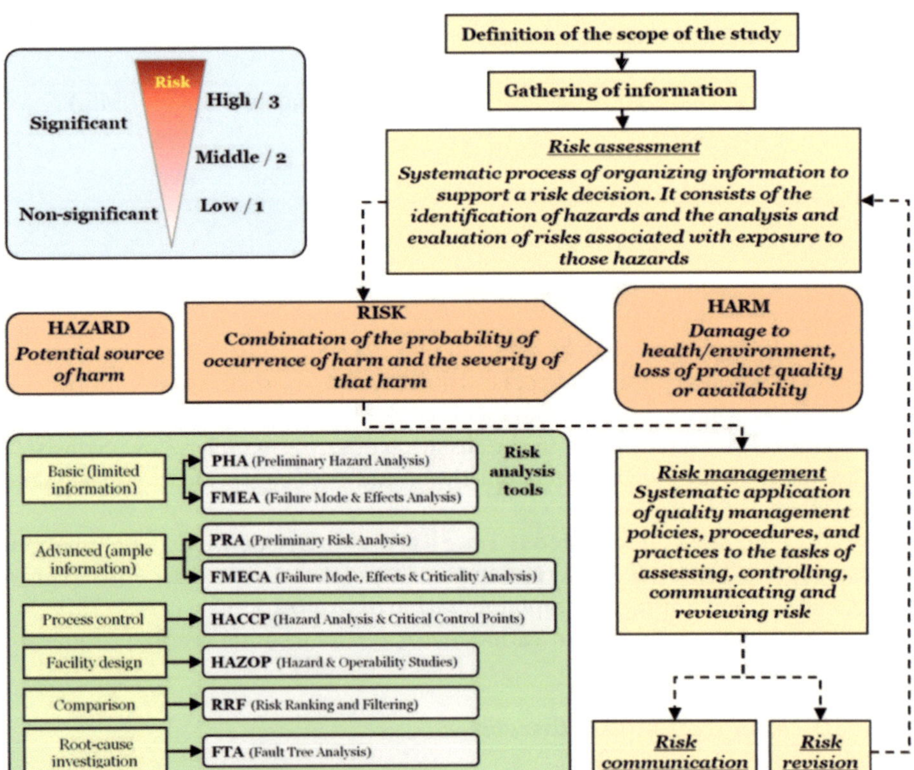

Figure 1.
RM: concepts and organization.

information on it. With this information and some amount of experience, it is possible to detect potential problems (hazards or failure modes) and assess their respective level of significance or criticality.

Risk analysis tools facilitate the organization and assessment of the existing data. The objective is to be able to list the critical hazards or failure modes that require control actions. Those considered non-critical, because of their low level of significance, can be left aside and, thus, we can concentrate our resources and efforts to manage the critical ones.

This process is a cyclical one, because the objects of study can be subjected to technological and methodological improvements or regulatory amendments, which can modify our risk assessment and, thus, affect risk management. In the lower part of **Figure 1** are shown different tools that we can use in risk analysis. All are perfectly valid, although they provide the best performance when used in the most appropriate manner. It is important to keep in mind that they are not miraculous weapons that reveal to us what we do not know. They only organize the information we already have [3].

The level of knowledge and experience determines, in general, the worth of the risk assessment and, in particular, the accuracy of the determination of risk. As it is well known, this can be done either qualitatively or quantitatively. If there are enough data, a quantitative risk estimation is, evidently, preferable, but if this is not the case, a qualitative estimate will do. We should bear in mind that "inventive determination" of risk values does not help and can mislead. It is also possible that as our analysis progresses we get more information, allowing more accurate risk assessments. In all this process, common sense is a very valuable ally.

Regarding risk analysis tools, there is a certain tendency to assimilate risk analysis to Failure Mode, Effects & Criticality Analysis (FMECA) and to privilege this tool in an abusive way. FMECA is an excellent tool for well-known processes and items, because it allows quantifying the risk, and this is a powerful ally in case of continual improvement, where it visualizes the evolution, which is achieved. However, it is easy to come to too subjective risk assessments when applying FMECA to situations for which there is little knowledge and experience [4, 5].

In emergency situations, which are by definition little known, we propose to analyze risk by using simpler tools such as Primary Hazard Analysis (PHA) or Failure mode and effects analysis (FMEA) and to appraise it qualitatively at two levels: "low" (insignificant or non-critical) and "high" (significant or critical).

Table 1 shows a model of chart for PHA. As we can see, the first column serves to indicate the item that is studied. Then, in the second column are listed all the possible hazards that loom on the item. In the following columns are described the possible causes and effects of the identified hazards. With the information written in the former four columns, it is possible to assess the importance of the hazards. If they are deemed significant, it is necessary to take actions, which are described in the last column.

Item	Hazard	Cause	Effect	Assessment	Actions

Table 1.
Example of PHA table.

Process stage	Failure mode	Cause	Effect	Assessment	Actions

Table 2.
Example of FMEA table.

Table 2 shows a model of chart for FMEA. The first column serves to indicate the process stage that is studied. Then, in the second column are enumerated all the possible modes of failure. The following columns are the same that we described above for PHA.

As one can see, both tools are similar, although FMEA focusses on processes, whereas PHA is more general and centers on items.

The main obstacle to overcome while using these tools is to be able to detect all existing hazards or failure modes.

When using PHA, there is no general rule for determining the possible hazards. Each case has a particular approach and it is necessary to use a comprehensive rationale to determine hazards and not to leave aside any of them. Below, are given some practical examples of how to tackle this issue.

Instead, it is possible to say that FMEA is more straightforward, because the key-element for the analysis of a process is its flowchart, which decomposes the process in stages. Then, each stage is studied in order to identify possible failure modes.

PHA and FMEA contain columns intended for the examination of "causes" and "effects". However, they are not always necessary, as shown in the examples that we provide below. When you are assessing, for instance, a disaster, the cause is obvious (the same disaster or an evident consequence of it) and the effect is manifest too (the damage). In these cases, when it is clear that the information contained in one or in both of the columns is worthless, they can be set aside.

3. Application of RM to draft an emergency management plan

It is impossible to draft a detailed contingency plan for incidents that might disrupt normality in a manufacturing plant without taking into account the particular characteristics of the unit, which can be very varied. This is why we just provide an example of the kind of rationale that can be applied to these situations.

In the present example, our object of study will be the effect of a disaster on the production of a manufacturing plant. We are not going to focus on the incident itself but on its effects on manufacturing. Consequently, the factors or elements that we will take into account are the following:

- Documentation: The incident can affect or destroy both paper and computer files.
- Premises and equipment: Here, we include utilities produced in the plant (HVAC, demineralized/purified water, steam, vacuum and compressed air).
- Utilities coming from outside: Electricity, gas and mains water.
- Supplies. Materials, products, chemicals, consumables, etc., which are necessary for manufacturing.

- Personnel
- Production: Processes used for the manufacture of products.
- Quality control (QC)
- Distribution: Shipping and transportation of products.
- Pollution: The disaster can lead to the accidental and uncontrolled liberation of substances to the environment

Next, as we previously said, we detect the hazards that are associated with each factor/element, we assess their significance and finally, we determine the necessary actions.

Table 3 develops these ideas. It goes without saying that real cases require real data and that corrective actions should be carefully described in reports ad hoc.

Factor/ Element	Hazard	Assessment	Actions
Documentation	Loss of data	No effect on production	---
		The loss affects production	If it is possible to recover the missing information, go ahead taking the necessary precautions
			If it is not possible, analyze how to reconstruct necessary information. Draft an action plan regarding data and production recovery
Premises and equipment	Loss of functionality	Evaluate the situation of the site	Develop a recovery plan taking into account affected areas, needed/ existing resources, product priorities, feasibility of outsourcing, etc.
			Try to restart production in the unaffected areas considering possibilities/priorities and outsourcing
Utilities	Lack of supply	Assess delay and consider alternative solutions	Electricity: Restore transmission line or install a generator Water: Restore piping or us a tanker truck for transportation of water Gas: Restore piping. Consider alternative systems or use of cylinders
Supplies	Loss of stock of supplies	Is it possible to restart production with the existing supply stock?	Study the situation and act accordingly. Consider the need of repeating quality controls of the existing supply stock
		Consider delivery time and get new supplies	Draft accordingly a new production schedule
		Will the new supplies suppose a change with respect of those previously received?	In case of change, consider the need of increased analysis and monitoring. If necessary ask for change authorization

Personnel	Has the situation affected the existing personnel?	No	---
		Yes. There is lack of staff	Hire new staff considering training needs and use old trained personnel as supervisors
Production	Does the resumption of production mean changes in methods, monitoring, or data recording?	Can these changes be made acceptable by increased control, monitoring and "concurrent validation"?	Establish a plan to cope with these changes. If necessary ask for change authorization
Quality control			
Distribution	Stock of products affected by the incident	Inspect state of products	Discard products out of specification
			Contact purchasers to evaluate the situation and define production priorities
Pollution	Stocked materials, chemicals or products accidentally liberated to the environment	See the situation and assess severity on a case by case basis	Put in practice control measures (recovery or inactivation and, if required, inform authorities)

Table 3.
Study of effects on products of incidents that disrupt normality.

4. Application of RM to cope with PHEC-19

4.1 An unexpected health emergency

Manufacturing plants were not prepared to face a problem like PHEC-19. The effects of PHEC-19 are less evident that those of a "typical disaster" and this means that problems might pass undetected. We must keep in mind that to have problems is not good, but not to be aware of them is even worst!

Still, the situation created by the COVID-19 is far from being an "unimaginable surprise". In fact, both science and history show that this is a "normal" event.

On the one hand, we know that living beings are constantly evolving and that mutations are the engine of this evolution. A new organism, caused by a mutation, may challenge its environment until the necessary adaptation occurs. Either it loses virulence or the other beings develop defenses against it.

On the other hand, the arrival of a novel infectious agent is nothing new. We can easily remember, for example, what happened several centuries ago when the black plague arrived in Europe. Then, it was an unknown disease, for which there was no treatment, and it caused a very high mortality. This "unforeseen health emergency" came from the Asian steppes, where the causal agent, *Yersinia pestis*, is endemic among groundhogs. The initial diffusers of this bacillus were the Mongol hordes that invaded large areas of the Eurasian continent. Afterwards, however, diffusion took place along trade routes [6].

It is interesting to recall that, in the absence of effective medicines or vaccines, black plague was fought, and finally controlled, by applying confinement and separation measures.

Black plague is just an example but we could mention many other. The human immunodeficiency virus (HIV), which causes acquired immunodeficiency syndrome (AIDS), was also a newcomer in the last years of the 20th century. We also know that in past centuries many people from outside Europe died because of "new" (for them) pathogenic agents diffused by European explorers and colonizers.

4.2 SARS-CoV-2 diffusion

As far as we know, the basic system of SARS-CoV-2 infection is transmission from person to person by air (aerosols) or by direct person-to-person contact. This is why the main preventive action is keeping distance between people, a measure that has a relevant impact on society.

Because of the limited viability of the virus on surfaces, the risk of contamination by coming into contact with an infected surface and then running your hand over your mouth, nose, and possibly eyes is restricted primarily to those surfaces and objects that are very frequently touched by people (e.g. handles, counters, push buttons, etc.).

The incubation period of COVID-19 is estimated between 2 and 14 days [1, 7].

4.3 Practical effects of PHEC-19 on the industry

So far, no case of contamination by the virus of raw materials or products is known [1, 7].

Outside from the first and more evident direct effect of SARS-CoV-2, disease and death of many people, there are other important side effects, which can be grouped in three areas:

- Absenteeism, both because of illness or because people cannot move freely (confinement, travel restrictions, curfew, etc.).

- Breaks of stock, because of absenteeism, which can affect any stage of the supply chain.

- Behavior deviances, for the reason that people are afraid and do not want to be contaminated by the virus. This type of changes can be very varied and have different kinds of effects: shunning of public transportation, staying longer at home, diminishing consumption, etc. [7].

4.4 COVID-19 prevention

Presently, waiting for the practical results of vaccination, we cannot control the virus itself. Thus, the first and paramount defense measure, as far as it is applicable, is the detection and separation of infected people.

Unfortunately, as it is difficult to detect all infected people, because of the lack of testing or symptoms, our basic preventive measures possess passive character [1, 7]:

- Social distancing (minimum approx. 2 m).

- Use of masks.

- Restriction as much as possible on the number of people.

- Frequent disinfection of hands, washing or alcohol-based disinfectants (at least 60%).

- Proper behavior, covering coughing and sneezing.

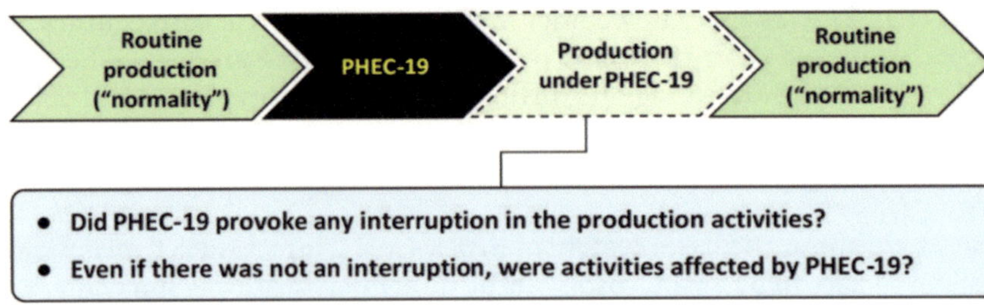

Figure 2.
Effect of PHEC-19 on manufacture.

- Prevent people from sharing objects and surfaces as much as possible.
- Increase cleaning and disinfection practices.
- Apply technical measures where appropriate and possible (increased air renewal rate in rooms, HEPA air filtration, installation of separation screens, etc.).

4.5 PHEC-19 and RM

During this emergency, the industry has two main objectives. On one side, ensuring normal market supply and, on the other, at the same time impede the contamination of personnel and products by SARS-Cov-2.

As shown in **Figure 2**, the objective of the RM process that we are describing is determining if PHEC-19 has led to an interruption or a disturbance of the manufacturing activities and, if this occurred, assess its importance and, accordingly, apply the appropriate corrective actions in order to ensure product quality. Following is described a practical approach to this process.

As, in principle, we can suppose (and hope) that PHEC-19 will be time-limited, the need for revisions can be deemed as restricted. However, any change in the data used for the risk assessment has to be known and evaluated.

5. Practical example of RM for PHEC-19 in a manufacturing unit

The present object of analysis is a manufacturing unit. The situation that we consider is PHEC-19, for which we do not have much information. Thus, PHA is our risk analysis tool of choice.

Here, we are going to use the same approach discussed above for establishing an emergency management plan, as shown in **Figure 3**.

The effect of PHEC-19 in a plant is exerted at two levels. The main one is the lack of staff produced because of increased absenteeism. The second one is the effect of preventive measures to impede virus diffusion.

A manufacturing unit should be seen in terms of a supplying chain. Supplies (materials, products, chemicals, consumables, electricity, drinking water, etc.) arrive and are used in manufacture. Production takes place within premises provided with facilities. Manufacturing processes are monitored. A specific QC department analyzes product samples. Finished products are distributed.

PHEC-19, in principle, should not affect Documentation and this is why here it is not considered. However, some operating procedures might require a review to introduce preventive measures.

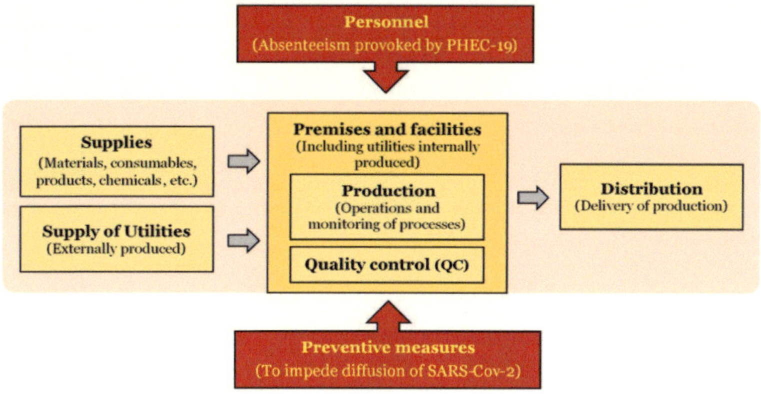

Figure 3.
Possible effects of PHEC-19 in a manufacturing plant.

It is necessary to point out that in the following example we are not interested in production itself but on the effects of PHEC-19 on it.

5.1 Personnel

We should not forget that the PHEC-19 focuses on people because persons diffuse the virus. Neither diseased nor infected persons should be allowed into the manufacturing premises [1].

This means that absenteeism can increase and diminish without prior notice the work force at disposal. It is necessary to ensure that this will not affect the quality standard of production.

5.2 Preventive measures

They can have an indirect effect on manufacturing. On one side the need to limit personnel and to isolate them, can provoke a shortage of personnel, as discussed in the previous bullet. On the other, preventive measures might affect production processes in terms of increased duration (because supplementary sanitization requirements or personnel controls) or modified schedules (e.g. because of lack of catering services).

5.3 Supply of materials, reagents and consumables

Items and utilities supplied to a manufacturing plant can be affected by PHEC-19 and be unavailable or suffer losses of quality.

In fact, as shown in **Table 4**, the problems derived from PHEC-19 can belong to three categories:

- Lack of supply or irregular and delayed arrival of supplies.
- Modification of the attributes of the materials and products supplied. This can be the consequence of using alternative raw materials, of manufacturing under nonstandard conditions, or of diminishing monitoring or controls
- Loss of control on the suppliers (e.g. delayed auditing, reduction of monitoring and analysis)

Hazard	Cause	Effect	Evaluation	Actions
Shortage of supplies	Supplier stopped or reduced production	Production in the plant is disturbed	Study on a case by case basis	Depending on each case: • Stop production if there is enough stock • Reduce production • Establish priorities • Look for another supplier • ...
Delayed supply	Transport unavailable or hindered			
Changes in materials	Supplier switched to other sources of raw materials	Quality of products is jeopardized	Study on a case by case basis	Depending on each case: • Skip the material • Increase monitoring • Increase QC • Look for another supplier • ...
	Supplier unable to meet all requirements			
Unqualified supplier	Supplier could not be adequately approved/ qualified	Materials might be out of specification	Study on a case by case basis	• Well known suppliers could be considered accepted (maybe with additional controls) • Ask for more information and increase controls

Table 4.
PHA of supply of materials, chemicals, products, consumables, etc.

Thus, it is necessary to evaluate in detail each one of these situations to see if they could really affect the quality of the products manufactured in the plant. Changes in attributes could require additional controls to understand their possible effects in properties, stability, etc. The lack of supplies could unleash a chain of shortages.

A regular exchange of information between supplier and manufacturer is essential. The former should understand that changes are likely to affect the manufactured products. The latter should be informed about changes and be aware to detect changes.

5.4 Supply of utilities

We should also consider the possible effect of PHEC-19 on the supply of utilities such as electricity, water or gas, even if this is unlikely (**Table 5**).

5.5 Premises and facilities

In manufacturing plants where sanitization was already a product requirement, the new measures introduced by PHEC-19 do not purport sensible changes. They knew very well that persons are sources of contamination and acted accordingly (use of special attire, sanitization, health control, separation, training, etc.). They also had HVAC systems that controlled the quality of air by ventilation and filtration.

However, in other industrial branches the preventive measures can be more difficult to implement, because personnel is neither familiar nor trained in these procedures. They also do not have HVAC systems prepared for an adequate control of the air quality (**Table 6**).

Have the changes performed in the plant to implement preventive measures affected the approved operational procedures? If the answer is yes, are these changes likely to affect the quality of the products? Logically, the aim is to detect all

Hazard	Cause	Effect	Evaluation	Actions
Power supply cuts	PHEC-19	Production stop	How long will they last?	• Consider alternative supply (if this is feasible) • Use electric generators • Protect equipment from likely voltage changes
Mains water supply cuts	PHEC-19	Depending on water requirements, capacity of storage and alternative sources	How long will they last?	• Consider using other water supplies (wells, streams, tanker trucks, etc.)
Gas supply cuts	PHEC-19	Stoppage of equipment using gas	How long will the restrictions last?	• Consider using gas cylinders or alternative equipment.

Table 5.
PHA of supply of utilities.

Hazard	Cause	Effect	Evaluation	Actions
Uncontrolled changes	Preventive measures to cope with SARS-Cov-2	Is production disturbed?	Yes, if changes affect the approved working procedures	Discover deviations from procedures and evaluate if actions are required
Skipping commissioning/ qualification programs	Lack of staff Technicians cannot travel to the plant	Reliability of equipment under suspicion	Old equipment can be deemed safe based on history and monitoring, but this is not the case with new equipment	Look for alternative ways to ensure the performance of old equipment. For new equipment either wait for the availability of the expected technicians or look for alternative solutions (e.g. on-line communication)
Maintenance program not respected	Lack of staff Technicians cannot travel to the plant	Reliability of equipment under suspicion	Depending on experience	Increase monitoring Skip affected equipment
Calibration program not respected	Lack of staff Technicians cannot travel to the plant	Reliability of equipment under suspicion	Depending on experience	Increase monitoring Skip affected equipment

Table 6.
PHA of premises and facilities.

changes, determine their effects and, if necessary, apply the necessary corrective and preventive measures.

In addition to operational changes, absenteeism and confinement measures may have altered the scheduled maintenance, calibration, commissioning, and qualification/validation programs. Here, cases can be very varied. Usually old equipment is well known and the effect of these alterations can be better assessed. This is not the case with newer equipment, which might require production under increased monitoring or simply, be left aside until situation improves.

5.6 Production

Absenteeism has a direct influence on the manufacturing processes. The lack of personnel and the protective measures for personnel and products can affect production in several modes:

- Modification of the established operating procedures (e.g. to include preventive measures).
- Diminution of the level of in-process control (reduction in the number of samples and in the frequency of sampling).
- Decrease of process monitoring (less intensive surveillance)
- Curtailing the recording of data during the processes.
- Inability of detecting problems in due time.
- Delayed response to problems and deferred application of solutions.

Hazard	Cause	Effect	Evaluation	Actions
Uncontrolled operational changes	Lack of staff Preventive measures to cope with SARS-Cov-2	Approved operational procedures are not faithfully followed	In principle they should be considered significant	Detect deviations from procedures, evaluate their importance and evaluate if actions are required
In process control reduction Decrease of monitoring	Lack of staff	Product quality endangered	In principle it should be considered significant	See if increased QC controls can compensate these deficiencies
Uncomplete process data recording	Lack of staff	Lack of traceability	In principle it should be considered significant	Determine if the missing data affect the procedure used for the approval of the batch of product and/or can be compensated by other means (e.g. QC)
Delayed detection/solution of deviations	Lack of staff	Increased importance of the problems	In principle it should be considered significant	Detect the problem and apply risk analysis to assess its importance and the need of remedial solutions

Table 7.
PHA of production.

Any change affecting operations and its related monitoring has to be detected and assessed (**Table 7**).

Consider the need to inform customers and, if appropriate, authorities, on product supply shortages and quality problems in products.

Revision of production programs and schedules might be inevitable and then it is necessary to establish priorities using RM too, as seen in **Table 5**.

5.7 Quality control (QC)

The QC laboratory is a unit and as such, it shares, in small scale, almost all the problems that we have mentioned for the plant as a whole. The unit needs supplies (reactives, culture media, standards, etc.) and develops operations. Thus, it is necessary to assess all these aspects.

Here absenteeism has a direct influence on quality control products. The lack of personnel and the protective measures for personnel and products can affect analysis in several modes (**Table 8**):

Hazard	Cause	Effect	Evaluation	Actions
Lack of /delayed supplies	Suppliers affected by PHEC-19	Analysis are disturbed	Study on a case by case basis	Depending on each case: • Delay analysis, if possible • Look for another supplier • Look for an alternative method, if there is one
Uncontrolled changes in supplies	Preventive measures to cope with SARS-Cov-2	Production is disturbed	See if they affect the approved analytical procedures	Detect deviations from procedures and evaluate if actions are required
Validation, qualification, maintenance and calibration programs	Lack of staff Technicians cannot travel to the plant	Reliability of equipment and procedures under suspicion	Depending on experience	If analysis cannot be delayed, consider control systems like repeated analyses on the same sample or use of reference standards
Uncontrolled changes in analytical procedures	Lack of staff Preventive measures to cope with SARS-Cov-2	Approved analytical procedures are not faithfully followed	In principle, they are significant	Detect deviations from procedures, evaluate their importance and evaluate if actions are required
Uncomplete analytical data recording	Lack of staff	Lack of traceability	In principle, it is significant	Determine if the missing data affect the procedure used for issuing the analysis certificate and/or if data can be compensated by other means
Delayed detection/ solution of deviations	Lack of staff	Increased importance of the problems	In principle, it is significant	Detect the problem and apply risk analysis

Table 8.
PHA of quality control.

Hazard	Cause	Effect	Evaluation	Actions
Disturbance of distribution logistics	Lack of staff	Delayed delivery	It depends on the product	Increase control on distribution Look for other distributors
	Preventive measures			
Loss of control on the distribution	Lack of staff	Loss of quality	It has to be considered significant	Increase control on distribution Inform clients
	Preventive measures			

Table 9.
PHA of distribution.

- Modification of the established analytical procedures
- Diminution of the level of control (reduction in the number of samples and in the assays)
- Restricting the recording of data during the processes
- Inability of detecting problems in due time
- Delayed response to problems and deferred application of solutions

5.8 Distribution

The objective of a manufacturing plant is not simply releasing production but delivering these products or materials to those who require them. Thus, products and materials should arrive timely and without loss of quality to the intended destinations.

During PHEC-19, absenteeism and, above all, preventive measures (e.g. confinement, curfew, movement limitations) are likely to affect the logistics of distribution and the control on the distribution process. Products that require special conditions during transport (e.g. cold chain) are particularly vulnerable to the distortions caused by PHEC-19 (**Table 9**).

5.9 Pollution

Contamination incidents because of PHEC-19 are very unlikely. However, it is possible that the emergency disrupts services like waste collection and recycling. It is necessary to determine how to increase storage capacity and, maybe, to look for alternative companies.

6. Discussion

Disasters affecting a manufacturing plant can be very varied in both characteristics and effects. This is why they have to be handled at two levels. On one side, it is necessary to detect the damages and understand the problems that they pose. On the other, it is essential to provide solutions to them.

It is evident that concrete actions depend on each type of plant and require specialized knowledge. RM tools, such as those described above, do not increase knowledge but allow for a logical and systematic organization of data.

Manufacturing plants should all possess emergency management plans for emergencies like fire and, if located in accident-prone areas (e.g. seismic activity), for the likely disaster.

As an extension of these plans, any plant should have an agenda to manage unforeseen disasters. RM tools are very useful in these tasks.

Unfortunately, PHEC-19 is a kind of unforeseen disaster, which presents particular characteristics because it has direct and indirect effects on manufacturing production. These effects are not always evident and thus, they require careful analysis.

Emergency management plans based on RM tools can be readily adapted to cope with PHEC-19.

7. Conclusions

In view of what has been written above, it is possible to form the following conclusions:

1. All manufacturing units should prepare an emergency management plan. In the best of cases, they will never use it, but in the event of an emergency, it will facilitate recovery establishing a roadmap and averting disproportionate measures.

2. Risk management (RM) allows for the creation of a rationale to control unknown situations.

3. Risk can only be managed if it has been previously assessed. Risk assessment requires good knowledge of the "object" affected by the emergency and some amount of experience.

4. We have several tools that can facilitate our risk assessment. Anyway, in cases with little experience, such as emergencies, it is preferable to use simpler tools, such as PHA or FMEA.

5. PHA is the tool of choice for items or units, but it requires identifying all existing hazards and this is not an easy task. This is why it is recommended to use a systematic and comprehensive approach.

6. FMEA is the tool of choice for processes. It necessitates an updated flowchart, in order to determine failure modes in each of its steps.

7. Risks can be assessed as significant or critical, which require actions, and non-significant or non-critical, which do not require them.

8. Emergency management plans are a good base to establish a PHEC-19 management plan, but they have to be adapted to the very particular characteristics of it (absenteeism, changes in behavior, social distancing, etc.).

9. The effects of disasters are so evident that to overlook them is very unlikely. However, in the PHEC-19 this is not the case and, thus, it is necessary to analyze accurately the situation.

10. A very important component of PHEC-19 management is to understand how it has affected your manufacturing plant.

Conflict of interest

The author declares no conflict of interest.

Author details

Jordi Botet
GMP Consultant, Barcelona

*Address all correspondence to: jbotetfregola@gmail.com

References

[1] U.S. Food and Drug Administration. Good Manufacturing Practice Considerations for Responding to COVID-19 Infection in Employees in Drug and Biological Products Manufacturing. Guidance for Industry. June 2020.

[2] U.S. Food and Drug Administration. Resuming Normal Drug and2Biologics Manufacturing Operations during the COVID-19 Public Health Emergency. Guidance for Industry. September 2020.

[3] ICH. Quality Risk Management. Q9. Geneva, Switzerland, 2005.

[4] Botet, J. Calidad total farmacéutica: Procesos y controles. Planeta Perú, Lima. 2021.

[5] Botet, J. Good Quality Practice (GQP) in Pharmaceutical Manufacturing: A Handbook". Bentham Science Books, Sharjah, U.A.E. 2015. 490 p. ISBN 978-1-68108-115-1/e-book: 978-1-68108-114-4.

[6] Becker, J. The Lost Country: Mongolia Revealed. Hodder and Stoughton. London, 1992.

[7] U.S. Department of Labor, Occupational Safety and Health Administration. Guidance on Preparing Workplaces for COVID-19. OSHA 3990-03 2020.

Chapter 9

Risk Communication in the Age of COVID-19

Isabell Koinig

Abstract

Literature describes a pandemic as a unique form of health crisis, which requires intensive communicative efforts. The government is a key actor in such situations for it is not only particularly trusted to manage a crisis, but also can obtain compliance on part of the affected population. Scholars agree that health messages are important tools to create awareness for the (health) threat. Particularly during health emergencies, information on which preventive measures should be taken is most valuable. With measures often concerning "disruptive actions", messages must be carefully crafted to counteract negative emotions and controversial arguments. The present chapter presents a checklist for successful campaign design in health risk situations by paying specific attention to COVID-19. To this end, we conduct an extensive literature review and highlight how scientific information should be presented, as well as which message appeals and design features should be utilized to provide the population with targeted and timely information. This is essential against decreasing health literacy rates, which have to be considered in the message design process. To illustrate our case, we will refer to selected national health campaigns which were successfully utilized to manage the risk associated with the COVID-19 pandemic. The chapter will conclude with some limitations and directions for future research.

Keywords: health risk communication, COVID-19, health campaigns, health message design, literature review

1. Introduction

A pandemic presents a special kind of health crisis that requires "collective responsibility" together with changes in communication techniques ([1], p. 515). Previous research has confirmed that communication during a health crisis is crucial [2] in order to create awareness for the existence of a health threat [3, 4]. Hence, health risk messages disseminated during the crisis should be both instructing and adjusting, informing the public of which precautionary measures to take to reduce physical harm and the virus from spreading, while also providing individuals with guidance as to how to deal with the psychological threats of the crisis [5].

In the event of a pandemic, the government becomes a key actor in managing the (health) crisis [6, 7]. Conditioned by high degrees of trust, messages distributed on part of the government can drive the general population to comply with its recommended actions [8–11]. This is the case, since health messages for which the government is the identified source are perceived as both credible and relevant [7, 12], for individuals are convinced that the government can control the crisis [13]. This is in line with previous research, which suggests that controllability and responsibility for the health threat influence the public's risk perceptions and, consequently, responses to these risks [14].

The primary aim of this chapter is to present some guidelines for effective health risk message design, drawing input from established crisis communication literature in general and some recent studies on COVID-19 risk communication in particular. To this end, recommendations regarding message presentation and design will be presented, before limitations and directions for future research are addressed.

2. Communicating during a health crises

Pandemics qualify as a form of health crisis [1]. As crises present situations for which individuals are neither prepared nor possess knowledge of how to deal with the uncertain circumstances [15], they actively seek support and guidance [16, 17]. In order to mobilize the affected public as a partner [18, 19], individuals' need for information must be satisfied. Useful information is usually based on scientific facts. Following the Office and Science and Technology [20], science communication comprises all communication activities between different stakeholder groups, and, as in the case of a health crisis, takes place between "the government and the public". In line with Burns et al. [21], one of the many objectives of science communication is to raise awareness for and create familiarity with new aspects of science. Consisting of three separate processes – i.e. communication, consultation and participation [22] – science communication needs to be designed strategically to fill existing (knowledge) gaps and present information in an appealing manner [23]. Only this way, the public's understanding of science can be assured [21][1].

Media messages afford individuals with instruction and, thus, present respondents' primary sources of information in crises [26–28]. Message credibility and trust is elevated, if the government is the identified source [12, 29], highlighting its central role in the crisis management process [6, 7]. On the one hand, it can help sensitize people for the risks associated with the crisis and, on the other hand, encourage them to adopt preventive measures [30]. For this reason, governmental officials are advised to invest in "well-coordinated health communications" to assist individuals in managing their daily lives in times of upheaval [31]. Previous studies have investigated how the public responds to a government's overall health risk communication, for instance during the avian influenza [12], SARS [32], or Ebola [33]. Findings confirm that the government is perceived to be in the position to mitigate potential health risks [13].

In the event of a crisis, governments are advised to engage in intensified communication [9, 10]. In order to build community trust and engagement, communication must be open and transparent, as well as scientifically based in order to facilitate the public's preparedness to deal with the health threat [9, 16, 34]. This call seems to be expressive of recent social developments towards a knowledge or information society [35]. Thereby, knowledge (re)production centers on documented scientific knowledge (e.g., scientific findings), which no longer solely has its origin in natural sciences but is also based on social sciences [29]. Moreover, this kind of knowledge is increasingly discussed in the media. While science communication is concerned with raising awareness for and creating familiarity with new aspects

[1] The arguments presented in this chapter build on a "Public Understanding of Science" and "Public Awareness of Science", both of which attest to the general public's attitudes, behaviors, or opinions towards science and scientific knowledge [24, 25].

of science (as part of a "Public Understanding of Science" and "Public Awareness of Science", [24, 25]), messages disseminated during any (health) crisis need to be designed strategically to present information in an appealing manner in order to draw respondents to (scientific) message content [21].

3. Health campaigns in crisis situations

Effective risk communication is a requirement in case of health emergencies and crises [2] and can assist the public in managing the crisis [36]. Health crises, including epidemics and pandemics, do not present an exception to this trend. For this reason, governments throughout the world heavily depend on health campaigns, described as "a systematic effort to change health behaviors (or attitudes and beliefs about health and/or social and environmental conditions that mediate health behaviors) within a target population of people who are at risk for a health problem or problems" [37]. Health messages by the government are also known as Public Service Announcements (PSAs, [38]). Contrary to traditional advertising messages, these materials set out to change individual behaviors. For this reason, they have been commonly used in health crises [39].

With PSAs appealing to individuals to change their behaviors and instructing them on how to achieve these proposed behavioral changes, they are in line with health campaigns' three communicative objectives: awareness, instruction or persuasion [37, 40]. In case of a health crisis, health campaigns primarily intend to raise awareness for the severity of the threat amongst the affected population and offer instruction to individuals on how to utilize self-protective measures [41, 42]. As such, PSAs appeal to individuals' self-efficacy [16, 43, 44]. For instance, health messages spread during the H1N1 influenza emphasized the need to take up hygiene measures, such as "hand washing, sanitizer use, covering of coughs and sneezes, and staying at home" ([16]: p. 5). Similar message content was also employed as part of national COVID-19 health campaigns.

Albeit different campaign themes exist, amongst them community building [16], messages typically center on risk reduction strategies [5, 30]. Particularly during health emergencies, information on which preventive measures should be taken is valuable [45]. These measures, for instance, could be nonpharmaceutical interventions (NPIs), which are nation-wide actions proposed by the government to resolve the health crisis [31]. NPIs are useful in controlling the pandemic and are, thus, often labeled "community mitigation strategies". With measures often concerning "disruptive actions" ([44], p. S2), individuals are forced to reconfigure their daily lives and routines [46]. For this reason, health risk messages must be carefully designed to prevent controversial arguments and negative emotions from surfacing [19, 47, 48].

Campaigns advocating NPIs rely on media messages to reach diverse publics in crisis situations [49]. While an increasing amount of research is available on how health messages are used to create awareness amongst the population during risk situations [33, 50–53]. In this chapter we review articles pertaining to health risk message design and focus on the special case of pandemics and emerging infectious diseases [8].

4. Method

The purpose of this paper is to present the cumulated results of an excessive literature review, looking at propositions for and examples of health risk messages disseminated during previous epidemics and pandemics, as well as during COVID-19. Hence, this review will only include articles from the field of risk communication and health communication which were released between 2000 and 2020, even though parallels to messages addressing ongoing pandemics, such as HIV/AIDS and Cholera, can be found.

We used keywords such as risk, health risk, risk communication, health communication, epidemic, pandemic and a combination thereof to compose our sample. With this scope in mind, we conducted a search using national library databases. We covered the major journals in strategic communication, risk communication, and health communication, such as *The Journal of Risk Research, Environmental Research, The Journal of Business Research, The Journal of Public Relations Research, Public Relations Review, The European Journal of Communication, Public Health, Health Communication, The Journal of Health Communication, Health Education and Behavior, The Journal of Allergy and Clinical Immunology, The Journal of Communication in Healthcare, The Journal of Health Management, The American Journal of Public Health, The Journal of Urban Health* and *Public Understanding of Science.* From these sources, we limited our selection to articles dealing with any type of health crisis, including Zika, Ebola, H1N1, the avian influenza and COVID-19. We screened them to a list of 115 pertinent references on health risk communication and message design, which constituted our sample.

With the above considerations we have now summed up some recommendations for designing health risk messages. For government officials, it is now of great interest to learn more about how health risk messages can be designed to benefit not only their own agenda, but also whole populations affected by crisis situations. After reviewing relevant (and recent) literature, it becomes obvious that scholars have devoted their research to studying communication during crisis situations in detail. In the following, several recommendations for designing and drafting health risk messages will be presented.

5. Recommendations for designing health risk messages

5.1 Be open and transparent

The availability of timely and transparent information allows the public to derive at a realistic assessment of the health threat [3, 4, 54]. Building on previous research, messages disseminated in times of disruption should "[e]mphasize the rationale and importance of adherence to public health measures that some people may consider intrusive (e.g., quarantine)" (US Department of Health and Human Services 2008). Providing a solid reasoning is seen as paramount, given that in recent years, individuals trust in the validity of scientific findings has decreased considerably [55]. Hence, PSAs must address the necessity for specific crisis mitigation strategies and actions.

5.2 Focus on relevant message content

Experts have determined that ensuring public access to information – and thus engaging in a process of constant communication – is seen as essential in crisis situations [56]. Thereby, different forms of information need to be distinguished: instructing information, preventive information, and reactive information [57]. Instructing information covers three areas: information on the pandemic, the public's primary needs, and precautionary measures [57]. Through preventive information, public opinion regarding the crisis is sensitized, whilst through reactive information,

Figure 1.
Austrian PSAs advising grandparents to refrain from visiting their grandchildren (left) and social distancing (right). (Source: https://www.bmkoes.gv.at/).

the affected population is informed about the crisis progression, and a potential panic and the spread of rumors can be prevented [1]. *For instance, public health campaigns in Austria, Australia and the U.S. (New York) highlighted the necessity to either stay at home, socially distance or wear masks. For instance, the example in* ***Figure 1*** *emphasizes the necessity to cut back on visits from grandparents or social distancing.*

5.3 Present information consistently and "straight to the point"

In the process of encouraging individuals to follow the proposed preventive actions [58–60], information should be presented in a straight-forward manner [16] and in "one voice". Moreover, messages should use simple language [61], and be consistent in terms of message content, as inconsistency can lead to confusion and undesired health outcomes: "A well-crafted national message [has] the potential to build unity around the goal of defeating the virus through behavior change, preferably with clear, unambiguous recommendations of what actions to take" ([61], 1736). *For example, when the crisis first surfaced, the Austrian government stressed the importance of staying home; after the first lockdown, when social distancing was in order, the campaign commonly referenced the baby elephant as a metaphor to remind individuals to keep their distance (of 1.5 m; see* ***Figure 2****).*

5.4 Appeal to individuals' self-efficacy

According to Fishbein and Ajzen [62], effective communication should stress which behaviors have to be changed, further providing the public with clear instruction as to how this change can be obtained [3]. Therefore, message should appeal to individuals' self-efficacy [63, 64]. Self-efficacy is activated if identification with message content is high [43, 44]. Clear communication can boost individual self-efficacy and help mitigate the risks associated with the health threat [61]. If individuals feel empowered, this can then improve the relationship between the public and the government lastingly [10]. *Governments throughout the world familiarized individuals with how they could contribute to preventing the virus from spreading, e.g. through personal hygiene, reducing their social contacts, or self-isolating. Examples of Australian campaign resources are presented in* ***Figure 3****.*

Figure 2.
Austrian PSAs featuring the baby elephant. (Source: https://www.bmkoes.gv.at/).

Figure 3.
Australian PSAs presenting risk mitigation strategies. (Source: https://www.health.gov.au/resources/).

5.5 Align message content with social norms

As individual behavior is influenced by social norms, i.e. how people in one's immediate environment react [65], health communication messages should promote these norms [29, 39], which can induce behavioral change. Besides the relevance of collective norms[2] [67], norms that require personal investment (e.g., social distancing, personal hygiene) are presumed to predict behavioral intentions even more strongly [68]. *Apart from stressing individual benefits, governments also highlighted how individual actions would contribute to the overall social good (e.g., "Let's be COVIDSAFE together" in Australia or "Because your mask doesn't protect you. It protects me" as part of the Mask Up America Campaign; see* ***Figure 4****).*

5.6 Use prosocial appeals

The risks associated with any crisis have been renowned to elicit negative emotions in individuals [69], further influencing their risk perceptions [70–72]. Therefore, the negative emotions associated with the pandemic should be

[2] Collective norms describe "prevailing codes of conduct that either prescribe or proscribe behaviors that members of a group can enact" ([66], p. 29).

Figure 4.
Prosocial Appeal as part of #MaskUpAmerica. (Source: https://www.idsociety.org/public-health/covid-19/)

Figure 5.
Austrian PSAs emphasizing prosocial and collective action, such as staying at home if feeling unwell (left) and shopping for at risk groups (right). (Source: https://www.bmkoes.gv.at/).

counterbalanced with positive emotional appeals [29, 73]. This, for instance, can be achieved through "prosocial motivation" or a collective orientation, in the course of which the positive impact of a certain behavior on the community elicits hope in recipients [74, 75]. Likewise, higher intentions to comply with proposed behaviors can be achieved if prosocial appeals are used [76]. *In addition to the examples mentioned above, also the Austrian and German government emphasized the need for collective action (e.g. Austria's Schau auf Dich, Schauf auf Mich campaign and Germany's #besonderehelden video campaign; see* ***Figure 5****).*

5.7 Emphasize the necessity of proposed measures

Besides stressing the necessity for engaging in selected NPIs, messages also must point out why it is essential to do so [3, 77]. This builds upon previous research, which has demonstrated that increased efficacy levels are reliable in predicting individual behavior [78]. One potential way, for instance, could be to increase the perceived

Figure 6.
#MaskUpAmerica featuring Everyday Heroes. (Source: https://www.governor.ny.gov/).

relevance of message content or the similarity to the source, which have proven successful in mitigating negative message consequences [79–81], e.g., the spread of the virus.

5.8 Evoke positive emotions

Individuals' risk perceptions usually incorporate emotional aspects [53] that have been found to drive individuals to take up protective behaviors in crisis situations [82–84]. Hence, the use of (positive) emotion has been found to be conducive to behavioral change [85], also in times of crisis, where emotions have been found to drive (health) risk message reception, e.g., by impacting individuals' willingness and motivation to take up precautionary measures (e.g., [86–89]). *Positive emotions can be evoked, for instance, by presenting individuals as heroes, as it is the case in both the German public health campaign and the New York #maskupamerica campaign (see* ***Figure 6****).*

5.9 Emotionalize message content

While some audiences seek out facts and scientific information, others are more drawn to emotional and personalized message content [37]. Thereby, message appeals describe promotional cues that are used to drive both recipients' interest and attention [90]. While i*nformative appeals* utilize rational arguments in a matter-of-fact presentation [91], e*motional appeals,* on the other hand, are based on images or videos to facilitate comprehension amongst message recipients [92]. Emotional appeals allow organizations to gain support from the affected public in times of crisis [93–95], and researchers have identified a number of advantages associated with the use of an emotional message presentation, such as an increased "attention to messages, recall, positive attitudes, and compliance to recommended behaviors" ([37]: p. 249). *In this context, stories or personal recounts are recommended, and have been employed in numerous countries, such as Austria, the U.S. and Germany.*

Figure 7.
Austrian PSAs featuring individuals in their domestic settings. (Source: https://www.governor.ny.gov/).

5.10 Employ strong visuals

Health risk communication's reliance on an emotional (visual) presentation might stem from the fact that visuals drive risk perceptions more than factual information [96, 97]. In case of strong emotional reactions, individuals' likelihood to ignore factual information is increased [98, 99]. Therefore, the use of pictures is recommended and can increase the likelihood of a message receiving fixation [100]. *For example, the Austrian government decided to feature individuals in their domestic environments when encouraging them to stay at home (see **Figure 7**).*

5.11 Create Identification

As pandemics evoke negative emotional responses – first and foremost, fear [29] - that affect whole populations, crisis communication itself should not only center on people [101] but also familiarize them with proper behavior, e.g., by featuring role models [102, 103]. If identification is high, people are driven into compliance, which can positively effect crisis management [104, 105]. *Governments have featured a number of role models in their campaigns, including health-care workers (U.S.), or celebrities (as narrators in the U.S.).*

Figure 8.
Austrian PSAs with strong visuals but low in complexity. (Source: https://www.governor.ny.gov/).

5.12 Feature community members

Besides medical experts or celebrities [39], a number of studies has highlighted the importance of featuring nonpolitical sources, whose statements are perceived as credible and trustworthy [77, 106, 107]. For instance, people have been found to easily relate to individuals who are similar to them (i.e. "community ambassadors"; [16]). Previous research has been able to demonstrate that similarity with the testimonial featured in a promotional or risk message can be a useful tool to increase message effectiveness [108, 109], as well as message credibility and acceptance [110]. As community members resemble real people, individuals are also more likely to follow their lead and take up proposed behaviors [111]. *This strategy has been employed in several countries, including the U.S., Germany, and Austria (for examples, see **Figure 7** above).*

5.13 Take individual health literacy levels into account

Messages also must be reflective of individuals' respective health literacy levels[3] [48, 72, 114]. Numerous studies determined individual's health literacy is rather low [48, 114–116]. "Barriers that keep the people we want to become more scientifically literate from understanding what we do [is that] they do not know the terminology". For this reason, messages must ensure that people do not feel overwhelmed with the information they are presented with. *Governments seem to have taken this advice to heart by predominantly broadcasting simple messages, such as it was the case in Austria, Germany, and Australia.*

5.14 Reduce message complexity

While low health literacy levels can result in unintended health outcomes [51], messages low in complexity can enhance both individuals' message processing and willingness to act on the recommendations presented therein [51]. More complex messages, however challenge individuals as they require more elaborate health literacy skills for individuals to not only understand the message, but also align message content with existing knowledge [117]. *Examples for reduced and simplified messages can be found for Germany, Austria, as well as for UNICEF and FIAF, who heavily relied on visual (instructive) information. For examples from Austria, see **Figure 8**.*

5.15 Present information in dual mode

Health campaigns have been found to increasingly rely on videos [118], which present information in dual form, meaning in both textual and visual form. In the first instance, facts can be both presented in written and auditory form (voiceover or narration) and might be supported by illustrations and pictograms (e.g., [51]). Narration particularly caters to individuals with low health literacy levels, who can process spoken information more readily than written information [119]. Personal stories that are directly linked to the health-cause and narrated by testimonials, can increase identification and message impact [108, 110]. Videos' dual-mode presentation information processing and message recall [120, 121]. *For example, campaign videos in Germany and Austria were dubbed, while textual information was complemented with pictograms in Austria and Australia (see **Figure 9**).*

---

[3] In general, *health literacy* is defined as an individual's ability to process and comprehend health information [112]. A more broadly speaking, health literacy encompasses individuals' reading and writing skills, their ability to distinguish relevant from irrelevant information as well to critically analyze and reflect upon the information retrieved [113].

Figure 9.
Austrian PSAs utilizing information and pictograms. (Source: https://www.governor.ny.gov/).

5.16 Tailor information to individual needs

If individuals act upon the proposed actions by the government depends on the impact – both in economic and social terms – associated with the health risk [18, 44], as well as their ability to make sense of the information they are presented with [122]. Governments are, therefore, advised to tailor their communications to individual information needs [123–125]. *In Austria, for example, campaign messages differed, depending on the message's designated target group (e.g., elderly at-risk people, general population, etc.).*

5.17 Utilize switch buttons

According to previous research, individual message preferences vary, and different message formats are preferred [16, 54]. For this reason, messages must be provided where individuals are likely to encounter them [126, 127], taking generational differences and media preferences into consideration. *For instance, campaign messages in Austria and Germany concluded with links to the Government's website, where additional information could be retrieved.*

6. Conclusion

If crisis strikes, government officials are called upon to act quickly and engage in increased communication [6, 7]. The present study reviewed some existing literature and combined it with insights from health communication, in an attempt to provide some recommendations for effective COVID-19 health risk message design. This is crucial, for individuals' risk perceptions have been found to predict their likelihood of engaging in preventive behaviors, also in the case of pandemics [82] and in the case of emerging infectious diseases (EID) [8].

At any time during the crisis, message complexity should be reduced [122, 128], requiring lesser cognitive capacities on behalf of individuals to process message [51]. This is specifically important, if scientific evidence is presented. Only if message match the audience's cognitive capacities, individuals can play an active role in managing health risks. Moreover, visual (affective) stimuli can elicit emotions in individuals, and enhance message acceptance and learning, specifically if new information is presented [121].

Communication strategies are further recommended to take audiences' attitudes and inherent needs for comprehensive and instructional information – which appeals to their self-efficacy [43] – into account [129]. Hence, government officials are advised to optimize message presentation, especially when the problem or risk addressed in this message affects whole populations. As such, it is important to increase both the identification with and the relevance of message content, evoking individuals into compliance. In order to increase identification and create familiarity with proper crisis behavior, communication should center on the affected population [18, 80, 104] and feature community members [43]. In order to increase message comprehensibility, information needs to be presented in simple language and in a straight-forward-manner, while also reducing message complexity [100, 120], e.g., through the inclusion of visuals. If message content is too complex, effectiveness can be enhanced by presenting information in dual form, i.e. by combining visual/auditory and textual elements [51]. For instance, narration can increase a message's persuasive impact [130], while also aiding respondents' identification with the message [131]. A dual-more presentation can thus help overcome respondents' potential resistance to message content [132], while also favoring those with low health literacy rates – a problem, that still challenges health communication in the age of COVID-19 [48, 114].

There are several limitations to the list of recommendations presented herein. Even though the study is based on a comprehensive literature review, it only focused on research articles from the field of strategic communication and health communication. Moreover, the national campaign examples only offer insights into the communication strategies utilized by the German, Austrian, U.S. American (New York) and Australian government. PSAs might be conceptualized differently in other parts of the world. Future research should also emphasize how campaign messages have changed as the COVID-19 pandemic progressed.

Acknowledgements

The author acknowledges the financial support by the University of Klagenfurt.

Author details

Isabell Koinig
University of Klagenfurt, Klagenfurt, Austria

*Address all correspondence to: isabelle.koinig@aau.at

References

[1] Saliou, P. (1994). Crisis communication in the event of a flu pandemic. European Journal of Epidemiology *10,* 515-517.

[2] Reynolds, B. (2007). Crisis Emergency Risk Communication Pandemic Influenza. Retrieved from https://emergency-origin.cdc.gov/cerc/resources/pdf/cerc-pandemicflu-oct07.pdf

[3] Covello, V.T. (2003). Best practices in public health risk and crisis communication. *Journal of Health Communication 8(supplement 1),* 5-8.

[4] Tinker, T.L., Zook, E., & Chapel, T.J. (2001). Key challenges and concepts in health risk communication: perspectives of agency practitioners. Journal of Public Health Management and Practice *7(1),* 67-75.

[5] Coombs, W.T. (2007a). *Ongoing crisis communication: Planning, managing, and responding.* 2nd ed. Thousand Oaks, CA: Sage.

[6] Shuaib, F., Gunnala, R., Musa, E.O., Mahoney, F.J., Oguntimehin, O., Nguku, P.M. et al. (2014). Ebola virus disease outbreak – Nigeria: July – September 2014. MMWR: Morbidity and Mortality Weekly Report *63(39),* 867-872.

[7] Wabba, A.P. (2014). Statement by the medical and health workers' Union of Nigeria regarding the Ebola Virus Disease (EVD) outbreak in west Africa. Retrieved from https://www.world-psi.org/sites/default/files/attachment/news/nigeria_mhwunstatement_ebola2014.pdf

[8] Gesser-Edelsburg, A., Stolero, N., Mordini, E., Billingsley, M., James, J.J., & Green, M.S. (2015). Emerging Infectious Disease (EID) Communication during the 2009 H1N1 Influenza Outbreak: Literature Review (2009-2013) of the Methodology Used for EID communication analysis. Disaster Medicine and Public Health Preparedness *9(2),* 199-206.

[9] Menon, K.U. (2008). Risk Communications: In Search of a Pandemic. Annals of the Academy of Medicine Singapore *37(6),* 525-534.

[10] Paton, D. (2008). Modeling societal resilience to pandemic hazards in Auckland. GNS Science Report *13,* 23.

[11] Tay, J., Ng, Y.F., Cutter, J., & James, L. (2010). Influenza (H1N1-2009) Pandemic in Singapore – Public Health Control Measures Implemented and Lessons Learned. Annals of the Academy of Medicine Singapore *39,* 313-324.

[12] Li, R., Xie, R., Yang, C. & Frost, M. (2016). Perceptions on the risk communication strategy during the 2013 avian influenza A/H7N9 outbreak in humans in China: a focus group study. WPSAR *7(2),* 1-8.

[13] Goodwin, R. & Sun, S. (2014). Early responses to H7N9 in Southern Mainland China. BMC Infectious Diseases *14(1),* 8.

[14] Jin, Y., Iles, I., Austin, L., Liu, B. & Hancock, G. (2020). The Infectious Disease Threat (IDT) Appraisal Model: How perceptions of IDT 310 predictability and controllability predict individuals' responses to risks. International Journal of Strategic Communication *14(4),* 246-271.

[15] Pfefferbaum, B. & North, C.S. (2020). Mental health the COVID-19 pandemic. The New England Journal of Medicine *383(6)*, 510-512.

[16] Gray, L., MacDonald, C., Mackie, B., Paton, D., Johnston, D., & Baker, M.G. (2012). Community responses

to communication campaigns for influenza A (H1N1): a focus group study. BMC Public Health *12*. doi: 10.1186/1471-2458-12-205.

[17] Rains, S.A., Crane, T.E., Iyengar, S., Merchant, N., Oxnam, M., Sprinkle, M.M. & Ernst, K.C. (2020). Community-Level Health Promotion during a Pandemic: Key Considerations for Health Communication. *Health Communication 35(14),* 1747-1749.

[18] Blendon, R.J., Koonin, L.M., Benson, J.M. et al. (2008). Public response to community mitigation measures for pandemic influenza. Emerging Infectious Diseases *14,* 778-786.

[19] Rasmussen, S.A., Jamieson, D.J., & Bresee, J.S. (2008). Pandemic influenza and pregnant women. Emerging Infectious Diseases *14*, 95-100.

[20] OST. (2000). Science and the Public: A review of science communication and public attitudes to science in Britain. Public Understanding of Science, *10*(3), 315-330. https://doi.org/10.3109/a036873

[21] Burns, T.W., O'Connor, D.J. & Stocklmeyer, S.M. (2003). Science Communication: a contemporary Definition. Public Understanding of Science *12,* 183.

[22] Rowe, G. and Frewer, L. (2005). A typology of public engagement mechanisms. Science Technology and Human Values 30, 251-290.

[23] Fischhoff, B. & Scheufele, D.A. (2012). The Science of Science Communication. PNAS *116(16),* 7632-7633.

[24] Bodmer, W. (2010). Public Understanding of Science: The BA, the Royal Society and COPUS. Notes and Records of the Royal Society 64S151–S161. http://doi.org/10.1098/rsnr.2010.0035

[25] Bowater, L. & Yeoman, K. (2013). Science Communication: A Practical Guide for Scientists. Oxford: Wiley-Blackwell.

[26] Brug, J., Aro, A.R., Oenema, A., De Zwart, O., Richardus, J., and Bishop, G. (2004). SARS risk perception, knowledge, precautions, and information sources, the Netherlands. Emerging Infectious Diseases *10(8).* 1486-1489. doi: 10.3201/eid1008.040283

[27] Gaglia, M.A., Cook, R.L., Kraemer, K.L., and Rothberg, M.B. (2008). Patient knowledge and attitudes about avian influenza in an internal medicine clinic. Public Health *122(5)*, 462-470.

[28] Paek, H.J., Hilyard, K., Freimuth, V.S., Barge, J.K., & Mindlin, M. (2008). Public support for government actions during a flu pandemic: Lessons learned from a statewide survey. Health Promotion Practice *9(S4),* 60-72.

[29] Van Bavel Baicker, K., Boggio, P.S. et al. (2020). Using social and behavioural science to support COVID-19 pandemic response. Nature – Human Behavior *4,* 460-471. https://doi.org/10.1038/s41562-020-0884-z

[30] Coombs, W.T. (2007b). Protecting organization reputations during a crisis: The development and application of situational crisis communication theory. Corporate Reputation Review, *10(3),* 163-176.

[31] Reynolds, B., & Quinn, S.C. (2008). Effective communication during an influenza pandemic: the value of using a crisis and emergency risk communication framework. *Health Promotion Practice 9(4) – supplement,* 13S-17S.

[32] Lee, K. (2009). How the Hong Kong Government lost the public trust in SARS: Insights for governmental communication in health crisis. Public Relations Review *35,* 74-76.

[33] Nelson, O. & Namtira, B.-J. (2017). Measuring media campaigns effectiveness for environmental health for sustainable development: A Study of Ebola Outbreak in Lagos State, Nigeria. Journal of Health Management *19(4),* 553-562.

[34] Liu, B.F. & Horsely, J.S. (2007). The government communication decision wheel: toward a public relations model for the public sector. Journal of Public Relations Research *19(4),* 377-393.

[35] Sowka A. (2016) *Wissenschaftskommunikation zwischen Sozialforschung und Praxis.* Wiesbaden: Springer. https://doi.org/10.1007/978-3-658-11354-4_3

[36] Reynolds, B. (2006*). Crisis and emergency risk communication: Pandemic Influenza*. Atlanta, GA: CDC.

[37] Wright, K.B., Sparks, L., & O'Hair, H.D. (2008). *Health Communication in the 21st century*. Oxford: Blackwell.

[38] Murry, J.P., Stam, A., & Lastovicka, J.L. (1996). Paid-Versus Donated-Media Strategies for Public Service Announcement Campaigns. Public Opinion Quarterly, *60(1).* 1-29.

[39] Manganello, J., Bleakley, A. & Schumacher, P. (2020). Pandemics and PSAs: Rapidly Changing Information in a new Media Landscape. Health Communication *35(14),* 1711-1714.

[40] Salmon, C., & Atkin, C.K. (2003). Media campaigns for health promotion. In T.L. Thompson, A.M. Dorsey, K.I. Miller, and R. Parrott (ed). *Handbook of Health Communication* (pp. 285-313). Mahwah, NJ: Lawrence Erlbaum.

[41] Covello, V.T. et al. (2001). Risk communication, the West Nile virus epidemic and bioterrorism: responding to the communication challenges posed by the intentional and unintentional release of a pathogen in an urban setting. Journal of Urban Health *78(2),* 382-391.

[42] Fitzpatrick-Lewis, D. et al. (2010). Communication about environmental health risks: a systematic review. Environmental Health *9(1),* 67.

[43] Heymann, D. (2020). COVID-19: what is next for public health? The Lancet *395.*

[44] Vaughan, E. & Tinker, T. (2009). Effective health risk communication about pandemic influenza for vulnerable populations. American Journal of Public Health *99(S2),* 324-332.

[45] Wray, R.J. et al. (2008). Communicating with the public about emerging health threats: lessons from the Pre-Event Message Development Project. American Journal of Public Health 98(12), 2214-2222.

[46] Stephens, K.K., Jahn, J.L.S., Fox, S., Charoensap-Kelly, P., Mitra, R., Sutton, J., Waters, E.D., Xie, B. & Meisenbach, R.J. (2020). Collective sensemaking around COVID-19: Experiences, concerns, and agendas for our rapidly changing organizational lives. Management Communication Quarterly *34(3),* 426-457.

[47] Holmes, B.J. (2008). Communicating about emerging infectious disease: the importance of research. Health, Risk and Society *10,* 349-360.

[48] Paakkari, L. & Okan, O. (2020). COVID-19: health literacy is an underestimated problem. *The Lancet* 5, DOI:https://doi.org/10.1016/S2468-2667(20)30086-4

[49] Nelson, O. (2011). Mass media strategies for creating awareness of breast cancer. Public Knowledge Journal *3(1),* 1-18.

[50] Hendriks, H., van den Putte, B., de Bruijn, G. J., & de Vreese, C. H. (2014). Predicting health: the interplay between interpersonal communication and health campaigns. Journal of Health Communication, *19(5),* 625-636.

[51] Meppelink, C.S., van Weert, J. C.M., Haven, C.J., & Smit, E.G. (2015). The effectiveness of health animations in audiences with different health literacy levels: An experimental study. Journal of Medical Internet Research 17(1), e11. doi: 10.2196/jmir.3979

[52] Moorhead, S.A., Hazlett, D.E., Harrision, L., Carroll, J.K., Irwin, A., & Hoving, C. (2013). A new dimension of health care: systematic review of the uses, benefits, and limitations of social media for health communication. Journal of Medical Internet Research *15(4),* e85.

[53] Freeman, A.L.J., Kerr, J., Recchia, G., Schneider, C.R., Lawrence, A.C.E., Kinikarides, L., Luoni, G., Dryhurst, S., & Spiegelhalter, D.J. (2020). Communicating personalised risks from COVID-19: guidelines from an empirical study. *medRxiv 2020.10.05.20206961;* doi: https://doi.org/10.1101/2020.10.05.20206961

[54] Fischhoff B. (2005). Scientifically sound pandemic risk communication. In D. Kamien (ed.). *McGraw Hill Handbook of Terrorism and Counter-Terrorism*. (p. 14). New York: McGraw Hill.

[55] Browne, M., Thomson, P., Rockloff, M., & Pennycook, G. (2015). Going against the herd: psychological and cultural factors underlying the vaccination confidence gap. PloS One 10(9). https://doi.org/10.1371/journal.pone.0132562

[56] Wallis, P. & Nerlich, B. (2005). Disease metaphors in new epidemics: The UK media framing of the 2003 SARS epidemic. Social Science and Medicine *60(11),* 2629-2639.

[57] Kim, S. & Fisher Liu, B. (2012). Are all Crisis Opportunities? A Comparison of How Corporate and Government Organizations Respond to the 2009 Flu Pandemic. Journal of Public Relations Research *24(1),* 69-85.

[58] Novac, A. (2001). Traumatic stress and human behavior. Psychiatric Times. Retrieved from https://www.psychiatrictimes.com/view/traumatic-stress-and-human-behavior

[59] Seeger, M.W., Sellnow, T.L., & Ulmer, R.R. (2003). *Communication and organizational crisis.* Westport, CT: Praeger.

[60] Wray, R. & Jupka, K. (2004). What does the public want to know in the event of a terrorist attack using plague? Biosecurity and Bioterrorism: Biodefense Strategy, Practice, and Science *2(3),* 208-215.

[61] Noar, S.M. & Austin, L. (2020). (Mis)communicating about COVID-19. Insights from Health and Crisis Communication. Health Communication *35(14),* 1735-1739.

[62] Fishbein, M. & Ajzen, I. (2010). *Predicting and changing behavior: The reasoned action approach.* New York, NY: Taylor & Francis.

[63] Chou, W.-Y. S. & Budenz, A. (2020). Considering Emotion in COVID-19 vaccine communication: addressing vaccine hesitancy and fostering vaccine confidence. Health Communication *35(14),* 1718-1722.

[64] Witte, K. & Allen, M. (2000). A meta-analysis of fear appeals: Implications for effective public health campaigns. Health Education and Behavior *27(5),* 591-615.

[65] Cialdini, R.B. & Goldstein, N.J. (2004). Social influence: compliance and conformity. Annual Review of Psychology 55, 591-621.

[66] Lapinski M.K. & Rimal R.N. (2005). An explication of social norms. Communication Theory *15(2),* 127-147.

[67] Sedlander, E. & Rimal, R.N. (2019). Beyond individual-level theorizing in social norms research: How collective norms and media access affect adolescents' use of contraception. Journal of Adolescent Health *64(4),* 31-36.

[68] Rimal, R.N. & Storey, J.D. (2020). Construction of Meaning during a Pandemic: The Forgotten Role of Social Norms. Health Communication *35(14),* 1732-1734.

[69] Slovic, P., Fischhoff, B. & Lichtenstein, S. (1981). Perceived risk: psychological factors and social implications. *Proceedings of the Royal Society of London. Series A,* Mathematical and Physical Sciences *376(1764),* 17-34.

[70] Abrams, E.M. & Greenhawt, M. (2020). Risk Communication during COVID-19. The Journal of Allergy and Clinical Immunology *8,* 1791-1794.

[71] Slovic, P., Finucane, M.L., Peters, E. & MacGregor, D.G. (2007). The affect heuristic. European Journal of Operative Research *177,* 1333-1352.

[72] Smith, R.D. (2006). Responding to global infectious disease outbreaks: Lessons from SARS on the role of risk perception, communication and management. Social Science and Medicine *63,* 3113-3123.

[73] Lwin, M.O., Lu, J., Sheldekar, A., Schulz, P.J., Shin, W., Gupta, R. & Yang, Y. (2020). Global sentiments surrounding the COVID-19 pandemic on twitter: Analysis of twitter trends. JMIR Public Health and Surveillance *6(2),* e19447. DOI: 10.2196/19447

[74] Jordan, J., Yoeli, E. & Rand, D. (2020). Don't get it or don't spread it? Comparing self-interested versus prosocially framed COVID-19 preventing messaging. *PsyArXiv Preprints.* 10.31234/osf.io/yuq7x

[75] Ojala, M. (2012). Hope and climate change: The importance of hope for environmental engagement among young people. Environmental Education Research *18(5),* 625-642.

[76] Heffner, J., Vives, M. & Feldman Hall, O. (2020). Emotional responses to prosocial messages increase willingness to self-isolate during the COVID-19 pandemic. Personality and Individual Differences *170,* https://doi.org/10.1016/j.paid.2020.110420

[77] Noar, S.M. (2006). A 10-year retrospective of research in health mass media campaigns: Where do we go from here? Journal of Health Communication *11(1),* 21-42.

[78] Avery, E. & Park, S. (2016). Effects of crisis efficacy on intentions to follow directives during crisis. Journal of Public Relations Research *28(2),* 72-86.

[79] Kreuter, M. W., & Wray, R. J. (2003). Tailored and targeted health communication: Strategies for enhancing information relevance. American Journal of Health Behavior, *27*(Suppl. 3), 227-232.

[80] Kreuter, M.W., Green, M.C., Capella, J.N., Slater, M.D., Wise, M.E., Storey, D. et al. (2007). Narrative communication in cancer prevention and control: a framework to guide research and application. Annals in Behavioral Medicine *33,* 221-235.

[81] So, J., & Nabi, R. (2013). Reduction of perceived social distance as an explanation for media's influence on personal risk perceptions: A test of the risk convergence model. Human Communication Research, *39*(3), 317-338.

[82] Bish, A. & Michie, S. (2010). Demographic and attitudinal determinants of protective behaviours during a pandemic: a review. British Journal of Health Psychology *15,* 797-824.

[83] Dryhurst, S., Schneider, C.R., Kerr, J., Freeman, A.L.J., Reccahia, G., van der Bles, A.M., Spielgelhalter, D. & van der Linden, S. (2020). Risk perceptions of COVID-19 around the world. Journal of Risk Research *23(7-8),* 994-1006.

[84] Leppin, A. & Aro, A.R. (2009). Risk perceptions related to SARS and avian influenza: Theoretical foundations of current empirical research. International Journal of Behavioral Medicine *16(1),* 7-29.

[85] Perugini, M. & Bagozzi, R.P. (2001). The role of desires and anticipated emotions in goal-directed behaviours: Broadening and deepening the theory of planned behavior. British Journal of Social Psychology *40(1),* 79-98.

[86] Betsch, C., Ulshöfer, C., Renkewitz, F. & Betsch, T. (2011). The influence of narrative vs. statistical information on perceiving vaccination risks. Medical Decision Making *31(5),* 742-753.

[87] Morgul, E., Bener, A., Atak, M., Akyel, S., Aktas, S., Bhugra, D., Ventriglio, A. & Jordan, T.R. (2020). COVID-19 pandemic and psychological fatigue in Turkey. International Journal of Social Psychiatry. doi: 10.1177/0020764020941889

[88] Qui, J., Shen, B., Zhao, M., Wang, Z., Xie, B. & Yu, Y. (2020). A nationwide survey of psychological distress among Chinese people in the COVID-19 epidemic: Implications and policy recommendations. General Psychiatry *33(2),* doi: 10.1136/gpsych-2020-100213

[89] Wang, C., Pan, R., Wan, X., Tan, Y., Xu, L., Ho, C.S. & Ho, R.C. (2020). Immediate psychological responses and associated factors during the initial stage of the 2019 coronavirus (COVID-19) epidemic among the general population in China. International Journal of Environmental Research and Public Health *17(5)*, 1-25.

[90] Kinnear, T. C., Bernhadt, K. L. & Krentler, K. A. (1995). *Principles of marketing*. 4th ed. New York: Longman.

[91] Aaker, D.A. & Norris, D. (1982). Characteristics of TV Commercials Perceived as Informative. Journal of Advertising Research *22.* 61-70.

[92] Wilson, E.A. & Wolf, M.S. (2009). Working memory and the design of health materials: A cognitive factors perspective. Patient Education and Counseling *74(3),* 318-322.

[93] Dillard, J.P. & Nabi, R.L. (2006). The persuasive influence of emotion in cancer prevention and detection messages. *Journal of Communication 56(supplement 1),* 123-139.

[94] Lang, A. & Yegiyan, N.S. (2008). Understanding the interactive effects of emotional appeal and claim strength in health messages. Journal of Broadcasting and Electronic Media *52(3),* 432-447.

[95] Stephens, L.K. & Malone, P.C. (2009). If the organization won't give us information. The use of multiple new media for crisis technical translation and dialogue. *Journal of Public Relations Research 21,* 229-239.

[96] Loewenstein, G.F., Weber, E.U., Hsee, C.K. & Welch, N. (2001). Risk as Feelings. Psychological Bulletin *127,* 267-286.

[97] Slovic, P, Finucane, M.L., Peters, E., & MacGregor, D.G. (2004). Risk as analysis and risk as feelings: some thoughts about affect, reason, risk and rationality. Risk Analysis *24,* 311-322.

[98] Hsee, C.K. & Rottenstreich, Y. (2004). Music, pandas, and muggers: o the affective psychology of value. Journal of Experimental Psychology (General) *133,* 23-30.

[99] Rottenstreich, Y. & Hsee, C.K. (2001). Money, kisses, and electric shocks: on the affective psychology of risk. P Money, kisses, and electric shocks: on the affective psychology of risk. Psychological Science *12,* 185-190.

[100] Houts, P.S., Doak, C.C., Doak, L.G., & Loscalzo, M. J. (2006). The role of pictures in improving health communication: A review of research on attention, comprehension, recall, and adherence. Patient Education and Counseling *61,* 173-190.

[101] Ratzan, S.C., Sommarivac, S., & Rauh, L. (2020). Enhancing global health communication during a crisis: lessons from the COVID-19 pandemic. Public Health Research & Practice 30(2), https://doi.org/10.17061/phrp3022010

[102] Grant, A.M. and Hofmann, D.A. (2011). It's not all about me: motivating hand hygiene among health care professionals by focusing on patients. Psychological Science 22, 1494-1499.

[103] Feinberg, M. & Willer, R. (2019). Moral reframing: a technique for effective and persuasive communication across political divides. Social and Personality Psychology Compass 13. https://doi.org/10.1111/spc3.12501

[104] Kahan, D.M. et al. (2012). The polarizing impact of science literacy and numeracy on perceived climate change risks. Nature Climate Change *2*, 732-735.

[105] Drummond, C. & Fischhoff, B. (2017). Individuals with greater science literacy and education have more polarized beliefs on controversial science topics. PNAS 114, https://doi.org/10.1073/pnas.1704882114

[106] Boynton, M.H., O'Hara, R.E., Tennen, H. & Lee, J.G.L (2020). The impact of public health organization and political figure message sources on reactions to coronavirus prevention messages. American Journal of Preventive Medicine *60(1),* 136-138.

[107] Jin, Y., Austin, L., Vijaykumar, S., Jun, H. & Nowak, G. (2019). Communicating about infectious disease threats: Insights from public health information officers. Public Relations Review *45(1),* 167-177.

[108] Ahn, S. J., Fox, J., & Hahm, J. M. (2014). Using virtual doppelgängers to increase personal relevance of health risk communication. In T. Bickmore, S. Marsella, & C. Sidner (Eds.), *Intelligent virtual agents* (IVA 2014) (pp. 1-12). Cham: Springer.

[109] Kresovich, A. & Noar, S.M. (2020). The power of celebrity health events: Meta-analysis of the relationship between audience involvement and behavioral intentions. Journal of Health Communication *25(6),* https://doi.org/10.1080/10810730.2020.1818148

[110] Lasker, R.D. (2004). Redefining readiness: terrorism planning through the eyes of the public. New York: The New Work Academy of Medicine.

[111] Phua, J. & Tinkham, S. (2016). Authenticity in obesity public service announcement: influence of spokesperson type, viewer weight, and source credibility on exercise, information seeking, and electronic word-of-mouth intentions. Journal of Health Communication *21(3),* 337-345,

[112] Ratzan, S.C. & Parker, R.M. (2000). Introduction. In C.R. Selden, M., Zorn, S. Ratzan and R. M. Parker (eds.). *National library of medicine current bibliographies in medicine: health literacy*. Bethesda, MD: National Institute of Health.

[113] Nutbeam, D. (2000). Health literacy as a public health goal: A challenge for contemporary health education and communication strategies into the 21st century. Health Promotion International *15(3)*, 259-267.

[114] Nguyen, A. & Catalan-Matamoros, D. (2020). Digital Mis/Disinformation and Public Engagement with Health and Science Controversies: Fresh Perspectives from Covid-19. Media & Communication *8(2)*, 323-328.

[115] Hickey, K.T., Masterson Creber, R.M., Reading, M., Sciacca, R.R., Riga, T.C., Frulla, A.P., and Casida, J.M. (2018). Low health literacy: Implications for managing cardiac patients in practice. Nurse Practioner *43(8)*, 49-55.

[116] Sonderheimer, J. (2019). Low Health Literacy: A Guide for Public Health Advocates. Retrieved from https://www.glcsophe.org/single-post/2019/06/10/Low-Health-Literacy-A-Guide-for-Public-Health-Advocates

[117] Squiers, L., Peinado, S., Berkman, N., Boudewyns, V. and McCormack, L. (2012). The health literacy skills framework. Journal of Health Communication 17(S3), 30-54.

[118] Tseng, C.-H. & Huang, T.-L. (2016). Internet advertising video facilitating health communication: Narrative and emotional perspectives. Internet Research *26(1)*, 236-264.

[119] Höffler, T.N. & Leutner, D. (2007). Instructional animation versus static pictures: A meta-analysis. Learning and Instruction *17(6)*, 722-738.

[120] Lang, A. (2000). The limited capacity model of mediated message processing. Journal of Communication *50*, 46-70.

[121] Mayer, R.E. & Moreno, R. (2002). Animation as an aid to multimedia learning. Educational Psychology Review *14(1)*, 87-99.

[122] Sorensen, K., Van den Broucke, S., Fullam, J., Doyle, G., Pelikan, J., Sonska, Z. et al. (2012). Health literacy and public health: A systematic review and integration of definitions and models. BMC Public Health *12*, 80. https://doi.org/10.1186/1471-2458-12-80

[123] Lwin, M.O., Vijaykumar, S., Fernando, O.N.N., Cheong, S.A., Rahnayake, V.S., Lim, G., Theng, Y.-L., Chaudhuri, S. & Foo, S. (2014). A 21st century approach to taking dengue: Crowdsourced surveillance, predictive mapping and tailored communication. Acta Tropica *130(Feb)*, 100-107.

[124] Rousseau, C., Moreau, N., Dumas, M.-P., Bost, I., Lefebvre, S., and Atlani-Duault, L. (2015). Public media communications about H1N1, risk perceptions and immunization behaviors: A Quebec-France comparison. Public Understanding of Science *24(2)*, 225-240.

[125] Stolow, J.A., Moses, L.M., Lederer, A.M. & Carter, R. (2020). How Fear Appeal Approaches in COVID-19 Health Communication may be harming the Global Community. Health Education & Behaviour *47(45)*, 531-535.

[126] Kim, K.S., Sin, S.C.J. & Tsai, T.I. (2014). Individual differences in social media use for information seeking. The Journal of Academic Librarianship *40(2)*, 171-178.

[127] Young, D. & Bleakley, Y. (2020). Ideological health spirals: An integrated political and health communication approach to COVID-19 interventions. International Journal of Communication *14*, 3508-3524.

[128] Mazor, K.M., Calvi, J., Cowan, R., Costanza, M.E., Han, P.K., Greene, S.M. et al. (2010). Media messages about cancer: What do people understand? Journal of Health Communication 15(S2), 126-145.

[129] George, A. & Selzer, J. (2007). Kenneth Burke in the 1930s. Columbia; SC: University of South Carolina Press.

[130] Escalas, J.E. (2004). Narrative processing: Building consumer connections to brands. Journal of Consumer Psychology 14, 168-180.

[131] Green, M.C. & Brock, T.C: (2000). The role of transportation in the persuasiveness of public narratives. Journal of Personality and Social Psychology 79, 701-721.

[132] Dillard, J.P. & Shen, L. (2005). On the nature of reactance and its role in persuasive health communication. Communication Monographs 72, 144-168.

Section 2

Financial Sector and Governance

Chapter 10

Corporate Governance and ERM for SMEs Viability in Italy

Patrizia Riva, Maurizio Comoli and Ambra Garelli

Abstract

Family Small and Medium-sized Enterprises (Family SMEs) in Italy have been asked by the new Insolvency and Crisis Code (IC-Code) to establish organizational, management and accounting bodies and tools appropriate to their nature and size. They need to be able to face early warning of company's crisis and potential loss of going concern and to be able to implement strategies provided by the law to recover viability. The peculiarity of the Italian System is the joint existence of two levels of controls. A "downstream" one carried out by Auditors in charge of the accounting control and an "upstream" one carried out by the Supervisory Board in charge for the surveillance of directors' behaviour. The board of statutory auditors (*Collegio Sindacale*), which has been defined as the watchdog distinguishing Italian corporate governance system, plays a fundamental role in reaching the goal. Its supervisory activities are played *ex-ante* over directors and are set with independence and competence. Auditors, instead, operate when everything has already been decided or even implemented concentrating on the accounting issues. The IC-Code sets up new corporate governance rules for a huge number of Family SMEs requiring the appointment of independent control bodies, Board of Statutory Auditors and Auditors and demanding therefore for more attention to risk monitoring and managing.

Keywords: viability, going concern, corporate governance, board of statutory auditors (*Collegio Sindacale*), auditors, internal audit, ERM, ESG risks, overlapping, insolvency directive (Directive EU 2019/1023), IC-code, Italy, early warning system, SMEs, family firm

1. Introduction

In the current scenario Covid-19 pandemic has undermined many Family Small and Medium-sized Enterprises (Family SMEs) viability. Those entities are characterised by few formalisms and important decisions are mainly in the family hands. This can represent an important element of weakness and can lead to situations of serious difficulty both for the family, which increasingly finds itself having to guarantee company commitments with its personal assets, and for the workers who risk being overwhelmed by the consequences of an unmanaged crisis [1, 2]. The work focuses on factors crucial to preserve going concern and to be able to intercept the signs of the crisis well in advance presenting the "*italian way*". Companies urge to be able to face early warning of financial distress and to implement strategies provided by the law to recover viability [3, 4]. The new Italian Insolvency and Crisis Code (IC-Code) tries to answer those needs requiring Family SMEs to implement external and independent control systems that make it possible to identify the major risks and to deal with them in time and in a more rational way.

Some of these tools are known internationally – such as the introduction of compulsory audits - while others are typical of the Italian national Corporate Governance system. The peculiarity of the Italian System is the joint existence of two levels of controls. A "downstream" one carried out by Auditors in charge of the accounting control and an "upstream" one carried out by the Supervisory Board in charge for the surveillance of directors' behaviour. The last is the Board of Statutory Auditors (*Collegio Sindacale*) which has been defined as the watchdog distinguishing Italian corporate governance system. It plays a fundamental role in reaching the goal as its supervisory activities are played *ex-ante* over directors and are set with independence and competence. Auditors, instead, operate when everything has already been decided or even implemented concentrating on the accounting issues. The relevance of these two different roles is the subject of further study in the first part of the work, where, after having better defined SMEs viability, the two levels of controls are analysed and compared.

The appointment of independent control bodies required by the IC-Code entails the need for companies to pay greater attention to identifying risks and to monitoring and managing them. This is particularly true for family SMEs in which we often navigate on sight and strategies selection is based more on the entrepreneurial instinct of the founder and the family than on a structured analysis of what exists and possible options for the future. The second part of the work explores the theme on the Internal Control (IC) and Risk Management System (ERM). In this context a focus on ESG risk is proposed.

2. SMEs viability

Suitable corporate governance is a fundamental prerequisite for maintaining business viability as it allows mapping and a greater awareness of risk management which structurally characterise the corporate context, so they can be understood at an early stage to seek to prevent and if necessary deal with crisis factors [5]. It is important to note that the concept of business viability is formulated and central to Directive (EU) 2019/1023, most commonly known as the Insolvency Directive, and is specified as a distinctive concept (there is an explicit introduction to the concept of a "viability test") to define and rank companies in order to assess their resilience and ability to deal with issues while also finding sustainable solutions to them [6].

The issue of setting up appropriate organisational structures, i.e. the implementation of a corporate governance model which is consistent and proportionate to the business reality, is a particularly sensitive one in the case of family SMEs [7]. In these companies, the formalisation of decision-making processes is often seen as dispossession and a way to reduce the family's decision-making powers [8–12]. In the world of SMEs, there is a widespread belief that the idea of control systems and the professional contribution of administrative- and control-type skills is only a cost and not, on the contrary, an important support to achieve objectives [13]. The widespread style of entrepreneurship that characterises the Italian productive sector, but also of many other countries, leads to the existence of a very high number of small businesses typically run by one or a small number of people who over time identify completely with the company they founded, thus becoming themselves the absolute centre of their entrepreneurial creature. It's a business governance model that often struggles to change even when the business gains market recognition and thus the size of the company grows at the same pace as the complexity which is to be managed [14]. The fear of opening up their management model and listening to instructions from others who introduce new and different skills in many cases wins out, despite the numerous external stimuli [15].

With the introduction in the Italian legislation of the Insolvency and Crisis Code (IC-Code) [16], which will coincide with the timelines indicated in the Insolvency Directive, but which precedes it in terms of its conception, the issue of "organisational structures" is highlighted for all companies including SMEs [17]. It introduces in particular a modification of the law which "requires entrepreneurs to establish an appropriate organisational, management and accounting structure proportionate to the nature and size of the company, which would also pursue the timely detection of a company crisis and the loss of going concern, as well as to take immediate action to adopt and implement one of the instruments provided for by the law to overcome the crisis and recover viability".

The legislation underlines and strengthens the tasks and duties which already existed in the Italian Civil Code and codes of conduct issued by professional organisations. But the most significant feature in the legislation is the obligation to appoint supervisory and audit bodies in SMEs, which to date had only been touched on marginally on the issue of governance. In particular, the acknowledgment of the control role of the Board of Statutory Auditors – a characteristic figure in the Italian context - and that of Auditors through the significant widening of the range of companies required to appoint them, is undoubtedly revolutionary. The compulsory introduction of independent professionals should lead, as a consequence, especially in family businesses, as most Italian companies are, on the one hand to a greater focus on processes and on the other hand to a more regular reporting of company figures and a more formal implementation of budgeting and planning systems.

3. The role of the board of statutory auditors

In order to protect stakeholders, the Board of Statutory Auditors manages an extensive system of controls related to, first of all, compliance with the reference standards for the preparation of financial statements and, second, compliance with the law and the Articles of Association [18]. Of particular importance is overseeing the timely implementation of mandatory requirements in the event of significant losses, such as to jeopardise business viability [19]. Originally, the "control of the financial statements" was included tout court among the duties of the Board of Statutory Auditors pursuant to Article 2403 of the Italian Civil Code; subsequently, this concept was replaced by the "audit", understood as a function distinct from overseeing. The Board of Statutory Auditors may also perform the audit, but only in smaller companies and only if the Board is composed of auditors who are members of the appropriate register. Above all, however, in a situation of going concern, it is the responsibility of the Board of Statutory Auditors to monitor the conduct of the directors. They therefore check if there is an effective dashboard of indicators and if it is reliable and if it can therefore allow them, among other things, to monitor the risks taken by the company, the actual and projected performances. It is indeed necessary for the Board of SA to calculate with constant frequency the parameters and thresholds identified in the new IC-Code to check if there are signs of the beginning of a crisis phase and a risk for company viability.

It is worth noting that statutory auditors are professionals who act autonomously and independently, including vis-à-vis the shareholders who elected them. The Board of Statutory Auditors verifies compliance with its independence both after its appointment and annually thereafter, reporting its findings to the Board of Directors. They accept the appointment when they judge that they can devote the necessary time to the diligent performance of their duties, as required by the

2020 Italian Corporate Governance Code. It is in fact a challenging position the performance of which, in addition to their skills, requires to play a number of tasks. An indispensable component of their work is, therefore, a commitment and the possibility of taking part in the activities of the Board of directors and, if they have been appointed, of the committees (i.e.: Control and Risk Committee) set up within it and of interacting with the other key players in corporate governance, including Auditors and the Internal Auditor, who, when appointed, is responsible for setting up and monitoring the Internal Control and ERM system. The remuneration of the statutory auditors is commensurate with their skills, competence, the commitment required and the size and sector characteristics of the company. As for all independent auditors, it must be determined *ex-ante* by the shareholders' meeting and cannot be changed for the duration of the mandate [20].

For the system to work, a significant and structured dialogue among the parties involved in the process [21] must be developed, which should ideally take place: a) on a daily basis among the directors, the managers and the Internal Auditor; and b) periodically, but not intermittently, between these parties - in particular the directors appointed in the Control and Risk Committee and the Internal Auditor - and the corporate control bodies that is the Board of Statutory Auditors (or the Sole Statutory Auditor in case of sitting alone appointment).

The 2020 Italian Corporate Governance Code devotes space to the issue of coordination among control bodies. In particular it establishes that the Board of Directors shall define the principles concerning coordination and information flows among the various entities involved in the internal control and the risk management system in order to maximize the efficiency of the system itself, reduce activities duplication and ensure effective conduct of the tasks of the control bodies. As part of their activities, the Statutory Auditors may ask the internal Auditor to carry out checks on specific areas or corporate operations [20]. Moreover, the law provides that the Board of Statutory Auditors and Auditors must promptly exchange information related to the performance of their respective duties.

The Board of Statutory Auditors has the fundamental function of a communications hub as it manages and drives information flows to ensure their efficient circulation and to oversee the timely identification of any threats to business viability [17]. The Board of Statutory Auditors is, in fact, the central hub in the information flow system; it simultaneously plays the role of "recipient, researcher and source of information" [22]. The law establishes the obligation of the Board of Directors to report to the Board of Statutory Auditors at least quarterly in listed companies and at least every six months in unlisted companies, with an initial flow of information which is essential for the effective performance of the control functions over the administration. The Board of Statutory Auditors, however, is the recipient of a more complex information flow, i.e. not only "downstream" from the Board of Directors but also "upstream" due to the information flows coming from the auditors and from the internal audit function. On its own initiative, it can also set in motion information channels to obtain the information needed for the exercise of its supervisory function [23]. It thus assumes in fact the function of coordinator of the numerous players in the system of internal corporate controls.

4. The role of auditors

During the year, the auditor verifies that the accounts are duly kept and the company's transactions in the book entries are recorded properly. To do this, they collect evidence related to the transactions and compare it with the contents of the financial statements [17]. In their report, they illustrate the findings of their checks and express their professional opinion. The audit report is related to actual accounting documents, i.e. the financial statements and the consolidated financial statements, if they have been prepared. It also contains the auditor's conclusions on the existence of going concern, indicating any uncertainties related to events or circumstances that may give rise to significant doubt, but this is done only with the precise purpose of assessing the fairness of the criteria used to prepare the financial statements figures.

Auditor functions are, therefore, limited to expressing a professional opinion on the fairness of the financial statements, and comply with auditing standards published in the European Union Official Journal. The functions are in no way comparable to the supervisory functions attributed to the Board of Statutory Auditors by the Italian Civil Code. Specifically, the auditor – unlike the Board of Statutory Auditor – does not participate in Board of Directors meetings and does not oversee the directors behaviours, nor the appropriate organizational, management and accounting structures and tools. Such as appropriateness – or even existence - of the internal control system and the corporate risk mapping system. The auditor cannot express an opinion on the interim accounting situation. The auditor does not assume the role of a corporate information "hub", but rather contributes as a supplier of specific information only on the accounting figures already processed. In short, the auditor's checks are *ex-post* on the actual accounting documents prepared by the company, while the Board of Statutory Auditors oversight role is more complex, in that it is an *ex-ante* systemic guarding role and it works from a forward looking perspective.

5. The Internal Auditor (IA) and the Internal Control (IC) and Risk Management System (ERM)

The Internal Control (IC) and Risk Management System (ERM) consists of the processes executed by the Board of directors, managers and other corporate structure entities to: i) provide a reasonable assurance on the reliability of the financial statement figures; ii) achieve compliance with organisational conduct, i.e. compliance with the law and regulations in force; and iii) achieve greater awareness of business risks and allow continuity in achieving operational efficacy and efficiency objectives [17]. The Internal Control and Risk Management System is basically represented by the lines of action and by the control and procedure system adopted by the management to achieve the efficient and orderly conduct of corporate activities basing choices on reliable data and consciously monitoring the important risks. The internal control system must be seen as the process put in place by the company to achieve a reasonable assurance that the corporate goals will be achieved. It supports the company in identifying and analysing the risks connected to achieving those goals. It allows management to stay focused on the business and achieve its objectives in compliance with the regulations. It is, in short, made up of the rules, procedures and organisational structures aimed at allowing the identification measurement, management and constant verification of the main company risks.

More specifically – focusing on the issue of risk and therefore on the Enterprise Risk Management model – it ensures that the directors have activated an appropriate process to define business and governance objectives which are consistent with the corporate mission and are in line with the levels of risk appetite (i.e. with the overall exposure to risk the organisation is willing to accept) and acceptable risk (satisfactory residual risk after mitigation measures of the individual risk situations). It is divided into three phases: identification of the events, risk assessment and identification of response to the risk itself. The ERM supports the organisation in identifying the risks associated with the adopted strategy and, if necessary, alternative strategies. In assessing the potential risks that can arise from a specific strategy, the underlying critical assumptions are considered. The risk management process monitors and provides valuable information on changes in the assumptions and their effect of achieving the strategy. Pursuing every strategy entails risk that can change depending on the context dynamics. At times the risk is so important that an organisation may want to review the strategy chosen or possibly replace it with another one characterised by a more appropriate risk profile.

In most Italian family SMEs – but not only Italian ones –, the system described above is not implemented at all, or its implementation is insufficient or self-referential.

In this regard, the introduction of the IC-Code represents a considerable element of discontinuity because obliging significant external controls on these entities means forcing these entities to put their administrative and accounting processes in order or strengthen them. Undoubtedly, in many cases this cannot but lead to a greater focus on the internal control system, and therefore to the introduction in their staff of internal – or even outsourced figures initially – figures with skills typical of Internal Auditors.

The introduction of a risk mapping and assessment process takes on particular relevance in small and medium enterprises as it allows them to make more informed decisions. In fact, the risks identified must be analysed and acknowledged in terms of importance, thus allowing management to focus on those that have a higher future probability of occurring and which thus have a greater impact. This also allows enterprises to identify responses which are more structured and not random ones to each identified risk. A risk can be accepted if it is in line with the sustainable risk, or can be avoided by, say, transferring it to third parties through an insurance policy, or even reduced with interventions using the internal control system or, finally, shared through partnership agreements to reduce the impact in the event a negative event occurs.

What should be noted is the fact that the proper operation of the Internal Control (IC) and Risk Management System (ERM) involves several corporate governance parties (**Figure 1**) [20].

The first party in the system is the Board of Directors, which has an interest in basing its decisions on robust data. To best achieve this purpose, it is useful that a Control and Risk Committee composed of non-executive and independent directors (IA) is identified within the board itself when possible and considering the size of the board in an SME, with the task of supporting, with appropriate preliminary activities, the Board of Directors assessments and decisions. Tailoring the issue to

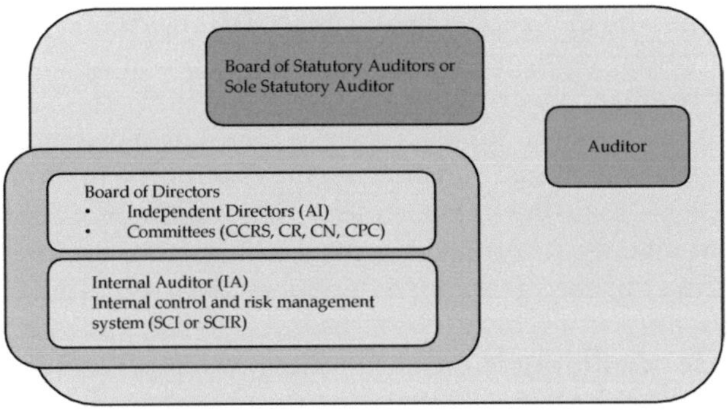

Figure 1.
Map of relevant administration and control roles in a going concern situation.

family SMEs we can say that the simple introduction of a sole independent director in SMEs can have a considerable impact in this regard.

Secondly, especially in cases where it is not possible to set up committees within the Board of Directors, the figure of the Internal Auditor (IA) is primary. Once identified, he or she assumes a central role in the internal control process as the main person responsible for the implementation, operation and monitoring of the system itself. He or she must be included in the company's organisational chart, directly under the Board of Directors as it reports directly to the Board and is responsible for verifying that the Internal Control (IC) and Risk Management System (ERM) is appropriate and that, consequently, the accounts and the information made available in general are complete and reliable. As mentioned above, it is precisely this figure that, in our opinion, will take on significantly greater importance with the introduction of the new IC-Code regulations.

Thirdly, of course, the Board of Statutory Auditors is an active party in the Internal Control and Risk Management System, albeit with a different vantage point, namely with a senior role within the control system. As mentioned above, the Board of Statutory Auditors oversees the appropriateness of the organisational structures and therefore also the effectiveness of the internal control and ERM by interfacing with the Board and the Internal Auditor. It should be underlined that this role is explicitly recognised in new 2020 Italian Corporate Governance Code.

Finally, it should be added that, if present, the Auditor too will appreciate the setting up of an effective Internal Control and Risk Management System as it will allow them to reduce detailed analyses by relying mainly on walk through procedures and consistency checks for the pursuit of their objectives.

6. Monitoring ESG risks in SMEs

It is worth noting that in October 2018 the Committee of Sponsoring Organizations of the Treadway Commission (COSO) developed, in collaboration with the World Business Council for Sustainable Development (WBCSD), the guidelines "Environmental, Social & Governance - Enterprise Risk Management. Applying enterprise risk management to environmental, social and governance related risks" for the application of Enterprise Risk Management also to Environmental, Social & Governance risks (hereinafter "ESG risks").

ESG risks concern the following issues: environmental, such as climate change, pollution and the protection of natural resources; social, such as the defence of human rights and working conditions or relations with local communities; governance, such as remuneration policies, the composition of the board of directors, control procedures and conduct in terms of compliance with laws and ethics.

In recent years, media and investor attention on environmental and social issues has increased considerably, making it more and more important to manage these risks, also in view of increasingly ESG-oriented national and international legislation. Institutional investors themselves are showing increasing interest in responsible investment and the way companies are addressing social and environmental changes to achieve long-term, sustainable growth. ESG has also been addressed at the regulatory level. This is the framework of Legislative Decree 254/2016 which, by introducing "non-financial reporting", requires, albeit currently only for large, listed companies, to disclose annually, among other aspects, risks and policies adopted in the environmental, social, personnel, human rights and anti-corruption fields. It is our opinion that the spread of a general and shared focus on these issues is set to bring them into SMEs reporting and language. The process of integrating ESG issues into these settings will probably be more gradual and, as usual, at the beginning acting on a voluntary basis by following the reference benchmark represented by listed companies.

However, the increasing disclosure of ESG issues highlights the lower attention recognized to ESG risk management, even in larger companies, compared to the concern with more checked out operational, strategic and financial risks.

According to the World Business Council for Sustainable Development (WBCSD), the main reasons for this are: i- the difficulty in quantifying ESG risks in monetary terms, as they are long-term risks with uncertain impacts; ii- the lack of knowledge of the ESG risks which characterise a company and the scarcity of cross-functional collaboration between the risk manager and those dealing with sustainability; iii- the fact that ESG risks are often managed by a team of specialists and seen as separate or at least less important than strategic, operational and financial risks.

The COSO [24] and WBCSD Guidelines therefore propose the redesign of the following specific objectives:

a. Governance & Culture: increase the Board's and management's awareness of ESG issues, promoting a culture of collaboration across functions;

b. Strategy & Objective: anticipate short, medium and long-term ESG risks already in the business strategy and objectives definition phase;

c. Performance: identify and assess ESG risk and related treatment measures based on risk severity;

d. Review & Revision: develop indicators to alert management to changes that impact on risks and treatment measures;

e. Information, Communication & Reporting: identify the information to be communicated internally and externally, involving every level of the organisation.

It is our opinion that these are valuable indications necessary for an effective assessment of business viability. They can therefore be addressed when SMEs are called upon to implement new or renewed internal control and risk management systems to take account of the IC-Code indications. It is worth noting that the Italian Organism Business Reporting (OIBR) has recently set up a Study Group to assess the inclusion of non-financial indicators, including ESG, in the parameters for assessing and identifying corporate crises for early-warning purposes provided for by the IC-Code.

7. Risk of overlapping and possible remedies

To be efficient and effective, the system of controls and their distribution among the various players that make it up, with different roles, functions and responsibilities, must necessarily reduce areas of overlaps and systematically structure the methods of interaction between the various players involved. The control functions can be described by identifying three different levels of subdivision:

1. *First level controls* – these manage and define the "line" controls of the operational processes, i.e. the checks carried out both by those who perform a given activity, and by those who have direct supervisory responsibility for it: in other words, these are the analytical accounting, management, budgeting, planning

and reporting systems that allow the administration and control of the business activities;

2. *Second level controls*, which monitor the correct conduct of the risk assessment and control process put into place by management, ensuring consistency with corporate goals and meeting organisational segregation criteria sufficient to allow effective monitoring;

3. *Third level controls*, whose goal is to assess the overall functionality of the company's internal control system.

It is precisely on the latter that the activities of the parties mentioned in the previous paragraphs are concentrated. Polycentric control systems, like those described, present areas for improvement, but overlapping is a risk that, like other risks, must be monitored, can be reduced and, in some cases, can be an opportunity. This objective can and must be pursued by means of instruments necessarily operating *ex-ante* and involving all the bodies involved, which are asked to pay specific attention and be aware of potential issues and of the need/opportunity to manage them.

The following tools can be used:

- the definition of a language common to the general internal control system and risk management;

- the definition and adoption of harmonized methodologies and instruments;

- the integrated planning of activities seeking to limit redundancies and duplication, focusing on areas of greater complexity or risk;

- the management of the company in line with the objectives defined by the Board of Directors, fostering the taking of fully informed decisions, based on the awareness of risks and the necessary safeguards for their monitoring.

As far as control roles and functions are concerned, integration can only be achieved with the establishment of procedures that facilitate an in-depth exchange of information between the various players and the planning of an integrated activities plan. The text of 2020 Italian Corporate Governance Code is also working in this direction, taking an important step forward. On the one hand, the document stresses the centrality of the Board of Directors as the entity responsible for the internal control and risk management system. On the other hand, it goes further by recognising the need for structured coordination between the various parties involved to avoid inefficiencies and duplications. This implies to formulate and set up procedures that allow periodic and systematic exchanges of information among all the parties involved in various capacities and tasks in the system.

Recommendation included in the 2020 Italian Corporate Governance Code for listed companies and those aiming to be listed represent a relevant benchmark for all companies, regardless of their size, called to comply in the next future with the IC-Code.

8. Results, limits and further researches

The work has proposed an examination of the "*Italian way*" to face Family SMEs financial distress situations. As described it is characterized by the introduction of the Board of Statutory Auditors which has a central role in identifying possible hazards to business viability. Its control *ex-ante,* as a matter of fact, allows the independent professionals involved in this special Board to interact in time with Directors - which in Family SMEs are usually are Family members - detecting signal of crisis and helping them to become aware of their relevance and potential impact. It is therefore asked to family SMEs to walk through this new path albeit implementing tools proportionate to the company's complexity. The aim is the development of a full awareness of corporate risks, the construction of a map that identifies and explicitly represents them so that they can be brought to the Family members attention and can be better monitored.

The importance of a constant constructive dialogue between experienced independent professionals and family members involved in the management of the company has been highlighted. The more the dialogue takes place before and when the decisions are taken the more the possibility of a positive influence will be high and therefore the more the probability of taking risks unknowingly will be reduced. For this to be possible, however, it is necessary on one side that independent professionals are able to use a convincing language and on the other side that family members are willing to listen their voices without feeling subjected to their presence. Experts ability to bring value, by focusing attention to the critical issues of choices and therefore forcing deeper and more rational reflections by tracing the intuition to a more structured and complex decision-making grid need to be recognized in the field.

Another point which resulted here emphasized is the necessity, when different control roles are defined, to reduce areas of overlaps and systematically structure the methods of interaction between the various players involved. This is essential to be able to convey clear and consistent messages and finally to reach efficacy of controls themselves. It is a relevant consideration as the proper operation of the Internal Control (IC) and Risk Management System (IC and ERM) involves, as seen in details in the chapter, several entities of corporate governance and consequently a risk is structural due to the increase of the complexity to manage.

A first limit of the work can be considered the qualitative approach of the analysis. Indeed this is a descriptive work that aims to provide a first analysis of the new Italian legislation that will come into force on 1st September 2021. It will be possible in the very near future to verify whether what is here described will actually bring benefits to Family SMEs. It will be possible to collect data and to proceed with the measurement of the effects of the introduction of the mechanisms examined, in particular of the Statutory Board, on the ability to promptly intervene and avoid or at least to face situations of financial economic distress at an earlier stage.

A second limit could be considered the lack of explicit international comparisons. In this regard, however, it should be reported that the researches carried out has allowed to detect that no similar mechanisms have been introduced in other Western countries. It will be therefore interesting, in future researches, to widen and to go deeper with this part of the analysis. In particular it will be certainly necessary to consider, with reference to the European context, if the implementation of the EU Insolvency Directive, which emphasizes the need to provide early warning tools in national legislation, will lead in the near future to the introduction of corporate governance rules comparable to the Italian ones.

Moreover the work highlights that the "*Italian way*" introduced by the IC-Code provides some financial specific indexes to be monitored by both the Directors and the Statutory Board, but some non-financial information are also taken in consideration. Some of these can be considered forward-looking and can be traced back to

DOI: http://dx.doi.org/10.5772/intechopen.96688

the categories of Governance information. It is our opinion that monitoring a more complete ESG information dataset could have an effective assessment of business viability. Future research could explore the possible inclusion of non-financial indicators, including ESG, in the parameters to identify corporate crises for early-warning purposes provided for by the IC-Code.

Author details

Patrizia Riva*, Maurizio Comoli and Ambra Garelli
DISEI, Department of Economics and Business Studies, Piemonte Orientale University, Novara, Italy

*Address all correspondence to: patrizia.riva@uniupo.it

References

[1] Riva P., Provasi R., The ability of the turnaround index to assess going concern assumptions: evidence from its application to Italian listed companies, in Global Business & Economic Review, 2016, ISSN: 1097-4954

[2] Riva P., Provasi R., Assessment of going concern for the Italian listed companies: an empirical study, in Review of Business & Finance Case Studies, 2015, ISSN: 2150-3338

[3] Riva P., Provasi R., An Overview about Italian companies facing the financial and economic crisis. A cultural revolution, in International Journal of Economics And Business Research, 2014, ISSN: 1756-9850

[4] Riva P., Provasi R., Accounting for debt restructuring in the current crisis. Italian experience by Italian legal conditions, in EKONOMSKA ISTRAžIVANJA, 2013, ISSN: 1331-677X

[5] Parisi G., L'adeguato assetto organizzativo e il rafforzamento degli obblighi e dei doveri dell'organo amministrativo e di controllo dopo il D.Lgs. 14/2019, Available from www.osservatorio-oci.org

[6] Stanghellini L., Mokal R., Paulus C. G., Tirado I., Contractualised distress resolution in the shadow of the law, Best practices in European restructuring, 2018, Wolters Kluwer

[7] Riva P., Comoli M., The impact of the new Italian early warning system provided by the Ic-code on family SMEs governance, in Corporate Ownership and Control, Virtus Interpress, 2019, DOI:10.22495/cocv16i3art6

[8] Anderson R. C., Reeb D. M., Founding family ownership and firm performance: Evidence from the SandP500, in The journal of Finance, 2003, https://doi.org/10.1111/1540-6261.00567

[9] Stein L. C., Takeover threats and managerial myopia, in Journal of Political Economy, 1988, https://doi.org/10.1086/261524

[10] Stein J. C., Efficient capital markets, inefficient firms: A model of Myopic corporate behaviour, in The Quarterly Journal of Economics, 1989, https://doi.org/10.2307/2937861

[11] James H., Owner as manager, extended horizons and the family firm, in International Journal of the Economics Business, 1999, https://doi.org/10.1080/13571519984304

[12] Anderson R., Sattar A., Mansi E., Reeb D. m., Founding family ownership and the agency cost of debt, in Journal of Financial Economics, 2003, https://doi.org/10.1016/S0304-405X(03)00067-9

[13] Colarossi F., Giorgino M., Steri R., Viviani D., A corporate governance study on Italian family firms, in Corporate Ownership & Control, 2008, http://doi.org/10.22495/cocv5i4p8

[14] Di Toma P., Strategic dynamics and corporate governance effectiveness in a family firm, in Corporate Ownership & Control, 2012, https://doi.org/10.22495/cocv10i1art3

[15] Songini L., Gnan L., Family involvement and agency cost control mechanisms in family small and medium-size enterprises, in Journal of Small Business Management, 2015, https://doi.org/10.1111/jsbm.12085

[16] Danovi A., Riva P., Azzola M., Avoiding bankruptcy in Italy: preventive arrangement with creditors, in Contemporary Issues in Finance:

Current Challenges from Across Europe, Emerald, 2017, ISBN: 978-1-78635-907-0

[17] Riva P., Corporate Governance Roles and Non Financial Information. Milano: Egea; 2020. 4: 274: 18: 19

[18] Riva P., Danovi A., Comoli M., Garelli A., Corporate Governance in Downturn Times: Detectionand Alert – The New Italian Insolvency and Crisis Code, in Crisis management. Theory and practice, IntechOpen, 2018. Available from: http://dx.doi.org/10.5772/intechopen.74964

[19] Difino M., Riva P., Ruolo, compiti e responsabilità del Collegio Sindacale. La rilevanza strategica dell'attività di vigilanza e l'organo di controllo nelle PMI, in I nuovi compiti degli organi sociali a cura di Riva P., Collana Crisi d'impresa diretta da Danovi A., Acciaro G., Il Sole 24 Ore, aprile 2019.

[20] Codice della Corporate Governance, Raccomandazione 30: 26, l. c):32

[21] Riva P., Provasi R., Crisis and controls: the Italian model, in Corporate ownership & control, Volume 11, 2013

[22] Caterino D., Poteri dei sindaci e governo dell'informazione nelle società quotate, Cacucci editore, Bari, 2012

[23] Stampelli G., I flussi informativi nelle società quotate: poteri e doveri del Collegio Sindacale, rivista di Diritto Privato, saggi e pareri, 1/2017

[24] Riva P., Provasi R., The Updated COSO Report 2013, Journal Of Modern Accounting And Auditing, 2015

Chapter 11

The Management of Tax Risks in Mergers and Acquisitions - The Importance of Tax Due Diligence

Arnaldo Marques de Oliveira Neto

Abstract

The purpose of this chapter is to demonstrate the importance of tax risk management in mergers and acquisitions processes by conducting an investigative work called due diligence. To achieve this objective, bibliographic and documentary research was used, as part of exploratory research. In topic 1 it is evidenced that the complexity of tax systems around the world has demanded increasing attention from companies to avoid undesirable cash disbursements for payment of infringement notices arising from questioning by tax authorities related to improper procedures of companies when paying taxes. Additionally, it has required them to be diligent in identifying lawful tax planning alternatives to optimize the tax burden on their operations. In topic 2 the responsibility of company administrators in the management of tax risks is exposed. Topic 3 explains the importance of accounting, tax and legal due diligence in merger and acquisition processes. Finally, topic 4 analyzes the main aspects of due diligence in the tax area. In view of all the exposed in this chapter, it will remain clear to readers the importance of the tax due diligence of the target company, as a way to minimize risks in the decision-making process of the managers of the purchasing company that may compromise the success of the merger and acquisition operation, as well as not subjecting them to administrative and judicial suits, for non-compliance with their fiduciary duties of diligence and loyalty in relation to the company of which they are executives. Additionally, the study's results suggest that companies—in compliance with the guidelines and limits set by the board—choose the appropriate and specific techniques of risk management, especially those related to minimization, immunization, and transferring these risks. The recommendations derive from the need to identify and manage tax risks, from the point of view of good corporate governance practices. This study may serve as a reference to companies in general, when studying, developing, and implementing recommendations for the identification and minimization of tax risks, as well as in the development of a work program that allows them to conduct due diligence work in target companies.

Keywords: tax system, tax risks, tax due diligence, managers responsibilities, merger and acquisition

1. Introduction

The complexity of tax systems around the world, as well as their constant changes, has demanded increasing attention from companies and their managers to avoid undesirable cash disbursements for payment of infringement notices arising from questioning by tax authorities related to improper procedures of companies when paying taxes. Additionally, it has required them to be diligent in identifying lawful tax planning alternatives to optimize the tax burden on their operations [1].

In the case of Brazil the complexity and dynamism of the its tax system is growing in sophistication, especially after the implementation of the Public Digital Bookkeeping System (SPED) and has occasioned the need for companies to organize their business under appropriate tax governance for effective and efficient tax compliance, in order to maximize the legitimate economy of taxes and minimize the risk of possible questioning by the tax authorities, which may result in identification of tax contingencies and the consequent issuance of notices of violation (infringement notification), with a corresponding recovery of punitive fines and penalty interest [2].

SPED was established by Presidential Decree No. 6022/2007 and regulated by Normative Instruction of Internal Revenue Service of Brazil No. 787/2007, such as a smart tool that unifies the activities of receipt, validation, storage, and authentication of books and documents that comprise the commercial and fiscal bookkeeping companies through unique and computerized information flow.

The globalization, a typical feature of modern society, made the concept of risk society that, from the perspective of taxation and in relation to its aspects of ambivalence, indeterminacy, and uncertainty, affects taxpayers, creating juridical insecurity and confusion in meeting their tax obligations [3].

Risk can simply be defined as exposure to change. It is the probability that some future event or a set of events will occur. Therefore, risk analysis involves identifying potential adverse changes and the expected impact as a result in the organization [4].

The term 'risk' comes from the word *risicu* or *riscu*, in Latin (which means 'to dare', in English). It is customary to understand 'risk' as the possibility of 'something does not work,' but its current concept involves the quantification and qualification of uncertainty, both regarding 'loss' as the 'earnings,' in relation to the course of events planned, either by individuals or by organizations [5].

When investors buy stock, surgeons perform operations, engineers design bridges, entrepreneurs open their businesses, and politicians run for elected office, the risk is an unavoidable partner. However, their actions reveal that the risk need not be so feared today: managing it has become synonymous with challenge and opportunity [6].

The objective of the study contained in this chapter is to demonstrate the importance of tax risk management in mergers and acquisitions processes by conducting an investigative work called due diligence.

To achieve this objective, bibliographic and documentary research was used, as part of exploratory research, since information and previous knowledge were collected about the problem for which the answer was sought, as well as materials that have not yet received analytical treatment, such as laws, regulations, and official decrees [7].

So, in this topic 1 it is evidenced that the complexity of tax systems around the world has demanded increasing attention from companies to avoid undesirable cash disbursements for payment of infringement notices arising from questioning by tax authorities related to improper procedures of companies when paying taxes. Additionally, it has required them to be diligent in identifying lawful tax planning alternatives to optimize the tax burden on their operations.

In topic 2 the responsibility of company administrators in the management of tax risks is exposed. This topic initially demonstrates that good corporate governance practices attributed to the board of directors and, in its absence, the senior management of the organization, the fundamental task of identifying, prioritizing, and ensuring effective management of various risks that may affect its business and even its continuity. It points out that through tax governance, the company aims to identify the most beneficial tax incidence hypothesis, to allow their activities may be lawfully benefited by the reduction in tax burden or inserted in the context of no tax levy. The company should also minimize the generation of tax contingencies. Finally, it points out that managers—in compliance with the guidelines and limits set by the board—should choose the appropriate and specific techniques of risk management, especially those related to minimization, immunization, and transferring these risks.

Topic 3 explains the importance of accounting, tax and legal due diligence in merger and acquisition processes. He points out that the due diligence work has some important functions. Firstly, it serves to uncover risks of various natures and helps in the decision-making process in terms of shaping the agreement and finding a realistic price for the acquisition, because it allows for a better assessment of the target object. The slighting of asymmetries of information may be seen as a direct effect of due diligence. Then, he comments on the relationship between the parties involved, the need to hire a multidisciplinary team of specialists, the areas to be examined, the preparation of the pro forma balance sheet, the writing of the report and the sizing of the guarantees.

Topic 4 analyzes the main aspects of due diligence in the tax area. It highlights issues to be observed as measurement of liabilities and assets accounted for, identification of unaccounted assets and liabilities and disclosure of contingencies not quantified.

2. The responsibility of company administrators in the management of tax risks

Regarding 'risk management', there are regulations in Brazil, for example, that are in line with the Sarbanes–Oxley Act (SOX) and the Basel Agreement (for financial institutions). The SOX was published in 2002 in the USA, in response to some corporate scandals. It introduced important changes for the regulation of financial practice and corporate governance of companies. It emphasized the critical role of internal controls [8].

Internal controls include the organization plan and all methods and measures adopted in the company to safeguard its assets, verify the accuracy and fidelity of accounting data, develop efficiency in operations and stimulate the follow-up of prescribed executive policies [9].

This is one of the reasons the administration, notably of the large companies, have become more complex and difficult, requiring professionals with expertise in various areas of knowledge, causing the separation of ownership (owners) and management (executives) to allow business to be conducted in a more professional manner [10].

2.1 Good corporate governance practices

The Organization for Economic Co-Operation and Development (OECD) emphasizes that a good corporate governance system enables corporations to operate for the benefit of the community, with investor confidence, and attract stable long-term capital. It stands out for the range of topics dealt with and their influence on the global dissemination of the principles of good corporate governance practices. According to the OECD, governance fixes as a link of development of bond markets, corporations, and nations [11].

The adoption in 2002 of US Law SOX, printing new coherence to the rules of corporate governance, as renewal element of good practices of legal compliance, provision accounts (accountability), transparency (disclosure), and sense of justice (fairness) [12].

Good corporate governance practices attributed to the board of directors and, in its absence, the senior management of the organization, the fundamental task of identifying, prioritizing, and ensuring effective management of various risks that may affect its business and even its continuity. In this vein, the responsibility of the board and the senior management members—from both a corporate and a tax perspective—loomed in the risk society. From the tax point of view, there may be the extent of the responsibility of the legal entity to its partners, directors, officers, or legal representatives in some situations, which may even result in the blocking of their personal property, including their bank accounts, among other measures [13].

For example, the article 135 of the Brazilian tax code prescribes that "they are personally responsible for claims relating to tax liabilities arising from acts performed with excess of power or violation of law, article of incorporation or bylaw: directors, managers, or representatives of legal persons of private law".

2.2 Tax governance to optimize the company's tax burden

A species of the genus corporate governance, tax governance is the way in which organizations are led, directed, and managed to optimize their tax burden, identifying opportunities for their reduction, and minimizing the possibility of tax contingencies (risks) [14].

Through tax governance, the company aims to identify the most beneficial tax incidence hypothesis, to allow their activities may lawfully be benefited by the reduction in tax burden or inserted in the context of no tax levy. The company should also minimize the generation of tax contingencies [15].

The tax governance considers all aspects of the issue, from a legal, tax, accounting, financial, and economic outlook considering domestic and international experience in order to minimize risks and maximize the legitimate tax savings, following high ethical standards and in full compliance with the letter and spirit of applicable laws [16].

The international surveys by large accounting firms indicate that the management of tax risks has been gaining more importance on the board. Senior executives are increasingly looking for information about taxes, because of its potential material impact on the financial statements and the tax issue can no longer focus exclusively on tax compliance and managing the effective rate of taxes. CEOs and board members are doing more complex questions about how your organization manages its exposure to tax risk [17].

The OECD has stressed the importance of the involvement of the board in tax strategies of multinational companies: 'Encourage the board, the CEO, and the audit committees from the large companies to have more interest and responsibility for their tax's strategies'. There is a clear expectation that the OECD will expand its guidelines on corporate governance for the tax area of the companies soon [18].

2.3 Tax risks management

Tax risks include the risk of paying more or less tax than legally required. Damage to reputation resulting from such errors may cause additional costs which are difficult to measure. Errors in assessing the tax effects of transactions may lead to wrong business decisions. For many companies, the tax is a cost factor which may be important for their competitiveness. Tax risks consist primarily of compliance, transactional, operational, and reputational risks. These are good reasons for the board is involved in the management of tax risk [19].

The risk appetite is associated with the level of risk that the organization can accept in the pursuit and achievement of its mission/vision (activity more associated with prior risk analysis). The risk tolerance is in line with acceptable levels of variability in achieving the goals and objectives defined (activity more associated with risk monitoring). Together, these two components defining the organization's risk profile, in relation to the exposure to the risk that it accepts, as **Figure 1** displays [20].

Managers—in compliance with the guidelines and limits set by the board—should choose the appropriate and specific techniques of risk management, especially those related to minimization, immunization, and transferring these risks [21].

The tax governance will have to cover the tax philosophy and strategy of the company, internal policies, and procedures regarding tax risks and external communication regarding all tax matters. The board of directors will be responsible for defining a direction, the implementation of a tax system of governance and of course for enhancement of company value, through tax reduction [22].

Therefore, efficient, and sustainable company from the tax point of view (regardless in which country it is located) is one that seeks to identify with the requisite notice the legal and tax alternatives less costly to achieve their business objectives and adopt a set of coordination procedures, control and review in order to minimize the possibility of generating tax contingencies. We remind you that from the owners' point of view the obligation of senior management of the company to plan its business, to increase—in a continuous, permanent, and sustainable manner—its revenues and reduce their costs (including taxes), to make it increasingly profitable [23].

The corporate sustainability can be defined as the ability of companies of creating value for its owners over the long term, through proper management of risks associated with economic, social, and environmental factors, as shown in **Figure 2**. Soon, the company, concerned with sustainability, investing in its continued ability to continue growing. There is a natural convergence between sustainability and

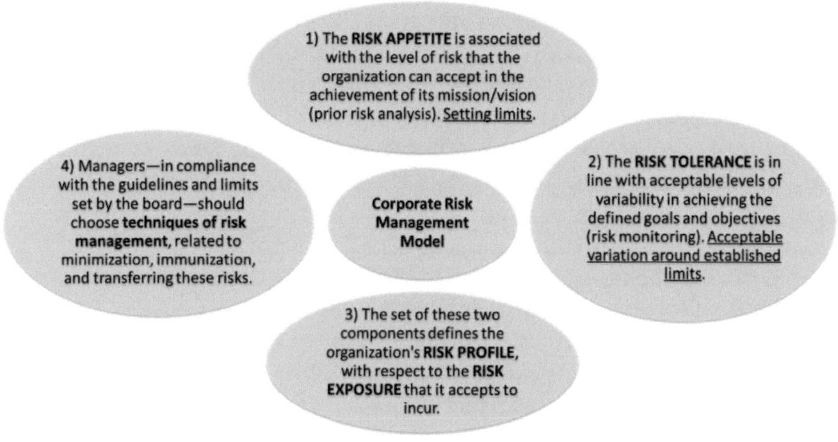

Figure 1.
Corporate risk management model resulting from appetite and tolerance to risk. Source prepared by the author.

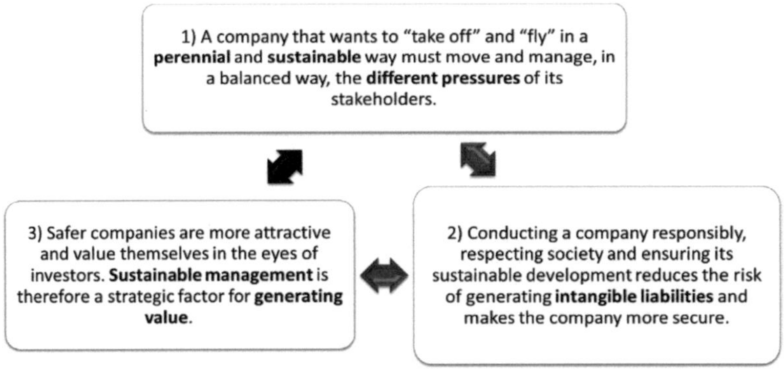

Figure 2.
Convergence between sustainability and implementation of corporate governance practices. Source prepared by the author.

implementation of corporate governance practices. From an economic standpoint, we can say that there is no sustainability without profitability [24].

Intangible liabilities (mentioned in the above **Figure 2**) mean the requirement whose information about its existence remains hidden from the user of the financial statements and, in some cases, even from its managers [25].

Because of all that has been exposed so far in this chapter, considering the responsibility of company administrators in the management of risks it is especially important do carry out a due diligence procedure, on which we come to deal with in the next topic.

3. The importance of accounting, tax and legal due diligence in merger and acquisition (M&A) processes

It is usual in commercial practice, mainly in mergers & acquisitions, to carry out a procedure for collecting information and reviewing and analyzing documents, with the function of verifying the legal and economic situation of the companies involved in the business, called due diligence [26].

Due diligence, used in mergers and acquisitions processes, as one of the last stages of the transaction, from the accounting, tax, and legal point of view, aims primarily to identify contingencies that are capable of affecting the value of the assets involved in the business, as is outlined in **Figure 3**. It is not too much to remember that, in the legislation of several countries, there are several situations in which the buyer becomes responsible for the seller's liabilities [27].

From a tax perspective, the economic advantage of an M&A transaction depends on the potential tax risks and opportunities of the targeted transaction that are identified during the transaction stage, the costs that are incurred on account of conducting the due diligence itself, as well as the tax savings that may be realized when consuming the target transaction, minus the requisite restructuring costs that are incurred during the integration stage. The latter are determined by the extent of pre-acquisition and post-acquisition measures [28].

From the seller's point of view, due diligence, prior to the signing of the closing of the transaction, may be used as a defense against future (any) claims by the buyer. Thus, it aims to ensure that the information has been audited by the buyer, serving to protect the seller from any claim of ignorance from the part of the buyer [29].

Due diligence is of the buyer's priority interest, as it is verified, at this stage, whether the data provided in the information memorandum are compatible with

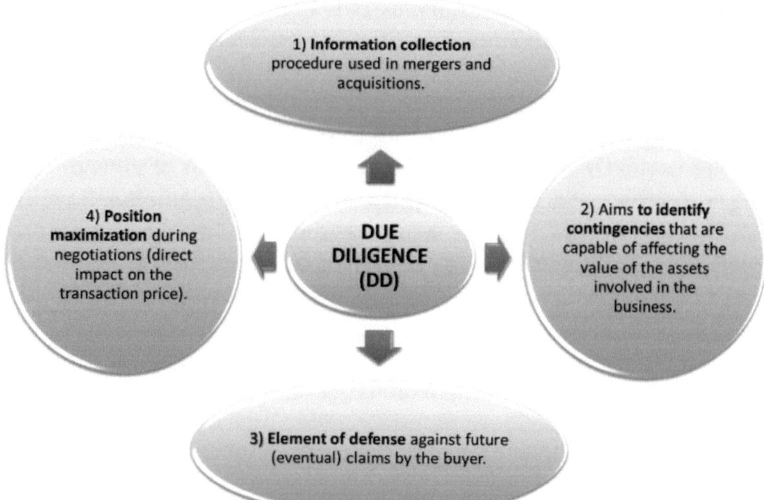

Figure 3.
Verifying procedure company's situation from several angles. Source prepared by the author.

the reality. Buyers seek to protect themselves from optimistic projections from sellers through earn out mechanisms and possible non-compliance of current and past data through due diligence. Due diligence grants the acquirer access to sensitive information about the object to be acquired, for the purpose of being able to conduct a comprehensive audit [30].

Due diligence is conducted by the buyer and accompanied by the seller. The latter should be diligent in the provision of information so that the earn out mechanisms are not applicable at a future date. It is therefore advisable to conduct the work in such a way as to ensure that the parties have extensive knowledge of what is being negotiated and the risks involved [31].

In that regard, due diligence has some important functions. Firstly, it serves to uncover risks of various natures and helps in the decision-making process in terms of shaping the agreement and finding a realistic price for the acquisition, because it allows for a better assessment of the target object. The slighting of asymmetries of information may be a direct effect of due diligence [32].

3.1 The relationship between the parties involved

The opposition of interests between the parties involved ends up being reflected in the performance of due diligence work. Generally, the due diligence is interested in detailing the legal, accounting, tax, labor, social security, financial, etc. situation of the target company. On the other hand, the latter always has the interest to protect itself [33].

The wear and tear in the relationship can be minimized through the establishment of confidentiality agreements, agreed before the start of the due diligence work, as well as by the stipulation of rules for the flow of documents and information between the parties, to avoid delays and conflicts [34], as summarized in **Figure 4**.

3.2 The formation of a multidisciplinary team of specialists

Given the scope and diversity of aspects to be observed during due diligence for the purpose of conducting a work of this nature, it is necessary to hire a multidisciplinary team of professionals, usually composed of auditors, tax consultants and lawyers (specialized in the most diverse areas of law) [35], as show in **Figure 5**.

The role of accounting auditors, objectively speaking, is to verify how the operations of the investigated company are processed (through its accounting system, which gives rise to the financial statements), from the point of view of meeting the fundamental principles of accounting and accounting agreements. For this, they will perform, among others, the following steps: examination of corporate documentation, operational plans, product description, financial statements, contracts, accounts relating to suppliers and customers, physical inspection of facilities, etc., addressing of matters to be analyzed in more detail by tax consultants and legal advisors, as well as receipt of inputs from the latter, which may represent adjustments for the purposes of the pro forma balance sheet [36].

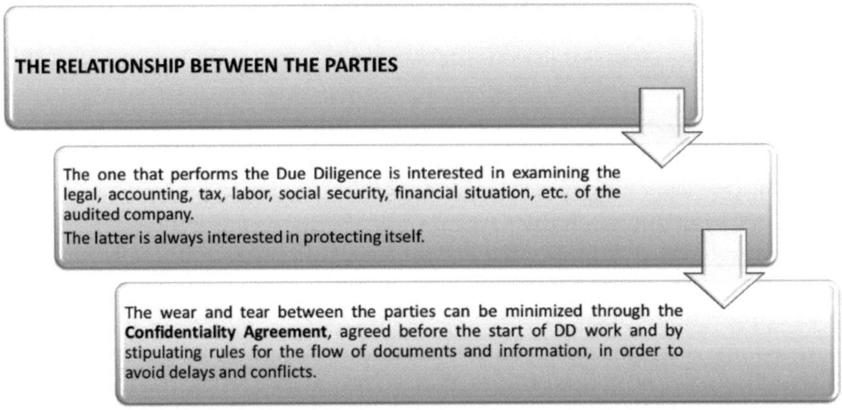

Figure 4.
The relationship between the parties involved. Source prepared by the author.

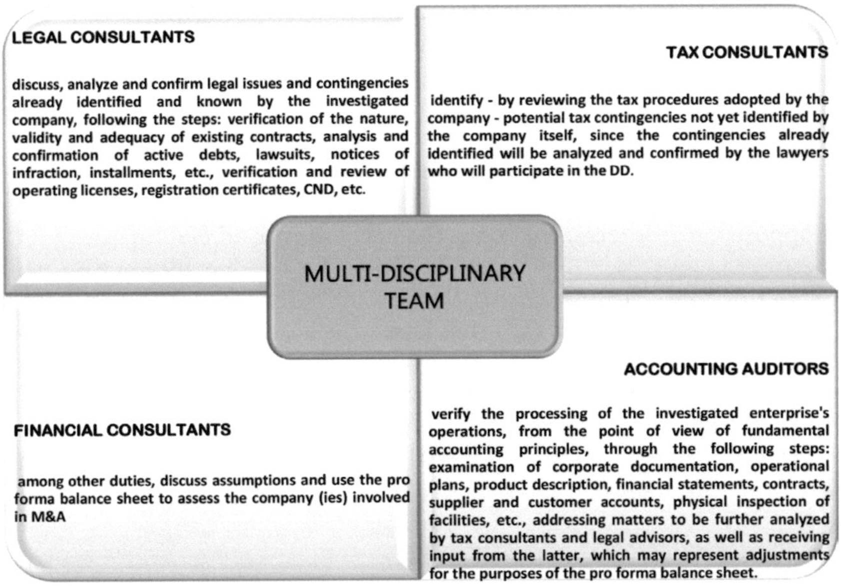

Figure 5.
Multidisciplinary team of specialists. Source prepared by the author.

Speaking specifically of the due diligence work in the tax area, it can be said that the primary objective of tax consultants will be to identify - through the review of the tax procedures adopted by the company under review (compliance) - potential tax contingencies not yet identified by the company itself, since the contingencies already effectively identified will be analyzed and confirmed by the lawyers who will participate in the due diligence process [37].

The main role of legal advisors will be to discuss, analyze and confirm judicial issues and contingencies already effectively identified and known by the company investigated. They must comply, among others, with the following steps: verification of the nature, validity and adequacy of existing contracts, analysis and confirmation of active debts, lawsuits, infringement notices, installments, etc., verification and review of operating licenses, registration certificates, tax authority negative certificates, etc. [38].

3.3 Areas to be examined

The multidisciplinary team will examine from the various angles of observation that their academic background and professional experience allow to evaluate, the following aspects of the target company, among others, as **Figure 6** displays:

3.3.1 Corporate aspects

Counsel for the buyer will invariably undertake a careful review of the organizational documents and general corporate records of the target company, including (among others): charter documents (certificate of incorporation, bylaws, etc.), good standing and (if applicable) tax authority certificates, list of subsidiaries and their respective charter documents, list of jurisdictions in which the company and its subsidiaries are qualified to do business, stockholder and voting agreements, minutes of stockholders' meetings since inception, including written consents to action without a meeting and minutes of board of directors and any board committees since inception, including written consents to action without a meeting [39].

Figure 6.
Areas of the target company to be examined. Source prepared by the author.

3.3.2 Contractual relations

It refers to the examination of contracts signed by the company, which have their execution in progress, with emphasis on financial and operational contracts, with a view to identifying possible default clauses in the event of disposal of controlling interest or other clauses that may affect the business. Legal proceedings involving the discussion of contracts should also be analyzed, with a view to identifying and quantifying possible contingencies [40].

The buyer will be concerned with all the target company's historical financial statements and related financial metrics, as well as the reasonableness of the target's projections of its future performance. One of the most time-consuming (but critical) components of a due diligence inquiry is the review of all material contracts and commitments of the target company. The categories of contracts that are important to review and understand include the following: guaranties, loans, and credit agreements, customer and supplier contracts, agreements imposing any restriction on the right or ability of the company (or a buyer) to compete in any line of business or in any geographic region with any other person, equity finance agreements and non-competition agreements [41].

3.3.3 Property

A review of all property owned by the target company or otherwise used in the business is an essential part of any due diligence investigation, with such review including deeds, leases of real property, deeds of trust and mortgages, title reports, other interests in real property, financing leases and sale and leaseback agreements, conditional sale agreements and operating leases [42].

This is the assessment of the documentary regularity of the main assets and the possible costs for the correction of irregularities found. Identification of the burden and encumbrances (mortgages, penhoras, servitudes, disposals, etc.) that fall on the properties. Supporting documents of the ownership of the main movable property should be analyzed to identify contingencies, burdens and encumbrances that may fall on them [43].

3.3.4 Environmental issues

Environmental due diligence is the other common workstream in a typical due diligence approach and focus on exposure in this area, as well as potential changes in run rate costs post-acquisition [44]. The buyer will want to analyze any potential environmental issues the target company may face, the scope of which will depend on the nature of its business [45].

The situation of environmental permits required for the exercise of the activity of the target undertaking should be examined. It is also necessary to analyze the judicial and administrative proceedings, to identify possible responsibilities for the repair of damage caused by it to the environment, as well as the regularity of the practices adopted in the context of its operations [46].

3.3.5 Consumer right

It is necessary to verify the situation of the relations maintained by the company with its consumers and with the consumer protection agencies. The existing cases against the company, whether in the administrative or judicial sphere, should also be analyzed to establish contingencies and the effects arising from possible irregular practice [47].

3.3.6 Labor aspects

Human resources due diligence typically includes a detailed review of the company's relationships with its employees, such as union agreements, regular benefits, executive compensation, and post-employment obligations. In addition to flushing out exposures, it can help identify cost structure changes that can occur if the target's employees join the buyer's benefit plans post-acquisition [48].

It refers to the evaluation of administrative and judicial processes, their routines adopted to identify possible contingencies and possible problems that may arise from the changes arising due to the proposed operation [49].

3.3.7 Tax and social security aspects

Tax due diligence may or may not be critical, depending on the historical operations of the target company, but even for companies that have not incurred historical income tax liabilities, an understanding of any tax carryforwards and their potential benefit to the buyer may be important [50].

This is the analysis of administrative and judicial processes, their tax and social security routines, to verify any problems, and those that may arise from the changes made with the implementation of the business [51].

Thus, in addition to the legal aspects, financial, strategic, technical, operational issues are analyzed, among others, so that, at the end of the entire analysis, a report is prepared that reflects the combination of the results found in all these different matters [52].

3.4 The pro forma balance sheet

After the completion of the exams by the multidisciplinary team engaged in the due diligence work, it is necessary to propose the appropriate adjustments in order to arrive a pro forma balance sheet, which will serve as the basis for financial projections (which will feed the business plan), the negotiation of the acquisition price, as well as the establishment of guarantees and escrow-account (in the case of acquisition), or for the determination of the exchange of shares (in the case of merger). A pro forma balance sheet is a financial document that discloses a business's assets, liabilities, and equity at a specific point in time. This financial statement is not prepared in accordance with Generally Accepted Accounting Standards (GAAP). It is considered more of a balance sheet projection [53].

3.5 The report

Due diligence work usually results in the preparation of a report, the form of which may vary depending on the interests of its recipient. Should the report describe the contingencies found, including, where possible, an estimate of theirs.

A due diligence report is the final report of the review conducted by the company in which the summary of the research done by the company is included [54].

Among the main objectives of due diligence are the identification of the main characteristics of the company; identification of possible obstacles to the conduct of the business and the quantification of existing contingencies; risk assessment; assistance in setting the price of the business; and assistance in the negotiation of contractual clauses [55].

Due diligence report is one of the most important records of conducting due diligence as it will be the final report that you will send to members of the executive team who will evaluate it. Without proper due diligence reporting, all the effort that you have put in conducting the due diligence will go astray [56].

It is necessary to highlight the agreed upon procedures scope used in the evaluation of the analyzed information, since the content of the report involves the evaluation of possible future effects of the situations, in fact, found, which rarely allows absolutely accurate estimates [57].

The agreed upon procedures scope differs from that of an annual audit [58]. A due diligence inspection must be quite separate from the annual audit because it is less profound [59].

Agreed upon procedures engagement is a type of engagement which auditor performs certain procedures that are agreed upon in advance. In this engagement, the auditor and specified parties agree that the auditor will perform specific procedures and report the findings. Likewise, there are usually three parties involved in the engagement, including the auditor, the client, and another third party. Unlike an audit, auditors do not give an opinion on subject matters in the agreed upon procedures. Auditors only report of findings based on the agreed procedures performed on the subject matter. Hence, the clients need to make their own conclusion on the subject matter [60].

Often, the interested party ends up assuming the risks of a limitation of scope due to its budget constraints or even the obligation to comply with time limits – an important fact, because due diligence is a time-consuming procedure, although it must be subject to the imposition of relatively short deadlines. Due diligence is also expensive for the party that must bear its costs, which increase in proportion to the size of the business and the number of problems found in it [61].

3.6 The sizing of the guarantees

The report shall indicate what guarantees would be required in the final contract to be signed between the parties. Thus, contingencies that are not quantifiable can be subject to specific guarantees, with a view to specifying value references to them, to be subject to subsequent adjustments, if they prove to be inaccurate. Those quantifiable can be directly deducted from the price, or in the event of uncertain occurrence, may be the subject of escrow accounts – a kind of deposit account, administered by a third party, whose values are released in the circumstances that the parties agreed to [62].

Where the purchaser determines that the seller is unlikely to have the resources to meet potential liability claims in connection with the transaction, the purchaser may seek the ability to hold-back (or escrow) a portion of the purchase price until the indemnity period (or as is more likely the case, a portion of the indemnity period) has expired [63].

Escrows are another common feature of transaction document, both the amount and duration of which can be increased as necessary to provide protection. Sometimes potential exposures can be so significant or clear as to the outcome if the target is audited that escrows will not provide a sufficient remedy. In these circumstances, alternate transaction structures, purchase price reductions, installment sales, and earn outs can all provide effective protection to a buyer.

The earn out clauses are defined by the parties and are detailed in the final contract. The payment method is detailed, and the use of escrow account can be established to ensure that if the earn out mechanisms are triggered, the buyer will obtain the adjustment in the amount to be paid [64].

Alternatively, when none of these remedies are sufficient, desirable, or obtainable (due to seller objections), buyers can consider purchasing tax risk insurance [65].

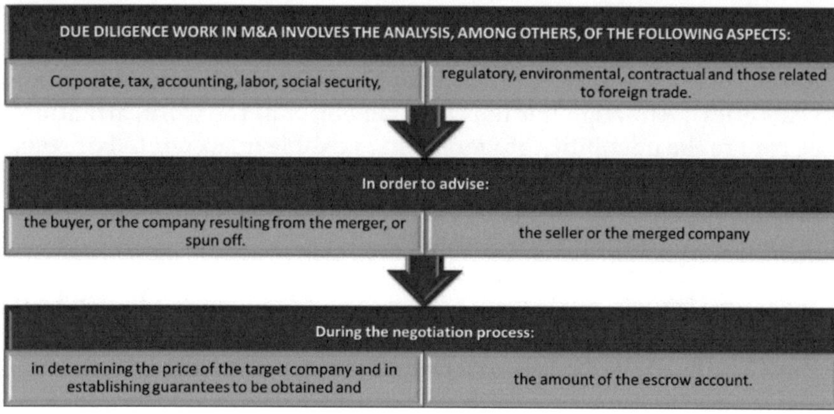

Figure 7.
Due diligence process flow. Source prepared by the author.

Thus, we can summarize the due diligence process through the flow shown in **Figure 7** above.

4. The main aspects of due diligence in the tax area

In today's corporate environment, acquisition transactions often occur on an aggressive time schedule or not at all. In addition, tax practitioners are often not consulted with respect to the tax sensitive aspects of the transaction until the final stages of the transaction, i.e., at the closing. For these reasons, familiarity with the basic tax framework for analyzing acquisition documents is essential [66].

Tax due diligence has its own importance, for two reasons. Firstly, tax risks often present significant hindrances for transactions [67]. Uncovering tax risks must be of special interest to the management of the corporation. Secondly, contrary to other fields of due diligence, tax law is subject to frequent, dynamical changes and puts rather complex demands on the inspection. It may not only have to deal with significantly different past, current and future tax regimes, but, in the case of international concern structures, it also must take the tax requirements of other countries into account. Therefore, efficient inspecting and auditing is of paramount importance in the tax arena.

Tax is one of the most important components that determine the overall profitability of a company. It is so important that it has its own place in the company's financial report in the name of items such as net profit before tax, net profit after tax, deferred tax, etc. Therefore, it goes without saying that the tax aspect cannot be overlooked in the due diligence during mergers and acquisitions [68].

Specifically, regarding the aspects to be observed in a due diligence work in the tax area, to be conducted by tax consultants, we could highlight the following.

4.1 Measurement of liabilities and assets accounted for

This is the due diligence of a research work, whereby the procedures and strategies of the tax area of the company under examination are evaluated, to verify whether the assets and tax liabilities accounted for are properly measured or if they are undervalued or overvalued [69].

4.2 Identification of unaccounted assets and liabilities

It seeks due diligence, also, to identify and measure unaccounted liabilities (hidden liabilities). Although it is not the main object of the work, attention should be paid to the possibility of identifying possible unaccounted or recognized tax assets that may be relevant to the negotiation process [70].

4.3 Disclosure of contingencies not quantified

Due diligence should report all tax procedures and strategies adopted by the company under investigation that may result in contingencies, but which, for various reasons (usually, lack of information and data), could not be quantified [71].

5. Conclusion

In view of the foregoing, it can be noted that the accounting, tax and legal due diligence consists of a work of investigation and analysis of the procedures, practices and strategies of the company under examination in several areas, carried out within the scope and materiality agreed upon procedures, in order to determine whether the assets and liabilities were properly recognized, the degree of realization of these assets, the degree of risk of these liabilities, as well as identifying the existence of other unrecognized liabilities or unidentified assets, thus providing the company that is demanding due diligence, with the elements necessary for a correct pricing, negotiation and overall assessment of the merger or acquisition operation [72].

The tax review essentially begins with the following question: “Has the seller paid all its tax liabilities on a current basis, and has a reasonable reserve been accrued for known and anticipated adjustments likely to arise in current and future audits by various taxing authorities?” Although the procedures used to examine these questions will vary depending on the size of the deal and the complexity of the target’s particular tax situation, these inquiries will generally entail a review and analysis of tax returns for all open years with special emphasis on the reconciliation between financial statement and taxable income and analysis of book and tax basis balance sheets, together with a review of the most recent revenue agent’s reports made by relevant taxing authorities [73].

Once completed, these results are then compared to reserves for taxes, or the so-called “cushion”, to determine whether the seller has adequately provided for any tax exposures. When representing financial buyers, another analysis that will often need to be done is a determination of when contingent tax liabilities may become due and payable. This obviously can tie into determining whether the buyer’s cash flow projections with respect to the target are correct [74].

Succession to the seller’s tax attributes is also an important area to review. Many companies today have net operating loss carryforwards and unutilized investment tax, foreign tax, and other credits. Depending on the type of acquisition structure, these tax attributes can represent significant cash savings to the buyer after the acquisition [75].

In view of all the exposed in this chapter, it remains clear the importance of the tax due diligence of the target company, as a way to minimize risks in the decision-making process of the managers of the purchasing company that may compromise the success of the merger and acquisition operation, as well as subjecting them to administrative and judicial processes, for non-compliance with their fiduciary duties of diligence and loyalty in relation to the company of which they are executives.

Additionally, the study's results suggest that companies—in compliance with the guidelines and limits set by the board—choose the appropriate and specific techniques of risk management, especially those related to minimization, immunization, and transferring these risks. The recommendations derive from the need to identify and manage tax risks, from the point of view of good corporate governance practices.

This study may serve as a reference to companies in general, when studying, developing, and implementing recommendations for the identification and minimization of tax risks, as well as in the development of a work program that allows them to conduct due diligence work in target companies.

Author details

Arnaldo Marques de Oliveira Neto
Fundação Getulio Vargas, São Paulo, Brazil

*Address all correspondence to: amarques@fgvmail.br

References

[1] De Oliveira Neto AM. Governança tributária e sustentabilidade. Revista Brasileira de Administração, n. 316, p 34. Conselho Federal de Administração, São Paulo; 2012.

[2] De Oliveira Neto, AM. Governance and risk management in taxation. Ed. Springer Science + Business Media, Singapore; 2017. 171 p. DOI: 10.1007/978-981-10-2297-5.

[3] Tributação na sociedade de risco. Revista Ciências Sociais, Rio de Janeiro, vol. 12, n. 1, pp 211-254 [Internet]; 2009. Available from: www.ugf.br/files/editais/Artigo%209%20Vol%2012%20n%201%20e%202.pdf [Accessed 1 Dec 2012].

[4] Paxson D, Wood D. The Blackwell Encyclopedic Dictionary of Finance, Oxford, United Kingdom; Blackwell Publishers, 1997. 240 p. ISBN10 155786912X and ISBN13 9781557869128.

[5] IBGC—Instituto Brasileiro De Governança Corporativa. Guia de orientação para gerenciamento de riscos corporativos. (Série cadernos de governança corporativa, n. 3). IBGC, São Paulo; 2007. 48 p. ISBN: 978-85-99645-04-8.

[6] Bernstein, PL. Desafio aos deuses: a fascinante história do risco, 3rd. Ed. Campos, Rio de Janeiro; 1996. 402 p.

[7] Beuren IM (Org.). Como elaborar trabalhos monográficos em contabilidade – 3. ed. São Paulo: Ed. Atlas, 2012. 195 p. ISBN: 978-85-224-4391-8.

[8] De Oliveira Neto, AM. Governance and risk management in taxation. Ed. Springer Science + Business Media, Singapore; 2017. 171 p. DOI: 10.1007/978-981-10-2297-5.

[9] Assi, M. Gestão de Riscos com controles internos. São Paulo: Ed. Saint Paul, 2012. 165 p. ISBN: 978-85-8004-050-0.

[10] De Oliveira Neto, AM. Governance and risk management in taxation. Ed. Springer Science + Business Media, Singapore; 2017. 171 p. DOI: 10.1007/978-981-10-2297-5.

[11] De Oliveira Neto AM. Relacionamento com os acionistas. In: Rocha T e Goldschmidt A, coordinators. Gestão dos stakeholders. Ed. Saraiva; 2011. p. 53-80. ISBN 978-85-02-10263-7.

[12] De Oliveira Neto AM. Relacionamento com os acionistas. In: Rocha T e Goldschmidt A, coordinators. Gestão dos stakeholders. Ed. Saraiva; 2011. p. 53-80. ISBN 978-85-02-10263-7.

[13] De Oliveira Neto, AM. Governance and risk management in taxation. Ed. Springer Science + Business Media, Singapore; 2017. 171 p. DOI: 10.1007/978-981-10-2297-5.

[14] De Oliveira Neto, AM. Governance and risk management in taxation. Ed. Springer Science + Business Media, Singapore; 2017. 171 p. DOI: 10.1007/978-981-10-2297-5.

[15] De Oliveira Neto AM. Governança tributária e sustentabilidade. Revista Brasileira de Administração, n. 316, p 34. Conselho Federal de Administração, São Paulo; 2012.

[16] Governança tributária: um estudo de caso sobre a importância e a viabilidade de implementação de suas práticas na empresa Alfa Ltda. 2011. 68f. Trabalho de Conclusão de Curso (Monografia)—Curso de Ciências Contábeis, Faculdade de Ciências Aplicadas, Petrolina [Internet]. Available from: (www.lapisletras.ba.gov.br/uploads/publicacoes/docs/governanca_tributariaLapis_e_Letras1339547364.pdf) [Accessed in 1 Dec 2012].

[17] Good corporate governance: the tax dimension—OECD forum on tax administration—July 2009 [Internet]. 2009. Available from: (http://www.oecd.org/tax/administration/43239887.pdf) [Accessed 22 May 2015].

[18] Erle B. Tax risk management and board responsibility. In: Drexl J, Hilty RM, Schön W, Straus J, editors. Tax and corporate governance. Ed. Springer, Berlin, Heidelberg; 2008. 423 p. DOI 10.1007/978-3-540-77276-7.

[19] Erle B. Tax risk management and board responsibility. In: Drexl J, Hilty RM, Schön W, Straus J, editors. Tax and corporate governance. Ed. Springer, Berlin, Heidelberg; 2008. 423 p. DOI 10.1007/978-3-540-77276-7.

[20] IBGC—Instituto Brasileiro de Governança Corporativa. Código de melhores práticas de governança corporativa. IBGC, São Paulo; 2009. 73 p. ISBN 978-85-99645-14-7.

[21] Governança empresarial, riscos e controles internos: a emergência de um novo modelo de controladoria. Revista Contabilidade e Finanças, São Paulo, v. 15, n. 34, Jan–Apr 2004 [Internet]. 2004. Available from: (www.scielo.br/phpw?pid=S1519-70772004000100001escript=sci_arttext) [Accessed in 1 Dec 2012].

[22] Erle B. Tax risk management and board responsibility. In: Drexl J, Hilty RM, Schön W, Straus J, editors. Tax and corporate governance. Ed. Springer, Berlin, Heidelberg; 2008. 423 p. DOI 10.1007/978-3-540-77276-7.

[23] De Oliveira Neto, AM. Governance and risk management in taxation. Ed. Springer Science + Business Media, Singapore; 2017. 171 p. DOI: 10.1007/978-981-10-2297-5.

[24] IBGC—Instituto Brasileiro De Governança Corporativa. Uma década de governança corporativa – Histórias do IBGC, marcos e lições de experiência. Ed. Saraiva, São Paulo; 2006. 224 p. ISBN 9788598838144.

[25] Handout "Corporate Governance" by Prof. Rubens Mazzali, p. 4 and 5, Dec/2016.

[26] Wald A, Moraes LR de, Waisberg I. Fusões, incorporações e aquisições – aspectos societários, contratuais e regulatórios. In Warde Jr WJ, coordinators. Fusão, cisão, incorporação e temas correlatos. Ed. Quartier Latin, São Paulo; 2009. p 29-76. ISBN 85-7674-391-4.

[27] De Oliveira Neto AM. Reponsabilidade tributária dos Sucessores. Revista Informe Performance, n. 50, p.6. Grupo Performance Alliot Brasil, Salvador; 2003.

[28] Gröger, H (2010) Planungsaspekte aus Erwerbersicht. In Kneip, Chr., Jänisch, Chr., editors, Tax Due Diligence. Steuerrisiken und Steuergestaltungen beim Unternehmenskauf. 2. Edition. München; 2010. p 545-558. ISBN 9783406597640.

[29] De Oliveira Neto AM. A importância do due diligence nos processos de fusão e de aquisição (merger and acquisition). Revista Informe Performance, n. 49, p.4 and 5. Grupo Performance Alliot Brasil, Salvador; 2003.

[30] Improving the acquisition profit of cross border transactions by adjusting the tax due diligence process – a theoretical model based on a german target. Periodica Polytechnica Social and Management Sciences, pp. 41-50 [Internet]. 2015. Available from: (https://www.researchgatc.nct/publication/277568541_Improving_the_Aquisition_Profit_of_Cross_Border_Transactions_by_Adjusting_the_Tax_Due_Diligence_Process_-_a_Theoretical_Model_Based_on_a_

German_Target) [Accessed 25 November 2019].

[31] Rossi, LEM. Manual de private equity e venture capital: passos para a atração de investidores e alocação de recursos. Ed. Atlas, São Paulo; 2010. 235 p. ISBN 978-85-224-5969-8.

[32] Improving the acquisition profit of cross border transactions by adjusting the tax due diligence process – a theoretical model based on a german target. Periodica Polytechnica Social and Management Sciences, pp. 41-50 [Internet]. 2015. Available from: (https://www.researchgate.net/publication/277568541_Improving_the_Aquisition_Profit_of_Cross_Border_Transactions_by_Adjusting_the_Tax_Due_Diligence_Process_-_a_Theoretical_Model_Based_on_a_German_Target) [Accessed 25 November 2019].

[33] Nejm E e Bruna SV (2002). Due diligence – identificando contingências para prever riscos futuros. In Saddi J, organizer. Fusões e aquisições: aspectos jurídicos e econômicos. Ed. IOB, São Paulo; 2002. p 203-219. CDD-338.83.

[34] Nejm E e Bruna SV (2002). Due diligence – identificando contingências para prever riscos futuros. In Saddi J, organizer. Fusões e aquisições: aspectos jurídicos e econômicos. Ed. IOB, São Paulo; 2002. p 203-219. CDD-338.83.

[35] De Oliveira Neto AM. A importância do due diligence nos processos de fusão e de aquisição (merger and acquisition). Revista Informe Performance, n. 49, p.4 and 5. Grupo Performance Alliot Brasil, Salvador; 2003.

[36] De Oliveira Neto AM. A importância do due diligence nos processos de fusão e de aquisição (merger and acquisition). Revista Informe Performance, n. 49, p.4 and 5. Grupo Performance Alliot Brasil, Salvador; 2003.

[37] Accounting Due Diligence Checklist [Internet]. 2020. Available from: (https://yourbusiness.azcentral.com/prepare-memo-revenue-cycle-problems-27943.html) [Accessed 3 February 2021].

[38] The Scope of Due Diligence in Mergers and Acquisitions [Internet]. 2017. Available from: (https://capitalorigination.net/insights/entry/the-scope-of-due-diligence-in-mergers-and-acquisitions) [Accessed 3 February 2021].

[39] 20 key due diligence activities in a merger and acquisition transaction [Internet]. 2014. Available from: (https://www.forbes.com/sites/allbusiness/2014/12/19/20-key-due-diligence-activities-in-a-merger-and-acquisition-transaction/?sh=70e2442f4bfc) [Accessed 11 November 2020].

[40] Nejm E e Bruna SV (2002). Due diligence – identificando contingências para prever riscos futuros. In Saddi J, organizer. Fusões e aquisições: aspectos jurídicos e econômicos. Ed. IOB, São Paulo; 2002. p 203-219. CDD-338.83.

[41] 20 key due diligence activities in a merger and acquisition transaction [Internet]. 2014. Available from: (https://www.forbes.com/sites/allbusiness/2014/12/19/20-key-due-diligence-activities-in-a-merger-and-acquisition-transaction/?sh=70e2442f4bfc) [Accessed 11 November 2020].

[42] 20 key due diligence activities in a merger and acquisition transaction [Internet]. 2014. Available from: (https://www.forbes.com/sites/allbusiness/2014/12/19/20-key-due-diligence-activities-in-a-merger-and-acquisition-transaction/?sh=70e2442f4bfc) [Accessed 11 November 2020].

[43] Nejm E e Bruna SV (2002). Due diligence – identificando contingências para prever riscos futuros. In Saddi J, organizer. Fusões e aquisições: aspectos jurídicos e econômicos. Ed. IOB, São Paulo; 2002. p 203-219. CDD-338.83.

[44] Due diligence [Internet]. 2020. Available from: (https://www.bestarcorporation.com/post/due-diligence) [Accessed 11 November 2020].

[45] 20 key due diligence activities in a merger and acquisition transaction [Internet]. 2014. Available from: (https://www.forbes.com/sites/allbusiness/2014/12/19/20-key-due-diligence-activities-in-a-merger-and-acquisition-transaction/?sh=70e2442f4bfc) [Accessed 11 November 2020].

[46] Nejm E e Bruna SV (2002). Due diligence – identificando contingências para prever riscos futuros. In Saddi J, organizer. Fusões e aquisições: aspectos jurídicos e econômicos. Ed. IOB, São Paulo; 2002. p 203-219. CDD-338.83.

[47] Nejm E e Bruna SV (2002). Due diligence – identificando contingências para prever riscos futuros. In Saddi J, organizer. Fusões e aquisições: aspectos jurídicos e econômicos. Ed. IOB, São Paulo; 2002. p 203-219. CDD-338.83.

[48] Due diligence [Internet]. 2020. Available from: (https://www.bestarcorporation.com/post/due-diligence) [Accessed 11 November 2020].

[49] Nejm E e Bruna SV (2002). Due diligence – identificando contingências para prever riscos futuros. In Saddi J, organizer. Fusões e aquisições: aspectos jurídicos e econômicos. Ed. IOB, São Paulo; 2002. p 203-219. CDD-338.83.

[50] 20 key due diligence activities in a merger and acquisition transaction [Internet]. 2014. Available from: (https://www.forbes.com/sites/allbusiness/2014/12/19/20-key-due-diligence-activities-in-a-merger-and-acquisition-transaction/?sh=70e2442f4bfc) [Accessed 11 November 2020].

[51] Nejm E e Bruna SV (2002). Due diligence – identificando contingências para prever riscos futuros. In Saddi J, organizer. Fusões e aquisições: aspectos jurídicos e econômicos. Ed. IOB, São Paulo; 2002. p 203-219. CDD-338.83.

[52] Wald A, Moraes LR de, Waisberg I. Fusões, incorporações e aquisições – aspectos societários, contratuais e regulatórios. In Warde Jr WJ, coordinators. Fusão, cisão, incorporação e temas correlatos. Ed. Quartier Latin, São Paulo; 2009. p 29-76. ISBN 85-7674-391-4.

[53] What is a pro forma balance sheet? [Internet]. 2021. Available from: (https://www.wisegeek.com/what-is-a-pro forma-balance-sheet.htm) [Accessed 3 February 2021].

[54] Nejm E e Bruna SV (2002). Due diligence – identificando contingências para prever riscos futuros. In Saddi J, organizer. Fusões e aquisições: aspectos jurídicos e econômicos. Ed. IOB, São Paulo; 2002. p 203-219. CDD-338.83.

[55] Wald A, Moraes LR de, Waisberg I. Fusões, incorporações e aquisições – aspectos societários, contratuais e regulatórios. In Warde Jr WJ, coordinators. Fusão, cisão, incorporação e temas correlatos. Ed. Quartier Latin, São Paulo; 2009. p 29-76. ISBN 85-7674-391-4.

[56] How to write a due diligence report and what to include in it [Internet]. 2009. Available from: (https://www.darbaar.com/how-to-write-due-diligence-report/) [Accessed 11 November 2020].

[57] De Oliveira Neto AM. A importância do due diligence nos processos de fusão e de aquisição (merger and acquisition). Revista Informe Performance, n. 49, p.4 and 5. Grupo Performance Alliot Brasil, Salvador; 2003.

[58] Lück W (2000). Quality Control. Maßnahmen zur Qualitätssicherung in der Wirtschaftsprüfer-Praxis. Der Betrieb. 53; 2000. p 1-6. ISBN 3-486-27513-5.

[59] Hogh M. Due Diligence und Unternehmenskauf. In: Kneip, Chr., Jänisch, Chr., editors, Tax Due Diligence. Steuerrisiken und Steuergestaltungen beim Unternehmenskauf, 2. Edition. München; 2010a. p 1-7. ISBN 9783406597640.

[60] Agreed Upon Procedures [Internet]. 2020. Available from: (https://accountinguide.com/agreed upon-procedures/) [Accessed 3 February 2021].

[61] Wald A, Moraes LR de, Waisberg I. Fusões, incorporações e aquisições – aspectos societários, contratuais e regulatórios. In Warde Jr WJ, coordinators. Fusão, cisão, incorporação e temas correlatos. Ed. Quartier Latin, São Paulo; 2009. p 29-76. ISBN 85-7674-391-4.

[62] Nejm E e Bruna SV (2002). Due diligence – identificando contingências para prever riscos futuros. In Saddi J, organizer. Fusões e aquisições: aspectos jurídicos e econômicos. Ed. IOB, São Paulo; 2002. p 203-219. CDD-338.83.

[63] The tax due diligence process and negotiating and drafting tax provisions in acquisition agreements, pp. D-3, D-4 and D-32 [Internet]. 2000. Available from: (https://www.law.uh.edu/faculty/bwells/cit/duediligence.pdf) [Accessed 11 November 2020].

[64] Rossi, LEM. Manual de private equity e venture capital: passos para a atração de investidores e alocação de recursos. Ed. Atlas, São Paulo; 2010. 235 p. ISBN 978-85-224-5969-8.

[65] Tax due diligence: because what you do not know can hurt you [Internet]. 2019. Available from: (https://efinancemanagement.com/mergers-and-acquisitions/tax-due-diligence) [Accessed 11 November 2019].

[66] The tax due diligence process and negotiating and drafting tax provisions in acquisition agreements, pp. D-3, D-4 and D-32 [Internet]. 2000. Available from: (https://www.law.uh.edu/faculty/bwells/cit/duediligence.pdf) [Accessed 11 November 2020].

[67] Gerber, Chr, König, J (2009) Controlling steuerlicher Risiken in M&A Transaktionen. Controlling & Management. 53 (1); 2009. p 59-63.

[68] Tax due diligence [Internet]. 2019. Available from: (https://efinancemanagement.com/mergers-and-acquisitions/tax-due-diligence) [Accessed 11 November 2019].

[69] De Oliveira Neto AM. A importância do due diligence nos processos de fusão e de aquisição (merger and acquisition). Revista Informe Performance, n. 49, p.4 and 5. Grupo Performance Alliot Brasil, Salvador; 2003.

[70] De Oliveira Neto AM. A importância do due diligence nos processos de fusão e de aquisição (merger and acquisition). Revista Informe Performance, n. 49, p.4 and 5. Grupo Performance Alliot Brasil, Salvador; 2003.

[71] De Oliveira Neto AM. A importância do due diligence nos processos de fusão e de aquisição (merger and acquisition). Revista Informe Performance, n. 49, p.4 and 5. Grupo Performance Alliot Brasil, Salvador; 2003.

[72] De Oliveira Neto AM. A importância do due diligence nos processos de fusão e de aquisição (merger and acquisition). Revista Informe Performance, n. 49, p.4 and 5. Grupo Performance Alliot Brasil, Salvador; 2003.

[73] The tax due diligence process and negotiating and drafting tax provisions in acquisition agreements, pp. D-3, D-4 and D-32 [Internet]. 2000. Available from: (https://www.law.uh.edu/faculty/bwells/cit/duediligence.pdf) [Accessed 11 November 2020].

[74] The tax due diligence process and negotiating and drafting tax provisions in acquisition agreements, pp. D-3, D-4 and D-32 [Internet]. 2000. Available from: (https://www.law.uh.edu/faculty/bwells/cit/duediligence.pdf) [Accessed 11 November 2020].

[75] The tax due diligence process and negotiating and drafting tax provisions in acquisition agreements, pp. D-3, D-4 and D-32 [Internet]. 2000. Available from: (https://www.law.uh.edu/faculty/bwells/cit/duediligence.pdf) [Accessed 11 November 2020].

Chapter 12

Fuzzy Approach Model to Portfolio Risk Response Strategies

Yaser Rahimi

Abstract

Risk management and control of project risks have been the intrinsic characteristics of high-rise building projects in a changing built environment. In this research, a novel bi-objective model for the best mixture of projects is proposed. The first objective focuses on maximizing profits and efficiency of risk responses, and the second objective aims at minimizing project direct cost including machinery, human, and material costs to implement proper risk responses over a planning horizon under uncertainty. In this model, risks of the projects are controlled by time, quality, and cost constraints, and the most optimum risk response strategies (RRSs) are selected to eliminate or reduce the impacts of the risks. Thus, the combination of optimum projects with the best RRSs can be selected for an organizational portfolio model. Finally, to assess the solution method and the proposed model, the empirical result and sensitivity analysis are carried out. Ten large-scale high-rise building projects and their associated risks are evaluated as cases in this study.

Keywords: building engineering, fuzzy system, portfolio selection, project risk management

1. Introduction

The purpose of the risk management framework is to assist the organization in integrating risk management into significant activities and functions. The effectiveness of risk management will depend on its integration into the governance of the organization, including decision-making. This requires support from stakeholders, particularly top management. Framework development encompasses integrating, designing, implementing, evaluating and improving risk management across the organization.

Managing risks at all levels is an active process involving continuous planning, analysis, response, and monitoring and control. The execution of response strategies should be anticipatory and implemented by trigger events that launch response actions before the risk materializes so that opportunities (positive risks) may be enhanced or threats (negative risks) may be diminished. Even within an active process of continuous risk identification, risk management at the program, project, and operations areas are traditionally approached from a prescriptive, process-based perspective. However, within complex systems such as portfolios, risks may not be managed in the traditional or simple sense. Complexity requires a less prescriptive approach. In many cases, the execution of risk response strategies at the portfolio level involves the establishment of projects within the portfolio's component programs or as part of continuing operations to address specific opportunities or threats (positive or negative risks) that have either materialized or have had a significant increase in the probability of occurrence as indicated by a trigger event occurring. There is an important distinction between portfolio risk management and risk management at the program or project level. In many cases, the portfolio manager should delegate risk response measures to subordinate programs or projects within the portfolio. A desired outcome from portfolio risk management is to utilize a structured risk planning and response effort in order to reduce management inaction and decision delay. Risk identification analysis and response planning acknowledge the limits of data and the lack of clear, unambiguous, and actionable information concerning many management factors at the portfolio level. Various possible risk scenarios are studied and response plans developed to limit the impact of the data and information disconnect described above. Through portfolio risk management, senior leadership and portfolio management staff are provided with courses of action or management options that assist in making decisions involving risk with incomplete information.

The importance of an appropriate selection of one project due to the combination of the selected projects for successful portfolio management is inevitable. Many companies try to implement a group of relevant projects as a portfolio to satisfy their synergy and economize their cost through efficient project management. Furthermore, it is needed to manage the risks of each project through the standard risk management process after the creation of the appropriate portfolio. The portfolio has an important role in managing a group of relevant projects so that they bring benefits and values. In the portfolio level, risk management requires a balanced attitude and management judgment exercises in two stages: the first stage is associated with the portfolio creation phase and the second one is allocated to the implementation phase of portfolio projects. We only benefit from the synergy and saving resulted from the portfolios projects management in the case of active risk management. A risk strategy response (RSS) is one of the most important processes of risk management. Therefore, selecting the appropriate projects and managing project risks are simultaneously two appropriate approaches to increase both revenue and profits of project-based organizations. In this research, the main aim is to choose an optimum portfolio of project investment considering its risk response cost and multi-term planning. Project portfolio selection observes the organization's objectives in a planning horizon without outpacing available resources. Schniederjans and Santhanam [1] classified the system's objectives and preferences as financial benefits, intangible benefits, availability of resources, and risk level of the project portfolio, so project risk assessment was a key element in their study [2].

Badri et al. [3] presented a binary goal programming model for the project selection of an information system. Wei and Chang [4] presented a portfolio choice model based on enterprise strategy considering customer's resource and capability, project performance and project delivery, and project risk constraints. Project risks are categorized into three types: market risk, technical risk, financial risk. In any aspect of a project, risk can emerge. The nature of risk is uncertainty. For each project, risks should be identified and analyzed, and to cope with these risks, proper RRSs must be employed [5–11]. Tang et al. [9] developed a new solution method to the lean 6-sigma portfolio management as a binary quadratic programming problem. Muriana and Vizzini [12] presented a certain method to determine the risk of the Work Progress Status for assessing and preventing project risk.

On the other hand, Rahimi et al. [13] proposed a mathematical model, in which different risks are considered for activities so that different responses can be selected for each risk. Also, the risk responses are not considered as independent, and responses are associated with each other. Indeed, choosing the responses, which overlap each other, can affect their results, time, cost, and quality of the project. The objective function used different evaluation criteria and tried to choose the optimum responses, which maximizes these evaluation criteria. Ben-David and Raz

[14] considered the cost of implementing strategies and incorporated them into an RRS selection problem. Ben-David et al. [15] extended their previous work by providing a mathematical model that facilitates computer implementation of the model. Because of the risk abatement actions, a selection problem is a complex one. Therefore, they proposed a branch-and-bound algorithm and two heuristic algorithms [16, 17]. Zhang and Fan [18] integrated all three key elements in project management (i.e., project expenditure, project planning horizon, and project quality). They proposed a new efficient solution for the mathematical model of the RRS.

Reviewing the aforementioned discussions and literature, we understand that there are gaps in (1) selecting the best projects portfolio that the effect of risk in selected projects is controlled [18], and (2) selecting projects to check the balance between the total cost of the selected projects and the profit of the selected projects, and all the predicted risk response effects. Furthermore, some of the parameters in the real-world are uncertain and can cause a high degree of uncertainty on a designed network [19].

To overcome and fulfill these gaps, for the first time, we develop a mathematical model for selecting the best projects and control risks of each selected projects under uncertainty. In this research, we investigate the trade-off between the total cost of the selected projects including all three types of resources (e.g., human, machine, raw materials) and implanting proper risk responses-and the net profit of the selected projects, and all the approximated risk response effects. The important items which this research contributes are as follows:

- Presenting a new two-objective binary mathematical model to choose an optimum portfolio and control risks of the selected projects.

- Introducing a new objective function for selecting projects with the maximum net profit and all the estimated risk response effects for each project.

- Developing a new multi-period, multi-project, and multi-resource model to control risks of the selected projects.

2. Problem description

We present a new model to select an optimum project portfolio tacking into account many constraints in the multi-period planning horizon. Also, this model can be used to select the RRSs. The portfolio selection problem of the project RRSs is combined with four basic concepts (i.e., project opportunity, work breakdown structure, risk event, and risk responses) as well as three key elements (i.e., schedule, quality, and cost) are considered in these concepts. These concepts are described as project scope, work breakdown structure, risk event, risk response. There is a strategy to respond r risk events. On the other hand, N project should be evaluated with their risk responses' effects to select an optimum portfolio. The optimal portfolio will be top j projects. All parameters of the mathematical model change dynamically. In this model, an optimum portfolio is selected considering its risk response expenditure. The most enticing RRSs can be acquired by solving the mathematical model. **Figure 1** depicts the process of portfolio RRSs.

In this section, we present notations and mathematical modeling in Sections 2.1 and 2.2, respectively.

It should also be mentioned that the definition of parameters of s_{ar}^{w}, $s_{r}^{w}, q_{ar}^{w}, \varepsilon^{w}, \delta^{w}, \acute{T}_{max}, Q_{max}, \tilde{e}_{ar}, q_{r}^{w}, \overline{M}, \overleftrightarrow{M}$ can be found in Rahimi et al. [13]. Following is the mathematical mode.

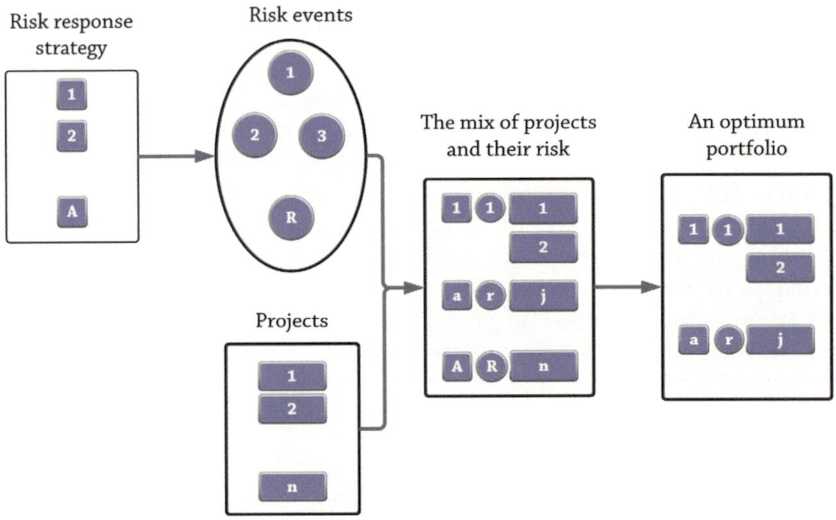

Figure 1.
Process of portfolio RRSs.

2.1 Mathematical programming

$$\text{Max}Z_1 = \sum_{t=1}^{T}\sum_{j=1}^{n} x_{jt} \times \tilde{p}_{jt} + \sum_{j=1}^{n}\sum_{a=1}^{A}\sum_{r=1}^{R} z_{jar} \times \tilde{e}_{ar} \tag{1}$$

$$\text{Min}Z_2 = \sum_{t=1}^{T}\sum_{j=1}^{n} x_{jt} \sum_{i=1}^{m} h_{ij}.\tilde{C}_{it} + \sum_{t=1}^{T}\sum_{j=1}^{n} x_{jt} \sum_{k=1}^{s} m_{kj}.\tilde{C}_{kt} + \sum_{t=1}^{T}\sum_{j=1}^{n} x_{jt} \sum_{o=1}^{z} r_{oj}.\tilde{C}_{ot} + \sum_{j=1}^{n}\sum_{a=1}^{A} \tilde{C}_a \max_r z_{jar} \tag{2}$$

s.t.;

$$\sum_{t=1}^{T} x_{jt} \leq 1; \quad \forall j \tag{3}$$

$$\sum_{t=1}^{T} (t + d_{jt}).x_{jt} \leq T + 1 + T_{max}; \quad \forall j \tag{4}$$

$$\sum_{j=1}^{n} h_{ij} x_{jt} \leq H_{it}; \quad \forall i, t \tag{5}$$

$$\sum_{j=1}^{n} m_{kj} x_{jt} \leq M_{kt}; \quad \forall k, t \tag{6}$$

$$\sum_{j=1}^{n} r_{oj} x_{jt} \leq R_{ot}; \quad \forall O, t \tag{7}$$

$$\left(\sum_{i=1}^{m} h_{ij}.\tilde{C}_{it} + \sum_{k=1}^{s} m_{kj}.\tilde{C}_{kt} + \sum_{o=1}^{z} r_{oj}.\tilde{C}_{ot}\right) \times x_{jt} < \tilde{p}_{jt}, j = 1, 2, \ldots, n; \quad \forall t \tag{8}$$

$$\sum_{j=1}^{n}\sum_{a=1}^{A}\tilde{C}_a \max_r z_{jar} + \left[\sum_{i=1}^{m} h_{ij}\tilde{C}_{it} + \sum_{k=1}^{s} m_{kj}\tilde{C}_{kt} + \sum_{o=1}^{z}\tilde{C}_{ot}r_{oj}\right] \times x_{jt} \le \tilde{B}_{jt}; \quad \forall r, j, t \quad (9)$$

$$\sum_{r=1}^{R} s_r^w - \sum_{r=1}^{R}\sum_{a=1}^{A}\left(s_{ar}^w z_{jar}\right) \le \varepsilon^w; \quad \forall j, w \quad (10)$$

$$\sum_{r=1}^{R} q_r^w - \sum_{r=1}^{R}\sum_{a=1}^{A}\left(q_{ar}^w z_{jar}\right) \le \delta^w; \quad \forall j, w \quad (11)$$

$$\sum_{r=1}^{R} s_r^W - \sum_{r=1}^{R}\sum_{a=1}^{A}\left(s_{ar}^W z_{jar}\right) \le \acute{T}_{max}; \quad j = n \quad (12)$$

$$\sum_{r=1}^{R} q_r^W - \sum_{r=1}^{R}\sum_{a=1}^{A}\left(q_{ar}^W z_{jar}\right) \le Q_{max}; \quad j = n \quad (13)$$

$$\sum_{j=1}^{n} x_{jt}.\left(MARR_t - I_{jt}\right) \le 0; \quad \forall t \quad (14)$$

$$\sum_{j=1}^{n} x_{jt} \ge 0; \quad \forall t \quad (15)$$

$$z_{jar} + z_{j\acute{a}\acute{r}} \le 1 \left(A_a, A_{\acute{a}}\right) \in \overset{\leftrightarrow}{M}; \quad \forall j, a, \acute{a}, r, \acute{r} \quad (16)$$

$$z_{jar} + z_{j\acute{a}\acute{r}} = 1 \left(A_a, A_{\acute{a}}\right) \in \overset{\leftrightarrow}{M}; \quad \forall j, a, \acute{a}, r, \acute{r} \quad (17)$$

$$z_{jar} - z_{j\acute{a}\acute{r}} \le 0 \left(A_a, A_{\acute{a}}\right) \in \overline{M}; \quad \forall j, a, \acute{a}, r, \acute{r} \quad (18)$$

$$z_{jar}, z_{j\acute{a}\acute{r}} \in \{0, 1\}; \quad \forall j, a, \acute{a}, r, \acute{r} \quad (19)$$

$$x_{jt} \in \{0, 1\}; \quad \forall j, t \quad (20)$$

Objective function value (OFV) (1) maximizes the NP of the selected portfolio and effects on all RRSa for each project of the selected portfolio. Objective function value (2) is minimizing the total cost of the chosen projects consisting of four terms. These terms are the human resource expenditure, the machine resource expenditure, the raw materials resource cost, and implementing the RRSs, respectively.

Constraint (3) ensures that each project selection will happen only one time on the planning horizon. Constraint (4) states that the completion time of each selected project is less than the planning horizon plus the upper bound for project delivery delay. Constraints (5)–(7) define the maximum limits of all three resources. Constraint (5) states that the number of human resources of all types needed for projects during selection cannot exceed the maximum available human resources for all types and all planning terms. Constraint (6) ensures that all machine-hour resources of all types needed for projects during selection do not exceed the maximum available machine-hour resources for all types and all planning terms. Constraint (7) ensures that all raw materials resources of all types needed for projects during selection do not exceed the maximum available raw materials resources of all types and for all planning terms. Constraint (8) certifies that the total cost of each selected project is less than its net profit for all planning terms. Constraint (9) certifies that the total cost of a selected project including human resource expenditure, machine resource expenditure, raw material cost, and implementing the RRSs, is less than its budget for all projects and all planning terms.

Constraint (10) certifies that, in each project, each work packages (except the last one) is completed in the due date, otherwise (if it takes more), it does not affect the schedule of its successors' start times. Constraint (11) ensures that, in each project, each work packages (except the last one) maintain a certain level of quality. Constraint (12) indicates that, in each project, the last work package must be finished in the project deadline. Constraint (13) indicates that in each project, the last work packages must conform to project quality standards. Constraint (14) ensures if a project is selected, it is attractive and that means the internal RoR of the chosen projects should be greater than or equal to the MARR. Constraint (15) indicates that in each period, projects can be chosen. Constraints (16)–(18) are about strategies. Constraint (16) ensures that strategies A_a, and $A_{\acute{a}}$prevent each other for each project. Constraint (17) ensures that for each project, only one strategy must be selected if strategiesA_a, and $A_{\acute{a}}$exclude each other. Constraint (18) states that projects cooperate if one strategy is chosen another strategy must be chosen too. Also, in constraint (19) attributes a binary variable for each project. Constraint (20) refers to binary decision variables.

2.2 Proposed uncertainty programming

Uncertainty in data can be grouped into two categories: randomness and fuzziness. Randomness originates from the random nature of data and Fuzziness refers to the vague parameters Infected with epistemic uncertainty-ambiguity of these parameters stems from the lack of knowledge regarding the exact value of these parameters. The proposed model for this problem is a fuzzy multi-objective nonlinear programming (FMONLP). There are a number of adopted methods to transform this model into its equivalent crisp match, from which a two-phase approach is offered [13–20]. Firstly, using an efficient method introduced by Jimenez et al., [21], the basic model is transformed into an equivalent auxiliary crisp multi-objective model. Secondly, the fuzzy aggregation function, developed by [20], is used to solve the crisp multi-objective mode. To do this, a single-objective parametric model to find the final preferred compromise solution replaces the crisp multi-objective model.

Several methods have been proposed to convert a probabilistic model into an equivalent non-probabilistic one. Probabilistic constraints transform into non-probabilistic ones using fuzzy measures, which was introduced, in the literature review section. The possibility (Pos) and necessity (Nec) are the general fuzzy measures respectively showing the optimistic and pessimistic attitudes of the decision maker. The Pos measure shows the possibility degree of occurrence of a probabilistic event, and the Nec measure indicates the minimum possibility degree of occurrence of a probabilistic event. Certainty degree of occurrence of an uncertain event is measured by credibility (Cr), which equals the average of the Pos and Nec measures [22]. New fuzzy measure Me, which is a developed Cr measure is presented by [23]. The main advantage of this measure is its flexibility to avoid excessive views. In the following, the three measures of a fuzzy event, including possibility, necessity and credibility, are described. Variable ξ is determined as a fuzzy variable on probabilistic space $(\Theta, P(\Theta), Pos)$and its membership function, obtained from the probability measure Pos, is as follows:

$$(X) = Pos\{\theta \in \Theta | \xi(\theta) = x\}, x \in R \tag{21}$$

Set A is in $P(\Theta)$. The necessity and credibility measures of are defined as follows:

$$Nec\{A\} = 1 - Pos\{A^c\} \tag{22}$$

$$Cr\{A\} = \frac{1}{2}(Pos\{A\} + Nec\{A\}) \tag{23}$$

More details and descriptions of the fuzzy theory are explained in [22]. In this research, the Me-based probabilistic programming method is selected to deal with the uncertain parameters of the presented model. The fuzzy measure Me is defined, according to [22], as follows:

$$Me\ \{A\} = Nec\{A\} + \mathcal{E}\ (Pos\{A\} - Nec\{A\}) \tag{24}$$

Where ε as a parameter shows the optimistic-pessimistic attitude of a decision maker. Mathematical programming problem (25) with fuzzy parameters is as follows:

$$Min\, f(x, \tilde{c})$$

Subjected to

$$\tilde{A}x \geq \tilde{b} \tag{25}$$

$$\tilde{N}x \leq \tilde{d}$$

$$x \geq 0$$

In this notation $\tilde{c} = (\tilde{c}_1, \tilde{c}_2, \dots, \tilde{c}_n)$,$\tilde{A} = [\tilde{a}_{ij}]_{m\times n}$,$\tilde{N} = [\tilde{n}_{ij}]_{m\times n}$, $\tilde{b} = \left(\tilde{b}_1, \tilde{b}_1, \dots, \tilde{b}_n\right)^t$ and $\tilde{d} = \left(\tilde{d}_1, \tilde{d}_1, \dots, \tilde{d}_n\right)^t$ represent the triangular fuzzy numbers which are used in the objective function and constraints, respectively. Furthermore, the fuzzy number $x = (x_1, x_1, \dots, x_n)$ is the crisp decision vector, which shows the possibility distribution for fuzzy parameters.

To deal with the probabilistic objective functions and constraints, the expected value and chance-constrained operators based on the Me measure in this method are used. Accordingly, we can rewrite this model (26) as below:

$$Min\ E[f(x, \tilde{c})]$$

Subjected to

$$Me\left\{\tilde{A}x \geq \tilde{b}\right\} \geq \alpha \tag{26}$$

$$Me\left\{\tilde{N}x \leq \tilde{b}\right\} \geq \beta$$

$$x \geq 0$$

In this notation, E is the expected value operator, α and β are respectively the decision maker's minimum confidence level for satisfaction of probabilistic constraints. Jiménez et al. [21] defined the expected value operator based on Me measure as follows:

$$E[\xi] = \frac{1-\varepsilon}{2}\xi_1 + \frac{1}{2}\xi_2 + \frac{\varepsilon}{2}\xi_3 \tag{27}$$

According to [22] we can transform the aforementioned model (26) into two approximation models including the upper approximation model (UAM) and the lower approximation model (LAM). These models are presented as follows:

$$(UAM)\begin{cases} \min\left(\frac{1-\varepsilon}{2}c_1+\frac{1}{2}c_2+\frac{\varepsilon}{2}c_3\right)x \\ A_{(2)}x+(1-\alpha)\left(A_{(3)}-A_{(2)}\right)x\geq b_2-(1-\alpha)\left(b_{(2)}-b_{(1)}\right) \\ N_{(2)}x-(1-\beta)\left(N_{(2)}-N_{(1)}\right)x\leq d_2+(1-\alpha)\left(d_{(3)}-d_{(2)}\right) \end{cases} \tag{28}$$

$$(LAM)\begin{cases} \min\left(\frac{1-\varepsilon}{2}c_1+\frac{1}{2}c_2+\frac{\varepsilon}{2}c_3\right)x \\ A_{(2)}x+\alpha\left(A_{(3)}-A_{(2)}\right)x\geq b_2+(1-\alpha)\left(b_{(3)}-b_{(2)}\right) \\ N_{(2)}x+(1-\beta)\left(N_{(3)}-N_{(2)}\right)x\leq d_2+\beta\left(d_{(2)}-d_{(1)}\right) \end{cases} \tag{29}$$

Where ε is the optimistic-pessimistic parameter. Solving the LAM and UAM models provides the decision maker with the lower and upper bound of the optimal decision respectively. In this research, we use UAM models to solve problem. Accordingly, the auxiliary crisp equivalent of the presented model with triangular fuzzy parameters is presented as follows:

UAM:

$$Max\ Z_1=\sum_{t=1}^{T}\sum_{j=1}^{n}x_{jt}\times\left(\frac{1-\varepsilon}{2}p_{jt(1)}+\frac{1}{2}p_{jt(2)}+\frac{\varepsilon}{2}p_{jt(3)}\right)+\sum_{j=1}^{n}\sum_{a=1}^{A}\sum_{r=1}^{R}z_{jar}$$
$$\times\left(\frac{1-\varepsilon}{2}e_{ar(1)}+\frac{1}{2}e_{ar(2)}+\frac{\varepsilon}{2}e_{ar(3)}\right) \tag{30}$$

$$Min\ Z_2=\sum_{t=1}^{T}\sum_{j=1}^{n}x_{jt}\sum_{i=1}^{m}h_{ij}.\left(\frac{1-\varepsilon}{2}C_{it(1)}+\frac{1}{2}C_{it(2)}+\frac{\varepsilon}{2}C_{it(3)}\right)$$
$$+\sum_{t=1}^{T}\sum_{j=1}^{n}x_{jt}\sum_{k=1}^{s}m_{kj}.\left(\frac{1-\varepsilon}{2}C_{kt(1)}+\frac{1}{2}C_{kt(2)}+\frac{\varepsilon}{2}c_{kt(3)}\right)$$
$$+\sum_{t=1}^{T}\sum_{j=1}^{n}x_{jt}\sum_{o=1}^{z}r_{oj}.\left(\frac{1-\varepsilon}{2}C_{ot(1)}+\frac{1}{2}C_{ot(2)}+\frac{\varepsilon}{2}C_{ot(3)}\right)$$
$$+\sum_{j=1}^{n}\sum_{a=1}^{A}\left(\frac{1-\varepsilon}{2}C_{a(1)}+\frac{1}{2}C_{a(2)}+\frac{\varepsilon}{2}C_{a(3)}\right)\max_{r} z_{jar} \tag{31}$$

Subjected to

$$\left(\sum_{i=1}^{m}h_{ij}.\left(C_{it(2)}x-(1-\beta)\left(C_{it(2)}-C_{it(1)}\right)\right)\right.$$
$$+\sum_{k=1}^{s}m_{kj}.\left(C_{kt(2)}x-(1-\beta)\left(C_{kt(2)}-C_{kt(1)}\right)\right)$$
$$\left.+\sum_{o=1}^{z}r_{oj}.\left(C_{ot(2)}x-(1-\beta)\left(C_{ot(2)}-C_{ot(1)}\right)\right)\right)\times x_{jt} \tag{32}$$
$$\leq p_{jt(2)}+(1-\beta)\left(p_{ij(3)}-p_{ij(2)}\right)$$

$$\sum_{j=1}^{n}\sum_{a=1}^{A}\left(C_{a(2)}x-(1-\beta)\left(C_{a(2)}-C_{a(1)}\right)\right)\max_{r} z_{jar} + \left[\sum_{i=1}^{m}h_{ij}\left(C_{it(2)}x-(1-\beta)\left(C_{it(2)}-C_{it(1)}\right)\right) + \sum_{k=1}^{s}m_{kj}\left(C_{kt(2)}x-(1-\beta)\left(C_{kt(2)}-C_{kt(1)}\right)\right) + \sum_{o=1}^{z}\left(C_{ot(2)}x-(1-\beta)\left(C_{ot(2)}-C_{ot(1)}\right)\right)r_{oj}\right]\times x_{jt} \leq B_{jt(2)}+(1-\beta)\left(B_{ij(3)}-B_{ij(2)}\right) \tag{33}$$

Other Constraints

2.3 LAM

$$Max\ E[Z_1] \tag{34}$$

$$Min\ E[Z_2] \tag{35}$$

Subjected to

$$\left(\sum_{i=1}^{m}h_{ij}.\left(C_{it(2)}+(1-\beta)\left(C_{it(3)}-C_{it(2)}\right)\right) + \sum_{k=1}^{s}m_{kj}.\left(C_{kt(2)}+(1-\beta)\left(C_{kt(3)}-C_{kt2}\right)\right) + \sum_{o=1}^{z}r_{oj}.\left(C_{ot(2)}+(1-\beta)\left(C_{ot(3)}-C_{ot(2)}\right)\right)\right)\times x_{jt} \leq p_{jt(2)}-(\beta)\left(p_{ij(2)}-p_{ij(1)}\right) \tag{36}$$

$$\sum_{j=1}^{n}\sum_{a=1}^{A}\left(C_{a(2)}+(1-\beta)\left(C_{a(3)}-C_{a(2)}\right)\right)\max_{r} z_{jar} + \left[\sum_{i=1}^{m}h_{ij}\left(C_{it(2)}+(1-\beta)\left(C_{it(3)}-C_{it(2)}\right)\right) + \sum_{k=1}^{s}m_{kj}\left(C_{kt(2)}+(1-\beta)\left(C_{kt(3)}-C_{kt(2)}\right)\right) + \sum_{o=1}^{z}\left(C_{ot(2)}+(1-\beta)\left(C_{ot(3)}-C_{ot(2)}\right)\right)r_{oj}\right] \times x_{jt} \leq B_{jt(2)}-(\beta)\left(B_{ij(2)}-B_{ij(1)}\right) \tag{37}$$

Other Constraints

2.4 Experimental results

The select Portfolio RRSs proposed in this study is a mixed-integer linear programming model. It worth noting that the general algebraic modeling system (GAMS) software is used to solve the mathematical model. In this section, a P.G. company (One of the huge companies in the field of construction) in Iran is investigated as a real-case study to validate the performance of the proposed select Portfolio RRSs model.

An efficient multi-objective method can be done as an efficient method for obtaining the satisfaction level for each OFVs according to the decision maker's preferences. For further explanations, the interested reader can refer to TH [20]. Two parameters in this method are very critical: relative importance of OFVs (i.e., weight factor) and coefficient of compensation. Details of the distribution functions of the parameters and the size of test problems are listed in **Table 1**. After that, the results on test problems for diverse values of ϑ andφ are shown in **Table 2**.

According to **Table 2**, the values of objective functions change based on the value of ϑ. The results indicate that satisfaction degrees displaying each objective function change based on the value of ϑ. In this table, the values of satisfaction degree of objective functions (1) and (2) for test problem 2 fluctuate between 0.841 and 0.965, and 0.848 and 0.961, respectively. The results show that by manipulating the value of ϑ, the decision-maker can make trade-offs between two objective functions and select an optimal pair. Generally, increasing the value of ϑ leads to higher allocated weights to acquire a higher lower bound for the satisfaction degree of objectives (λ_0).

Based on the acquired results and considering the budget and time limitations, the most appropriate strategy for responding to the risk work packages is provided in **Table 3**. In this test problem project 8 and 3 are selected. Appendix A. shows the amount of maximum allowed time reduction (day) and the quality of each activity (in percentage). The obtained quality of each activity under acceptable and ideal condition is assumed 90% and 99% respectively ($\delta^w \in [1\%, 10\%]$). Appendix B. illustrates the effect of implementing risk response strategies on risks cost reduction (if occurs).

Parameters	Values		
	First Problem	Second Problem	Third Problem
J	3	3	3
I	20	20	20
K	3	3	3
O	2	2	2
T	5	5	5
W	12	12	12
R	12	12	12
A	8	8	8
p_{jt}	(2 × 104,3.5 × 104)	(4 × 104,6 × 104)	(6 × 104,9 × 104)
e_{ar}	(5 × 103,104)	(8 × 103,2 × 104)	(1.8 × 104,5 × 104)
C_a	(103,5 × 103)	(104,2 × 104)	(3 × 104,5 × 104)
B_{jt}	(5 × 103,1.5 × 104)	(3 × 104,5 × 104)	(5 × 104,7.5 × 104)
C_{it}	(500,700)	(800,1000)	(1500,2000)
C_{kt}	(800,1500)	(2000,3000)	(4000,8000)
C_{ot}	(1000,2000)	(1000,2000)	(1000,2000)

Table 1.
Amount of the parameters by random generation.

Problem No.	ϑ	φ	$\mathcal{Z}_1$	$\mu_1(\mathcal{Z})$	$\mathcal{Z}_2$	$\mu_2(\mathcal{Z})$
1	0.6	0.3,0.7	33218.2	0.924	781.08	0.973
	0.6	0.5,0.5	32039.2	0.958	817.20	0.930
	0.6	0.7,0.3	31287.4	0.981	826.98	0.919
	0.4	0.3,0.7	34838.8	0.881	772.35	0.984
	0.4	0.5,0.5	32791.6	0.936	805.93	0.943
	0.4	0.7,0.3	30909.3	0.994	867.57	0.876
2	0.6	0.3,0.7	50448.4	0.892	1317.2	0.911
	0.6	0.5,0.5	48966.2	0.919	1345.3	0.890
	0.6	0.7,0.3	46632.1	0.965	1415.0	0.848
	0.4	0.3,0.7	53507.7	0.841	1248.6	0.961
	0.4	0.5,0.5	51903.1	0.867	1295.8	0.926
	0.4	0.7,0.3	47418.3	0.949	1393.7	0.861
3	0.6	0.3,0.7	70806.1	0.918	2098.6	0.953
	0.6	0.5,0.5	69370.3	0.937	2164.5	0.924
	0.6	0.7,0.3	67427.3	0.964	2171.5	0.921
	0.4	0.3,0.7	71982.2	0.903	2044.9	0.978
	0.4	0.5,0.5	69817.4	0.931	2148.2	0.931
	0.4	0.7,0.3	66598.3	0.976	2229.6	0.897

Table 2.
Results of test problem 1 ($\beta = 0.5$).

2.5 Managerial insights

Large construction companies mainly use the project to carry out their activities. Due to the limited resources of these companies, which can be considered project-based organizations, they have to decide on selecting, stopping projects and allocating resources, and have using portfolio management tools, consequently. Portfolio Risk Management is one of the common knowledge scopes in portfolio management with project portfolio decisions application. The primary purpose of risk management is to protect the organization against damages and to prepare the organization for possible future damage. Therefore, the risks should be met with proper risk responses. Risk management at the portfolio level supports the aforementioned goals in different ways.

Firstly, enables the portfolio manager to compare the risks of single projects in terms of risk feature reduction actions. This comparison allows to make difference between options and the single risk levels are clarified and the results of risk responses actions are reflected and facilitate the transfer of experiences between the projects. Secondly, the comparison of the public risks of the portfolio and its trend according to the life cycle of the project has been revealed. Clarity growth leads to preventing other project risks or increasing focus on risks that are prevalent in most of the projects. Thirdly, risk management reduces uncertainty by providing enough information to make decisions. As a result, estimations are more accurate, reliable, and reduce the chance of surprise and the rate of failures. Therefore, risk management should increase information clarity, detecting and clarifying problems, risk response capacity, and depth of information for decision making.

Optimal allocation in project 3	Risks	Work Packages (WP)
RR 27	R1	WP 1- WP 10
RR 17	R 5	WP 5- WP 10
RR 21	R 8	WP 5- WP 10
RR 10	R 9	WP 3- WP 4
RR 12	R 12	WP 1, WP 9, WP 10
RR 7	R 24	WP 2- WP 8
RR 22	R 25	WP 4- WP 6
RR 1	R 26	WP 6, WP 7, WP 9
Optimal allocation in project 3	Risks	Work packages
RRS 27	R 1	WP 1- WP 12
RRS 13	R 2	WP 1, WP 3- WP 10
RRS 14	R 4	WP 2- WP 12
RRS 11	R 7	WP 3- WP 12
RRS 21	R 8	WP 5- WP 12
RRS 10	R 9	WP 5- WP 12
RRS 30	R 10	WP 8, WP 10, WP 11
RRS 16	R 11	WP 3- WP 12

Table 3.
Solution allocation of RRs for projects 8 and 3.

3. Conclusion

In this research, a linear mixed-integer model was proposed to solve a project selection problem and provide RRSs. According to objective functions, this model firstly aims to select projects with the highest net profit and risk response effects. Secondly, these projects should be carried out with minimum resource and implanting risk responses costs. The model is solved to select the most desirable projects and risk response strategies to deal with risk events. The main contribution of this research is combining of project selection from a portfolio and calculation of risk response effect. In addition, because of environmental effects, some parameters (including the cost of human, machine, material, risk response effect, etc.) were considered as fuzzy numbers. Fuzzy Me measure is considered to deal with the uncertain parameters of the proposed model. To solve the model ten building project were studied, and Net profit and resources costs were considered as objective functions. Finally, optimal allocation of risk response strategies was determined. TH method was used to solve the model, which was coded in GAMS. Results showed that increasing budgets in sample problem, led to higher net profit and less projects costs. The sensitivity analysis of the case study showed the necessity of the trade-offs between maximizing profit and minimizing projects cost. At last, Pareto frontier was analyzed. Results indicate that this model can act as a powerful criterion and help project managers to increase desirable impacts of a solution before implementing the project. Also, uncertain parameters like robust programming can be determined to cover the limitations of the designed model. Moreover, since the presented model is categorized as an NP-hard problem, meta-heuristic algorithms may be utilized to solve the model.

Notations

Sets

j	Projects $j = 1, 2, \ldots, n$).
i	Human resources (HR) ($i = 1, 2, \ldots, m$).
k	Machinery ($k = 1, 2, \ldots, s$).
O	Material ($O = 1, 2, \ldots, z$).
t	Time period ($t = 1, 2, \ldots, T$).
w	Work packages($w = 1, 2, \ldots, W$).
r	Risk events (RE)($r = 1, 2, \ldots, R$).
a	Candidate RRSs($a = 1, 2, \ldots, A$).

Parameters

H_{it}	Max accessible HR i in time t (person-hours).
h_{ij}	Demand of HR i in j (person-hours).
$\tilde{M}_{kt}$	Max available machine-hour k in time t.
m_{kj}	Demand of machine-hour k in j.
R_{ot}	Max accessible material o in time t.
r_{oj}	Demand of material o in j.
B_{jt}	Maximum available project budget for j in period t.
$\tilde{C}_{it}$	Hourly cost of HR i in period t.
$\tilde{C}_{kt}$	Hourly cost of machine k in time t.
$\tilde{C}_{ot}$	Unit cost of material o in time$t$.
W_w	Work packages w.
R_r	Risk response (RR) r.
A_a	Candidate RRS a.
C_a	Cost of implementing risk response strategy a.
$\tilde{p}_{jt}$	Total Net Profit (NP) worth of j in time t.
I_{jt}	RoR for j in time t.
$MARR_t$	MARR during period t.
d_{jt}	Period of project j in time t.

Decision variables

x_{jt}	if project j is chosen for investment in time t, 1; otherwise, 0.
z_{jar}	1 if RRS a is applied for RE r for project j; 0, otherwise.

Appendix A: Projects activities, budget, costs, Maximum allowed time reduction (day) and the quality of each activity (percentage)

Appendix A.1

	Project 1									Project 2						
	W1	W2	W3	W4	W5	W6	W7	W8	W9	W1	W2	W3	W4	W5	W6	W7
δ^w	10%	10%	10%	10%	10%	10%	10%	10%	10%	10%	10%	10%	10%	10%	10%	10%

	Project 1									Project 2						
	W1	**W2**	**W3**	**W4**	**W5**	**W6**	**W7**	**W8**	**W9**	**W1**	**W2**	**W3**	**W4**	**W5**	**W6**	**W7**
ε^w	14	8	10	15	10	8	14	14	12	14	11	14	11	11	11	8
C_{it}	22,000 (USD)									25,000(USD)						
C_{kt}	35,000 (USD)									30,000(USD)						
C_{ot}	30,000 (USD)									38,000(USD)						
B_{jt}	200 million (USD)									250 million (USD)						

Appendix A.2

	Project 3											
	W1	**W2**	**W3**	**W4**	**W5**	**W6**	**W7**	**W8**	**W9**	**W10**	**W11**	**W12**
δ^w	10%	10%	10%	10%	10%	10%	10%	10%	10%	10%	10%	10%
ε^w	11	12	14	10	12	13	9	13	15	10	8	14
C_{it}	20,000 (USD)											
C_{kt}	35,000 (USD)											
C_{ot}	28,000 (USD)											
B_{jt}	270 million (USD)											

Appendix A.3

	Project 4							Project 5						Project 6				
	W1	W2	W3	W4	W5	W6	W7	W1	W2	W3	W4	W5	W6	W1	W2	W3	W4	W5
δ^w	10%	10%	10%	11%	10%	10%	10%	10%	10%	10%	10%	10%	10%	10%	10%	10%	10%	10%
ε^w	10	10	12	12	13	9	10	12	13	9	13	14	10	10	12	12	14	9
C_{it}	25,000 (USD)							25,000 (USD)						20,000 (USD)				
C_{kt}	30,000 (USD)							35,000 (USD)						35,000 (USD)				
C_{ot}	35,000 (USD)							35,000 (USD)						38,000 (USD)				
B_{jt}	200 million (USD)							200 million (USD)						250 million (USD)				

Appendix A.4

	Project 7							
	W1	**W2**	**W3**	**W4**	**W5**	**W6**	**W7**	**W8**
δ^w	10%	10%	10%	10%	10%	10%	10%	10%
ε^w	8	11	14	11	13	13	12	14
C_{it}	25,000 (USD)							
C_{kt}	45,000 (USD)							
C_{ot}	28,000 (USD)							
B_{jt}	300 million (USD)							

Appendix A.5

	Project 8										Project 9						
	W1	**W2**	**W3**	**W4**	**W5**	**W6**	**W7**	**W8**	**W9**	**W10**	**W1**	**W2**	**W3**	**W4**	**W5**	**W6**	**W7**
δ^w	10%	10%	10%	10%	10%	10%	10%	10%	10%	10%	11%	11%	11%	11%	11%	11%	11%
ε^w	14	15	14	16	14	11	12	9	14	14	10	12	13	9	13	15	9
C_{it}	20,000(USD)										20,000(USD)						
C_{kt}	35,000(USD)										38,000(USD)						
C_{ot}	25,000(USD)										40,000(USD)						
B_{jt}	200 million (USD)										200 million (USD)						

Appendix A.6

	Project 10								
	W1	**W2**	**W3**	**W4**	**W5**	**W6**	**W7**	**W8**	**W9**
δ^w	10%	10%	10%	10%	10%	10%	10%	10%	10%
ε^w	11	11	8	11	12	14	10	12	13
C_{it}	25,000(USD)								
C_{kt}	35,000(USD)								
C_{ot}	28,000(USD)								
B_{jt}	250 million (USD)								

B: the effect of implementation of risk response strategies on risks cost reduction (*10 USD)

Appendix B.1

		Risks									
		Risk 1	Risk 2	Risk 3	Risk 4	Risk 5	Risk 6	Risk 7	Risk 8	Risk 9	Risk 10
Risk responses strategies	Risk Response 1	3320	7260	—	—	—	—	—	—	—	—
	Risk Response 2	—	—	4530	—	—	—	—	7310	—	—
	Risk Response 3	—	—	9480	4790	5460	—	4450	—	—	10,020
	Risk Response 4	—	5230	—	—	—	5960	—	—	—	—
	Risk Response 5	3800	—	—	—	—	—	5010	—	—	—
	Risk Response 6	—	—	—	—	6140	5630	—	6730	—	—
	Risk Response 7	5840	5040	—	—	—	—	—	—	8300	—
	Risk Response 8	—	—	—	4800	—	—	—	7100	—	—
	Risk Response 9	—	7100	—	—	3960	—	—	6200	—	—
	Risk Response 10	—	—	7980	—	—	4560	—	—	9200	—
	Risk Response 11	—	—	—	4320	5070	—	8900	4070	—	8090
	Risk Response 12	—	—	—	—	9750	10,450	—	6470	5300	—
	Risk Response 13	—	7890	4600	4800	—	—	4500	—	—	4750

		Risks									
	Risk Response 14	4200	6540	—	9800	6540	4890	—	—	4750	9640
	Risk Response 15	—	—	—	6940	—	—	7310	4800	—	—
	Risk Response 16	5470	—	—	4580	6700	11,230	4500	4980	—	—
	Risk Response 17	—	4860	—	—	9870	7800	6940	7500	—	—
	Risk Response 18	—	7560	—	—	7460	8600	7120	—	—	—
	Risk Response 19	—	3980	4690	—	—	—	6400	—	—	—
	Risk Response 20	—	—	7310	4600	—	5600	—	—	—	—
	Risk Response 21	—	—	5740	—	9000	—	—	7510	4500	4500
	Risk Response 22	—	—	6210	—	4670	4810	6070	—	—	—
	Risk Response 23	—	4670	—	7900	9800	—	7240	—	—	—
	Risk Response 24	—	4120	3980	5600	—	—	—	3650	—	—
	Risk Response 25	—	—	7820	—	4680	7800	—	—	—	10,110
	Risk Response 26	—	—	6450	8210	—	8090	8000	—	—	—
	Risk Response 27	9200	—	6480	4040	—	—	5200	—	4860	—
	Risk Response 28	—	6390	—	—	4920	—	—	7500	—	—
	Risk Response 29	—	5890	—	6400	—	—	7560	—	—	—
	Risk Response 30	—	4620	3980	—	6540	—	4890	4040	—	10,200
	Risk Response 31	7200	—	7560	—	7560	—	3960	—	—	7200

Appendix B.2

		Risks					
		Risk 11	Risk 12	Risk 13	Risk 14	Risk 15	Risk 16
Risk responses strategies	Risk Response 1	9300	—	—	—	7200	4620
	Risk Response 2	—	—	4550	3500	—	—
	Risk Response 3	—	—	3900	—	—	—
	Risk Response 4	7220	—	7890	—	3560	4780
	Risk Response 5	—	9520	—	—	—	8630
	Risk Response 6	—	—	—	—	—	—
	Risk Response 7	—	9700	—	7560	—	—
	Risk Response 8	8200	9200	—	—	4560	—
	Risk Response 9	—	—	9400	5670	—	7200
	Risk Response 10	7500	10,400	11,630	4750	9600	7450
	Risk Response 11	5040	—	—	—	7500	8040
	Risk Response 12	—	11,230	—	—	—	7400
	Risk Response 13	—	—	—	7800	—	—
	Risk Response 14	8750	—	—	4620	10,400	—
	Risk Response 15	—	—	12,400	4590	6870	4700
	Risk Response 16	9500	—	—	10,400	—	—
	Risk Response 17	—	7800	—	—	—	9500
	Risk Response 18	—	8600	—	7500	—	—

	Risks						
	Risk Response 19	8620	—	—	—	—	—
	Risk Response 20	—	5600	—	—	9500	8720
	Risk Response 21	—	—	—	7120	—	—
	Risk Response 22	—	4810	9450	—	—	—
	Risk Response 23	8200	—	—	—	8620	—
	Risk Response 24	—	—	10,410	—	—	8300
	Risk Response 25	—	—	—	10,420	—	—
	Risk Response 26	—	—	7800	4860	—	—
	Risk Response 27	—	—	8600	—	8200	—
	Risk Response 28	—	—	—	—	—	8400
	Risk Response 29	4680	—	5600	4560	11,110	12,300
	Risk Response 30	—	7510	—	8600	—	—
	Risk Response 31	—	—	4810	—	—	—

Appendix B.3

		Risks								
		Risk 17	Risk 18	Risk 19	Risk 19	Risk 20	Risk 21	Risk 22	Risk 23	Risk 24
Risk responses strategies	Risk Response 1	3320	7260	—	—	—	—	—	—	—
	Risk Response 2	—	—	4730	4120	—	—	—	8510	—
	Risk Response 3	—	—	4850	4670	4230	—	4450	—	—
	Risk Response 4	—	5630	—	—	—	7640	—	—	—
	Risk Response 5	5700	—	—	—	—	—	5410	—	—
	Risk Response 6	—	—	—	—	5100	—	—	6730	—
	Risk Response 7	5220	4040	—	—	—	—	—	—	8300
	Risk Response 8	—	—	—	4210	—	—	—	7100	—
	Risk Response 9	—	9000	4690	—	10,200	—	9000	3320	4800
	Risk Response 10	4250	4670	7450	—	—	7310	4870	—	—
	Risk Response 11	—	9800	—	—	8510	4700	7200	—	—
	Risk Response 12	—	—	9600	—	—	4840	—	—	4500
	Risk Response 13	—	4680	—	7890	—	7120	4680	5700	—
	Risk Response 14	5600	—	—	—	—	6400	—	—	—
	Risk Response 15	—	—	—	4680	6730	—	—	5220	—
	Risk Response 16	—	4920	—	7420	—	—	4920	—	—
	Risk Response 17	—	—	4760	6900	7100	6070	—	—	6780
	Risk Response 18	6230	—	—	—	—	7240	—	4250	—
	Risk Response 19	5520	—	—	—	12,400	—	—	—	4700
	Risk Response 20	—	4890	—	—	—	—	4870	—	6970
	Risk Response 21	—	—	—	9640	—	8010	—	—	—

	Risks								
Risk Response 22	—	—	6710	—	10,700	5400	—	—	—
Risk Response 23	6200	—	—	—	—	7800	4790	9870	—
Risk Response 24	3750	—	—	—	—	—	8920	6540	5470
Risk Response 25	—	4790	—	—	—	3450	—	—	—
Risk Response 26	—	9760	4500	—	11,450	—	—	4800	—
Risk Response 27	—	7450	—	—	—	—	7890	—	—
Risk Response 28	—	8960	—	4750	—	9700	—	—	—
Risk Response 29	4200	4300	—	—	—	4780	7450	—	4600
Risk Response 30	—	—	6710	—	10,010	—	—	4500	—
Risk Response 31	—	—	7890	7200	9800	—	—	8040	—

Appendix B.4

		Risks									
		Risk 24	Risk 25	Risk 26	Risk 27	Risk 28	Risk 29	Risk 30	Risk 31	Risk 32	Risk 33
Risk responses strategies	Risk Response 1	—	—	9500	—	—	—	—	7800	7800	—
	Risk Response 2	—	—	—	—	9000	—	4200	—	3320	—
	Risk Response 3	—	9320	—	—	4670	—	—	—	—	—
	Risk Response 4	—	—	8620	—	9700	4230	—	—	—	—
	Risk Response 5	—	—	—	9520	—	—	—	10,400	—	—
	Risk Response 6	—	—	—	—	—	—	—	—	5700	—
	Risk Response 7	8300	—	—	9700	—	5100	—	7890	—	—
	Risk Response 8	—	—	8200	9200	—	—	—	5470	5220	8090
	Risk Response 9	4800	4580	—	—	4920	—	—	—	—	—
	Risk Response 10	—	7400	—	—	—	7500	—	—	—	4750
	Risk Response 11	—	6520	—	6970	6870	—	—	—	4250	9840
	Risk Response 12	4500	—	—	4580	—	8510	8090	12,300	—	—
	Risk Response 13	—	—	—	—	6980	—	—	—	—	—
	Risk Response 14	—	—	7310	—	—	—	4750	—	—	—
	Risk Response 15	—	—	4500	—	4120	—	9640	—	7560	—
	Risk Response 16	—	—	—	7450	3640	4800	—	7540	4520	—
	Risk Response 17	6780	—	7120	6420	—	9200	—	6420	—	—
	Risk Response 18	—	—	6400	—	—	3480	—	4120	—	7890
	Risk Response 19	4700	8090	—	—	—	5800	—	—	—	3320
	Risk Response 20	6970	—	—	4780	—	6700	—	—	6340	—
	Risk Response 21	—	4750	6070	—	6980	—	—	—	4120	—
	Risk Response 22	—	9640	7240	—	—	—	—	10,230	—	—
	Risk Response 23	—	—	—	—	—	—	4890	—	7890	5700
	Risk Response 24	5470	—	—	—	—	—	—	11,100	6420	—
	Risk Response 25	—	—	8000	—	6980	—	9560	—	—	5220

	Risks									
Risk Response 26	—	—	—	7890	—	4780	6340	—	—	—
Risk Response 27	—	—	—	—	—	—	7800	—	—	—
Risk Response 28	—	—	7450	—	—	—	9870	—	—	10,500
Risk Response 29	4600	8000	6320	—	—	8970	—	—	6740	—
Risk Response 30	—	—	—	7120	9780	—	6700	—	—	—
Risk Response 31	—	—	—	—	5700	—	—	7400	—	—

Author details

Yaser Rahimi
School of Industrial Engineering, College of Engineering, University of Tehran, Tehran, Iran

*Address all correspondence to: yaser.ie87@gmail.com

References

[1] Schniederjans, M. J., & Santhanam, R. (1993). A multi-objective constrained resource information system project selection method. European Journal of Operational Research, 70(2), 244–253.

[2] Ahmad, Z., Thaheem, M. J., & Maqsoom, A. (2018). Building information modeling as a risk transformer: An evolutionary insight into the project uncertainty. Automation in Construction, 92, 103–119.

[3] Badri, M. A., Davis, D., & Davis, D. (2001). A comprehensive 0–1 goal-programming model for project selection. International Journal of Project Management, 19(4), 243–252

[4] Wei, C.-C., & Chang, H.-W. (2011). A new approach for selecting portfolio of new product development projects. Expert Systems with Applications, 38 (1), 429–434.

[5] Zou, P. X., Zhang, G., & Wang, J. (2007). Understanding the key risks in construction projects in China. International Journal of Project Management, 25(6), 601–614.

[6] Ebrahimnejad, S., Mousavi, S. M., & Mojtahedi, S. M. H. (2008, December). A fuzzy BOT project risk evaluation model in Iranian power plant industry. In Industrial Engineering and Engineering Management, 2008. IEEM 2008. IEEE International Conference on (pp. 1038–1042). IEEE.

[7] Mousavi, S. M., Malekly, H., Hashemi, H., & Mojtahedi, S. M. H. (2008, December). A two-phase fuzzy decision-making methodology for bridge scheme selection. In Industrial Engineering and Engineering Management, 2008. IEEM 2008. IEEE International Conference on (pp. 415–419). IEEE.

[8] Alborzi, S., Aminian, A., Mojtahedi, S. M. H., & Mousavi, S. M. (2008, December). An analysis of project risks using the non-parametric bootstrap technique. In Industrial Engineering and Engineering Management, 2008. IEEM 2008. IEEE International Conference on (pp. 1295–1299). IEEE.

[9] Tang, W., Qiang, M., Duffield, C. F., Young, D. M., & Lu, Y. (2007). Risk management in the Chinese construction industry. Journal of construction engineering and management, 133(12), 944–956.

[10] Mousavi, S. M., Tavakkoli-Moghaddam, R., Hashemi, H., & Mojtahedi, S.M.H. (2011). A novel approach based on non-parametric resampling with the interval analysis for large engineering project risks. Safety Science, 49(10), 1340–1348.

[11] Ebrahimnejad, S., Mousavi, S.M., Tavakkoli-Moghaddam, R., & Heydar, M. (2014). Risk ranking in mega projects by fuzzy compromise approach: A comparative analysis. Journal of Intelligent and Fuzzy Systems, 26(2), 949–959.

[12] Muriana, C., & Vizzini, G. (2017). Project risk management: A deterministic quantitative technique for assessment and mitigation. International Journal of Project Management, 35(3), 320–340.

[13] Rahimi, Y., Tavakkoli-Moghaddam, R., Iranmanesh, S. H., & Vaez-Alaei, M. (2018). Hybrid approach to construction project risk management with simultaneous FMEA/ISO 31000/ evolutionary algorithms: Empirical optimization study. Journal of Construction Engineering and Management, 144(6), 04018043.

[14] Ben-David, I., & Raz, T. (2001). An integrated approach for risk response development in project planning. Journal of the Operational Research Society, 52(1), 14–25.

[15] Ben-David, I., Rabinowitz, G., & Raz, T. (2002). Economic optimization of project risk management efforts. Project Risk Management Optimization.

[16] Khodemani-Yazdi, M., Tavakkoli-Moghaddam, R., Bashiri, M., & Rahimi, Y. (2019). Solving a new bi-objective hierarchical hub location problem with an M/ M/ c queuing framework. Engineering Applications of Artificial Intelligence, 78, 53–70.

[17] Roshan, M., Tavakkoli-Moghaddam, R., & Rahimi, Y. (2019). A two-stage approach to agile pharmaceutical supply chain management with product substitutability in crises. Computers & Chemical Engineering, 127, 200–217.

[18] Zhang, Y., & Fan, Z.-P. (2014). An optimization method for selecting project risk response. International Journal of Project Management, 32(3), 412–422

[19] Zhalechian, M., Tavakkoli-Moghaddam, R., & Rahimi, Y. (2017). A self-adaptive evolutionary algorithm for a fuzzy multi-objective hub location problem: An integration of responsiveness and social responsibility. Engineering Applications of Artificial Intelligence, 62, 1–16.

[20] Torabi, S. A., & Hassini, E. (2008). An interactive possibilistic programming approach for multiple objective supply chain master planning. Fuzzy sets and systems, 159(2), 193–214.

[21] Jiménez, M., Arenas, M., Bilbao, A., & Rodrı, M. V. (2007). Linear programming with fuzzy parameters: an interactive method resolution. European Journal of Operational Research, 177(3), 1599–1609.

[22] Pishvaee, M. S., Torabi, S. A., & Razmi, J. (2012). Credibility-based fuzzy mathematical programming model for green logistics design under uncertainty. Computers & Industrial Engineering, 62(2), 624–632.

[23] Xu, J., & Zhou, X. (2013). Approximation based fuzzy multi-objective models with expected objectives and chance constraints: Application to earth-rock work allocation. Information Sciences, 238, 75–95.

Chapter 13

Determinants of Job Satisfaction of Accounting Professionals in Tunisia

Lassaad Abdelmoula and Sami Boudabbous

Abstract

This study aims to identify the factors that affect the job satisfaction of professional accountants. It examines the relative effects of intrinsic and extrinsic factors on job satisfaction among accounting professionals. Our methodology was applied to 232 accounting professionals working in Tunisia. The methods of data analysis are principal component analysis (PCA) and multiple regression. The results show that intrinsic and extrinsic factors have a positive and significant effect on job satisfaction. However, promotion, growth and recognition do not have effect on job satisfaction.

Keywords: job satisfaction, intrinsic factors, extrinsic factors, achievement, promotion, the work itself, recognition, growth, salary, relationship with the supervisor and co-workers, working conditions, the company policy, accounting professionals

1. Introduction

The specific attitude of employees to job satisfaction is of major interest in the field of organizational behavior and human resource management practice today [1]. This interest stems from the belief that satisfied employees are more productive than those who are dissatisfied. An employee with a high level of job satisfaction has a positive attitude toward the job, while one who is dissatisfied with his job has a negative attitude toward the job [2]. Indeed, job satisfaction is defined as an affective or emotional response to various facets of one's job. This definition means that job satisfaction is not a unitary concept: an individual can be relatively satisfied with one aspect of their job and dissatisfied with one or more others [3].

Job satisfaction is defined as "a pleasant or positive emotional state resulting from the evaluation of one's work or professional experience" [4]. Workers do their jobs in defined areas and assess the environment according to their values. When the experience in the work environment is consistent with an employee's values, the employee expresses satisfaction with the job [4, 5].

The drivers of job satisfaction have been a controversial topic in previous literature [6]. Several studies have treated them, but the results are mixed. Most of these studies focused on various professions, such as teachers [7], doctors [8], nurses [9], and employees in general [10]. However, the results of these studies cannot be applied to the accounting profession in which very little research has been done. Therefore, the objective of our study is to fill this gap by studying the job satisfaction of accounting professionals in the Tunisian context.

The theory of [11] identified several determinants of satisfaction at work, namely achievement, promotion, the work itself, growth, recognition company policies, relationship with supervisor and co-workers, working conditions, and salary.

The objective of this study is to identify the factors affecting job satisfaction in Tunisia. Specifically, the study examines the relative effects of intrinsic and extrinsic factors on job satisfaction among accounting professionals.

The rest of the article is structured as follows. The following section presents a brief review of the literature on the determinants of job satisfaction. Subsequently, the method section describes the sampling method and the steps followed to develop the study instrument. The following analysis section presents the results of the study.

2. Literature review and hypotheses development

Relatively few studies have used Herzberg's theory to examine the job satisfaction of employees in the field of public administration [12]. Herzberg et al. [11] proposed motivating factors related to job satisfaction (intrinsic factors), such as success, recognition, advancement or promotion, work itself and responsibility, and hygiene factors (extrinsic factors), including company policy, job safety, relationship with supervisor, salary, peer relations and working conditions. According to [11], the absence of motivating factors does not necessarily lead to job dissatisfaction, and the preferred level of hygiene factors does not necessarily result in job satisfaction.

According to [11] the absence of motivating factors does not necessarily lead to job dissatisfaction, and the preferred level of hygiene factors does not necessarily result in job satisfaction.

Therefore, job satisfaction and dissatisfaction are not elements of a single continuum, hence the following hypotheses:

Hypothesis 1: Intrinsic factors have a positive and significant effect on the job satisfaction of professional accountants, hence the following hypotheses:
Hypothesis 2: Extrinsic factors have a positive and significant effect on the job satisfaction of professional accountants.

Some sub-hypotheses corresponding to variables of these factors are stated in what follows:

2.1 The intrinsic job satisfaction factors

2.1.1 Achievement

Hur and Herzberg [12, 13] associated achievement with the feeling of success in performing a task or solving a problem. There is a significant relationship between extrinsic factors and the job satisfaction of accounting professionals. Employees who demonstrate a strong success orientation tend to work long hours accepting difficult tasks and demonstrating an ongoing commitment to doing whatever is necessary to achieve optimal results [6, 14]. In the same vein, many researchers [7, 15, 16] affirm the link between success and job satisfaction and believe that job satisfaction is an essential element that stimulates and encourages employees to achieve better results.

In this regard, we propose the following hypothesis:

Hypothesis 1-1: There is a positive and significant relationship between achievement and job satisfaction of accounting professionals.

2.1.2 Advancement or promotion

Malik et al. [17] argue that the remuneration and promotion contribute to job satisfaction. It can be concluded that employers could meet the needs of employees not only from the point of view of safety and social needs, but also physiological needs. Noor et al. [18] prove that job promotion and job advancement have a positive relationship with job satisfaction.

Similarly [19–21], revealed that promotion opportunity is a central factor in determining employee job satisfaction.

Hence, the following hypothesis:

Hypothesis 1-2: Promotion has a positive and significant effect on job satisfaction of accounting professionals.

2.1.3 The work itself

Work itself as a determinant of job satisfaction includes certain aspects, such as control over the method and pace of work, the use of skills and abilities and variety. People take pleasure in successfully coping with their environment. The use of valued skills and abilities gives workers a sense of pride, competence and self-confidence. Specialization and repetitiveness lead to consistency with job satisfaction.

According to [22], moderate stimulation provides great satisfaction to the worker [10, 23], showed that the work itself affects job satisfaction.

In this context, we formulate the following hypothesis:

Hypothesis 1-3: The work itself has a positive and significant effect on job satisfaction of accounting professionals.

2.1.4 Recognition

Canlan and Still [24] suggest that burnout was associated with lower job satisfaction and higher job satisfaction was associated with rewards (remuneration and recognition) as well as cognitively challenging work.

Imran et al. [25–27] assert a positive correlation between recognition and employee job satisfaction.

Let us propose the following hypothesis:

Hypothesis 1-4: The recognition has a positive and significant effect on job satisfaction of accounting professionals.

2.1.5 Growth

According to [28], employee job satisfaction is affected by several factors, some of which are intrinsic in nature, such as self-esteem, personal growth, accomplishment, and employee readiness.

Indeed, many previous studies, such as [29–32], concluded that growth contributes to job satisfaction.

Let us, therefore, pose the following hypothesis:

Hypothesis 1-5: The growth has a positive and significant effect on job satisfaction of accounting professionals.

2.2 The extrinsic job satisfaction factors

2.2.1 Salary

Salary is one of the basic elements used to motivate employees in a company. It helps in increasing workers' performance and productivity. Yong Yew et al. [9, 33–36] emphasized that salary is significantly correlated with job satisfaction. However, poor compensation will have negative effects on job satisfaction [37].

Nonetheless [38], showed that salary increases are directly related to decreased satisfaction.

From what has been advanced, the following hypothesis can be set:

> Hypothesis 2-1: There is a positive and significant relationship between salary and job satisfaction of accounting professionals.

2.2.2 Relationship with the supervisor and co-workers

For [39], the determinants of job satisfaction show that people have emotions toward all or certain aspects of their work, such as the relationship with colleagues and co-workers. Many previous studies (e.g., [8, 40–44] have shown that the level of satisfaction from the work is closely correlated with the relationship with the supervisor and co-workers.

Hence, the following hypothesis:

> Hypothesis 2-2: The relationship with the supervisor and co-workers have a positive and significant effect on job satisfaction of accounting professionals.

2.2.3 Working conditions

Khalifa and Truong [32] state that working conditions would not lead to an improvement in employee job satisfaction. However [22], find that "lone workers disliked their jobs and cited social isolation as the main reason". The absence of such working conditions, among others, can have a negative impact on the mental and physical well-being of the worker [45]. Likewise [2, 46, 47], proved that working conditions are an essential factor in job satisfaction.

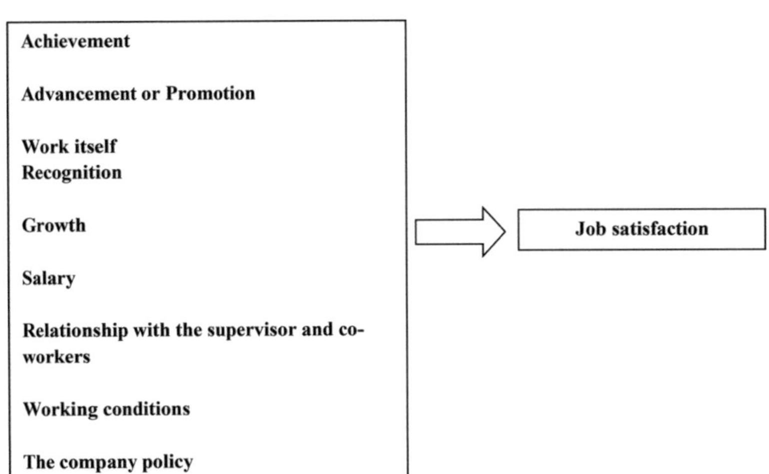

Figure 1.
The research model.

Indeed, employees prefer pleasant working conditions because they facilitate work efficiency. The right tools and equipment help employees achieve their work goals [4].

In this regard, we propose the following hypothesis:

> Hypothesis 2-3: Working conditions have a positive and significant effect on job satisfaction of accounting professionals.

2.2.4 The company policy

Locke et al. [4, 48, 49] emphasize that company policy contributes to job satisfaction and dissatisfaction. Holmberg et al. [50–54] showed that the company policy affects satisfaction.

Hence, the following hypothesis:

> Hypothesis 2-4: Company policy has a positive and significant effect on job satisfaction of accounting professionals.

Our research model is illustrated in **Figure 1**.

3. Research methodology

3.1 Methods of data collection

This research was entirely based on the answers received from 232 accounting professionals in Tunisia. In fact, out of 250 respondents, 232 accounting professionals were selected. Two administration methods: face-to-face and internet surveys were chosen in this work.

3.2 Measurement of the variables

Table 1 shows the measurements of the variables.

3.3 Data analysis method

The methods of data analysis are principal component analysis (PCA) and multiple regression. The former is used to analyze the relationship between quantitative

Variables	Measurements	Authors
Job satisfaction factors	Achievement (3 items)	[48]
	Advancement/promotion (2 items)	
	Work itself (3 items)	
	Recognition (3 items)	
	Growth (3 items)	
	Company policy: (3 items)	
	Relationship with supervisor and peers (6 items)	
	Salary (2 items)	
	Working conditions: (3 items)	
Job satisfaction	4 items	[48]

Table 1.
Measurement of the variables.

data. It is the most used among the descriptive methods for cleansing and validation of scales. It is conducted on mean-centered data. The variables then have the same variability and have the same influence in the calculation of the distance between the individuals. It reveals a factorial structure through which the components identified are related to items.

It should be recalled that for the study of the validation of the research hypotheses, we chose the methods appropriate to the reference samples. Thus, we resorted to the multiple regression tests.

4. Results and discussion

4.1 PCA

4.1.1 The intrinsic determinants of job satisfaction

From the 14 selected items, the factorial analysis highlighted a solution of five factors. The value of Kaiser – Mayer – Olkin (KMO) is 0.847, the anti-image correlation matrix, and the significance of Bartlett's sphericity test at the 1% threshold invite us to continue the analysis. The total explained variance is 74.8%, and the lowest factorial weight is 0.445. As a result, according to the scree-test and the Kaiser criterion, the PCA confirms a multidimensional structure with five factors [55, 56].

The determinant "Achievement" represents the first factorial axis which accounts for 29.2% of the total variance explained. However, "Advancement", which explains 15.7% of the total variance explained, is the second factorial axis. The variance explained by the determinant "Work itself" is 14.4% of the total variance explained. The fourth factorial axis, "Recognition", accounts for 12.8% of the total variance explained. Finally, the determinants related to "Growth" explains 12.7% of the total variance explained.

To confirm the consistency of each of these dimensions, we performed the Cronbach's alpha test. **Table 2** shows that the reliability coefficient α is slightly higher than the selected threshold (0.8799122); it is all the more acceptable because this scale is exploratory.

4.1.2 Extrinsic determinants of satisfaction

A first PCA based on the covariance matrix, on the 14 items, is launched without specifying the number of axes requested. According to the Kaiser criterion (eigenvalue greater than 1), five factors are extracted and allow to resituate 74.8% of the total variance. The results of the anti-image correlation matrix indicate that not all items are presented by two diagonally opposite points, and this indicates that they are not linked by a strong correlation, and therefore no item is duplicated. Furthermore, the factor analysis conducted on the 14 items shows that the first factorial axis is the "relationship with supervisor and colleagues", which explains 22.3% of the total variance explained. The second is the "company policy", explaining 19.4% of the total variance explained. The "working conditions" is the third factorial axis accounting for 16.1% of the total variance explained, and "Salary" is the fourth factorial axis explaining 11.9% of the total variance explained (**Table 3**).

4.1.3 Job satisfaction

To study the factor structure of job satisfaction, we used the KMO and Bartlett tests. The value of KMO which is of the order of 0.72284, the examination of the

Items	Fact 1	Fact 2	Fact 3	Fact 4	Fact 5
I am proud to work in this company because it recognizes my achievements	**0.535**	0.062	0.043	0.013	−0.06
I feel satisfied with my job because it gives me a feeling of accomplishment	**0.464**	0.011	−0.08	−0.038	−0.113
I feel I have contributed to my firm in a positive manner	**0.445**	0.172	0.033	0.038	−0.012
I will choose career advancement rather than monetary incentives	0.025	0.155	0.061	−0.04	**0.775**
My job allows me to learn new skills for career advancement	0.167	0.157	0.009	0.07	**0.657**
My work is thrilling and I do diverse tasks	−0.140	−0.024	**0.751**	−0.02	0.019
I am empowered enough to do my job	−0.026	0.107	**0.610**	−0.04	−0.079
My job is challenging and exciting	−0.071	0.092	**0.808**	−0.08	−0.014
I feel appreciated when I achieve or complete a task	−0.113	0.031	−0.131	**0.725**	0.212
My manager always thanks me for a well-done job	−0.143	−0.054	0.031	**0.568**	0.228
I receive adequate recognition for doing my job well	−0.013	−0.284	−0.089	**0.435**	−0.162
I am proud to work in my company because I feel I have grown as a person	−0.074	**0.642**	0.023	−0.14	−0.031
My job allows me to grow and develop as a person	−0.022	**0.746**	0.046	−0.18	0.048
My job allows me to improve my experience, skills, and performance	−0.019	**0.677**	−0.083	−0.07	−0.018
Variance explained	19.2	15.7	14.4	12.8	12.7
Eigenvalue	3.4578	2.8307	2.5961	2.309	2.277
Total variance			74.8%		
KMO			0.847		
Bartlett (p-value)			19.325 (0.000)		
Cronbach 's alpha			0.8799122		

Table 2.
PCA of intrinsic determinants (standardized Varimax).

anti-image matrix of correlations, and the significance of Bartlett's sphericity test at the threshold of 0.01 invite us to continue the analysis. The factorial structure obtained is satisfactory and explains 89.36% of the results. The lowest factorial score is 0.599 (**Table 4**).

To properly analyze the joint link between intrinsic and extrinsic determinants and job satisfaction, we used a multiple regression [57].

4.2 Analysis and discussion of multiple regression results

To test the validity of our nine research hypotheses, we chose modeling the job satisfaction of accounting professionals using the Fully Modified Ordinary Least Square (FMOLS) approach, which allows us to estimate a set of relationships by taking into account the problem of the autocorrelation of errors and the presence of omitted variables [57].

Items	Fact 1	Fact 2	Fact 3	Fact 4
The attitude of the administration is very accommodative in my firm	0.142	**0.766**	0.05	−0.04
I am proud to work for this firm because the company policy is favorable for its workers	0.126	**0.893**	0.052	0.138
I completely understand the mission of my firm	0.174	**0.515**	0.186	0.138
I feel my performance has improved because of the support from my supervisor	**0.754**	0.003	−0.65	0.132
I feel satisfied at work because of my relationship with my supervisor	**0.607**	0.122	0.059	0.069
My supervisors are strong and trustworthy leaders	**0.504**	0.011	0.099	0.073
It is easy to get along with my colleagues	**0.773**	0.093	0.531	0.160
My colleagues are helpful and friendly	**0.696**	0.149	0.057	0.055
Colleagues are important to me	**0.797**	0.209	0.709	0.065
I am encouraged to work harder because of my salary	0.311	0.042	0.09	**0.714**
I believe my salary is fair	0.130	0.040	0.02	**0.867**
I feel satisfied because of the comfort I am offered at work	0.120	0.244	**0.805**	0.10
I am proud to work for my firm because of the pleasant working conditions	0.184	0.195	**0.676**	0.139
Variance explained	22.3	19.4	16.1	11.9
Eigenvalue	4.0078	2.471	2.008	2.031
Total variance		69.7%		
KMO		0.899		
Bartlett (p-value)		29.338 (0.000)		
Cronbach's alpha		0.88195		

Table 3.
PCA of extrinsic determinants (standardized Varimax).

Items	Fact 1
I am satisfied with my job	0.8213
I am happy with the way my colleagues and superiors treat me	0.6332
I am satisfied with what I achieve at work	0.599
I feel good at work	0.7325
Variance explained	89.36
Eigen value	6.897
KMO	0.72284
Bartlett (p-value)	18.88 (0.00)
Cronbach's alpha	0.83364

Table 4.
PCA of Job satisfaction (standardized Varimax).

The relationships between the intrinsic/extrinsic variables and job satisfaction are estimated using the following two tests:

- Ramsey Regression Equation Specification Error Test (RESET) that consists of verifying the presence of omitted variables in the model.

- Durbin Watson (DW) test shows if we will accept the hypothesis of the existence of an auto correlated error.

The results of these two tests are presented in **Table 5**. As can be seen in this table, the problem of the autocorrelation of errors for all intrinsic and extrinsic variables is verified.

Indeed, the Durbin-Watson statistic shows a value of 2.31, this indicates that we will accept the hypothesis of the existence of autocorrelated errors problem. The Ramsey Reset test confirms the absence of omitted variables in our model, which implies a good prediction of the job satisfaction of the accounting professionals in our sample.

The overall significance of the model is also verified using the Fischer statistic at the 0.1% threshold.

Hypothesis (H2–4) regarding the positive and significant effect of the company policy on job satisfaction is validated ($\alpha = 0.41105$; $p = 0.000$), which corroborates this result of [56].

Hypothesis (H2–2) regarding the positive effect of relationship with supervisor and co-workers on job satisfaction is corroborated ($\alpha = 0.18456$; $p = 0.084$, $p < 0.1$). This result is in line with that of [8].

The hypothesis related to the positive effect of salary on job satisfaction (H2–1) is validated ($\alpha = 0.3841$; $p = 0.0011$). Thus, confirming a previous result by [36].

Moreover, the result related to Hypothesis (H2.3) postulating the relationship between working conditions and job satisfaction shows a positive and significant relationship ($\alpha = 0.3382$; $p = 0.064$, $p < 0.1$). This last finding is consistent with the result found by [46].

Variables	**Coefficient**	**t-stat**	**p-value**
The company policy	0.4110548	2.32	**0.000**
Relationship with the supervisor and co-workers	0.1845661	1.72	**0.084**
Salary	0.384122	2.02	**0.0011**
Working conditions	0.338201	1.88	**0.064**
Achievement	0.28227	1.74	**0.088**
Advancement (promotion)	−0.043652	−0.87	0.922
The work itself	0.65541	3.06	**0.000**
Growth	−0.007447	−0.7123	0.544
Recognition	0.000745	0.76	0.84
Number	232		
R2 adjusted	0.67		
Fisher (p-value)	142.186 (0.000)		
Durbin	2.31		
Ramsey Reset (p-value)	13.28 (0.0014)		

Table 5.
Result of FMOLS estimation.

Hypothesis (H1–1) concerning the positive and significant effect of achievement on job satisfaction is validated ($\alpha = 0.2822$; $p = 0.088$, $p < 0.1$), which is consistent with the finding of [16].

The hypothesis of a positive effect of work itself on job satisfaction is also accepted (H1–3) ($\alpha = 0.6554$; $p = 0.000$). This result seems to be justified by the fact that work itself is the most important variable in predicting job satisfaction. This result is in agreement with that of [23].

Our results show the absence of a significant relationship between promotion (H1–2), recognition (H1–4), and growth (H1–5) and job satisfaction which have a $P > 0.1$. In fact, a survey of accounting firms revealed how intrinsic and extrinsic motivational factors can have an impact on the accounting professionals' job satisfaction. Therefore, faced with the competitiveness requirements, personal achievement, responsibility, initiative, recognition, as well as good working conditions and salary policy are ultimately important adjustment variables for professional accountants because they can contribute to the value creation. However, the survey results showed that variables, such as promotion, recognition and growth do not have any impact on the professional accountants' job satisfaction. More specifically, professional accountants seek personal growth and development much more than the desire for recognition or promotion.

5. Conclusion

The work aimed to investigate the determinants of the accounting professionals' job satisfaction in the Tunisian context. For this end, we posed two main hypotheses that deal with the relationship between the intrinsic and extrinsic factors and the accounting professionals' job satisfaction, respectively. The first hypothesis was subdivided into five sub-hypotheses, which present the intrinsic factors. The second was composed of four sub-hypotheses about the extrinsic factors. The results showed that three intrinsic factors, namely achievement, the work itself, recognition, along with four extrinsic ones, i.e., salary, relationship with supervisor and co-workers, working conditions, and the company policy, significantly affect the job satisfaction. However, we did not prove the existence of a significant relationship between growth, promotion, and recognition as well as job satisfaction. The research presented two limitations: The first was related to the small size of the sample. The second limitation concerned the imbalance in the composition of the sample and the selection of accounting professionals. Finally, new avenues of research could be explored by studying the relationship between the intrinsic and extrinsic factors, and the audit team job satisfaction.

A.Appendix

B.Intrinsic satisfaction factors

B.1 Achievement

1. I am delighted to work in this firm as it acknowledges my achievements.

2. I feel fulfilled with my job because it gives me a feeling of accomplishment.

3. I feel I have participated in my firm positively.

B.2 Advancement

4. I will choose career development rather than financial incentives.
5. My job enables me to learn new skills for career development.

B.3 Work Itself

6. My work is stimulating, and I do diverse tasks.
7. I am qualified enough to do my job.
8. My job is challenging and exciting.

B.4 Recognition

9. I feel appreciated when I achieve or complete a task.
10. My director always expresses recognition for a well-done job.
11. I receive adequate recognition for doing my job well.

B.5 Growth

12. I am proud to work in my firm because I feel I have grown as a person.
13. My job enables me to progress and develop as an individual.
14. My job enables me to improve my experience, skills and performance.

C. Extrinsic satisfaction factors

C.1 Company policy

1. The attitude of the administration is very accommodative in my firm
2. I am proud to work for this firm because the company policy is favorable for its workers
3. I completely understand the mission of my firm

C.2 Relationship with the supervisor

4. I feel my performance has improved because of the support from my supervisor
5. I feel satisfied at work because of my relationship with my supervisor
6. My supervisors are strong and trustworthy leaders

C.3 Relationship with the co-workers

7. It is easy to get along with my colleagues
8. My colleagues are helpful and friendly
9. Colleagues are important to me

C.4 Salary

10. I am encouraged to work harder because of my salary
11. I believe my salary is fair

C.5 Working conditions

12. I feel satisfied because of the comfort I am offered at work
13. I am proud to work for my firm because of the pleasant working conditions

D. Job satisfaction

1. I am satisfied with my job
2. I am happy with the way my colleagues and superiors treat me
3. I am satisfied with what I achieve at work
4. I feel good at work

Author details

Lassaad Abdelmoula* and Sami Boudabbous
Faculty of Economics and Management Sciences, University of Sfax, Tunisia

*Address all correspondence to: lassaad.abd86@gmail.com

References

[1] Tett RP, Meyer JP. Job Satisfaction, Organizational Commitment, Turnover Intention, and Turnover: Path analyses based on meta-analytic findings. Personal Psychology. 1993; 46: 259.

[2] Robbins SP. Organisational Behaviour. New Jersey. Prentice Hall. 2001

[3] Kinicki A, Kreitner R. Organizational Behavior: Key concepts, skills and Best Practices, McGraw-Hill Irwin. 2003.

[4] Locke E.A. The nature and causes of job satisfaction. In M.D. Dunnette (Ed.). Handbook of Industrial and Organizational Psychology, Rand McNally, Chicago. 1976:1297-1349.

[5] Davis R. S. Unionization and work attitudes: How union commitment influences public sector job satisfaction. Public Administration Review. 2013; 73(1): 74-84.

[6] Raza MY, Akhtar MW, Husnain M, Akhtar MS. The impact of intrinsic motivation on Employee's Job Satisfaction. Management and Organizational Studies. 2015; 2(3) 80-88.

[7] Monyatsi PP. The level of job satisfaction of teachers in Botswana. European Journal of Educational Studies. 2012; 4(2):219-232.

[8] Zaman S. Work life issues and Job Satisfaction of doctors: A gender based study. Amity Journal of Healthcare Management. 2018; 1(2):17-32.

[9] Yong Yew S, Chen Yong C, Peng Tey N, Cheok Cheong K, Tho Ng S. Work satisfaction among nurses in a private hospital. International Journal of Healthcare Management. 2018; 13(1): 156-163.

[10] Anin E.K, Ofori I, Okyere S. Factors affecting Job Satisfaction of employees in the construction supply chain in the Ashanti region of Ghana. European Journal of Business and Management. 2015; 7(6):72-81.

[11] Herzberg F, Mausner B, Snyderman B. The Motivation to Work, Wiley, New York. 1959.

[12] Hur Y. Testing Herzberg's two-factor theory of motivation in the public sector: Is it applicable to public managers? Public Organization Review. 2018; 18(3):329-343.

[13] Herzberg, F. Work and the nature of man, staple press. 1966. London.

[14] Scott KS, Moore K S, Miceli M P. An exploration of the meaning and consequences of workaholism. Human Relations. 1997; 50(3):287-314.

[15] Ahmed I, Nawaz MM, Iqbal, N, Ali I, Shaukat Z, Usman A. The effects of motivational factors on employees' job satisfaction: A case study of University of the Punjab, Pakistan. International Journal of Business and Management. 2010; 5(3):70-80.

[16] Raziq A, Maulabakhsh R. Impact of working environment on Job Satisfaction, Procedia Economics and Finance. 2015; 23: 717-725.

[17] Malik M E, Danish R Q, Munir Y. The impact of pay and promotion on Job Satisfaction: Evidence from higher education Institutes of Pakistan, American Journal of Economics. 2012: 6-9.

[18] Noor Z, Khanl A U, Naseem I. Impact of job promotion and job advancement on job satisfaction in universities of KPK Province of Pakistan. Science International Journal (Lahore). 2015; 27(2): 1499-1505.

[19] Naveed A, Usman A, Bushra F. Promotion: A predictor of job satisfaction a study of glass industry of Lahore (Pakistan). International Journal of Business and Social Science. 2011.

[20] Neog BB, Barua M. Factors influencing employee's Job Satisfaction: An empirical study among employees of automobile service workshops in Assam the SIJ transactions on industrial, financial and Business Management. 2014; 2 (7): 305-316.

[21] Abreham T. The Effect of Employee Promotion Practice on Job Satisfaction: The Case of Dashen Bank S.C, Thesis. 2017.

[22] Arnold HJ, Feldman DC. A multivariate analysis of the determinants of job turnover, Journal of Applied Psychology. 1982; 67: 350-360.

[23] Sowmya KR, Panchanatham N. Factors influencing job satisfaction of banking sector employees in Chennai, India, Journal of Law and Conflict Resolution. 2011;.3(5): 76-79.

[24] Canlan JN, Still M. Job satisfaction, burnout and turnover intention in occupational therapists working in mental health. Australian occupational therapy journal. 2013; 60, 310-318.

[25] Imran A, Ahmad S, Nisar Q A, Ahmad U. Exploring relationship among rewards, recognition and employees' job satisfaction: A descriptive study on libraries in Pakistan, Middle-East Journal of Scientific. 2014;21(9):1533-1540

[26] Amarasena T S M, Ajward AR, Ahasanul Haque AKM. Does social recognition impact Job satisfaction of academic faculty members of state universities in Sri Lanka. International journal of recent advances in organizational behavior and Decision Sciences. 2015; 1(4): 540-553.

[27] Kiruthiga V, Magesh R. Gears of Job Satisfaction among star hotel employee, international journal of innovative research in science. Engineering and Technology 2015; 4(1):18563-18567.

[28] Matthews B, Daigle J, Houston M. a dyadic of employee readiness and job satisfaction: Does there exist a theoretical precursor to the satisfaction-performance paradigm? International Journal of Organizational Analysis. 2018; 6(5):842-857.

[29] Bruce WM, Blackburn JW. Balancing Job Satisfaction and Performance, Westport, CT: Quorum Books. 1992.

[30] Ruthankoon R, Ogunlana SO. Testing Herzberg's two-factor theory in the Thai construction industry, Engineering. Construction and Architectural Management. 2003; 10(5):333-341.

[31] Nielsen I, Smyth R. Job satisfaction and response to incentives among China' surban work force. The journal of Socio-Economics. 2008; 37(5):1921-1936.

[32] Khalifa MH, Truong Q. The relationship between employee perceptions of equity and Job Satisfaction in the Egyptian private universities Eurasian, Journal of Business and Economics. 2010; 3 (5):135-150.

[33] Dulebohn J H, Werling S E. Compensation research past, present and future, Human Resource Management Review. 2007; 7(2):191-207.

[34] Shah M J. Job satisfaction and motivation of teachers of public educational institutions, International Journal of Business and Social Science. 2012; 3(8):271-282.

[35] Makena Muguongo M. Effects of compensation on job satisfaction among secondary school teachers in Maara

sub – County of Tharaka Nithi County, Kenya, Journal of Human Resource Management. 2015; 3(6):47.

[36] Linh L H. Researching on factors affecting job satisfaction of lecturers in universities of Ho Chi Minh City, Vietnam. American Journal of Educational Research. 2018; 6(7):1056-1062.

[37] Hee OC, Cheng TY, Yaw CC, Gee WV, Kamaludin SM, Prabhagaran J R. The influence of human resource management practices on career satisfaction: Evidence from Malaysia, International Review of Management and Marketing. 2016; 6(3): 517-521.

[38] Young L, Milner M, Edmunds D, Pentsil G, Broman M. The tenuous relationship between salary and satisfaction, Journal of Behavioral Studies in Business. 2014;7:1-9

[39] Spector PE. Job satisfaction: application, assessment, causes and consequences, Thousand Oaks, Calif, Sage Publications. 1997: p. 28.

[40] Crossman A, Abu-Zaki B. Job satisfaction and employee performance of Lebanese banking staff, Journal of Managerial Psychology. 2003; 18(4): 368-376.

[41] George JM, Jones GR. Understanding and Managing Organizational Behavior, Fifth Edition, Pearson/Prentice Hall, New Yersey. 2008: p. 78.

[42] Zhang Y, Yao X, Cheong J O. City managers 'job satisfaction and frustration: Factors and implications, The American Review of Public Administration. 2011;41(6): 670-685.

[43] Charoensukmongkol P, Moqbel, M. Gutierrez-Wirsching S. The role of coworker and supervisor support on job burnout and job satisfaction. Journal of Advances in Management Research. 2016; 13(1):4-22.

[44] Szromek AR, Wolniak R. Job Satisfaction and problems among academic staff in higher education. 2020. Sustainability, 2:1-38.

[45] Greenberg Baron R.A. Behavior in Organization: Understanding and Managing the Human Side of Work. 7th Edition, Prentice Hall, Upper Sadle River. 2003.

[46] Wubuli A A. Study on the Factors Affecting Job Satisfaction among Employees of Fast Food Restaurants. Masters of Human Resource Management, University Utara Malaysia, Kedah. -Yavuz, 2009.

[47] Bakotic, D. and Babic, T. Relationship between working conditions and Job Satisfaction: The case of Croatian shipbuilding company, International Journal of Business and Social Science. 2013; 4(2):206-213.

[48] Hong T, Waheed A. Herzberg's motivation-hygiene theory and job satisfaction in the Malaysian retail sector: The mediating effect of love of money, Asian Academy of Management Journal. 2011; 16(1):73-94.

[49] Alina M, Simona E. Pre-university teachers' professional satisfaction. Procedia–Social and Behavioral Sciences. 2013; 78, 110-114.

[50] Holmberg, C., Caro J, Sobis I. 2018. Job satisfaction among Swedish mental health nursing personnel: Revisiting the two-factor theory. International Journal of Mental Health Nursing. 2018;27(2):581-592.

[51] Ab Rahman N, Husin, M, Dahian, K, Noh K. M, Atun, R, Sivasampu, S. Job satisfaction of public and private primary care physicians in Malaysia: Analysis of findings from QUALICO-PC. Human resources for health. 2019; 17(1): 1-10.

[52] Jarupathirun, S, De Gennaro M. Factors of work satisfaction and their

influence on employee turnover in Bangkok, Thailand. International Journal of Technology. 2018;9(7):1460-1468.

[53] Kjeldsen A M, Hansen JR. Sector differences in the public service motivation–job satisfaction relationship: Exploring the role of organizational characteristics. Review of Public Personnel Administration. 2018; 38(1): 24-48.

[54] Phuong N ND, Khuong M N, Phuc L. H, Dong L NT. The effect of two-dimensional factor on municipal civil Servants' Job Satisfaction and public policy implications. The journal of Asian finance, Economics, and Business. 2018. 5(3): 133-142.

[55] Saporta G. Probabilités, Analyse des Données et Statistique", Technip. 2006.

[56] Abdelmoula L, The impact of intrinsic satisfaction factors on affective, normative, and continuance commitment of accounting professionals in Tunisia. Journal of Accounting and Management Information Systems. 2021;20 (2): 199-220.

[57] Baillargeon G. Méthodes d'analyse de régression linéaire simple et régression multiple Méthodes statistiques Tome 2. 1999.

Chapter 14

Discerning the Strategies for Exiting Your Business

Jeffrey M. Shepard

Abstract

For many business owners, strategies for operations are well thought out, whereas strategies for exit are not. Exiting a business does not need to occur due to a challenge or disaster. It is possible to plan and exit for the purposes of business growth, retirement, mergers and more. An exit affects the business owner, as it means that they are no longer involved in running or operations of the organization. The aim of this chapter is to identify common exit strategies and understand how they are of benefit to both the business owner or manager and the individual taking over the business. Secondary qualitative research is the research method used, with analysis of strategies and structures used across countries. These findings include differentiation between exit strategies with an understanding of their impact or influence on the business. These include the process of creating and exit strategy and the benefits for having one in place. The expectations of the investor and how they are to be paid back are taken into consideration. The chapter concludes with a solution for any business owner, including how to work with a qualified team to create a logical, well thought out exit plan.

Keywords: Exit Strategies, Business Owner, Investor, Next Generation Entrepreneurs, Succession

1. Introduction

Business owners work hard to build up their businesses in a bid to attain success. They experience incredible excitement and enthusiasm to get a business going right from the start. However, business owners need to think about what would happen if they were no longer able to be part of the business [1]. Numerous circumstances may occur which drive a business owner to exit their business. Exiting a business is not always negative. For this reason, the exit strategy should be in place as part of the long-term plan for the business. This will ensure that any future exit is well planned for, with a smooth transition or continuity where necessary. Also, a business exit may be an excellent option for a business owner seeking to make a significant return on their investment.

Certain circumstances precede the need to exit a business. These include the following: -

- A non – profitable business could require the business to be closed down entirely, or the business owner could consider exiting and allowing the next generation with fresh ideas to run the business and lead it to success.

- Changes in market conditions – The economic climate makes it challenging for the business owner to run and manage their business.

- Reduce business ownership – A business owner may be willing to reduce their ownership and also give up some control in the business to a family member or employee, if they can get financial value by doing so.

- Opportunity to sell – There are times when things fall into place and open up the opportunity for the business owner to sell their business, even if it was not their initial plan.

Other circumstances could precede an exit, with those mentioned above being the most recurrent.

The exit strategy is a plan more than a statement as several factors need consideration. They include clarity on the benefits of having the exit strategy in place, aligning the exit strategy with business goals and objectives, and determining the impact an exit will have on investors and successors. With a business exit strategy in place, it becomes clear what direction the business should take if or when a transition is necessary.

2. Understanding the scope of the exit strategy

In business, the exit strategy document is often a basic document that may only be referred to in the event of a change in business. For the most part, it is not well thought out unless there is an urgent need for it as a tool. For these reasons, businesses require education that explains how the exit strategy directly links with the health of a business.

Existing research touches on individual touchpoints of the exit strategy, without painting a full picture that will enable applicability in long term planning. From the research, it is clear that the following approaches have been explored in relation to exit strategies: -

- How the exit strategy affects the business owner

- Reasons and benefits of having an exit strategy

- The implications of the exit strategy on investors and other stakeholders

- The different types of exit strategies, and their potential influence on the business

- Key financial concerns for revenue continuation following an exit strategy

With exit strategies being shallow documents in most organizations, each of these approaches requires in in-depth review to determine how they fit into the overall picture of the organization. This information is particularly important for upper-level management who are tasked with decision making during an exit. This paper seeks to connect the dots of exit strategy, allowing any manager to craft a comprehensive exit strategy that evaluates present success and a potentially thriving future. Using analysis of qualitative research, key insights are revealed, as is how these insights affect the bigger picture for the business.

2.1 Key benefits of putting an exit strategy in place

An exit strategy is a positive tool that can be beneficial to the overall health of the business [2]. Here are a few reasons why: -

1. The exit strategy can help a business better define what success looks like and clarifies the goal that the company is working towards achieving. It also offers a timeline that can help with measuring progress.

2. The exit strategy also ensures that business leaders can create and execute insightful strategic decision making. Rather than getting stuck in the day to day running of the business, the plan focuses on achieving long term plans and objectives.

3. As a potential blueprint for business, the exit strategy indicates what should happen if certain events occur. These could include the sudden death of a business owner, or even an acquisition decision. When transitions are necessary, they are smoother and more efficient, saving both time and money when an exit strategy is in place.

4. The value of the business is flexible as it can change from one year to the next based on the business activities. With an exit strategy, it becomes possible to determine the current value and plan for future value. For the individual taking over, having a plan for the future increases the value of the business as it indicates there is guidance being used to meet goals.

2.2 The business owner and exit strategy

Businesses differ in terms of their size and operations, which means there are different factors business owners will consider for an exit strategy. The key elements that will affect the type of exit strategy chosen include the following: -.

- Time Frame

The exit strategy needs to be guided in terms of when it will take effect. Although not set in stone, it enables the business owner to negotiate where necessary and also ensures that adequate time is taken for a smooth transition. This information is especially important for the next generation investing in the business, who want to understand how long their investment will be giving them a return, and what factors could affect that return [3].

- Business Intention

As part of the exit strategy, it should be understood whether the business operations are meant to continue, or if the business will be dissolved to make way for a new entity. Understanding this will ensure that the successor of the business meets the intention and overall goal. This also gives all stakeholders an understanding of what to expect in the event of an exit.

- Business Objectives

The business owner needs to evaluate the objectives for starting the business and their individual goals. With these in mind, during the process of exit, it becomes clear if particular business objectives are a priority.

- Triggers

The business owner needs to understand triggers to determine what could happen to cause an exit or any conditions which may preclude an exit. This way, it will be clear what response should be taken.

- Next course of action

The business owner needs to clearly define what their intentions are after they exit the business. If they plan to open up a new business that provides the same product or services, a non-compete clause may be necessary for the exit strategy agreement. If the intention is to simply take the proceeds from the sale and go into retirement, this should be clear as well. The more comprehensive the exit strategy, the better for both the business owner and the investors [4].

As a business owner, several questions need thinking through when putting together the exit strategy [5]. Answers to these questions will help to ensure that plans within the business are aligned with business goals and objectives. These include the following: -

1. Would you like to remain involved in the business after exit?

   This question may seem ironic considering exit means leaving the business. However, it is worth answering to determine which would be the best exit strategy to use, particularly if a younger member of the family is taking over. Remaining involved may require a seat on the board, a management position, offering advice, or even staying in business as an employee. As the business continues to grow, it is worth reviewing this question at least once a year.

2. When exiting the business, will you make money?

   Answering this question will determine whether the exit strategy is based on going through tough times in business or exiting when experiencing growth and success. This requires looking at the long-term financial plan for the business and placing milestones that help measure their achievement. At the end of this process, the business owner will have a threshold to guide whether exit will mean some money received.

3. How much money would you like to make when you exit?

   This ties up with the purpose of the exit. Some business owners begin ventures with the sole purpose of selling the business at the point that it achieves a particular goal. Others are motivated to grow the business until it can qualify for an IPO, and they can make a massive return. For some, the exit strategy is the route to retirement, and the payoff they are seeking should help them cater to the rest of their lives. When clear about the amount of money expected, the time needed for the exit strategy to be effective becomes more apparent.

4. Should the business continue under new ownership?

   This question addresses the type of exit strategy that will be chosen. In the event of a merger or acquisition, the business will be altered to create a new entity. This means that it will not continue in the same way when under new ownership. When the business is being transitioned to family members or employees, it is possible to put in a clause that the business should continue in the same spirit.

5. How much time is needed to go through the exit process?

   The time taken to exit the business is highly dependent on the type of exit that is planned. Ideally, the minimum time required for proper exit is one year. Within this year, the business owner can ensure that the successors have been chosen, informed, and are ready to take on the business once the owner exits. Furthermore, this time is necessary to ensure a smooth transition, particularly with the employees that will remain in the business. The main reason that it should take at least a year is financial. This time is needed for all finances to be evaluated and for clarity on how much the business owner should receive upon their exit. Where finances are concerned, business owners also need the year to ensure that they go through all the required legal channels and sort out any taxes.

6. Is there a need to train staff members for a smooth transition?

   Yes, there is a need for training. A business owner exiting the business does not necessarily mean that the business is grinding to a total halt. It is typically just the business owner who is mandated to leave, while the other employees stay on to ensure the operations of the business continue. With new owners, updated systems and ways of working are likely to be put in place. To ensure that they can manage these situations, training should be done and evaluated so that there are no gaps in running the business.

2.3 Understanding the expectations of the investor

A business owner's decision to exit the business impacts the stakeholders, especially the investors of the business. Investors may end up making a profit or a loss, depending on how the business owner chooses to exit the business. Even when a family member or employee is taking over, they must know the business owner understands that they want to get their money back from the investment that they make [6]. In the event the business owner chooses to exit, the potential new owner will have the option to move on as well and remain unscathed in the process.

To meet the expectations of the chosen successor, there are several actions a business owner must take. These include the following: -

1. Profit monitoring – This should be done on an annual basis over several years, with three years being ideal. The main aim is to ensure that there is an increase in profits each year. With this monitoring, the value of the business can increase significantly. Also, keeping excellent financial books that reveal an accurate picture of what is happening within the business is essential.

2. Long-standing contracts – Even as the business owner is changing, some things should remain the same to ensure the continuity and stability of the business. This requires long term contracts to be in place. Those who receive these contracts should be critical suppliers, the best and most qualified staff members, top customers, and management staff.

3. Legal compliance – This is concerning legislation that touches on all aspects of the business. It is vital that the business is fully compliant and is not facing any

legal challenges. Legal compliance applies to all the different business licenses and certifications. With finances, ensuring that current audited accounts are available for scrutiny is necessary.

If the business is transitioning into the hands of a successor who wants to keep the business running, the business owner may have the option of keeping their shares. With this, the value of their shares may change, and it will be necessary to educate the successor on the new venture and its goals.

2.4 How do you pay back the successors?

Within the exit strategy plan, it is worth considering the motivations that drove the next generation, or employees to put their funds or even expertise into the business. Most new owners are looking for a way to get a good return. The return may be realized in the event the business being sold, recapitalization, or going public through an IPO. A new owner is interested in knowing the exit strategy for the business owner so that they can be clear on how they will realize a return [7].

To build confidence in the new owner, it is essential to share the plans for the future of the company, especially when it comes to value. It is expected that the value of the company will grow over time, meaning that new owners can look forward to increased returns.

Within the exit strategy, one needs to share the possible time frame for the exit to ensure the new owners can determine whether they will meet their return on the investment. One trap to avoid falling into as a business owner is to forecast what the rate of return will be. The new owner should work on making the calculations on their own based on their understanding and experience. As a business owner, you can support them by sharing financial documents and comprehensive projections.

It is also possible that as a part of the exit strategy, mainly if a deal is in place with another business, shareholders are offered the shares of the other company. The terms and conditions of such an agreement should be hashed out when planning an exit strategy.

2.5 The different types of exit strategies

It is now clear that there is more than one way to exit a business, and the exit strategy chosen is affected by the goals and intentions of the business owner [8]. Here are some of the strategies to choose from when exiting a business.

Transition to family members or employees

Many entrepreneurs visualize their business is still running if they may have to exit, passing it forward to family members or trusted employees. With this strategy, the business owner can take several years to train and groom their successors so that the transition is seamless. The challenge with this strategy is making sure that the person intended to take over the business can adequately manage the pressure of business operations. One advantage is that though the business owner exits and stops being part of the daily operations, they are often available after the transition in an advisory capacity [9].

- Selling with a broker, or employees

Employees of the business may share their interest in purchasing the business and keeping it running. This often happens when the business owner is retiring and seeking a way to exit the business and get a good return. As an exit strategy, a business owner can plan a long-term buyout, allowing the employees to purchase shares and increase their control over several years. This option can even be tied to their benefits or bonuses, which can be a fantastic motivator to ensure that the business attains success. This is referred to as an ESOP (Employee Share Ownership Plan), which clarifies how current employees can purchase stock. Business owners may also seek permission to remain with the business and support the working team from an advisory capacity [10].

- Mergers and acquisitions

Businesses go through ups and downs, and when a business is losing money, mergers and acquisitions can help bring stability to the business. A merger brings together companies that have complementary abilities so that they can create a new entity. Mergers offer incredible flexibility for a business owner, as the owner may choose to sell their stake in the business or remain involved with business management.

An acquisition involves the entrepreneur finding another business willing to purchase the entire entity from the business owner. It offers some flexibility in getting a good return as there are keen buyers and a willing seller. This opens up the opportunity for negotiation based on the value of the business. If the business is perceived to have high value, various acquirers can begin bidding to own, giving the business owner the chance to benefit significantly. These are a better option than simply closing the entire business by stopping operations.

- Private equity buyout

Private equity buyouts are an excellent option for young companies experiencing challenges in scaling their operations. They work by a private entity acquiring stakes in these young businesses either with financial injections or offering value in expertise. The private equity buyout aims to help the business scale up, thus increasing its value and to own the business while building their potential eventually. The equity bought is in small quantities over time, and there are often some operational conditions included within the agreement. The benefit for the investor is they purchase the company and can realize a good return as the value increases over time.

- Initial public offer (IPO)

Rapid business growth is excellent, though, in the process, the business owner may realize that they do not have adequate funds to take the business to the next level and maintain consistent growth. This issue occurs with a business that is several years old and appears to have achieved a peak in success. At this point, a key consideration is taking in public investors through an IPO. IPO stands for initial public offering, indicating the first time the shares of the company are available to the public, often at a low price that is bound to increase in value.

The business will need to have achieved a pre-determined minimum amount in pre-tax earnings over at least three years. Also, planning for an IPO is expensive, so the company should be stable enough to go through the entire process unscathed. Once the shares are sold, they will then be traded on the stock exchange, and a pool of numerous investors will become a part of the business. The entrepreneur may choose to sell all their shares, giving the business to the control of a management team and board, and therefore ending involvement with the business and getting a good return.

Any business owner who chooses an IPO as an exit strategy should be ready for scrutiny from business analysts who are determined to define the value of the company. Financial documents need to be clear and up to date, going back as far as the company has been in existence.

- Liquidation

This should be a last resort option as it is equivalent to simply closing the business down. When this is the option, there are often challenges around debt, revenue, and profit. Liquidation requires the sale of all the assets so that creditors can be repaid the amount they are owed. If there are any funds left once this is done, the balance is divided between different shareholders to return for their investment. With so many ways to keep a viable business operational, this is one exit strategy that should not be considered unless necessary, and there is no alternative.

2.6 How the exit plan influences the business

- Legal Structure

An effective exit strategy requires a legal agreement that outlines the terms and conditions of the potential exit. During the crafting of the legal agreement, an exit advisory team must go through all the parts of the agreement in detail. With the support of this team, the exit strategy agreement may be drafted several times before a final one that meets all criteria is done [11].

Within the exit strategy agreement, five essential documents should be included. These are: -

1. Letter of Intent

   This is a letter prepared by the successor to formally expresses their interest in making an offer for the business. It often requires specific information, including how the transition will be done to fit the structure of the business. This letter of intent becomes particularly important if the next generation owner intends to purchase the business from an exiting business owner. This is to allow for fair negotiation and can ensure there is a focus on the expectations of the business owner to reach an agreement.

2. Purchase and Sale Agreement

   This document is also referred to as the Definitive Purchase Agreement. It includes the final agreement between the parties and acts as a legally binding document for the ownership exchange. Within it, the shares and how they will be divided is outlined. Also, there will be details on how stocks and assets are to be purchased. This agreement should be drafted by an attorney who is well-versed in all the requirements and payments necessary. Furthermore, the attorney can support the exit strategy advisory team with their expertise. With the Definitive purchase agreement, the tax implications for each transaction are captured.

3. Earn-Out Agreement

   One aspect of an exit strategy is offering the successor a guarantee that the business will continue to grow and thrive even after the business owner has made their exit. For most business owners, getting a one-time cash payment to close the deal is the best strategy. This may not be ideal for the buyer. With the earn-out agreement, the buyer offers to make payments to the exiting owner after the exit for some time. This is highly risky for the business owner, as once they exit the business, they have little control over the operations and real success of the entity. If this agreement is used, it needs to have precise and careful wording that offers the exiting business owner some protection.

4. Non-Compete Agreement

   When a business owner chooses an exit strategy, there is one highly valuable asset that they take away with them. That is their expertise and knowledge on how to run the business. This can be of concern to the business successor who will want to take all the necessary steps to protect their new investment in the business. This is where the non-compete agreement is essential. This is a formal agreement that outlines that the exiting business owner will not create a competing business or be employed within the same industry in a competing organization for some time. Typically, the non-compete agreement will cover three years.

To ensure that the full legal process is followed, some documents need to be updated continuously for ease of transition. These include all intellectual property licenses, patents, trademarks, and copyrights. The same applies to any software that may hold sensitive or confidential information. These types of documents have an impact on royalties and the way they are collected.

Also, contracts with vendors and clients need filing and updating as they tie into the value of the business. They also provide information on the length of time these stakeholder relationships are valid.

2.7 Types of revenue models

Money and how to get a good return are top of mind when creating an exit strategy. From a financial standpoint, it is necessary to understand financial risks, any barriers to entry due to a change in the business owner, and also if there is any advantage that remains sustainable.

In financial reporting, it is ideal the business seeking to exit can reveal multiple income streams allowing for flexibility when it comes to beating the competition and being able to meet new goals. These income streams include: -

- Transactional Revenue Models
  - With this revenue model, it is easy to transition as part of the exit strategy. This is because, for the most part, the business will remain as usual, which is the most ideal scenario for a next generation successor. Revenue is earned through the company offering a product or service, and the customer making payments for it.
- Subscription Revenue Models
  - With this revenue model, customers pay a subscription fee to gain access to the product or service. It could also be a subscription model where customers pay for a product in installments over some time. For an exit strategy, it is crucial to determine whether this model is in place as it has a high risk.

Customers may not finish their payment or choose to unsubscribe in the event of a chance of the business owner. It remains an attractive option for next generation successors due to generating recurring revenue.

2.8 Trade-offs between long vs. short term exit strategy

When considering a long term or short-term exit strategy, the goals, as well as the sustainability of the company, can more easily be aligned. Consider the following example. A business wants to work towards an IPO option within five years. To meet this long-term goal, there are specific steps that will be taken with a short-term strategy. These could include the product or service offering and even pricing and competition. In effect, the long-term goal for investment is the primary consideration, while everything in the short term is viewed as a tactic towards meeting this goal.

The type of exit strategy that you choose, whether long term or short term, will also affect the value you can receive. This is why a business owner needs to select their preferred exit strategy. Exiting can take as little as one year, and even up to ten years to accomplish well.

3. Research methods

The research method that was used to collect data for analysis and discussion is secondary qualitative research. This data was collated from a range of journals, all of which were addressing a different touchpoint of exit strategies. The aim of seeking for information across different platforms was to identify joining factors as well as identify any patterns in approaching exit strategies. Therefore, the review and analysis have been carried out on existing literature, including literature that offers comparisons of exit strategy situations in different countries.

The data collected was non-numeric. The journals and other content sources that were referred to were based on small studies that offer insight into a business or section of industry. For this reason, this paper focuses on analysis of their conclusions, more so than their data sets. This allows for deductive reason, though may also be viewed as a practical limitation. Furthermore, this paper attempts to understand cultural nuances that may impact the exit strategy process, as explored through the literature studies.

The analysis focuses on the meaning of exit strategies, both for the business owner and the investors. Through research analysis, it became clear that from end to end, exit strategies begin with the owner and culminate with the potential effect on the investors. By seeking to analyze this process, this paper seeks to understand the implications of choosing one specific strategy, as well as how to ensure that the strategy is carried out from start to finish. The secondary qualitative research is interpretive in nature, as this paper offers exploration into the topic building on theoretic principles that are in existence within the literature [12].

3.1 Discussion

The research reveals that there are positive reasons for an exit strategy, and that this strategy should form a core component of any business documentation. The exit strategy guides decision making, both for the next generation owner and the exiting business owner. This means that it acts as a blueprint for what actions should be taken in the event that an exit is imminent. With this blueprint, it becomes easier to determine the factors that can affect any exit strategy including the time needed, intention and business objectives for the business. Furthermore, there are numerous courses of action that a business owner can take following the strategy that include being available for consultation within the business, or a full exit meaning the business and its operations are totally in new hands.

For the new owner, it touches on how they can ensure a return on the investment that they make with the business. By the business owner understanding the goal of the investor, the exit strategy can ensure that the business operations are competent and aligned to a certain exit strategy that is most likely. Money, or a return on investment is also essential for the business owner, and this may guide the number of months or years that the business owner works through making their exit.

Therefore, there are ongoing actions that the business owner needs to ensure take place, both for them and the investor. These including profit monitoring, staying legally compliant and setting up contracts with suppliers and stakeholders. From the literature, it becomes clear that ensuring these actions are in place will result in the right exit strategy being chosen.

4. Conclusion

A business owner who starts their venture may create five-year plans that seek to drive profits and sales. Also, business owners desire to achieve growth, taking their business from one level of success to the next. However, it is essential to create an exit strategy if things do not go according to the plan. Not only is this a plan that will guide business operations, but it is also a fail-safe to ensure that the business is never caught off guard in case of any operational challenges. The earlier in the life of the business, the easier the transition will be when it is necessary.

An exit strategy is vital to ensure that the company has the right revenue models and legal structure. Furthermore, it provides direction on investment, especially when looking at short and long-term growth goals and the types of investors that would be beneficial to the business. In the heat of the moment, putting together an exit strategy with tight time restraints may result in gaps that cost the business owner dearly. A logical and well-thought-out plan will ensure that there is minimal loss and that investments of all stakeholders are well protected.

To create the exit strategy, a finance professional like an accountant should be at the forefront of the draft plan. This finance professional should coordinate their work with a business attorney so that all due process is followed. Together, they will create the initial draft. Additional information can be added in from key managers and members of an exit strategy advisory committee. With all these contributions, it becomes possible to have a highly comprehensive document that can be updated when necessary.

Many people opt to write a will to ensure proper division of their assets should they pass away. This does not mean that they are planning to die. In fact, it is viewed as something highly responsible to do. It is similar to creating a business exit strategy. It does not speak to the commitment of the entrepreneur. It is merely a readiness tool to prepare for any eventuality [13].

There is something worth considering when creating an exit strategy, and that is how to react and respond to an unexpected offer by large companies who may be seeking an acquisition. This helps ensure that the business owner has some insight and can guide a negotiation well if a buyer is available. Sometimes exit is not voluntary, and even in this situation, significant benefits can be realized.

Future research should seek to analyze an actual exit strategy, seeking insights and opinions from all stakeholders. These should help to determine the planning phase effectiveness, those involved in the process, and the end result. Carrying out these end to end studies will help with understanding which processes are the most effective from start to finish. Furthermore, it will become easier to identify loopholes that may cause an interruption to executing an exit strategy.

Author details

Jeffrey M. Shepard
Union Institute and University, Cincinnati, Ohio, USA

*Address all correspondence to: jeffreymshepard@yahoo.com

References

[1] Leonetti, J. M. (2008). *Exiting your Business. Protecting your Wealth. A Strategic Guide for Owners and their Advisors.* John Wiley & Sons.

[2] DeTienne, D. R. (2010, March). Entrepreneurial exit as a critical component of the entrepreneurial process: Theoretical development. Journal of Business Venturing, *25*(2), 203-215. Retrieved September 24, 2020

[3] Talebi, K., Shakhdari, K., & Darijani, Z. (2016). Identify individual factors influenced the choice of exit strategy. International journal of physical and social sciences, *6*(8), 84 - 95.

[4] Headd, B. (2003). Redefining business success: Distinguishing between closure and failure. Small Business Economics, *21*, 51-61. Retrieved September 25, 2020

[5] Lane, J. (2018). The Exit Strategy: The difference between building a business and being an entrepreneur is what you can sell at the end of the day. *Strategic Finance, 99*(8), 23+. Retrieved September 23, 2020

[6] Onetti A, A. p. (2018). When start-ups exit comparing strategies in Europe and the USA. Journal of Business Strategy, *39*(3), 26 - 33.

[7] Bjerkestrand, K. E., & Helland, T. (2016). *Financing of Start-Ups-investors' Requirement for Exit Strategy; a Comparative Study of Norway and the United States.* Bergen: Norwegian School of Economics.

[8] DeTienne, D., McKelvie, A., & Chandler. (2015). Making sense of entrepreneurial exit strategies. A typology and test. *Journal of Business Venturing, 30*(2), 255.

[9] Hawkey, J. (2002). *Exit Strategy Planning: Grooming your Business for Sale or Succession.* Gower publishing Ltd.

[10] Brill, A. (2017). *Employees Stock Ownership Plans as an Exit Strategy for Private Business Owners.* Matrix Global Advisors White paper.

[11] Lee, B., & Cho, Y. (2020). The Legal Structure of Ventures and Exit Routes: A Study of Single-Founder Start-Ups in the United States. *The International Journal of Entrepreneurship and Innovation*.

[12] Jankowicz, D. (2011). *Research Methods for Business and Management.* Edinburgh Business School.

[13] Neneh, B.N. (2020). Why foreignness matters: The impact of business-family interference on the exit intentions of women entrepreneur. Journal of Small Business Strategy, *30(1), 83-96*

Chapter 15

Assessment of Top Management Commitment and Support on IS Risk Management Implementation in the Business Organization

Fasilat Aramide Sanusi and Satirenjit Kaur Johl

Abstract

Information system has become a strategic tool for business organization, its wide usage and acceptance has increased the flexibility of commercial activities and business sustainability. The use of internet technology has also promoted business networking, information sharing, knowledge acquisition, and prompt decision-making. Meanwhile, efficiency of IS is anchored on the commitment and support of top management in terms of policy and strategy formulation. This paper analyses the impact of top management commitment and support on IS risk management implementation in the business sector. The study employed a narrative method of literature review that critically analyzed the importance of top management commitment and support on information system risk management implementation within the business organization. Relevant information was obtained from Scopus, Web of Science, Research Gate and google scholar. It was found that IS improves task efficiency through effective communication and job automation. Therefore, organizations need to control and prevent the possibility of IS risk occurrence in their operations to promote competitive advantage and sustainable performance. Hence, and it is the responsibility of executive arm of organization to guide, direct, and control IS risk management implementation for performance advantage.

Keywords: top management, commitment and support, risk management, information system, business organization

1. Introduction

The development in information technology has enabled the business organizations to implement information system (IS) risk management as a method of protecting businesses as well as organization's confidential information. Nowadays, information technology (IT) has helped organizations to accomplished objective of automated information processing system. Information is considered valuable and intangible assets that has to do with knowledge acquisition, trade secret, organizational capability and innovative advantage, therefore, they need to be protected from any form of IS related threat or risk [1].

Recently, attention has been drawn to IS risk management implementation due to the common problem of cyber-attack and intellectual property theft.

Effective IS risk management implementation is significant to IS assets protection. Organizations need to focus on every area of risk management and not financial assets alone [2]. Top management must show commitment and ultimate responsibility towards accomplishment of IS risk management implementation. Senior management should include IS risk management as part of managerial function and ensure that all required resources are readily available to provide the capabilities needed to achieve IS risk management implementation objective [3]. Additionally, top management should evaluate IS risk management performance to know the failure or success of the program.

Moreover, in order to incorporate the result of risk assessment into organizational decision making, top management must show support and commitment to IS risk management implementation programmes to mitigate IS related risks. Both profit and not for profit organizations need to boost efficient and secure financial operations by remain proactive in managing various risks that are related to IS. The most common type of theft in our time is connected to intellectual property theft, information security breach, and online financial crime therefore, top management commitment and support for IS risk management implementation will enhance greater protection of business information.

However, IS risk management implementation should be based on criteria that successfully measure IS performance objective in all areas of corporate activities. IS is now a critical success factor that influenced number of performance outcomes, hence, managing its risk will promote competitiveness and performance of business organization. Studies have recommended risk management implementation as breakthrough in performance management [4, 5] also views risk management as the crucial area of managerial planning and action required to achieve performance efficiency. Ultimately, commitment and support of top management is a factor that measure organization's proactiveness in IS risk management implementation in relation to entire performance of business units. Top management commitment and support involves establishment of corporate objective on risk minimization, risk management policy formulation, financing, setting up committees for monitoring, supervision and training, as well as evaluation of risk management result [6]. However, IS is a combination of hardware, software and people in an organization who collect, filter and process data to generate useful information to support business processes [7]. Nowadays, both financial and non-financial operations relied on information processing using IT as a major tool. Hence; it is necessary to beware of various major risks associated with the usage of IS such as human error, scam, and natural disasters.

Therefore, this book chapter discusses the impact of top management commitment and support on IS risk management implementation in the business organization for sustainable business result. Meanwhile, IS risk include series of events associated with the usage of IS, examples are hardware and software failure, computer virus attack, human error, and other criminal risks like hackers, staff dishonesty, fraud, information security breach, passwords theft and denial of service. Including the occurrence of natural disasters like fire, flood and others that could cause complete damage to entire information processing operation. Thus, it is critical to prevent risk occurrence than waiting for the risk to occur and then try to get rid of it, this could be costly and have a devastating effect on performance outcome. Much has not been done in the area of academic research when it comes to IS risk management implementation [7, 8], unlike other areas of risk management studies. Researchers and practitioners should put efforts in understanding and assessing how organizations can implement effective IS risk management. In terms of combination of technical procedure with people-orientated component for the purpose of minimizing the likely risks of IS assets as well as enhancing organization's capacity in managing the risks [9].

2. Overview of information system

IS risk management implementation can be a foundation to effective business management initiative, businesses are processing tons of stakeholders information daily any, slack or weakness in IS management operation can expose the entire business operation to financial loss. Organization is a network of activities combined as one under the influence of IS. IS has become an essential tool that promote entire operation of an organization and it is crucial to performance. Specifically, organization must recognize the implication of IS risk management implementation to profitability. Risk management is like a catalyst to operational efficiency [10]. Nevertheless, IS risk management implementation should be a concentrated area of study especially in the financial institutions. Financial sectors have been trying to understand how to minimize customer's information theft and financial scam for the performance efficiency.

Literature review findings revealed limited studies on IS risk management implementation in the business organization [11]. Studies like [12] explained the process and the importance of managing risk in the business organization. Other studies discussed factors that drove effective IS risk management implementation [13]. The importance of IS risk management implementation to financial performance is worthy of exploration due to the present cashless policy in the global economy. The more the global reliance on internet services for business operations the higher the exposure to IS risk and the more the necessity for IS risk management implementation. Also, business organizations are operating under intense competitive pressure relating to trade secret and competitive advantage, organizations that failed to implement IS risk management implementation could lose sensitive information to competitors. This can reduce operational efficiency and slow down timely decision making. Additionally, the global economic efficiency is anchored on digital financial transaction and the volatility of information exposure via the internet further increased IS risk. This problem has hindered the effectiveness of IS usage. Organizations are rethinking of risk management policy to meet the current challenges of IS risk management. Therefore, top management must adequately play oversight function in the risk management implementation by setting up a risk management policy and framework and accept suggestions on IS risk management prevention and control.

The main reason for implementing IS risk management does not limited to risk minimization but to optimize it rewards and prevent probable failure in the long run [14, 15]. IS risk management implementation is a technical practice that influence the major area of business practice in recent time. Effective IS risk management implementation in the business operation is critical to both financial and sustainable performance. Development of effective capacity to measure and manage IS risks is also critical for organizations to effectively perform their duties in financing business activities, particularly, the role of continuous managing financial operations involving various stakeholders whose involvement underpin economic growth of the company. It is highly important to minimize losses and increase business performance.

IS supports the strategic decision of business organization. It also gives appropriate response to information aspect of business operation by promoting effectiveness in the coordination of different units of the business. IS promotes simple access to data and information in timely basis and in an arranged manner. Information becomes easily documented to enhance and improve the day-to day activities of organization. IS needs people and hardware to exercise functional activities of planning, directing, organizing, coordinating, controlling, and decision-making. However, IS risk management implementation is relevant to protect the functional activities of IS for better result and to correct the deviations in the system. IS creates appropriate condition for effective decision-making and information processing that improves organizational efficiency. IS risk management implementation help to predict and protect the future of IS usage in the organization with the view to make appropriate caution in the event of a limitation in attaining the goal of IT resource [1, 16]. Ability to take advantage of IS lies in risk management efficiency.

3. Do we have to measure economic effect of IS risk management implementation to promote pro-activeness in risk prevention?

IS is a tool that supported business connectivity within and outside the organization. It helps to generate information from data processing and analyzed it into meaningful services for managerial decision making. IS is people and service oriented activities that determine the method of gathering, processing, storing and transmitting business information to support managerial operations in the organization [17]. The success of IS risk management dependent on the result of evaluation and efficiency of business processes. The common measure for evaluating IS risk management implementation are quality of productivity and performance efficiency. Quality of productivity is a determent of how the organization utilizes it IS in the production of products and services. Meanwhile, efficiency of IS depends on employees' attitudes and behaviors towards IS usage, task effectiveness, and resource availability.

Technological development and expansion have promoted the recent industrial booming in terms of speedy information processing and decision making. Also, the whole activities in our everyday life has been impacted by IS and technology devices. In a nutshell, IS is a product of information and communication technology (ICT), which includes software, hardware, and other elements communication [18]. Nonetheless, IS involves combination of IT and its applications in the organization as well as the users who enables technology implementation for organizational benefit. Organizational information is related to customers, suppliers, products, operating procedures, equipment, competitors, financial transactions, and regulatory environments [19]. IS risk management implementation helps to safeguard customers' accounts, payroll information, information relating to trade secret, company' financial and non-financial assets and the efficiency of the branch operations [20].

Hence, IS consists of software, people, hardware communication devices, and data that enable information processing, storage, and usage for business purpose. Acemoglu et al. [21] described IS as a package of software connected within the organization to achieve performance efficiency. Abbas [8] also defined IS as a structural means of gathering, entering, processing, storage, managing, controlling, and disseminating business information to achieve business goals and objectives. Rai et al. [10] refers to IS as a system that promotes activities that are concentrated on managing, disseminating, and displaying information. Based on those definitions, IS can be referred to as an essential technology tool that improve performance and competitive advantage of business organization. IS risk management implementation is an emerging area of study and no generally accepted standard to guide organizations on successful implementation of IS risk management. Though, few of such standards exist but limited to certain practices which are limited to a small range of business organizations. Therefore, more studies will help to bridge this gap.

4. Do the components of IS matters to it designs and usefulness

Three components of IS was identified and explained in the following statements.

4.1 IS technology activeness

This is a dimension that is built on system and information quality. System and information quality is considered key factor affecting IS's usage and acceptance within the organization. However, system quality is characterized by device flexibility, software features, ease of use, system reliability, and employee's acceptance [22]. The success and prospect of IS was based on the perceived usefulness, user satisfaction, and the performance outcome. Moreover [23] concluded that system quality positively influenced user's satisfaction. In addition [24] also supported that system quality influenced IS user satisfaction. Whereas, information quality is the desirable end result of IS usage. It includes information relevant, clarity, accuracy, conciseness, completeness, and timeliness. Increase in information quality will lead to high IS usefulness. Premkumar and King [25] opined that information quality has a significant influence on IT usefulness and user satisfaction.

Nevertheless, service quality is the motivation and encouragement given to the system users usually from the IT or HRM department and technology personnel support. This includes responsiveness, device accuracy, software reliability, technical support, empathy, rewards and recognition. Victoria Lucas et al. and Al-Mamary et al. [6, 23] concluded that service quality positively affected perceived usefulness of IS. Meaning that increase in service quality will increase IS usefulness.

4.2 Internal organizational factor

Internal organizational factor is the top management commitment and support in terms of training given to IS users. That is, the support offered by top management in IS risk management implementation. Top management commitment and support activities aimed to realize the full benefits of IS by promoting the use of technology for job-related task, provision of necessary resources, rewards and recognitions, training and guidance on IS (Victoria Lucas [6]). IS training is relevant in Operation systems (OS), Spreadsheets, Word processing, and other software application packages.

Sudhakar [26] concluded that top management support positively affect IS usefulness and user's satisfaction. Al-Mamary et al. [23] also concluded that training has a direct positive influence on IS usefulness and user's satisfaction. Resource allocation is very important to IS risk management implementation and the functioning of business operation units. Resource allocation can be finance, people, technology devices etc. IS resource allocation is dependent on the size of business operation and the expected outcome. Organization that has a significant objective of IS risk management implementation is expected to have great IS resources to support their business operations. Also, participation of top management and users in the IS risk management planning and implementation will promote understanding and efficiency of the system.

4.3 People's factor

People's factor refers to computer user's efficacy (Self-efficacy) and experience in handling IS devices. Computer efficacy is the user's skills and abilities to perform a given task using IS devices. Computer efficacy measure individual's understanding of how the system work and confidentiality in the use of the system [27, 28]. Premkumar and King [25] agree that computer efficacy positively influence IS usefulness and users satisfaction. User's experience can be measure by previous knowledge and skill in the use of IS devices such as spreadsheet, OS, word processing and so on. Moh'd Al-adaileh [29] found positive interaction between computer experience and user's satisfaction.

5. Is there a fit between the role of IS and organization performance?

IS function stated that organization with significant impact on information processing need a high level of technology efficiency, because any interruption can have a devastating effect on business operation. For example, IS deficiency can caused significant level of revenue loss to organizations that are based on the use of computer for business processing e.g., airlines, banks et cetera [19]. In those organizations, performance is based on genuine service, relevant of information, and the consistency of the system. IS implementation is often established in the organization to achieve a key performance objectives. Integration of IS with business operation will improve communication efficiency and better identification of strategy that suit performance objectives. IS applications and good communication will also promote a user friendly environment. The achievement of these objectives can be considered as a measure of active IS risk management implementation. Organizations that play a significant role in IS risk management implementation is expected to have greater attainment of both mission and vision objectives. Success in IS risk management implementation is to a large extent dependent on the organization's culture and level of resistance to risk management and control [4, 5]. Organization's resistance to risk control and reduction can cause loss of revenue and profitability. The level of acceptance and usage of IS could be higher in organizations that are in the strategic position of competitiveness. Hence, the more the usage of IS the higher the exposure to potential risk of IS technology. A computer or system shutdown can has a great negative effect on the operations of organizations in the strategic IS businesses. For instance, sectors like Airlines can suffer significant revenue loss if their computers were to be breakdown for few hours. In those organizations, IS efficiency must be maintained to support accuracy of service, relevancy of information, and the efficiency of system to meet the critical needs of business operation.

IS has the capacity to impact business performance in many ways, such as return on investment (ROI), sales revenue, customer satisfaction, market share and competitive advantage. Studies have highlighted that the return from IS investment dependent on the system's strategic role [19]. Over the years, airline industries have been found to increase their sales revenue and market share through strategic IS implementation. Scholars like [29] provide evidences that IS can impact organizational performance. Therefore, since this study focuses on the top management commitment and support for IS risk management implementation, it is expected that organizations that have a significant reliance on IS for business operations need an active top management executives to implement and support IS risk management. This will have a great contribution to the development and economic sustainability of business organization.

6. Concept of risk management

Risk is a probability of bad occurrence and the anticipation of the degree of loss that is likely to occur. Probability of loss can emerge from the uncertainty, threat, vulnerability, and asset characteristics. Eboigbe [30] refers to risk as an unwanted event or circumstance that has a probability of occurrence resulting to bad result from a project. Technology, N. I. o. S. a. [31] described risk as any circumstance that is capable of affecting the goal of business objectives. Diverse opinions on the meaning of risk are what resulted into various identifications of risks and it outcomes, including the risk assessment. Looking at the definition of the risk, it nature is universal regardless of the context. Business organization is liable to incur some risks in the form of investment risk, market risk, credit risk, operational risk, liquidity risk, IS risk, competition risk, government policy risk, natural disaster's risk and other risks that are connected to commercial activities. Therefore, risks exposure required effective risk management. Risk management is one of the strategies required to achieve business goal.

7. IS risk management

Nowadays, technology serves as a blockbuster to business performance and automated information processing. IS is an asset to the organization thus, organizations are required to protect their assets from any form of risk. IS risk is an IT-related risk that can expose business process to significant loss. IS risk management played an important role in the management of business organization. An efficient IS risk management is necessary for the success of IT security in the organization. Hence, IS risk management should not be left to IT technicians/experts; rather it should be regarded as one of the critical managerial function [32, 33].

IS risk management allowed IT supervisor to evaluate operation and economic costs of information security to obtain the goal of IT investment. IS is an organizational system designed to process, store and distribute information to accomplish the mission and vision objectives. Every stage of those functions involved risk, for example, during information processing, sensitive information could be loss or stolen, it is in the capacity of business organization to manage such risk exposure. Also, financial data is one of the sensitive aspects of IS processing, organization needs to protect it from the risk of manipulation and false Figures. IS risk management encompasses security and conscious procedures in preventing and reducing IS risk. These risks include operational, usage, and implementation.

This book chapter however, concentrates on the role of top management commitment and support as a driver of IS risk management implementation in the business organization. Al-Wohaibi et al. [2] concluded that the main goal of IS risk management is to enhance active performance of business operation by reducing the running cost of the business [26] examined IS and software development in U.S. and found that IS risk management promote data and information processes within the organization. Standardization and integration of activities enabled organizations to coordinate operating processes and improve information generation capacity such that reduce the operating cost. Whale [34] conducted study on IS risk management in the bank sector in England and concluded that IS risk management is critical to the operation of bank institution than any other organization due to their stand as service delivery. Financial institutions processed a huge amount of customers' information daily. This information is exposed to a number of factors like theft, destruction, system failure, and information inaccuracy. These risks are threat to the performance of organization, therefore IS risk management implementation becomes critical for the survival of business.

8. Implementation of IS risk management

IS risk management implementation is the method of highlighting vulnerability in the IS and the protection of all the components of IS. Whale [34] argued that the fundamental concerns of IS risk management implementation is to support operating mission and vision of the organization. IS risk management implementation involves a series of steps like identifying, measuring, monitoring, and controlling IS related risks in an organization. The process ensures that individual clearly understand risk management procedures in order to achieve business strategic objectives. IS risk management implementation can also reduce the negative impact of business and increase the emerging market opportunities [35].

However, I concluded on the following as major objectives of IS risk management implementation in an organization: (1) building IS that process, store, and disseminate information; (2) allowing management to formulate useful decision that ensure judicious utilization of IS budget and (3) assist management to give necessary authority regarding the documentation of risk management performance. IS risk management implementation consists of different activities by which when undertaking in sequence will allow continual improvement in decision making. This includes establishing the content of the risk, identifying the risk, evaluating the risk, and risk treatment.

Al-Mamary [32] emphasized that effective IS risk management implementation should support the business operation objective. IS risk management is a vital component of business management and performance. Top management is enriched with two fundamental obligations, namely, obligation to dedicate and obligation to care in IS risk management implementation process. An obligation of dedication means that the IS risk management implementation decision will be made in the benefit of the business. Obligation of care is an indication that senior executive will safe guide the assets of the organization and make informed business decision. IS risk management implementation must be practical and control must be directed towards eradication of existing risks. Implementing a timely IS risk management can fulfill this objective [11] IS risk management implementation responsibility and accountability should be made specific and clear. IS risk management implementation policy should be based on the responsibilities of workforce. Also, for effective IS risk management implementation, efficient policy must be implemented, missions and objectives must be clearly communicated across the workforce and IT experts. The result of IS risk management implementation should always be evaluate to know the area that required improvement and to meet IS changing update. This should be done in respect to time, need, and objective. Efficient top management commitment and support will help to conduct routine inspection on IS risk management implementation and make changes where necessary.

9. Is top management commitment and support a necessity to IS risk management efficiency

Top management commitment and support played crucial role in IS risk management implementation, stating from budget approval, policy formulation, team appointment, supervision and monitoring to evaluation [36]. Effective IS risk management implementation and objective accomplishment can be compensated by top management as a reward for the success. Dembo and Freeman [37] conducted study in U.S. to examine the concept of critical success factor to be implemented in a business environment. Executive management support was considered the most successful critical success factor. Integrating risk management into decision-making process will create efficiency in procedure and control in a common risk management. Galorath [38] studied the importance of risk management and evaluate the process required for effective implementation of IS risk management in SMEs. Top-level executive support was also considered a success factor for risk management implementation. Risk management implementation protects the entire management structure and measure the pattern of performance in relation to risk management. Westerveld [39] investigate the relationship between project success and critical success factor using project designed model, top management support was found effective. Belassi and Tukel [40] identified critical success factors for Management Information System (MIS) project implementation, top management support was considered a crucial factor. Cereola [41] examined the critical success factors in complex industrial project management and highlighted top management support as major critical success factor.

An holistic survey conducted by [42] revealed that the most important elements of risk management implementation in the organizations include attitude towards risk monitoring and practice and support from executive board. Therefore, it can be concluded that top management commitment and support is a key component of IS risk management implementation because it improves and support decision making in IS risk management. Commitment from top management and support are crucial to IS risk management implementation. Successful implementation of risk management is thus, based on the commitment and support of the top management.

The commitment and support from top management plays a major role in the success of any form of project implementation within an organization. Top management has a broad range of actions that include effective decision-making in managing IS risk, developing training programs, supporting quality management, formulating objectives and strategies for IS risk management implementation, and establishing a project management office [43]. Commitment and support from top management is very essential in the management of any organization and its one of the key factors for IS risk management implementation. The level of capability in managing risk project administration in the organization has a connection with the implementation and risk control. Top management needs to be mindful of risk management control in terms of execution, device screening and selection, application prerequisites, and outcome measurement [44] Commitment and support can be in the forms of skill, monetary, and direct participation in organization's risk management implementation. Top management clearly has a key role in running business activities and concerns for organizational success. Fasilat [45] conducted study on the critical success factor for IS risk management implementation in the financial sector and found that top management commitment and support was critical to the success of IS risk management implementation. Victoria Lucas et al. [6] also found that top management support is critical to the success of diverse enterprise resource management. Top management competency, instruction, and awareness about IS risk management practice play significant role in building a strategy that promote risk management.

IS is considered importance in the production of goods and services in the recent time, production activities from raw material supply to the final consumption required communication processes both within and outside the scope of organization. Top management is expected to be committed to the process of formulating strategic decisions regarding the IS risk management implementation and performance efficiency. IS as a process of information and communication technology (ICT) that allows an organization to use and interact with technology in the business processing system. IS is a complete process that involves data process and management on the one hand and activity relating to information usage and management on the other hand. Hence, it can be concluded that successful IS risk management implementation depends on the commitment of top management officials and that if IS risk management is well implemented will enhance organizational performance.

10. Methodology

The architectural process of the method employed in this book chapter is logic that follows the sequence of highlights that clearly defines the title of the book chapter. However, [46] described research methodology as the process of considering and explaining the logic behind research method and technique which allowed the means to explore a phenomenon. Therefore, this study employs a narrative method of literature review, a comprehensive approach that critically analyzed the impact of top management commitment and support on information system risk management implementation in the business organization. It is essential to the study's objective because it helps to identify relevant information on what is matter in the research topic. This also allows identification of the importance and contributions of both top management commitment and support and IS risk management implementation to sustainable business performance in the existing body of knowledge [47]. This method was chosen due to its flexible approach which gives individual insight and opportunities for speculation that most quantitative review approaches never give. Google Scholar, Scopus, Web of Science, Research Gate were the main source of data collection.

11. Result and discussion

The desire to accelerate profit through sustainable performance does not come without an effort, organizations need to undertake some practical steps to enhance job standard and expectation. This will promote financial stability and commitment to performance objectives. Hence, top management commitment and support on information system risk management implementation is one of the channels through which an organization can truly achieve the desired goal and objective. Since IS has become the bedrock of business processing activities. Also, inability to managed IS risk has posed major challenges to sustainability of some organizations in the recent time. Sensitive information leakage, hard and software malfunctioning, attitude to IS usage, and online scammer constitute major IS risk. When IS risk management is affected, the sustainable performance of global business organizations will be hindered.

Additionally, IS promotes and sustained interaction between organization and its stakeholders. It is a key component that provide information to the right people at the right time in the favor of managerial activities. Additionally, it reduces the time spent in face-to-face communications among employees and supervisors thus, increasing efficiency of information responsiveness in the organization. IS is a user support system for management information which aims to provide understandable, reliable, accessible, and complete information in a timely basis. However, the risk of IS has been identified as one of the most critical issue in IS implementation. Few studies have been conducted to explore the influence of IS risk management implementation on the success of organizational performance. IS risk management implementation is a critical factor that determine organization's success in IT management. According to [48] successful implementation and usage of technology in the business processes depends on software characteristics, organizational characteristics, types of project, users perception, and value yield to the financial outcome. IS risk management can be evaluated from the users experience in terms of perceived usefulness, perceived ease of use and user satisfaction. IS implementation is a costly project, inability of organization to maximize it performance potential is a risk to financial stability. Hence, IS is a resource capability that can be used as tool for competitive advantage. Therefore, more studies are required to create awareness about the importance of top management commitment and support on information system risk management implementation to promote sustainable profit and performance across the globe.

12. Conclusion

IS has become a bedrock of organization's achievement in business administration and control. Therefore, efficient IS risk management implementation will help to achieve reliable information required for business processing. People like managers, employees and other related stakeholders need to connect through IS to coordinate business processing activities. IS analysis indicates that organizations have distinct roles to play in IS operations in terms of supporting various forms of strategic planning, performance, and evaluation. A great deal of administrative activities is been supported by IS software components, example is the Enterprise Resource Planning (ERP). It's obvious that modern organization cannot survive without technology particularly, in the area of Management Information System (MIS). MIS help to disseminate information relating to business administration and processes within the circle of corporate units for organizational success. It's also assists in timely process of business information for effective decision making. IS risk management implementation has not been a reality in the realm of research activity but it was valued by business organizations especially, the multi-million-dollar businesses. Telecommunication and financial sectors are most concerned with the problem of IS risk management. They are information service-oriented businesses that required information quality, service quality, and system quality to satisfy customers for profitability. Hence, top management commitment and support will enhance IS risk management and technology efficiency.

Author details

Fasilat Aramide Sanusi* and Satirenjit Kaur Johl
Universiti Teknologi PETRONAS, Bandar Seri Iskandar, Perak, Malaysia

*Address all correspondence to: fasilat17@gmail.com

References

[1] Westner, M., & Strahringer, S (2010). Determinants of success in IS offshoring projects: Results from an empirical study of German companies. Information & management, *47*(5), 291-299.

[2] Al-Wohaibi, M. A., Masoud, F. A., & Edwards, H. M. (2004). Fundamental risk factors in deploying IT/IS Projects in Omani government organisations. Advanced Topics in Global Information Management,, *3*(179).

[3] Roland, H. (2008). Using IT to drive effective risk management. Journal of Risk Management, *55*(1), 43-44.

[4] Dubois, É., Heymans, P., Mayer, N., & Matulevičius, R. (2010). A systematic approach to define the domain of information system security risk management *Intentional Perspectives on Information Systems Engineering* (pp. 289-306): Springer.

[5] Hubbard, D. W. (2020). *The failure of risk management: Why it's broken and how to fix it*: John Wiley & Sons.

[6] Victoria Lucas Mkonya, Yu Jintian, Stella Binauli Nanthuru, & Jinyevu, S. A. (2018). Analysis of Top Management Support and Individual Factors Influence on Accounting Information,. *International Journal of Management Science and Business Administration., 4*(3), 19-29. .

[7] Masuoka, Y., Naono, K., & Kameyama, S. (2004). Network monitoring method for information system, operational risk evaluation method, service business performing method, and insurance business managing method: Google Patents.

[8] Abbas, S. (2015). Factors Affecting ERP Implementation Success in Banking Sector of Pakistan. International Review of Basic and Applied Sciences, *3*(7).

[9] Ramasubbu, N., Bharadwaj, A., & Kumar Tayi, G. (2015). Software process diversity: Conceptualization, measurement, and analysis of impact on project performance. Management Information Sytem, *39*(4), 787-807.

[10] Rai, A., Maruping, L. M., & Venkatesh, V (2009). Offshore information systems project success: the role of social embeddedness and cultural characteristics. MIS quarterly, 617-641.

[11] Alicia, L. T., Tatiana, G. S., Laura, M. D., & Eugenio, P. (2019). *Risk Management as a Critical Success Factor in the International Activity of Spanish Engineering*. Retrieved from València, Spain:

[12] Acharya, V. V., L.H. Pedersen, T. Philippon, and M. Richardson. (2017). Measuring systemic risk. The Review of Financial Studies, *30*(1), 2-47.

[13] Mayer, N. (2009). *Model-based management of information system security risk.* University of Namur.

[14] Avison, D., & Torkzadeh, G. (2009). Information systems project management. *New York: Sage Publications, Inc.*

[15] Ali Yahya Gheni1, Y. Y. J., Marzanah A. Jabar and Norhayati Mohd Ali. (2017). The Critical Success Factors (CSFs) for IT Projects. *Journal of Telecommunication,* Electronic and Computer Engineering, *9*(3), 3-13.

[16] A. Mahfuth, S. Y., A. Baker, N. Ali (2017). A systematic literature review: information security culture *International conference on research and innovation in* information systems 1-6.

[17] Terlizzi, M. A., Albertin, A. L., & Moraes, H. R. (2017). IT benefits management in financial institutions:

practices and barriers. International Journal of Project Management, *35*(5), 763-782.

[18] Bhattacharjee, J., Sengupta, A., Barik, M. S., & Mazumdar, C. (2018). An Analytical Study of Methodologies and Tools for Enterprise Information Security Risk Management *Information Technology Risk Management and Compliance in Modern Organizations* (pp. 1-20): IGI Global.

[19] Kim, S.-B., & Kim, D. (2020). ICT Implementation and Its Effect on Public Organizations: The Case of Digital Customs and Risk Management in Korea. Sustainability, *12*(8), 3421.

[20] Selma, M. R. B., Abdelghani, E., & Rajhi, M. T. (2013). Risk management tools practiced in Tunisian commercial banks. Studies in Business and Economics, *8*(1), 55-78.

[21] Acemoglu, D., A.Ozdaglar, and A. Tahbaz-Salehi. (2015). Systemic risk and stability in financial networks. American Economic Review, *105*(2), 564-608.

[22] Giudici, P. (2018). Fintech risk management: A research challenge for artificial intelligence in finance. Frontiers in Artificial Intelligence, *1*, 1.

[23] Al-Mamary, Y. H., Shamsuddin, A., & Abdul Hamid, N. A. (2013). The impact of management information systems adoption in managerial decision making: A review. Management Information Systems, *8*(4), 010-017.

[24] Premkumar, G., & King, W. R. (1992). An empirical assessment of information systems planning and the role of information systems in organizations. Journal of Management Information Systems, *9*(2), 99-125.

[25] Premkumar, G., & King, W. R. (1991). Assessing strategic information systems planning. Long Range Planning, *24*(5), 41-58.

[26] Sudhakar, G. A. (2012). A model of critical success factors for software projects. Journal of Enterprise Information Management, *25*(6), 537-558.

[27] Singh, R., Baird, A., & Mathiassen, L. (2018). Collaboration risk management in IT-enabled asymmetric partnerships: Evidence from telestroke networks. Information and Organization, *28*(4), 170-191.

[28] Igbaria, M., & Iivari, J. (1995). The effects of self-efficacy on computer usage. Omega, *23*(6), 587-605.

[29] Moh'd Al-adaileh, R. (2009). An evaluation of information systems success: A user perspective-the case of Jordan Telecom Group. European Journal of Scientific Research, *37*(2), 226-239.

[30] Eboigbe, O. (2018). Analysis of Commercial Bank Risk Management, Strategies of Microfinance Banks. Journal of Financial Risk Management, *7*, 223-240.

[31] Technology, N. I. o. S. a. (2001). *Risk management guide for information technology systems*. Retrieved from

[32] Al-Mamary, Y. H., Shamsuddin, A., & Abdul Hamid, N. A. (2014). Factors affecting successful adoption of management information systems in organizations towards enhancing organizational performance. American Journal of Systems and Software, *2*(5), 121-126.

[33] Blakley, B., McDermott, E., and Geer, D (2001). Information Security Is Information Risk Management," Workshop on New Security Paradigms,. *Cloudcrodt, New Mexico: ACM New York, NY, USA,*, 97-104.

[34] Whale, N. S. (2005). *Risk management guide for small business*. Retrieved from Australia:

[35] Alicia L.T., T. G. S., Laura M. D., & Eugenio P (2019). *Risk Management as a Critical Success Factor in the International Activity of Spanish Engineering*. Retrieved from

[36] Remus, U., & Wiener, M (2009). Critical success factors for managing offshore software development projects. Journal of Global Information Technology Management, *12*(1), 6-29.

[37] Dembo, R. S., & Freeman, A. J. (1998). Seeing tomorrow: Rewriting the rules of risk. *Wiley and Sons, INC: New York*.

[38] Galorath, D. (2006). Risk management success factors. PM World Today, *8*(11).

[39] Westerveld, E. (2003). The Project Excellence Model: linking success criteria and critical success factors. International Journal of Project Management, *21*(6), 411-418.

[40] Belassi, W., & Tukel, O. I. (1996). A new framework for determining critical success/failure factors in projects. International Journal of Project Management, *14*(3), 141-151.

[41] Cereola, S. J., Wier, B., & Norman, C. S. (2010). Impact of Top Management Team on Firm Performance in Small and Medium-Sized Enterprises Adopting Commercial. *Enterprise Resource Planning. Behaviour & Information Technology, 31*, 889-907. .

[42] EIU, E. I. U. (2009). *Managing Risk in Perilous Times: Practical Steps to Accelerate Recovery.* Retrieved from

[43] Silver, N. R. f. (2010). Critical success factors in complex projects.

[44] A., M., & P, C. (2016). Critical Success Factors for Effective Risk Management in New Product Development, (Conference Proceeding). from International Conference on Industrial Engineering and System Management.

[45] Fasilat, S. (2015). *The critical success factors for information system (IS) risk management implementation in the Nigerian banking sector.* Universiti Utara Malaysia.

[46] Wilson, S. R., Whitmoyer, J. G., Pieper, T. M., Astrachan, J. H., Hair Jr, J. F., & Sarstedt, M. (2014). Method trends and method needs: Examining methods needed for accelerating the field. Journal of Family Business Strategy, *5*(1), 4-14.

[47] Baker, J. D. (2016). The purpose, process, and methods of writing a literature review. AORN journal, *103*(3), 265-269.

[48] Sun, S., Lee, P. C., Law, R., & Zhong, L. (2020). The impact of cultural values on the acceptance of hotel technology adoption from the perspective of hotel employees. Journal of Hospitality and Tourism Management, *44*, 61-69.